I0882120

International Developments and Practices in Investigative Interviewing and Interrogation

Techniques in the investigative interviewing and interrogation of victims, witnesses and suspects of crime vary around the world, according to a country's individual legal system, religion and culture. Whereas some countries have developed certain interview protocols for witnesses (such as the ABE Guidelines and the NICHD protocol when interviewing children) and the PEACE model of interviewing suspects, other countries continue to use physical coercion and other questionable tactics to elicit information.

Until now, there has been very little empirical information about the overall interview and interrogation practices in non-western countries, especially the Middle and Far East. This book addresses this gap, bringing together international experts from over 25 countries and providing in-depth coverage of the various interview and interrogation techniques used across the globe. Volume 2 focuses on the interviewing of crime suspects, aiming to provide the necessary information for an understanding of how law enforcement agencies around the world gain valuable information from suspects in criminal cases. Together, the chapters that make up this volume and the accompanying volume on interviewing witnesses and victims, draw on specific national case studies and practices, examine contemporary challenges and identify best practice to enable readers to develop an international, as well as a comparative, perspective of developments worldwide in this important area of criminal investigation.

This book will be an essential resource for academics and students engaged in the study of policing, criminal investigation, forensic psychology and criminal law. It will also be of great interest to practitioners, legal professionals and policy-makers around the world.

David Walsh is an Applied Criminologist and a Fellow of the UK's Higher Education Academy. He has published several articles and book chapters and co-authored a book on corruption. Prior to joining academia he was an investigation professional in government departments in the UK for over 20 years. Dr Walsh has presented his work at many national and international academic and practitioner conferences.

Gavin E. Oxburgh is a registered Forensic Psychologist with the UK Health and Care Professions Council, a Chartered Psychologist and Scientist, and a Fellow of the UK Higher Education Academy. Dr Oxburgh is an expert witness and has provided psychological advice in legal cases in the UK and overseas. Prior to academia, he had a highly successful 22-year career with the Royal Air Force Police where he was a senior detective specialising in crime management, child protection and sexual offences, serving throughout the UK and across Europe.

Allison D. Redlich, PhD, is an internationally-known researcher on police interrogation who began her career studying child victim/witnesses. She has published many peer-reviewed articles on these and related topics and is often asked to provide expert testimony in court and to educate law enforcement and court professionals. She has served on the Executive Committee of the American Psychology-Law Society and co-chaired their 2014 conference.

Trond Myklebust gained his Bachelor degree from the University of Oslo and an MSc in Investigative Psychology from the University of Liverpool while serving as a police officer. In 2009 he became the first police officer in Norway to obtain a PhD (Department of Psychology, University of Oslo). He holds a position as Assistant Chief of Police at the Norwegian Police University College and a Visiting Lectureship at Newcastle University in the UK. He is a Chartered Psychologist in the British Psychological Society and Co-Founder and Co-Director of the International Investigative Interviewing Research Group (iIIRG).

'Unprecedented in its coverage – a landmark text! A must-have for all psych-law academics and practitioners in the field.'

P. A. Granhag, *Professor of Psychology, Department of Psychology, University of Gothenburg, Sweden*

'This book provides a unique insight into the practice of interrogation techniques across the world. I strongly recommend it.'

Gisli Gudjonsson, *CBE and Emeritus Professor of Forensic Psychology, King's College London, UK*

'The scope and breadth of this compilation is extraordinary and unprecedented. The single best feature of this volume is that it provides the reader the ability to compare and contrast practices from different countries in an easy format, given that many chapters follow a similar structure and cover many of the same topics (e.g., training, age effects, common approaches, the role of a caution, etc.). This volume sheds a bright light on practices in countries we have previously known little about, while at the same time highlighting themes and practices that appear to be common across many cultures.

The sort of cross-cultural, international approach that this volume adopts towards the understanding of investigative interviewing is exactly what the research and operational communities need to move out of our cultural silos, learn from one another, and improve practice on a global scale.'

Melissa Russano, *Associate Professor, School of Justice Studies, Roger Williams University, USA*

'*International Developments and Practices in Investigative Interviewing and Interrogation (Volume 2: Suspects)* is a remarkable collection that is highly original and an important addition to the growing body of work on the interviewing and – even though we don't like to say it anymore – interrogation of suspects. In addition to chapters that bring us up to date with developments in the UK, USA, Canada and many other countries that are the mainstays of research on investigative interviewing, there are fascinating new chapters on interviewing in countries such as China, Italy, Germany, Japan, Iran, Israel, Mexico, Scotland and many more. The chapters are written to a consistent framework highlighting the historical, political and sometimes religious factors that have shaped investigative practices.

Students and researchers will find the wealth of case examples, statistical and legal information an invaluable resource. There is clear evidence here that scientific and ethical interviewing can and must be the cornerstone of all investigations. This book takes the entire field forward and is, without any exaggeration, truly essential reading.'

Stephen Moston, *Associate Professor, Department of Psychology, James Cook University, Australia*

Routledge Frontiers of Criminal Justice

1. **Sex Offenders: Punish, Help, Change or Control?**
   Theory, policy and practice explored
   Edited by Jo Brayford, Francis Cowe and John Deering

2. **Building Justice in Post-Transition Europe**
   Processes of criminalisation within Central and Eastern European societies
   Edited by Kay Goodall, Margaret Malloch and Bill Munro

3. **Technocrime, Policing and Surveillance**
   Edited by Stéphane Leman-Langlois

4. **Youth Justice in Context**
   Community, compliance and young people
   Mairead Seymour

5. **Women, Punishment and Social Justice**
   Human rights and penal practices
   Margaret Malloch and Gill McIvor

6. **Handbook of Policing, Ethics and Professional Standards**
   Edited by Allyson MacVean, Peter Spindler and Charlotte Solf

7. **Contrasts in Punishment**
   An explanation of Anglophone excess and Nordic exceptionalism
   John Pratt and Anna Eriksson

8. **Victims of Environmental Harm**
   Rights, recognition and redress under National and International Law
   Matthew Hall

9. **Doing Probation Work**
   Identity in a criminal justice occupation
   Rob C. Mawby and Anne Worrall

10. **Justice Reinvestment**
    Can the criminal justice system deliver more for less?
    Chris Fox, Kevin Albertson and Kevin Wong

11. **Epidemiological Criminology**
    Theory to practice
    Edited by Eve Waltermaurer and Timothy A. Akers

12. **Policing Cities**
    Urban securitization and regulation in a twenty-first century world
    Edited by Randy K. Lippert and Kevin Walby

13. **Restorative Justice in Transition**
    Kerry Clamp

14. **International Perspectives on Police Education and Training**
    Edited by Perry Stanislas

15. **Understanding Penal Practice**
    Edited by Ioan Durnescu and Fergus McNeill

16. **Perceptions of Criminal Justice**
Vicky De Mesmaecker

17. **Transforming Criminal Justice?**
Problem-solving and court specialization
Jane Donoghue

18. **Policing in Taiwan**
From authoritarianism to democracy
Liqun Cao, Lanying Huang and Ivan Y. Sun

19. **Reparation for Victims of Crimes against Humanity**
The healing role of reparation
Edited by Jo-Anne M. Wemmers

20. **Victims of Violence and Restorative Practices**
Finding a voice
Tinneke Van Camp

21. **Long-Term Imprisonment and Human Rights**
Edited by Kirstin Drenkhahn, Manuela Dudeck and Frieder Dünkel

22. **Working within the Forensic Paradigm**
Cross-discipline approaches for policy and practice
Edited by Rosemary Sheehan and James Ogloff

23. **Positive Criminology**
Edited by Natti Ronel and Dana Segev

24. **Inmates' Narratives and Discursive Discipline in Prison**
Rewriting personal histories through cognitive behavioral programs in prison
Jennifer A. Schlosser

25. **Municipal Corporate Security in International Context**
Kevin Walby and Randy K. Lippert

26. **Victims and Restorative Justice**
Edited by Ivo Aertsen, Inge Vanfraechem and Daniela Bolivar

27. **The Role of Community in Restorative Justice**
Fernanda Fonseca Ronseblatt

28. **Pre-crime**
Pre-emption, precaution and the future
Jude McCulloch and Dean Wilson

29. **Punishing the Other**
The social production of immorality revisited
Anna Eriksson

30. **International Developments and Practices in Investigative Interviewing and Interrogation**
Volume 1: Victims and witnesses
Edited by David Walsh, Gavin E. Oxburgh, Allison D. Redlich and Trond Myklebust

31. **International Developments and Practices in Investigative Interviewing and Interrogation**
Volume 2: Suspects
Edited by David Walsh, Gavin E. Oxburgh, Allison D. Redlich and Trond Myklebust

International Developments and Practices in Investigative Interviewing and Interrogation

Volume 2: Suspects

Edited by David Walsh, Gavin E. Oxburgh, Alison D. Redlich and Trond Myklebust

Routledge
Taylor & Francis Group
LONDON AND NEW YORK

First published 2016
by Routledge
2 Park Square, Milton Park, Abingdon, Oxfordshire OX14 4RN

and by Routledge
711 Third Avenue, New York, NY 10017

First issued in paperback 2017

Routledge is an imprint of the Taylor & Francis Group, an informa business

© 2016 selection and editorial material, David Walsh, Gavin E. Oxburgh, Alison D. Redlich and Trond Myklebust; individual chapters, the contributors.

The right of David Walsh, Gavin E. Oxburgh, Alison D. Redlich and Trond Myklebust to be identified as author of this work has been asserted by them in accordance with sections 77 and 78 of the Copyright, Designs and Patents Act 1988.

All rights reserved. No part of this book may be reprinted or reproduced or utilised in any form or by any electronic, mechanical, or other means, now known or hereafter invented, including photocopying and recording, or in any information storage or retrieval system, without permission in writing from the publishers.

British Library Cataloguing in Publication Data
A catalogue record for this book is available from the British Library

Library of Congress Cataloging-in-Publication Data
A catalog record for this book has been requested

ISBN 13: 978-1-138-06608-3 (pbk)
ISBN 13: 978-1-138-78175-7 (hbk)

Typeset in Times New Roman
by Deer Park Productions

Dedications

DW: For Joanna and Sue for such wonderful memories, and my love to Fiona, Emma and the newly arrived Jenson. To all those who have supported me in this and all my other endeavours.

GO: The journey from being a police officer in the Royal Air Force to entering academia has been enormously fulfilling. Many people along the way have greatly inspired me, not least my late father, Eric Oxburgh, my mother Hope Oxburgh, my devoted wife Laura and my daughter Susan. Your inspiration and belief in my ability has been unwavering and greatly appreciated. Thank you.

AR: My journey into researching the most effective and efficient methods to interview individuals in criminal contexts began with my first 'real' job. After college, I was fortunate enough to secure a position working with Michael Lamb at the National Institute of Child Health and Human Development (NICHD). While there, I assisted with his (and several others') research on interviewing alleged child sexual abuse victims – research that laid the foundation for the NICHD Interview Protocol. From there, I went on to graduate school where I (again fortunately) worked with the 'founding mother' of child victim-witness research, Gail Goodman. Gail is an exemplar mentor in all respects and much of what I know about interviewing I learned from her. During graduate school, I read an article by Saul Kassin on interrogating suspects. I was fascinated and the rest, as they say, is history. Thus I dedicate these volumes to Michael, Gail and Saul. All three have been wonderful mentors to me over the years and each played an important role in this never-ending journey in determining how and how not to interview and interrogate persons involved in the criminal justice systems as victims, witnesses and suspects.

TM: To Siren and Mathilde – for your never ending love, joy and support in my endeavours.

Contents

Figures, tables and boxes

Figures

Tables

Boxes

Contributors

Kamiar Alaei, MD, DrPH, MPH, MS, is a Public Service Professor in the Department of Public Administration and Policy and the founding Director of the Global Institute for Health and Human Rights. He and his brother Arash co-founded the first 'Triangular Clinic' for three target groups in Iran (drug users, HIV patients and STD cases), which was documented by the World Health Organisation as a 'Best Practice Model' for HIV/AIDS and injecting drug users' prevention and care. Dr Alaei's extensive experience in both global health policy and international human rights law allows him to focus on the intersections between international health and international law, while remaining sensitive to the needs and realities of vulnerable target groups, including the rights of prisoners. Kamiar Alaei received his Medical Doctorate (MD) from Isfahan Medical University and his Master of Public Health (MPH) in Epidemiology from Tehran Medical University, two of the most prestigious universities in Iran. He received his Master of Science in International Health from Harvard University and his doctoral degree on Health Policy and Management from the State University of New York at Albany. He is currently completing his degree in International Human Rights Law at the University of Oxford.

Igor Areh is a Senior Lecturer in Forensic Psychology at the Faculty of Criminal Justice and Security, University of Maribor, Slovenia. His lectures and research work focus mainly on interviews of crime victims and suspects. Having majored in psychology, he accepted a teaching position at the Faculty and narrowed his research work to the issues related to eyewitness testimony. In his successfully defended 2008 PhD thesis in psychology, he researched gender differences in eyewitness memory recall. In recent years, his research interests have moved towards suspect interrogation focusing on two main themes: detecting deceit with the polygraph (concealed information test) and the investigative interview. He has published over 70 articles and three books on forensic and investigative psychology issues. He also works as a criminal investigation advisor, mainly by evaluating the veracity of suspects' statements, as well as an expert witness in court.

Bianca Baker is a PhD student at the University of Derby in the United Kingdom where she is currently examining the employment of therapeutic methods during investigative interviewing settings across cultures. Her aim is to find methods of obtaining information that may culturally vary. Simultaneously, she is pursuing education in psychotherapy. Bianca Baker obtained her BA in Psychology at the University of Southern Maine, USA and her MS in Forensic and Legal Psychology at Leicester University in the United Kingdom. The focus of her research is largely on empathy, suggestibility, rapport-building methods and cultural differences in these areas.

Todd Barron is a Sergeant with the Royal Newfoundland Constabulary (RNC) with 24 years of service and is a graduate student in psychology at the Memorial University of Newfoundland. Todd is responsible for training members of the criminal investigation division and police recruits on all levels of the tier-based PEACE model of investigative interviewing. In addition to developing new interviewing courses as the Tier 5 interviewing advisor, he is also responsible for providing advice on major investigations. Todd's research interests pertain to the development of effective, professional and ethical interviewing standards.

Amanda Cain is a PhD student at the University of Auckland in New Zealand. Her PhD concerns how suspects are interviewed in New Zealand from a psychological perspective. She is also training as a clinical psychologist. Her research and practice interests include suspect interviewing and ensuring vulnerable suspects are interviewed fairly.

António Castanho is a clinical psychologist, psychotherapist, researcher and trainer at the Ministry of Home Affairs in issues related to domestic violence, risk assessment, and risk management and domestic homicide review. From 1992 to 2010, he was a police criminal investigator and clinical psychologist at the Portuguese Police (PSP).

Colin Clarke has wide-ranging experience of conducting investigative interviewing in a variety of roles, e.g. military, police and child protection, and has been conducting investigative interviewing research for nearly two decades. He co-authored the first 'Practical Guide to Investigative Interviewing' and was a founding member of the ACPO Investigative Interviewing Steering Group. His pioneering evaluation of PEACE training with Becky Milne laid the foundation for the tiered approach towards investigative interview development in the UK today. This research collected one of the largest ever samples of field interviews with the victims and witnesses of crime, which is still being examined today. Colin is currently employed as a senior lecturer at Kingston University where his interests include the role of individual differences in interviewing style.

Julie Courvoisier completed her academic career at the University of Lausanne in Switzerland. She earned a Bachelor's in Psychology in 2007 and then a Master's of Law (MLaw) in Criminal Justice (with Criminology and Security) in 2009. She then became an assistant at the Institute of Criminology and

Criminal Law of the School of Criminal Sciences at the university where she is now studying for her PhD regarding police interrogation in Switzerland. In addition, she has also worked as research manager on a preventative project regarding child sexual abuse.

Alexandra de Jong obtained a Master's degree in Social Psychology in 2010. Two years later she also obtained a Master's degree in Criminal Law and Criminology. As a junior researcher at Maastricht University she is currently involved in a research project on the impact of the lawyer on the value of the investigative interview in relation to other police investigative techniques. The project consists of an extensive international literature study and focus group interviews with police and legal profession in the Netherlands, Belgium, and England and Wales.

Laurent Delhalle, the manager of Segeco Consulting, began his career at the Ministry of Foreign Affairs in Paris and afterwards at UNICEF in New York, before being transferred to South Africa and Russia. He is now Head Teacher and Chair of Criminology-Psychology Education at the Lyon Faculty of Medicine teaching business intelligence at HEC Executive in France and abroad. He is co-author of *An Introduction to Business Intelligence* published by Grenoble University Press and several articles on the human dimension of business intelligence. Laurent holds a degree in international public law and international organisation law and a Master's in International Law from the University Pantheon-Sorbonne, Paris.

Samuel Demarchi, PhD, is an Associate Professor at the Université Paris 8. His research interests deal with some of the main factors in criminal investigation (description and identification of criminals, lie detection, witness interviewing). His current research studies concern the detection of criminals according to their description and the improvement of lie detection by the use of uncontrolled cues (e.g. pupil diameters). He is also interested in the strength of evidence in the trial process (line-up fairness, DNA vs line-ups, sequential vs simultaneous line-ups, etc.).

Ivar A. Fahsing is a Detective Superintendent and Assistant Professor at the Norwegian Police University College. He has earlier published in the fields of investigative interviewing, eyewitness testimony, detective skills, detectives' decision-making, knowledge management and organised crime. He has appeared as an expert witness in courts and has for several years conducted training of law-enforcement personnel throughout Europe and Asia. He has 15 years of experience as a homicide detective in the Oslo Police department and at the National Criminal Investigation Service of Norway.

Benjamin Flander, PhD, is Assistant Professor in the Theory of Law and the State at the University of Maribor, Faculty of Criminal Justice and Security, Slovenia. His areas of specialisation are constitutional law and human rights in criminal justice systems. His lectures and publications concern the power granted to the authorities in pre-trial procedure to detain, arrest, interrogate and search suspects as well as the degree to which a society is committed to the rule of law and fundamental rights of those who are suspected, accused or convicted of breaching criminal law. Lately his research interests also include Nietzsche, postmodernism, advanced critical legal studies and critical criminology/penology. He is the author of two books and several scientific articles. Since 2012 he has been active as evaluator of the Group of States Against Corruption (GRECO).

Gustavo Fondevila is Professor-researcher at the Centro de Investigación y Docencia Económicas (CIDE-Center for Research and Teaching in the Social Sciences) and National Researcher Level II of the Sistema Nacional de Investigadores (SNI) Comisión Nacional de Ciencia y Técnica (CONACYT). Gustavo holds a PhD in Law from the Buenos Aires University and a Magister Artium in Political Sciences from the Johannes Gutenberg University-Mainz (Germany) and is author of the following books: *Political Models of Social Integration* (Munich: Utz, 2002), *Institutions, Legality and the Rule of Law* (Mexico: Fontamara, 2005) and *Criminal Profile* (Mexico: CIDE, 2013 (with Carlos Vilalta)); he is also the author of several articles in national or foreign specialised academic publications.

Jane Goodman-Delahunty trained in law and experimental psychology and is currently a Research Professor at Charles Sturt University. Her research promotes evidence-based policies to enhance justice, informed by her experience as a litigator, administrative judge, third-party neutral investigator and part-time commissioner with the Law Reform Commission of New South Wales. She is an Associate Investigator of the Australian Research Council Centre for Excellence in Policing and Security. She served as Editor of *Psychology, Public Policy and Law* and was President of both the American Psychology-Law Society and the Australia and New Zealand Association of Psychiatry, Psychology and Law.

Alexandra R. Harrington, JD, LLM, Doctor of Civil Law, is Assistant Director and affiliated faculty at the Global Institute for Health and Human Rights. She is also adjunct faculty at Albany Law School, where her classes focus on international law topics. Dr Harrington serves as Lead Counsel for Cross-Cutting Legal Issues with the Centre for International Sustainable Development Law. Her more than three dozen publications address a variety of fields relating to international law, including international human rights law, international child's rights, environmental law, legal issues relating to climate change, natural resources regulation, international organisations, international trade law, corporate social responsibility and criminal law, as well as domestic fields such as constitutional law and military law. She routinely presents her work at domestic and international conferences, including a United Nations Academic Impact in Action panel. Dr Harrington has served as a Visiting Professor at

Albany Law School, as a Professor at the University of Montreal Centre d'Etudes et de Recherches Internationales summer programmes and as a Consultant to the Commission for Environmental Cooperation of the North American Agreement on Environmental Cooperation. She is also an ICTSD Expert for the International Centre for Trade and Sustainable Development.

Mohammad Hedayati-Kakhki graduated in Law from Shahid Beheshti University in Tehran in 1990 (LLB) and studied for a Master's in International Law at the University of Shiraz in 1999. He practised as a First-Class Attorney in Iran, within both civil and criminal litigation. Following completion of a PhD in International Law at Durham University (2008), he undertook various academic positions, including lecturing postgraduate subjects and continues to teach at Durham Law School. He was the co-founder of Islam Law and Modernity, a research centre at Durham University, and was its Associate Director from 2011 to 2014. He is currently a Special Advisor for the same research group, as well as advising the university's Centre for Criminal Law and Criminal Justice on Islamic jurisprudence.

Jos Hoekendijk is an investigative psychologist. Since 2013 he has been working as a behavioural consultant for the Dutch National Police. From 2000 to 2013 he was, among others, a lecturer for the Police Academy of the Netherlands in the training programme of investigative interviewing.

Stuart Houston is a Detective Chief Inspector with the Police Service of Scotland, based within the Edinburgh Division. He has been a police officer since 1996 and has been involved in various criminal investigation roles including senior investigating officer for a number of homicides. Between 2008 and 2010, he also worked within the Detective Training Unit.

Kristina Kepinska Jakobsen is a Psychologist and Assistant Professor at the Norwegian Police University College with responsibility for developing and conducting postgraduate studies in investigative interviewing. In addition, she is a PhD student at the Faculty of Law doing research on the investigative interviewing of traumatised witnesses. She has previously worked at the Danish National Police Board as a researcher and teacher.

Kristjan Kask has a PhD in Forensic Psychology from the University of Leicester, UK, and is currently a researcher at the Institute of Public Law at the University of Tartu as well as Associate Professor in Psychology in the Institute of Psychology at Tallinn University, Estonia. He is an accredited clinical psychologist specialising in cognitive-behavioural therapy. His research interests are the investigative interviewing of child and adult victims and witnesses, factors influencing eyewitness issues, adolescents' use of alcohol and issues regarding military psychology. He has conducted several training programmes with police investigators, prosecutors, judges and child protection workers about the principles of investigative interviewing of child victims and witnesses. He has published papers in several international peer-reviewed journals.

Carmit Katz is an Assistant Professor at the Bob Shapell School of Social Work at Tel Aviv University, Israel. She received her PhD in 2007 and continued to work as a research associate at Cambridge University, UK. Her studies have been published in leading journals, and she co-edited the updated version of the important book *Children's Testimony: A Handbook of Psychological Research and Forensic Practice* (2nd edn) by Wiley. Katz is intensively developing and disseminating practices and training for child forensic interviewers in Israel as well as practitioners within the forensic context (such as lawyers and judges).

Mark Kebbell's expertise and research is in the area of investigative psychology, particularly with regard to the investigation and prosecution of serious crime. His research has included writing the guidelines for police officers in England and Wales (with Graham Wagstaff) for the assessment of eyewitness evidence and developing a variety of applied risk assessment protocols for high-risk offenders. He is a Professor in the School of Applied Psychology and a Registered Psychologist with the Psychology Board of Australia.

Christopher E. Kelly, PhD, is an Assistant Professor in the Department of Sociology and Criminal Justice at Saint Joseph's University in Philadelphia, Pennsylvania, USA. Recently, Dr Kelly worked on three related data collection efforts funded by the High Value Detainee Interrogation Group (HIG) and was Principal Investigator of 'The Dynamic Process of Interrogation', a content analysis of video- and audio-recorded interrogations. Dr Kelly has been published in *Psychology, Public Policy and Law*, *Criminal Justice and Behavior* and *Policing and Society*, and is a member of the American Psychology-Law Society (APLS) and the International Investigative Interviewing Research Group (iIIRG).

David La Rooy received his BA, MSc and PhD degrees from the University of Otago in New Zealand. In 2004 he accepted a Post-Doctoral Research Fellowship at the National Institutes of Health (NIH) in Maryland, USA, and received specialist police training on child forensic interviewing, as well as training in the assessment of the quality of investigative interviews conducted with children alleging abuse. Dr La Rooy provides specialist training to police, social workers, solicitors, lawyers, advocates, sheriffs and judges. He was awarded a Scottish Institute for Policing Research Lectureship at the University of Abertay, Dundee, Scotland, in 2008, and in 2014 received the Academic Excellence Award from the iIIRG. He has co-edited two volumes for the Wiley Series in the Psychology of Crime, Policing and Law.

Kirk Luther is a PhD candidate at the Memorial University of Newfoundland. His research interests include false and coerced confessions; interrogation tactics; child interviewing practices; and distinguishing between science and pseudo-science in law enforcement. Kirk has published several articles within these areas, and has presented at both national and international conferences. His research has garnered international media attention and numerous national awards.

Christian A. Meissner is Professor of Psychology at Iowa State University. He holds a PhD in Cognitive and Behavioral Science from Florida State University (2001). His research focuses on applied cognition, including the role of memory, attention, perception and decision processes in real-world tasks and he studies phenomena in the areas of face recognition, forensic interviewing, deception detection, legal decision-making and comparative forensic sciences.

Rebecca Milne is a Reader in Forensic Psychology at the Institute of Criminal Justice Studies at the University of Portsmouth. She is Director of the Centre of Forensic Interviewing and works closely with the police and other criminal justice organisations (in the UK and abroad). Becky is a member of the Association of Chief Police Officers' Investigative Interviewing Strategic Steering Group and was part of a writing team which developed the 2007 version of the Achieving Best Evidence document. Becky was given the Tom Williamson award for her outstanding achievements in the field of investigative interviewing by ACPO in April 2009.

Annabelle Nicol is a PhD student at the University of Abertay, Dundee, Scotland. Her research focuses on the training of investigative interviewers of children and assessing the quality of role-play training interviews with adult actors as well as field interviews. She has been trained to analyse, code and assess the quality of forensic interviews. She works closely with a number of police jurisdictions in Scotland delivering inputs to their child forensic interviewing courses and participating in their practical role-play interviewing exercises.

Harriet Jakobsson Öhrn, BSc, MSc, PhD, is a former Senior Lecturer in Psychology at the Swedish National Police Academy, where she worked for over twenty years. She taught investigative interviewing on the basic police training programme as well as on advanced training courses. For nearly ten years she was course manager for courses in investigative interviewing for experienced police investigators. She received her PhD from Stockholm University in 2005 with a thesis on police interviews. Her main research interest concerns police interviewers' actions in police interviews and the impact those actions have on the outcome of the investigation. Since 2010 she has been assigned as an external training expert to Frontex, where she is involved in the development and implementation of interview training for border police officers within the European Union.

Raivo Öpik is a Lecturer in Forensic Science in the Academy of Security Sciences and teaches subjects in forensic science at the University of Tartu, Estonia. He graduated from the University of Tartu in law and is currently a PhD student researching using modelling in suspect interviewing. He has worked for many years as an investigator in the police and also as the leader of an investigation unit. He has carried out training in interviewing suspects in Estonia and also in Kyrgyzstan under the invitation of the OSCE.

Carlos Eduardo Peixoto has a PhD in Psychology from the University of Porto, Portugal. He is a Forensic Psychologist in the Northern Branch of the Portuguese National Legal Medicine and Forensic Sciences Institute (INMLCF, IP) with extensive experience on forensic psychological assessment of criminal, family, civil and labour law cases. He is also the lead researcher on a research project on the implementation of a forensic interview protocol for children who are victims, witnesses and offenders, supported by the Portuguese Science and Technology Foundation (FCT) and the Operational Programme for Competitive Factors (COMPETE) and conducted in the INMLCF and in the Faculty of Medicine of the University of Porto. Carlos is also a Researcher at the Centre for Studies in Human Development (CEDH) of the Catholic University of Portugal (Oporto Regional Centre), an Invited Auxiliary Professor at the Health Sciences High Institute – North/CESPU, and a trainer and consultant on investigative interviewing in the public and private sector in organisations such as the police, the judiciary and insurance companies.

Francesco Pompedda, MSc, graduated from the University of Turin, Italy, having specialised in forensic psychology and is currently pursuing his PhD in psychology at the Åbo Akademi University, Turku, Finland. He is also employed by the psychology department at the Åbo Akademi University as a research assistant. He is a member of LEPÅ: Legal Psychology Research Group at Åbo Akademi University, and is responsible for designing EIT software in the intensive professional training programme 'Interviewing Alleged CSA Victims with EIT (Empowering Interviewer Training)' at SSF Rebaudengo in Turin, Italy.

Vittorio Maria Rossini holds a Degree in Law and has been a lawyer of the Turin Bar since 2002, practising criminal law. In addition to his legal practice, he is an active participant of the Scientific Commission of the Turin Bar Association. He has experience in teaching for many organisations throughout the legal community. He works as a consultant and an instructor for UNICRI (the United Nations Interregional Crime and Justice Research Institute). He also teaches courses for the School of Professional and Legal Ethics Training of the Turin Bar Association and the 'Camera Penale' of Piedmont.

Massimo Scarabello is currently a Judge at the Court of Cuneo, dealing with civil law matters, from real estate law to contract law. Up until December 2014 Massimo served as a Judge for Preliminary Investigations at the Court of Turin. The author is involved in a collaboration with the intergovernmental institution Eurocontrol, which provides various services to air traffic management. He is counsel for the Just Culture policy and coordination between criminal investigations and safety investigations carried out when incidents or accidents occur. He offers a judiciary point of view and expertise on the matter of interactions between the two fields. Twice a year the author is invited to the Brussels headquarters of Eurocontrol to present seminars and courses covering this topic.

Alexandra Seabra graduated at ISPA, Lisbon, in Clinical Psychology in 1992. In 2000 she defended her Master's thesis in Health Psychology and in 2009 she defended her doctorate in Mental Health. Formerly a counsellor of sex workers and drug addicts, in 2002 she was appointed to coordinate and implement the Clinical Psychology service of the Centro Hospitalar de Torres Vedras, later the Centro Hospitalar do Oeste, where she coordinates and streamlines several projects in support of inpatient services,

Christophe Sellie, since beginning his police training in 1980, has successively worked as a police detective in various forces before being named Deputy Chief of the Police de Sûreté du Canton de Vaud in March 2012. Adding to his international experience, he participated in an exchange with the London Metropolitan Police in 1988. Then, in 1996, he completed, as a police observer, a mission led by the UN in Bosnia-Herzegovina. In 2004, he successfully completed the FBI National Academy. In 2007, in collaboration with Michel St-Yves, he created the first continuing education training programme in matters of investigative interviews in Switzerland.

Brent Snook is Professor of Psychology at the Memorial University of Newfoundland. He holds a PhD in Psychology from the University of Liverpool, UK. His research interests include decision-making, forensic psychology, investigative practices (e.g. interviewing) and pseudo-science in the criminal justice system. In addition to the implementation of PEACE in Canada, his current body of work involves how people understand their legal rights and refining the effectiveness of the various components comprising the PEACE model of interviewing.

Michel St-Yves is a forensic psychologist working with the Behavioural Analysis Service of the Sûreté du Québec (Quebec's provincial police force). He also teaches the psychology of investigative interviews at the École nationale de police du Québec (Quebec Police Academy) and is a lecturer at the Department of Criminology of the Université de Montréal. He has participated in the creation of the first continuing education training programme in matters of investigative interviews in Switzerland, where he has been a training instructor since 2007. He also acts as Deputy Chair of the Scientific Committee of the International Investigative Interviewing Research Group (iIIRG). His various publications are available in both French and English.

Nargess Tavassolian is a Legal Researcher and Legal Affairs Correspondent based in London. She holds a PhD in Law from SOAS, University of London, a Master's degree in International Criminal Law from McGill University in Canada and a Bachelor's degree in Law from Shahid Beheshti University in Tehran, Iran. She has conducted research and written reports and articles on various subjects related to freedom of thought and expression and its limits under various legal systems (international human rights law, Iranian law and Islamic law), religious intellectualism (in the area related to freedom of thought and expression, women's rights, minorities' rights and Islamic punishments) and the Iranian legal system in both English and Persian.

Martijn van Beek is an investigative psychologist working for the Police Academy of the Netherlands. Since 2014 he has been a lecturer in the Master's programme of Criminal Investigation. From 2008 to 2014 he was a lecturer in the training programme of investigative interviewing. Van Beek often advises the Dutch National Police on psychological topics such as the interviewing of witnesses and suspects.

Miet Vanderhallen finished her PhD on 'The Working Alliance in Police Interviewing' in 2007. Currently, she works as an Assistant Professor of Psychology and Law at Antwerp University, Belgium, and as Assistant Professor of Criminology at Maastricht University, the Netherlands. In addition, she is an affiliated Senior Researcher at KU Leuven, Belgium. She teaches psychology and law, criminology, and methods of empirical research at the faculty of law. Her main research interest concerns investigative interviewing. She is particularly interested in research regarding building rapport and research on the (evidential) value of suspects' statements. In the aftermath of the *Salduz* case law, she is currently involved in various (international) studies on legal advice at the police station. In addition to her research activities, she takes part in many (advanced) investigative interview training programmes at the national police academy on criminal investigation and regional police academies. Her latest projects address the supervision of interviewers at police stations as well as joint training for interviewers and lawyers. Miet Vanderhallen has published several (inter)national articles and book chapters on investigative interviewing.

Geert Vervaeke is a Full Professor in Psychology and Law, Chair of the Department of Criminal Law and Criminology and project officer for 'Management of Justice' at the Faculty of Law of the KU Leuven, Belgium. He is the former president of the High Council of Justice of Belgium and Executive Board Member of the European Network of Councils for the Judiciary. He is conducting research and training in the broad field of psychology and law, such as the police interrogation, judicial decision-making, explanatory models of crime and the selection of judges and prosecutors.

Renate Volbert is a Research Fellow at the Institute of Forensic Psychiatry, Charité Berlin, Germany, and a Professor in the Department of Psychology at the Free University Berlin, Germany. She got her diploma in psychology from the University of Bielefeld, her PhD from the Technical University of Berlin and the Venia legendi from the Free University of Berlin. She is licensed as a Specialist in Legal Psychology. Professor Volbert has been a member of the Executive Committee (1999–2009) and chair (2007–9) of the Psychology and Law Division of the German Psychological Association and is currently (since 2014) president elect of the European Association of Psychology and Law. Her main research interests are credibility assessment, suggestibility, secondary victimisation and false confessions. She often appears as a court-appointed expert witness on credibility assessment.

Taeko Wachi is a Senior Researcher at the National Research Institute of Police Science, Japan, and an instructor at the National Police Academy, Japan. Since beginning work with the Japanese police in 2005, she has been involved in offender profiling in serious criminal cases. Most recently, she has conducted research on investigative interviewing, and has been helping the Japanese police force by training and giving advice regarding their interviews. Taeko obtained a PhD in Psychology at the University of Cambridge under the guidance of Professor Michael E. Lamb. Her PhD dissertation on Japanese interrogation won her the 2013 American Psychology-Law Society Dissertation Award (First Place).

Kazumi Watanabe is a Section Chief in the Investigation Support Section at the Department of Criminology and Behavioral Science, National Research Institute of Police Science in Japan. She received her PhD in Forensic Psychiatry from Tokyo Medical and Dental University, becoming a clinical psychologist. She has over 20 years' experience working in the field of investigative psychology and psychological support for the police. Kazumi has recently contributed to the making of a National Police Agency's training manual of basic skills of police interviewing and interrogation based on psychological findings.

Nina J. Westera is a Research Fellow whose research examines how understandings in psychology can be used to improve criminal justice practice. Her area of expertise is investigative interviewing and criminal investigation, with a particular interest in the investigative and evidential interviewing of adult complainants in cases of sexual and violent offending. Nina's career began as an officer in the New Zealand Police, where she investigated serious crime and implemented evidence-based policy and practice for the interviewing of witnesses and suspects. She has educated and advised police officers, lawyers and judges about investigative interviewing.

Yuning Wu is an Assistant Professor in the Department of Criminal Justice at Wayne State University, Detroit, MI. Her research interests include citizen perceptions of crime and criminal justice, police behaviours and attitudes, victimisation and fear of crime. Her recent research has appeared in journals such as *Justice Quarterly*, *British Journal of Criminology*, *Crime and Delinquency*, *Journal of Interpersonal Violence* and *Journal of Criminal Justice*. She was a recipient of the National Institute of Justice's W. E. B. Du Bois Fellowship (2014–15). She also received the Dorothy Bracey/Janice Joseph Minority and Women New Scholar Award by the Academy of Criminal Justice Sciences in 2015.

Marvin Zalman is Professor of Criminal Justice at Wayne State University, Detroit, MI. He co-edited *Wrongful Conviction and Criminal Justice Reform:*

Making Justice (Routledge, 2014) with Julia Carrano. He is an editor, author or co-author of many peer-reviewed articles, books and book chapters on crime and criminal justice issues.

Angelo Zappalà is a psychologist, clinical criminologist, cognitive behavioural therapist and Honorary Judge Tribunal for Minors of Turin. He is also Professor of Criminal Psychology, CRIMELAB, SSF Rebaudengo, Torino, Italy, and Professor of Investigative Criminology, Università di Alessandria, Italy. In addition Angelo is a member of LEPÅ: Legal Psychology Research Group at Åbo Akademi University, and a co-founder and member of HYPOTHESES (Forensic Psychology Consulting).

Sabina Zgaga, PhD, graduated from the Faculty of Law, University of Ljubljana, Slovenia, in 2006 with the thesis 'The Relation Between the Constitution and the Theoretical Model of the Criminal Procedure'. In her doctoral study of criminal law at the same faculty she focused on international criminal law, especially its general aspect. For this she has been granted two Max Planck Institute for Foreign and International Criminal Law fellowships. Her doctoral thesis from April 2011 ('Necessity and Duress in International Criminal Law'), for which she received the United Nations Association for Slovenia award, focussed on the regulation of necessity and duress (and other related issues such as self-defence, military necessity and superior order) in international, comparative and Slovenian criminal law. Currently she is working at the Faculty of Criminal Justice and Security, University of Maribor, Slovenia, as a Senior Lecturer. Her research work is focused on international criminal law and criminal substantive and procedural law.

Acknowledgements

The editors would like to thank Anna Day, University of Derby, UK, for all her hard work from the start of this project in helping the editors and chapter authors to keep to deadlines and towards the final completion of the two volumes. In addition, special thanks must go to Millie Fuller, Newcastle University, UK, for helping to bring the project to completion. Thanks also to Mark Bisschop, Reed Business Information and Imke Rispens for their kind permission to reproduce previously published materials in Chapter 13 of this book. Finally, many thanks go to Heidi Lee at Routledge for all her work in ensuring that the editors were on course to complete this volume.

Abbreviations

ABE	Achieving Best Evidence
ACPO	Association of Chief Police Officers
aIAT	autobiographical Implicit Association Test
AP	Preliminary Investigation (Mexico)
APSAC	American Professional Society on the Abuse of Children
AVR	Audio and Visual Recording
BAI	Behavioural Analysis Interview
BARS	Behaviourally Anchored Rating Scale
BOQ	Behaviour Observation Questions
CAC	Child Advocacy Centres
CBCA	Criteria-based Content Analysis
CCP	Chinese Communist Party
CCP	Code of Criminal Procedure
CCTV	Closed-Circuit Television
CFIP	CornerHouse Forensic Interview Protocol
CGC	Child Guidance Centers
CI	Cognitive Interview
CIA	Central Intelligence Agency
CIB	Criminal Investigation Branch
CID	Criminal Investigation Department
CIDE	Center for Economic Research and Teaching (Mexico)
CLPS	Sri Lanka Police Service
CM	Conversation Management
COI	Case-oriented Interview
CoP	College of Policing
CPC	Canadian Police College
CPL	Criminal Procedure Law
CPP	Swiss Criminal Procedure Code
CPT	Committee for the Prevention of Torture
CPTU	Central Police Training Unit (UK)
CR	Cued Recall
CSA	Child Sexual Abuse
DCI	Detective Chief Inspector

DCM	Dialogical Communication Method
DFS	Dirección Federal de Seguridad
DIPD	Dirección de Investigaciones para la Prevención de la Delincuencia
DNA	Deoxyribonucleic Acid
DNE	Developmental Narrative Elaboration
DPER	Death Penalty Evidence Rules
ECHR	European Convention on Human Rights
ECI	Enhanced Cognitive Interview
ECtHR	European Court of Human Rights
ECTS	European Credit Transfer and Accumulation System
EEA	European Economic Area
FACV	Federal Act on Assistance to Crime Victims
FBI	Federal Bureau of Investigation
FLETC	Federal Law Enforcement Training Center
FNPP	First Nations Policing Program
GIS	General Interviewing Strategy
GNR	Republican National Guard
GQM	Griffiths Question Map
GSS	Gudjonsson Suggestibility Scale
GVG	Gerichtsverfassunggesetz
HIG	High-value Detainee Interrogation Group
HMA	Her Majesty's Advocate (Scotland)
HO	Home Office (UK)
HUMINT	Human Intelligence
ICCT	International Centre for Counter Terrorism
ICITAP	International Criminal Investigative Training Assistance Program
ICPC	Indonesian Criminal Procedure Code
iIIRG	International Investigative Interviewing Research Group
INP	Indonesian National Police
IQ	Intelligence Quotient
IRGC	Iranian Islamic Evolutionary Guard Corps
IRI	Investigation Relevant Information
IRRD	Interrogation-related Regulatory Decline
IVS	Interviewing Vulnerable Suspects
KNPA	Korean National Police Agency
KREATIV	K – communication; R – due process; E – ethical and empathetic; A – active awareness; T – trust through transparency; I – information access; V – based on science (Norway)
KRIPOS	National Criminal Investigation Service (Norway)
LCP	Law of Criminal Proceedings
LTE	Education Custody Law (Portugal)
MAI	Ministry of Home Affairs (Portugal)
MGEF	Ministry of Gender Equality and Family
MP	Ministerio Público
NAO	National Audit Office

NBI	National Bureau of Investigations
NCANDS	National Child Abuse and Neglect Data System
NCF	National Crime Faculty
NCO	Non-commissioned Officer
NEO PI-R	Neuroticism, Extraversion, Openness to experience, Personality, Inventory – Revised
NIAVE	Specific Victims Intervention and Support Team (Portugal)
NICA	National Intelligence Coordinating Agency
NICHD	National Institute of Child Health and Human Development
NP	National Police
NPA	National Police Agency
NPIA	National Policing Improvement Agency
NZ	New Zealand
NZMoJ	New Zealand Ministry of Justice
OD	Open Depth
OPD	Office of the Public Defender
OPP	Office of the Public Prosecutor
PACE	Police and Criminal Evidence Act
PCFQCE	Preparation, Contact and orientation, Free report, Questioning, Conclusion, Evaluation
PCPC	Portuguese Criminal Procedure Code
PCPI	Person Called to Provide Information
PEACE	Planning and preparation, Engage and explain, Account, clarify and challenge, Closure, Evaluation
PIDE	Policia Internacional e de Defesa do Estado
PIP	Professionalising the Investigation Programme
PJ	Judiciary Police
PM	Pubblico Ministero (public prosecutor)
PNP	Philippine National Police
POI	Person-oriented Interview
POLRI	Indonesian Republic National Police
POPP	Police Officers and Public Prosecutors
PP	Public Prosecutor
PPC-GRT	Procedure for Penal Codes in General and Revolutionary Trials
PPS	Prison Population Survey
PRC	People's Republic of China
PRI	Partido Revolucionario Institucional
PRICE	Preparation, Rapport, Information gathering, Confirming the content, Evaluation and action
ProGREAI	Processus General de Recueil des Entretiens, Auditions et Interrogatoires
PSB	Public Safety Bureau
PSP	Public Safety Police
PTI	Professional Training in Interviewing
PV	Professioneel Verhoor

RATAC	Rapport, Anatomy identification, Touch inquiry, Abuse scenario, and Closure
RCMP	Royal Canadian Mounted Police
RNC	Royal Newfoundland Constabulary
SAI	Self-administered Interview
SARCS	Sexual Assault Referral Centers
SCAN	Scientific Content Analysis
SCC	Supreme Court of Canada
SCPC	Swiss Criminal Procedure Code
SIP	Swiss Institute of Police
SLPS	Sri Lanka Police Service
SNS	Social Networking Services
SOP	Standard Operating Procedures
SPC	Supreme People's Court
STD	Sexually Transmitted Disease
STI	Sexually Transmitted Infection
SUE	Strategic Use of Evidence
SVA	Statement Validity Analysis
TID	Terrorist Investigation Department
TMC	Tribunal des Mesures de Contraintes
TMR	Tactical Method of Reasoning
TUE	Tactical Use of Evidence
UDP	Universidad Diego Portales
UK	United Kingdom of Great Britain and Northern Ireland
UNICEF	United Nations
USA	United States of America
ViCLAS	Violent Crime Linkage Analysis System
VKV	Verhoor Kwetsbare Verdachten
VRI	Video Recorded Interview
VWA	Victim/Witness Assistant
WPL	Witness Protection Law

Introduction

International developments in practice for suspects of crime

Allison D. Redlich, David Walsh, Gavin E. Oxburgh and Trond Myklebust

Investigative interviewing is a key feature both in the investigation of crime as well as in the way that it can enable justice. Given how essential interviewing and interrogation is to law enforcement agencies internationally, it is surprising how little we know of the techniques and practices used across the world. Policing has surely changed over the past century, but the majority of our general understanding is primarily stereotypical presentations from television shows or movies, many of which are unreliable as a means of understanding what actually happens when victims, witnesses and suspects are interviewed by law enforcement investigators. Those of us within the police and academic fields of police science, psychology, criminology, law and others see an urgent need for providing balanced information on the various techniques used in law enforcement.

In interviewing victims, witnesses and suspects, law enforcement is faced with a challenging task. It is beyond dispute that memory fades over time, that crimes often occur under conditions that impede accurate and complete recollections of events and that there are numerous reasons for people to be less than forthcoming (especially suspected offenders) and reluctant to speak with law enforcement. However, the need for victims, witnesses and suspects to share their experiences – that is, be interviewed and/or interrogated – has always been and will remain essential. Despite advancements in forensic science and technology, the need to rely on humans to both ask and answer questions is unlikely to diminish. Thus the ability to obtain accurate, comprehensive and up-to-date information about criminal happenings remains of great import.

In this volume concerned with the interviewing and interrogation of suspected offenders, the importance of effective questioning techniques was recently brought to the forefront with the release of the US Senate Select Committee on Intelligence 'torture report' in December 2014. The report documented many controversial – and by most accounts ineffective – interrogation techniques including mock executions, sleep deprivation and near drownings through waterboarding. As you will glean from reading this volume, many countries have abandoned and openly denounced the use of torture interrogation tactics. Indeed, several countries have banned psychologically coercive techniques. However, across the globe, some countries continue to use physically and psychologically coercive techniques, some legally and some illegally. As presented in the forthcoming chapters, it would appear that a paradigm shift is underway across the globe, from the traditional interrogation model, with an emphasis on persuading suspects to confess, to the investigative interviewing model, emphasising a search for the truth and the collection of accurate and reliable information from interviewees.

With both volumes, the editors and contributing authors aim to provide you with the necessary information for an understanding of how law enforcement agencies around the world gain valuable information from victims, witnesses and suspects in criminal cases. To this end, we have gathered a distinguished collection of authors from over 25 countries (including Asia, Australia, Europe, North and South America) around the world, culminating in many years of specialist knowledge and practice. We believe this volume provides readers with an in-depth coverage of the various interview and interrogation techniques used across the world, taking into account the two major types of legal system: adversarial and inquisitorial.

Adversarial versus inquisitorial legal systems

Between countries, there are many – and sometimes extensive – legal differences in the process of gathering forensically robust information. An inquisitorial system is where the court is actively involved in investigating the facts of the case. France is one country with an inquisitorial or non-adversarial[1] system. The main feature of the inquisitorial system is the function of the 'examining or investigating judge', who investigates serious crimes or complex inquiries in an inquisition or investigation of the crime. Judges can question victims, witnesses and suspects, order searches for evidence, declare the final verdict and decide on the punishment. Their role is not to prosecute the accused, but to gather facts to reach the correct verdict, and as such their duty is to look for any and all evidence, incriminating or exculpatory.

In contrast, in adversarial systems, judges focus on the issue of the law and procedure and act as a referee in the arguments presented by the defence and the prosecutor. Sometimes, juries decide on the matter of the presented facts according to the requirements in law. The prosecution services will be in charge of the cases presented for the court. However, the function of the prosecution services differs between countries. For most countries, the prosecution service is organised outside the police, as is the case in England and Wales, the USA and South Africa. In England and Wales the police will initiate the investigation and, when the case is completed, send it to the Crown Prosecution Service for a decision to be made regarding whether there is a realistic chance of conviction and whether it is in the public interest to proceed with a prosecution. In Sweden, for example, the police initiate the investigation and make preliminary enquiries, before sending it to the prosecutor who decides if there will be further investigation. In the Norwegian system, the police initiate the investigation with a representative of the prosecution authority as a formal leader in charge of the case. The present volumes do not intend to suggest whether an adversarial system is 'better' than an inquisitorial, but at this stage it is important to highlight to readers that a country's approach may well affect the interviewing practice found in that country.

The legal framework of the investigation will be one of the variables underlying differences in how investigative interviews or interrogations are conducted around the world. Other differences between practices in countries can be explained by a range of factors which may include economic, political, cultural, religious, socio-philosophical and historical traditions, which individually or collectively combine to shape the practices of investigators in any particular domain. Further, scientific advancements in our understanding of how victims, witnesses and suspects remember, discuss and choose to disclose events has played a large role in redefining interviewing and interrogation methods. However, as will become clear in these two volumes, countries are aware to differing extents of scientific advancements; whereas some countries' policies are seemingly unaware of the research literature, other countries' policies are developed from and entrenched in the literature.

The editors wish to thank the contributors for their efforts in shining a light on contemporary interviewing and interrogation practices throughout the world. Many of the chapters have not been extensively covered before (and some chapters not covered at all). Their contributions enable readers to develop both an international as well as a comparative perspective of developments world-wide in this important area of criminal investigation and its contribution to attaining justice.

Note

1. Some legal scholars consider inquisitorial misleading and prefer the word non-adversarial (Glendon *et al.*, 2008: 101).

Reference

Glendon, M. A., Carozza, P. G. and Picker, C. B. (2008) *Comparative Legal Traditions*. St Paul, MN: Thomson-West.

Asia

1 The interrogation of criminal suspects in China

Marvin Zalman and Yuning Wu

Introduction

This chapter describes and explains police interrogation of criminal suspects in the People's Republic of China (PRC). Interrogation is mandatory in criminal investigations, and confessions are present in the overwhelming majority of convictions. The widespread practice of torture to obtain confessions of guilt, while formally contrary to law, is officially acknowledged to exist, especially at local levels. We will examine interrogation in its social, institutional, legal, and political contexts. Like punishment, interrogation is a "complex cultural process" (Boulanger and Sarat, 2005) that helps to characterize and explain elements of the system within which it is embedded. Overlapping contextual aspects of police interrogation and torture include the balance of crime control and due process, concerns over wrongful convictions, the death penalty, structural features of China's criminal justice system, organizational characteristics of police departments, and the State's attempts to advance the rule of law. This contextual frame extends beyond technical justice process issues to consider the relationship between police interrogation practices and the nature of China's one-party state.

Interrogation practices and torture

McConville *et al.* (2011) analyzed a sample of 1,144 ordinary criminal cases tried between 2002 and 2006 in Basic and Intermediary Courts in 13 sites spread across China when the 1996 Criminal Procedure Law (CPL) was in effect. Police interrogation practices were assessed from case dossiers rather than from direct observations. They found that interrogations are conducted in all cases, producing very high confession rates: 92.1 percent full confessions and 5 percent partial admissions, with denials of guilt recorded in only 2.8 percent of cases. Data was missing in 51 of the 1,144 cases in McConville *et al.*'s (2011) study. In comparison, US and UK studies have found confession rates ranging from 60 to 80 percent (McConville *et al.*, 2011).

The CPL strictly forbade torture, coercion, inducement, and deceit to obtain confessions. Under the 1996 CPL, more than one officer is required to interrogate, and under Article 93 a suspect "shall answer the investigators' questions truthfully," with the proviso that "he shall have the right to refuse to answer any questions that are irrelevant to the case." Lawyers are not present during initial questioning and suspects are informed about access to attorneys only after a case is transferred to the prosecution (procuratorate). Police routinely monitor attorney–suspect meetings as was authorized by law (see McConville *et al.*, 2011: 67–70; Ma, 2003: 502). Under the 2012 amendments to the 1996 law, a few key changes were made: (1) the right against self-incrimination is recognized; (2) a stronger exclusionary rule was enacted; and (3) comprehensive video and audio recording throughout the police interrogation process was begun. In addition, suspects now have the right of access to lawyers at initial police questioning or detention. Police must now inform suspects of their rights to counsel during their first questioning or detention. Lawyer–suspect meetings should not be monitored by the police (Fan, 2013).

High confession rates may be explained by the structural features of China's inquisitorial criminal justice process, which places great weight on dossiers produced by the police (investigative dossiers), procurators (i.e. prosecutors) (criminal procedure dossiers), and the courts (trial dossiers). "Among them, investigation dossiers consist mainly of the documentation and evidence dossiers" and it is the evidence dossier that "plays a substantial role in the disposition of a case" (Zuo, 2008: 2). Virtually all evidence is produced by the state and multiple confessions are standard. Confessions accounted for a third of the dossier items (Zuo, 2008; Chen, 2011b). In contrast, an earlier study by Lu and Meithe (2003), drawing a non-random sample of 1,009 completed cases from published accounts of selected cases, found no confessions in 23.8 percent of cases decided before the 1996 CPL, and in 33.1 percent of cases after the CPL reform. Confessions – classified as sincere, remorseful, or self-initiated – reduced the counts and/or length of prison sentences. This study did not analyze the issue of police use of excessive force (Lu and Miethe, 2003).

An anonymous scholar quoted by McConville *et al.* (2011: 69–70) described police investigations as centered on the suspect's confession to such a degree that "… the case cannot be deemed to be detected without the suspect's confession." Interrogation and investigations, "… operated in a closed environment," and a confession is deemed sufficiently corroborated by the testimony of two witnesses. The anonymous respondent asserted that "… the quality of the investigation cannot be safeguarded, as it is a common phenomenon for the accused to change their confessions or testimonies in the proceedings." Another factor that encourages confessions is the promise and actuality of lenient sentences for those who show remorse (Lu and Miethe, 2003; McConville *et al.*, 2011).

The extensive use of torture to obtain confessions by police in China has been widely discussed and criticized (Belkin, 2011; Lewis, 2011b; Ma, 2003). Practicing lawyers report that "confession by torture is still prevalent" (Liu and Halliday, 2009: 935). Survey studies show that there is widespread belief among the general public as well as the police that confession by torture is a serious issue. Lin *et al.* (2006a) found that among 659 citizens surveyed, 47 percent thought that extorting confessions by torture occurred regularly and 33 percent thought that it happened occasionally. Among 487 surveyed police officers, 39 percent believed that confessions by torture occur on a regular basis and 52 percent believed that they happen occasionally (Lin *et al.*, 2006b). Ma (2003: 504, citations omitted) asserted:

> Both government officials and legal commentators admit that the police use of torture remains a serious problem in the police conduct of criminal investigations … There have been numerous reported cases where police torture has resulted in victims' injury or death.

McConville *et al.* also deduced the existence of torture from evidence provided in trials and from cited surveys reporting allegations of torture in more than half of all cases. They commented that "[f]requent reports coming out of China suggest that torture remains a favoured resource for interrogators" (2011: 338). Wrongful conviction studies provide additional estimates of the extent of torture, with all sources agreeing that the central government's attempts to constrain the routine use of torture have failed thus far.

Contexts

Contextual factors that help explain the nature of police interrogation, the widespread use of torture, failed attempts to contain abuse, and the consequences of abusive police practices interact and overlap. Although it is somewhat formulaic, we divide these contexts into separate headings for the purposes of exposition.

Wrongful convictions

Many research findings regarding the use of torture have stemmed from inquiries into convictions of the innocent (Wu and Zalman, 2013). Well publicized wrongful conviction cases, especially when an individual has been sentenced to death, have generated strong public criticism (see Huang, 2012a). The government responded to outcries by ordering the re-investigation of convictions, exonerating thousands of prisoners, and allowing research into false conviction (Wu and Zalman, 2013). Significant changes to the law and regulations subsequently followed (Belkin, 2011; Lewis, 2011b). Every wrongful conviction study conducted in China identified interrogation torture and false confessions as among the leading causes, if not the leading cause, of wrongful convictions (Chen, 2007; Dong, 2012; Huang, 2012b; He and He, 2012; Liu, 2007; Wu, 2011). These studies also identified sources of interrogation torture found in American surveys such as public pressure to solve cases, work pressures to maintain arrest rates, or evidentiary misinterpretation. There are also factors unique to China, such as the tremendous power of the Chinese police which are subject to only limited judicial and prosecutorial review.

Prior to 2010 and the notorious Zhao Zuohai wrongful conviction, "Chinese journalists and legal scholars had documented thirty-three cases of wrongful convictions for capital offences … and in each case, the defendant had been coerced to falsely confess to the crime" (Belkin, 2011: 275). Huang (2012b) identified false confessions and investigation-related torture in 22 out of 26 wrongful convictions that he selected for study. An empirical study of police investigation cases "filed in two research sites in China between 2002 and 2004" (Liu, 2007: 183) identified "coercive interrogation" by police in 66 percent of "minor" Basic Court cases in Site I, and in 36 percent of serious Intermediate Court cases in Site II (Liu, 2007). He and He (2012; see also He and He, 2013) report that 47 out of 50 wrongful convictions from which they collected information included false confessions, a rate far higher than the 25 percent reported by the Innocence Project (http://www.innocenceproject.org/understand/False-Confessions.php) for American wrongful convictions. In four of the 47 cases, the court or procuratorate admitted that torture occurred, and three abusive investigators were convicted of crimes for this. Although officials did not specifically find torture in 43 cases, the "conclusion that a confession was extorted by torture is possible" (He and He, 2012: 1288). Seven of the 43 defendants bore scars and other evidence of torture; 21 asserted torture but could not adduce proof, while 14 who confessed recanted at trial and were proven innocent by other evidence. Wu (2011) noted that every notorious wrongful conviction case was attended with torture and asserted that it is "arguably China's most common factor found at the center of many wrongful convictions" (p. 454).[1]

Death penalty

The death penalty and wrongful convictions are overlapping issues. China's status as the country that executes more convicts than all other nations combined has drawn substantial commentary, especially regarding its several waves of "strike hard" campaigns on crime from 1979 to 2010 (Trevaskes, 2007a, 2007b; MPS, 2010). More recently China eased its death penalty policy through a direction to "kill fewer, kill carefully", requiring the Supreme People's Court (SPC) to review all death sentences, and hiring scores of judges to review the appeals (Minas, 2009; Scott, 2010). Again, as with articles focused on wrongful conviction, several concerned with capital punishment highlighted the role of coercive interrogations and confessions, although the area is not fully transparent as China continues to treat the number of executions as a state secret (Jiang, 2013; Lewis, 2011a).

Exclusionary rules

Public outcries over wrongful convictions in death penalty cases led the Chinese government to shift from avoiding the torture issue (Peerenboom, 2010) to dramatically acknowledging the problem and modifying its laws in an attempt to control local police abuses (Belkin, 2011). This change reflects greater media and popular scrutiny of legal and political institutions, which allowed the government to tap into and mollify popular discontent (Liebman, 2009; Starr, 2010).

As explained by Margaret Lewis (2011b) the government chose to create legal rules to deter police from using torture by excluding such evidence from prosecution. China had enacted legal prohibitions on coerced confessions from at least 1996. Although SPC decisions do not set precedent in individual cases, they do provide "guidance to lower courts" (p. 653). Thus in 1998 the SPC offered guidance in regard to the 1996 CPL to the effect that verdicts should not be based on coerced statements of witnesses, victims or defendants (pp. 653–4). At a time when the public's faith in the government was undermined (Lewis, 2011b) the exclusionary rule, which is now part of the PRC government's official stance (particularly as it pertains to coerced confessions), is one way of showing that the national government is not influenced by corrupt local officials (Lewis, 2011b; see also Cohen, 2011). The 2012 amendments to the 1996 Criminal Procedure Law have reinforced the exclusionary rule. Yet "over 10 years of judicial practice have made it clear that this principle has not been effectively realized" (Chen, 2011a: 230). The odds of illegally obtained evidence being excluded by courts are extremely low, and even when illegal evidence was excluded in a small number of cases, the suspects were nonetheless convicted based on other evidence (Li, 2012).

Reasons for failures to prohibit torture lay in deficiencies in the written law and the criminal justice system's structure and practices. A problem was that earlier laws regarding police and prosecutors were vague, scattered among different procedural codes, jurisdictionally inapplicable, and filled with gaps. For example, Lewis (2011b) noted several areas in need of clarification, including "when an application to exclude evidence could be brought, what evidence was needed to support such an application, whether the defense was entitled to a live hearing on the application, who bore the burden of proof, and what standard of proof would be used to evaluate the application" (p. 654).

Another problem is that the Chinese criminal justice system is heavily police-centered. In the immediate post-Mao era, the 1979 CPL drew on the Soviet Union's inquisitorial model. Police, prosecutors, courts, and defense lawyers (when available) operated jointly with great discretion to decide cases with an eye towards crime control. In 1979, almost no court personnel had legal training. By 1996, China had experienced unprecedented economic growth, established law schools, and produced hundreds of thousands of lawyers, with many studying in Europe and the United States. In 1996, a new CPL modeled, in part, on American adversary procedures was enacted to great fanfare (Lan, 2010; Liu and Halliday, 2009). Yet, it failed to change a prosecutor- and police-dominated crime-control system in which torture to obtain confessions continued unabated.

These problems led the Chinese government to enact joint exclusionary rules in 2010 in the Evidence Rules promulgated by five agencies: the SPC and the central Ministries of Prosecution, Police, State Security, and Justice. The Chinese Communist Party's (CCP) Central Political-Legal Committee threw its weight behind the new rules in the name of its Politburo head, a highly unusual move (Belkin, 2011; Lewis 2011b). The exclusionary rules were included in two sets of rules: (1) the more detailed Death Penalty Evidence Rules (DPER); and (2) the less detailed Evidence Exclusion Rules. The DPER requires courts to verify the truth of each item of evidence and to ensure that no contradictions exist between items. Seven types of evidence are listed in the rules and for each type of evidence a list of factors that courts should consider is provided. Reliability, accuracy, and relevance are emphasized, and confessions or witness statements obtained by coercion are explicitly excluded. Procedures for enforcing the exclusionary rules include a pre-trial hearing, in which a defendant can challenge confessions, and, in a break from deeply embedded past practice, cross-examine interrogators (Lewis, 2011b; see also Belkin, 2011).

China's governmental and criminal justice systems

Space does not permit a detailed explanation of how China's police (Public Safety Bureau (PSB)), prosecutors (People's Procuratorate), courts, defense attorneys, defendants, the CCP, People's Congresses, the media, and the people interact to produce criminal justice (see Belkin, 2011; see also Chen, 2011a, 2011b, for a detailed explanation; see Lan, 2010; Landsman and Zhang, 2008; Lewis, 2011a, 2011b; Li, 2010; Liu and Halliday, 2009; Ma, 2003; McConville *et al.*, 2011, for extensive interviews and commentary; see also Sun and Wu, 2010; Trevaskes, 2007b). Yet an overview is needed to understand the complex structural context and cultural process of police interrogation and torture. In the most general terms, the kinds of power-separations and checks found in countries where the rule of law is more robust, and where courts exercise some degree of restraint on police and prosecutors, do not describe China. China's governing system is best described as a party-state where the CCP is the major force for organizing, mobilizing, directing, governing, and reforming Chinese society. If a 'constitution' is meant to describe the actual distribution of government power and authority in a state, then Suli (2010: 57) describes the CCP as "… a kind of alternative source of Chinese constitutionalism." China's written constitution enshrines the leadership of the Communist Party.

What this means for criminal justice in China is that the CCP plays a guiding role in an inquisitorial system that was built on memories of an imperial past, party-driven governing system in the twentieth century, and the demolition of legal authority during the Cultural Revolution. The criminal justice system has been described as a three-member family or iron triangle in which police, prosecution, and court work together to fight crime (Lewis, 2011a). They are frequently coordinated at all levels – national, provincial, county, and municipal – by the chief of the CCP Political-Legal Committee, who typically used to be the head of the PSB (i.e. police chief). Compared to their Western counterparts, Chinese courts are weak and assertions of judicial independence apply to the courts as an institution, but not to individual judges. In the past, many judges did not have law degrees and were often retired military officers. Today, judges and prosecutors are better paid than police and enjoy high social and political status. Lawyers were distrusted and viewed as helping criminals. Lawyers' organizations are supervised by the government, and attorneys can be imprisoned for overly aggressive advocacy.

Police still dominate the trial process and the verdict is based on the police evidence dossier (Zuo, 2008). A leading authority, Chen Ruiha (2011b), asserts that judges do not really find facts because witnesses rarely appear in court. Instead, they submit written testimony which is entered into the case dossiers and read out during the trial. To a great degree judges rubber-stamp the conclusions drawn by police creating a "dossier-centered style of adjudication" (p. 370). Indeed, judges and prosecutors who strictly follow the law suffer losses such as not receiving bonuses when issuing acquittals beyond an acceptable quota. Cases are pre-judged in consultation so as to avoid acquittals, with innocent defendants kept in "legal limbo" or given lighter penalties.

Yet, despite this police-dominated crime control system heavily weighted toward conviction and against challenging the PSB dossier, it is plausible that the central government's serious effort to enact a stronger exclusionary rule has had some traction. Only future practice, however, will tell whether the government's policy will actually influence police behavior at the local level (Lewis, 2011b). There are reasons for skepticism. Many defendants are not represented by lawyers and defendants are relatively ineffective in challenging police dossiers and police denials of torture (Lewis, 2011b; McConville *et al.*, 2011). Crime is indeed a serious problem and has increased since the beginning of China's enormous economic growth, due to growing crime opportunities, along with improved economic conditions, weakened informal social control, changed cultural values that highlight materialism, and the creation of an enormous floating population in the expanded market economy (Chen, 2011b; Liu, 2005; Liu and Halliday, 2009; Lu and Miethe, 2003; Starr, 2010; Trevaskes, 2007b). As Lewis noted, seeing criminals go free on technicalities is the flip side of undermining public trust by the use of torture. Inertia and the benefits of solving crimes via confessions will play a significant role. In addition, many people place a greater value on substantive justice and public safety than on due process and individual rights. For example, Lin *et al.* (2006a) found that about one-quarter of surveyed respondents thought that to protect public safety, the police can torture suspects (who may have placed a bomb on a major bridge) in order to locate the bomb. This finding is similar to the "Dirty Harry Syndrome"[2] identified in US policing (Klockars, 1980). Ten percent of Lin *et al.*'s participants even supported police torture to get a confession from a purse snatcher's accomplice, and 33 percent supported police torture if the accomplice refused to cooperate. Over half of the respondents reported that they would accept police extortion of confessions against such heinous criminals as murderers. Thus confession by torture seems to be less widely condemned in China than in the West. We may add that the exclusionary rules were enacted by the prior regime, and that the government under President Xi Jinping has been aggressively combating corruption, arguably the major source of popular discontent against the government and Party, but has also expressed hostility to Western legal values (Forsythe *et al.*, 2014; Buckley, 2014).

Conclusion

Pessimism about the central government's ability to restrain interrogation torture is rooted in the structure of China's criminal justice system. The enactment of more detailed exclusionary rules and adversary system procedures (e.g. court hearings in which attorneys cross-examine interrogators) fits a Western rule of law ideal, but does not fit the realities of China's governance. If the CCP is an alternative source of constitutionalism, a constitutional shift of authority in criminal investigations and trials requires CCP leadership. The newly enacted exclusionary rules suggest that the Party blessed an experiment furthering a judicial solution without fundamentally changing a deeply seated authoritarian and inquisitorial justice apparatus. Perhaps such reforms as enhanced exclusionary rules, counsel during interrogation, and videotaped interrogations can change the consciousness of PSB leaders, and perhaps increased adversarialism can check police excesses. These reforms raise revolutionary issues concerning judicial oversight of police procedures, which raises the controversy regarding judicial independence (Balme, 2010; Fu and Peerenboom, 2010; He, 2010; Peerenboom, 2010; Suli, 2010). The standard version of Western judicial independence connects it to the growth of republican, multi-party democracy in the eighteenth and nineteenth centuries. It is unlikely the CCP had this in mind when it slightly expanded judicial approaches to curbing police excesses. Perhaps the reforms were enacted only to placate external critics and pacify popular resentment. In any event, the success of China's experiment in controlling excesses in police interrogation and to strengthen the role of lawyers and courts will need to be assessed by future experience and further research.[3]

Notes

1. Additional studies on this point by Chen (2007) and Dong (2012) are described in Wu and Zalman (2013).
2. This is a reference to the fictional detective character played by Clint Eastwood in various movies whose unconventional methods are suggested as justifiable if they result in the arrest or killing of perpetrators.
3. As this chapter went to press Human Rights Watch published a detailed report, *Tiger Chairs and Cell Bosses: Police Torture of Criminal Suspects in China* (May 2015), that confirms this chapter's conclusions.

References

Balme, S. (2010) "Local courts in Western China: the quest for independence and dignity," in R. Peerenboom (ed.), *Judicial Independence in China: Lessons for Global Rule of Law Promotion*. Cambridge: Cambridge University Press, pp. 154–79.

Belkin, I. (2011) "China's tortuous path toward ending torture in criminal investigations," *Columbia Journal of Asian Law*, 24: 273–302.

Boulanger, C. and Sarat, A. (2005) "Putting culture into the picture: toward a comparative analysis of state killing," in A. Sarat and C. Boulanger, *The Cultural Lives of Capital Punishment: Comparative Perspectives*. Stanford, CA: Stanford University Press, pp. 1–48.

Buckley, C. (2014) "Leader taps into Chinese classics in seeking to cement power," *New York Times*, 11 October, p. A15.

Chen, R. (2011a) "China's new exclusionary rule: an introduction," *Columbia Journal of Asian Law*, 24: 229–46.

Chen, R. (2011b) "Initial research on the malfunctions of the criminal process" (trans. T. Webster), *Pacific Rim Law and Policy Journal*, 20: 359–97.

Chen, Y. (2007) "A perspective on China's wrongful conviction: using 20 shocking wrongfully convicted cases as a sample," *China Legal Science*, 3: 47–63. [陳永生（2007）。我國刑事誤判問題透視（節選）：以20起震驚全國的刑事冤案為樣本的分析。中國法學，*3*，47–63。]

Cohen, J. A. (2011) "Reforming China's Criminal Procedure: an introduction to this symposium," *Columbia Journal of Asian Law*, 24: 213–27.

Dong, K. (2012) *Quasi-empirical Analysis on Wrongful Convictions Caused by Specific Investigation*. Paper presented at the 2012 International Conference on the Prevention of Wrongful Convictions, Changchun, China. [董坤（2012，8月）。具體偵查行為誘發錯案的准實證分析。2012預防刑事錯案國際研討會，長春市，中國。]

Fan, C. (2013) "On the progress and development of the criminal procedural system in China," *Tribune of Political Science and Law*, 34: 72–85.

Forsythe, M., Buckley, C., and Ansfield, J. (2014) "Investigating family's wealth, China's leader signals a change," *New York Times*, 19 April, p. A1.

Fu, Y. and Peerenboom, R. (2010) "A new analytic framework for understanding and promoting judicial independence in China," in R. Peerenboom (ed.), *Judicial Independence in China: Lessons for Global Rule of Law Promotion*. Cambridge: Cambridge University Press, pp. 95–133.

He, J. and He, R. (2012) "Empirical studies of wrongful convictions in mainland China," *University of Cincinnati Law Review*, 80 (4): 1277–92.

He, J. and He, R. (2013) "Wrongful convictions and tortures confessions: empirical studies in mainland China," in M. McConville and E. Pils (eds), *Comparative Perspectives on Criminal Justice in China*. Cheltenham: Edward Elgar, pp. 73–90.

He, X. (2010) "The judiciary pushes back: law, power, and politics in Chinese courts," in R. Peerenboom (ed.), *Judicial Independence in China: Lessons for Global Rule of Law Promotion*. Cambridge: Cambridge University Press, pp. 180–95.

Huang, S. (2012a) "Chinese wrongful convictions: discovery and rectification," *University of Cincinnati Law Review*, 80 (4): 1195–218.

Huang, S. (2012b) "Chinese wrongful convictions: causes and prevention," *University of Cincinnati Law Review*, 80 (4): 1219–43.

Human Rights Watch (2015) *Tiger Chairs and Cell Bosses: Police Torture of Criminal Suspects in China*. USA: Human Rights Watch. Retrieved from: http://www.hrw.org/sites/default/files/reports/china0515_ForUpload.pdf.

Innocence Project (n.d.) Retrieved from: http://www.innocenceproject.org/understand/False-Confessions.php.

Jiang, N. (2013) "A comparison of wrongful convictions in death penalty cases between China and the United States," *International Journal of Law, Crime and Justice*, 41: 144–66.

Klockars, C. (1980) "The Dirty Harry problem," *Annals of the American Academy of Political and Social Science*, 452: 33–47.

Lan, R. (2010) "A false promise of fair trials: a case study of China's malleable criminal procedure law," *Pacific Basin Law Journal*, 27: 153–212.

Landsman, S. and Zhang, J. (2008) "A tale of two juries: lay participation comes to Japanese and Chinese courts," *Pacific Basin Law Journal*, 25: 179–227.

Lewis, M. K. (2011a) "Leniency and severity in China's death penalty debate," *Columbia Journal of Asian Law*, 24: 303–32.

Lewis, M. K. (2011b) "Controlling abuse to maintain control: the exclusionary rule in China," *New York University Journal of International Law and Politics*, 43: 629–98.

Li, C. (2012) "Effects of sanction for procedural violation: focusing on inadmissibility of illegally obtained oral evidence," *Modern Law Science*, 34 (3): 110–20.

Li, E. (2010) "The Li Zhuang case: examining the challenges facing criminal defense lawyers in China," *Columbia Journal of Asian Law*, 24 (1): 129–70.

Liebman, B. L. (2009) "Assessing China's legal reforms," *Columbia Journal of Asian Law*, 23: 17–34.

Lin, L., Zhao, Q., and Huang, Q. (2006a) "A survey on public perceptions of confession by torture," *Law Review*, 138: 117–35.

Lin, L., Yu, T., and Zhang, C. (2006b) "A survey on police perceptions of confession by torture," *Law Review*, 139: 123–40.

Liu, H. (2007) "A potential cause of miscarriages of justice: an empirical review of investigation techniques," *Journal of the Institute of Justice and International Studies*, 7: 179–95.

Liu, J. (2005) "Crime patterns during the market transition in China," *British Journal of Criminology*, 45: 613–33.

Liu, S. and Halliday, T. C. (2009) "Recursivity in legal change: lawyers and reforms of China's criminal procedure law," *Law and Social Inquiry*, 34: 911–50.

Lu, H. and Miethe, T. D. (2003) "Confessions and criminal case disposition in China," *Law and Society Review*, 37: 549–78.

Ma, Y. (2003) "The powers of the police and the rights of suspects under the amended Criminal Procedure Law of China," *Policing*, 26 (3): 490–510.

McConville, M., Choong, S., Wan, P. C. D., Hong, E. C. W., Dobinson, I., and Jones, C. (2011) *Criminal Justice in China: An Empirical Inquiry*. Cheltenham: Edward Elgar.

Minas, S. (2009) "'Kill fewer, kill carefully': an analysis of the 2006 to 2007 death penalty reforms in China," *Pacific Basin Law Journal*, 27: 36–70.

Ministry of Public Security of the People's Republic of China (MPS) (2010) *The MPS Starts Crack Down on Crime*, 13 June. Retrieved from: http://www.mps.gov.cn/n16/n1237/n1342/n803715/2442448.html.

Peerenboom, R. (2010) "Judicial independence in China: common myths and unfounded assumptions," in R. Peerenboom (ed.), *Judicial Independence in China: Lessons for Global Rule of Law Promotion*. Cambridge: Cambridge University Press, pp. 69–74.

Scott, K. (2010) "Why did China reform its death penalty?" *Pacific Rim Law and Policy Journal*, 19 (1): 63–80.

Starr, J. B. (2010) *Understanding China: A Guide to China's Economy, History, and Political Culture*, 3rd edn. New York: Hill & Wang.

Suli, Z. (2010) "The party and the courts," in R. Peerenboom (ed.), *Judicial Independence in China: Lessons for Global Rule of Law Promotion*. Cambridge: Cambridge University Press, pp. 52–68.

Sun, I. and Wu, Y. (2010) "Chinese policing in a time of transition, 1978–2008," *Journal of Contemporary Criminal Justice*, 26 (1): 20–35.

Trevaskes, S. (2007a) "Severe and swift justice in China," *British Journal of Criminology*, 47: 25–41.

Trevaskes, S. (2007b) *Courts and Criminal Justice in Contemporary China*. Lanham, MD: Lexington Books.

Wu, X. (2011) "An analysis of wrongful conviction in China," *Oklahoma City University Law Review*, 36: 451–69.

Wu, Y. and Zalman, M. (2013) "Wrongful convictions in China: analyzing the scholarship," *Crime and Criminal Justice International*, 21: 1–45.

Zuo, W. (2008) *An Empirical Study of the Chinese Criminal Dossier System – Focusing on the Evidence Dossier*. A paper delivered at the Kennedy School of Government, Harvard University. Retrieved from: http://www.google.com/url?sa=tandrct=jandq=andesrc=sandfrm=1andsource=webandcd=1andved=0CCYQFjAAandurl=http%3A%2F%2Fwww.hks.harvard.edu%2Fcriminaljustice-backup%2Fpublications%2FZuo_paper_English.docandei=hNhCU8aFF8a-sQSWkYGQCwandusg=AFQjCNEvw3CC-kBW_gKMZAMMfnNu8b1hTAandbvm=bv.64125504,d.cWc

2 Insights on investigative interviewing from practitioners and suspects in Indonesia, the Philippines and Sri Lanka

Jane Goodman-Delahunty

Introduction

A feature common to the Republic of Indonesia, the Republic of the Philippines and the Democratic Socalist Republic of Sri Lanka is that all three countries have faced home-grown terrorism in the past decades on a scale exceeding that in most other nations. Interest in global best interview practices has been intensified in these communities by the need to secure the cooperation of high-value detainees and informants and to communicate with them in ways that are not counterproductive. This chapter documents recent developments in investigative interviewing in those countries.

A limitation of much research on interrogation is its focus almost exclusively on police samples, without taking into account the suspects' views (Holmberg and Christianson, 2002), or interactional aspects of interview communication between interviewer and suspect (Goodman-Delahunty *et al.*, 2014). This chapter draws on original data from interviews conducted with non-random, purposive samples of police practitioners and with suspected terrorists from the Abu Sayyaf Group (Philippines), the Liberation Tamil Tigers of Eelam (Sri Lanka), and Bali bombing terrorist attackers (Indonesia). By sampling both interviewers and suspects, a more comprehensive picture was gained of contemporary interrogation practices in those communities. In addition, practitioners who conduct deradicalization interviews with violent extremists in Indonesia and Sri Lanka were asked about this emerging trend in police practice. Together, these interviews provided unique viewpoints on effective and ineffective interview strategies within the framework of the Interaction Process Model (Moston *et al.*, 1992).

Interview history and practice in Indonesia, Sri Lanka and the Philippines

General consensus exists that the focus of crime analysis is past events, whereas intelligence is focused on future threats and risks (Ball, 2007). In practice, these distinctions are compounded by jurisdictional variations regarding these functions. An overview of policing and intelligence functions performed by government agencies in Indonesia, the Philippines, and Sri Lanka is useful to specify the agencies primarily responsible for criminal investigative interviews with suspects, and those responsible for intelligence analysis by conducting HUMINT or intelligence interviews with other sources and informants.

The Republic of Indonesia

The Indonesian Republic National Police (POLRI) is responsible for arresting and interrogating suspects. Since its separation from the military in 1999, special divisions of POLRI, such as the Brigade Mobil and Detachment 88, have undertaken paramilitary police functions to maintain law enforcement and counter domestic terrorism. Badan Intelijen Negara (a national intelligence agency) is Indonesia's primary intelligence agency. Its role is to process and produce all intelligence information, coordinate all intelligence institutions, and report to the president and parliament.

Detachment 88 (Densus 88) is the special forces counter-terrorism squad of POLRI, formed in 2003 with ongoing funding and support from the USA and Australia. In keeping with Indonesian counter-terrorism measures aimed at disengagement (White *et al.*, 2014), Detachment 88 officers uniquely conduct both evidentiary and deradicalization interviews. Comprehensive legal safeguards for the treatment of suspects are undermined by the lack of penalty for their violation (Fitzpatrick, 2008) and by legislation permitting the detention of suspects for six months without charge. To date, this unit has killed over 90 suspects and arrested more than 900 persons. In the past five years, numerous reports of human rights abuses by Detachment 88 have been made, including allegations of extrajudicial killing of suspects and citizens (Cordell, 2012). Although the Chief of Police overseeing this squad admitted unlawful, violent tactics against terror suspects, in 2013 a videotape of a terrorist suspect who was shot after his surrender led to calls by Islamic organizations for further investigation of Detachment 88 (Priamarizki, 2013).

The Republic of the Philippines

The Philippine intelligence service is divided into four main agencies, the National Bureau of Investigation of the Department of Justice (NBI), the Philippine Drug Enforcement Agency, the National Counter-Terrorism Action Group, and the National Intelligence Coordinating Agency (NICA). The NBI is responsible for handling and solving cases in the interest of the nation. In conjunction with the NBI, the Intelligence Service undertakes internal security operations against terrorists and organized crime that threaten national security. NICA is the primary intelligence and analysis arm of the government and conducts investigations that can include the detention and arrest of potential terrorists. The Philippine National Police (PNP), whose main role is to prevent and control domestic crime through investigative processes prescribed by law, is separate from the intelligence services.

Since 2001, the Joint US Mutual Assistance Group and US Joint Special Operations Task Force Philippines provided training and advice to combat domestic terrorism, largely seen to have its origins in poverty and economic marginalization (White *et al.*, 2014). A reputation for poor interviewing techniques and reliance by the PNP on questionable confessions led to a shift in responsibility for the National Counter Terrorism Unit to specially trained civilian operatives and operations units of the Armed Forces of the Philippines (White *et al.*, 2014). These practitioners have received some interview training from the UK. Although the Anti-Torture Act (Republic Act 9745) proscribes torture or ill treatment of suspects and persons deemed a security threat, many suspects have been incarcerated for periods as long as ten years without charge.

The Democratic Socialist Republic of Sri Lanka

Sri Lanka's law enforcement agency combines specialized units and divisions. Each of these divisions has a particular focus, whether criminal investigation or terrorism investigation, etc. They are subject to legislation to safeguard against torture (Hampson *et al.*, 2009). The Sri Lanka Police Service (SLPS) is the national police force responsible for enforcing criminal law, maintaining the peace, and handling civilian complaints, minor crimes, and counter-terrorism investigations of a domestic nature. Special task forces branching from the SLPS include the Criminal Investigation Department (CID) and the Terrorist Investigation Department (TID). Investigations conducted by the CID involve serious crimes such as rape, murder, and organized crime and at times internal crimes pertaining to national security. In these cases, the mistreatment safeguards often fail, and when reported, are not investigated (Hampson *et al.*, 2009). The TID handles investigations into terrorism and sectarianism. In addition to these special divisions, Sri Lanka has a State Intelligence Service that combines intelligence units from the army, navy, air force and police to investigate both internal and external matters. Sri Lanka's armed forces have their own short- and long-term defensive strategic goals for internal and external threats but do not typically conduct investigative interviews.

Recently, high-ranking officers in the Sri Lankan Army, members of the CID, TID, the military, military intelligence, and the police were implicated in 40 independent sworn witness statements reporting postwar abductions, tortuous abuse and sexual violence against Tamils suspected of past association with LTTE (Sooka *et al.*, 2014). Reports of this nature documenting abuse by police and security forces in detention and rehabilitation centres run by police, the army or intelligence services led the United States to sponsor a Human Rights Council resolution calling for investigation of Sri Lankan war crimes (Howie, 2013).

In sum, variability exists in these three East Asian nations in terms of the purpose of interviews conducted (seeking information vs. evidence), the interview style or approach most commonly used (investigative vs. accusatory), and the agency jurisdiction (international vs. domestic).

Theoretical and practical background: interview methods and models applied

Research on approaches to investigative interviewing has identified as many as 71 strategies (Kelly *et al.*, 2013). Two major interview styles are distinguished: (1) a more coercive accusatorial approach, where the suspect is confronted by accusations to elicit evidence which can be used in court; and (2) a less coercive, information-gathering strategy using open questions that encourage suspects to talk (Moston *et al.*, 1992). One useful way to examine particular legalistic, physical, cognitive and social strategies is to situate them within a coercion continuum as illustrated in Table 2.1.

Best practice: support for non-coercive interview strategies

Practitioners endorsed a variety of non-coercive and rapport-building strategies in suspect interviews that have been shown to be effective (e.g. Alison *et al.*, 2013). In part this was because of the greater perceived reliability of suspect responses to this approach:

> If we can elicit information from the suspect without force, then the information given is based on facts, based on the truth. (Indonesian practitioner 7)

> A successful interview was characterized by: respect, no pressure, force, or coercion. (Indonesian practitioner 6)

Table 2.1 Social, cognitive, legalistic and physical interview practices

	Type of interview strategy			
	Social	*Cognitive*	*Legalistic*	*Physical*
Coercive practices	verbal threats, hostile, dominate, authoritarian	pretend to have evidence and know more, confront with evidence, surprise	presume guilty, accusatory, minimize crime or outline severe legal consequences	blindfold, use restraints, unpleasantly hot or cold temperatures, assault, isolate
Non-coercive practices	rapport-building, friendly, polite, respectful, considerate, reciprocity	provide explanations, use mnemonic aids use evidence for confirmation	obtain suspect's account, gather information, open-ended questions, remain neutral	comfortable setting, provide food and drink, take frequent breaks, soft furnishings

Adapted from Goodman-Delahunty *et al.* (2014).

Note. These distinctions for research purposes may not reflect legal definitions of unlawful coercion or torture.

Suspects interviewed in Indonesia, the Philippines and Sri Lanka confirmed that non-coercive strategies were effective, and offered this advice to interviewers:

> Interrogators should behave in a calm and friendly way, and sometimes make jokes or use humour with the suspect. (Indonesian suspect 23)
>
> The interviewer must not be harsh. They must be soft-spoken because people tend to be persuaded by soft-speaking people. (Filipino suspect 71)
>
> Interrogators should ask questions without harming their minds and their hearts. There are so many affected, so many people who are not engaged with those activities, so they should respect everyone. (Sri Lankan suspect 60)

Practitioners used rapport-building strategies to encourage suspects to exchange ideas and talk freely:

> The first thing I'm always doing is to let the interviewee be relaxed, maybe the atmosphere is relaxed. There's no pressure, you treat the person as a person in the real sense, to let them feel that you are there actually just to talk. Talk with each other, anything that you can talk about, and he will not feel that he's being interrogated actually. It's something like this one, just sharing information, something like that. (Filipino practitioner 8)

One Indonesian interrogator positioned himself as someone who wanted to learn about religion, and said that he needed to learn from the suspect who was more knowledgeable about religion than he. (Indonesian practitioner 14)

Another practitioner warned that a show of superiority would not result in cooperation:

> My ability to put myself in his place, because if you are an educated person, or an intellectual person, and you treat him in a way that he feels too inferior, you do not get the cooperation from the interviewee. But, if you put yourself at the same level as the interviewee, that is one of my abilities – putting myself at the level of the interviewee, but not necessarily losing my position as an interviewer. (Filipino practitioner 1).

Active listening skills and infinite patience were deemed essential:

> You listen, so you know that there's a relationship built, and it's a human bond. Even with the terrorists, or whoever – it's that human bond. (Sri Lankan practitioner 7)

Reciprocity was the most prevalent form of social persuasion applied to foster a reciprocal relationship reliant on the convention that suspects who receive favors or gifts feel an urge to reciprocate (Cialdini, 2001; Goodman-Delahunty and Howes, 2014). Advice from one detainee endorsed the effectiveness of this approach:

> If you want to befriend them and you want to extract information, provide them with good food to eat. Do not harm them or pay them money. Tell them "Do not worry, let us help each other," or "I will assist you in finding a job." Then, these individuals will voluntarily give secret information. (Filipino suspect 73)

Indonesian practitioners reported building trust and rapport with detainees by providing financial and social benefits such as accommodation, medical attention, educational opportunities and family visits. Suspects who receive these benefits may be more inclined to disclose information, and the provision of tangibles may also be used as a sign of good faith by practitioners, demonstrating to suspects that their relationship is genuine.

One notable feature of interviews by practitioners in the Asia-Pacific is that rapport-building strategies can lead to the development of genuine friendships between interviewers and detainees. Practitioners reported sincere and ongoing engagement with suspects, and did not approve of faking rapport to secure cooperation or behavior change. For instance, one practitioner emphasized "You don't lie. You can never lie" (Sri Lankan practitioner 9). The detrimental reciprocal impact of lying was highlighted by a suspect who candidly stated:

> Yes, of course there was information that I gave them that was not true … Because I was sure they were lying to me, I made up some lies too. (Filipino detainee 77)

The importance of police integrity in communicating with a suspect was further underscored by a practitioner who stated:

> Don't give anyone any false promises – to not be truthful – you have to be authentic. You should never promise someone something that you can't deliver … The detainee must feel that you are genuine. (Sri Lankan practitioner 10)

This perspective stands in contrast with the views of some Western interrogators who regard feigning similarity to create rapport as a legitimate means to achieve interview objectives.

Emerging practice: disengagement from violent extremism

Researchers have suggested that the process of radicalization observed in violent extremists can not only be halted, but also reversed (Porter and Kebbel, 2011). "Deradicalization" refers to desistance from extremist violence, and aims for substantive changes in ideology and attitudes (Neumann, 2010). Four principal modes of rehabilitation have been distinguished: religious or ideological, psychological, social and vocational (Gunaratna, 2011).

While deradicalization programs are auxiliary to policing in many nations, and are most frequently implemented in prisons in Indonesia, the Philippines and Sri Lanka (International Crisis Group, 2007; Jones, 2014) because of concerns that terrorist inmates will recruit and "radicalize" mainstream prisoners, or that the prison systems will undermine the rehabilitation programs in jails (Johnston, 2009), police in these countries are trained to perform both evidentiary and deradicalization interviews (Gunaratna, 2013).

A principal goal in interviews with high-value detainees in Indonesia and Sri Lanka is disengagement or deradicalization from terrorism-related activities. An important factor in this process is development of rapport and the formation of a trusting, respectful relationship with suspects (Dalgaard-Nielson, 2013).

> It's very crucial the rapport, because you establish and, you win them, you win the person. So to win the person, this person who has come before you, also has same kinds of likes and dislikes, just like me. He likes to have nice place and have good health and family, all that. You create a new link with this individual. And I think the rapport is primary, rapport is primary to further the rehabilitation of this man. (Sri Lankan practitioner 9)

> There have also been several times that I have built a relationship because I want to maintain and continue that connection, so that we can pull them over to the other side. (Sri Lankan practitioner 5)

Deradicalization interviewers reported the importance of tailoring the interview approach to the individual circumstances of the interviewee, the timing of questions, showing sensitivity to a detainee's emotional state, and avoiding confrontational questions. These approaches are consistent with best-practice guidelines that reject a one-size-fits-all approach (Global Counter-Terrorism Forum, 2012: 2), urging individualized consideration of detainees, and emphasizing that rushing interventions can be counterproductive to the deradicalization process (Hedayah and ICCT, 2013).

Many deradicalization interviewers mentioned the need for an interviewer to be empathic:

> … show that we are empathic. Because being a criminal is sometimes of no choice. Sometimes someone has to do criminal acts, they don't have choice in this life, so we should start to give empathy to him. (Indonesian practitioner 6)

> … interrogator should feel empathy of what has happened, and also the interrogator has to understand. Also empathy to the conditions of the suspect, not only the suspect, but also the suspect family's conditions. (Indonesian practitioner 9)

> … or an individual got into some cult or so, you must understand that. Especially a terrorist or extremist, you have to understand number one what made him to become that? That is going to be the success of your interview. (Sri Lankan practitioner 1)

The significance of interviewer empathy in promoting detainee behavior change is supported by research suggesting that clients' perception of their therapists as empathic is an important mechanism of change (Watson *et al.*, 2014). For example, therapist empathy improved clients' internal self-representations, and their level of security and close interpersonal relationships (Watson *et al.*, 2014).

Rehabilitation programs conducted with government and police sponsorship in Sri Lanka are devised by professionals with psychology training, and formally incorporate cognitive behavioral therapy techniques and motivational interviewing:

> Because whenever you interview someone, you must do what is called a motivational interview … Motivational interview is where you have to motivate him during your Q and A that he has done something bad, and the he needs to become a good human being … (Sri Lankan practitioner 10)

Just as tangible inducements were effectively used in securing suspect cooperation, they were critical to assist ex-detainees in rebuilding and developing new social identities, i.e. a socio-economic rather than a religious or ideological approach is preferred (International Crisis Group, 2007; Johnston, 2009). The success of rehabilitation and deradicalization activities has been documented in the new lives that ex-detainees create for themselves. These include working in civil defense, assisting young people with employment opportunities, and working with the deradicalization team on a voluntary or professional basis – even a former sharpshooter for the Liberation Tamil Tigers of Eelam (LTTE) who represented Sri Lanka on its national team (Dhami *et al.*, 2014). One Indonesian ex-terrorist manages a successful restaurant in Central Java with support from the Institute for International Peacebuilding which provides former terrorists with a place to work and develop new skills (Oktofani, 2012).

Specific techniques to use when interviewing detainees with the goal of deradicalization remain an emerging practice and topic of research (Global Counter-Terrorism Forum, 2012; Thomsen, 2012; Weilnböck, 2012), and require systematic evaluation (International Crisis Group, 2007).

Unsupported practice: psychological support and physical comfort

Two strategies that were described by practitioners have not yet been empirically or experimentally evaluated and validated, namely the mentoring of detainees such as terrorist suspects, and manipulation of the physical interview environment to make it as comfortable for the detainee as possible.

Mentoring high-value detainees

In Indonesia and Sri Lanka, police have implemented what they describe as a Mentor-Investigator model with suspected terrorist detainees. From the outset, the detainee is provided ongoing psychological support:

> After a terrorist suspect is arrested, he is assigned a mentor. The mentor is one of the police investigators. This police officer becomes the confidant of the terrorist. The focus of the police approach is on "winning hearts and changing minds." In other words, rehabilitation and deradicalization are goals of the interviewer. (Sri Lankan practitioner 3)

> One practitioner described how he kept a young suicide bomber with him constantly for the first two days following his arrest, speaking to him intermittently throughout the workday, asking how he was, etc. During this period, the detainee became more relaxed and said he had remembered something that he forgot to tell the interviewer earlier, and disclosed additional significant information. (Sri Lankan practitioner 2)

Support is provided to the mentee for periods as long as 18 months, and may include arranging for doctor's visits or providing care for the detainee's family members. To ensure continuing personal contact, the mentors prefer to keep the detainees at police headquarters rather than place them in the prison system (Johnston, 2009). The Sri Lankan police attributed the high rate of guilty pleas in terrorist cases to this model as it encouraged detainees to disclose information rather than respond with denials.

The impact of the physical interview environment

Practitioners in all three countries reported that the impact of the physical environment on the interviewee was an important consideration. For example, a comfortable and relaxed environment facilitated interviewer–interviewee rapport and helped interviewees to feel more comfortable about responding to questions:

> Firstly, the setting must be very comfortable. You must always treat the detainee with the utmost friendship and respect, with food, teach, coffee, juice – whatever he needs to make him feel comfortable. I feel that if you don't do that, you don't build a good connection with the detainee. That relationship is at the heart of a good interview. (Sri Lankan practitioner 10)

Others emphasized that there should be no interruptions or distractions:

> When I conduct the interrogation, the first thing is that the interrogation is conducted in a certain room. What I mean by certain room, there are no other

> activities apart from interrogation, so the interaction between the suspect and interrogator wouldn't be disturbed. (Indonesian practitioner 4)

Establishing a physically safe environment for the suspect was also of value:

> It took sometime before he spoke openly. I could see that he was hesitant during the first few days, so we had to get his confidence. I took the opportunity of his need for security; I took advantage of that. I kept him under our watch and, I think he appreciated that, and he spoke after a few days. (Filipino practitioner 40)

Contraindicated practice: coercive practices and lack of accountability

Hostility and threats

In the Philippines, despite endorsement of rapport-building techniques, the use of coercive tactics such as threats was justified by some practitioners as "the lesser evil," or because "the end justifies the means."

> Somebody will talk to them, intimidate. Then the other one will be very friendly, like "good-cop bad-cop." (Filipino practitioner 2)

> You should somehow convey to him that if he chooses not to help, "I will also make your life as miserable as it can be through legal means." (Filipino practitioner 6)

One Philippine Army interviewer traded on the reputation of the police for physical coercion:

> I told him, "You'd better cooperate with me, because if the police officer is the one who does the interrogation …" sort of giving him some fear that the police would be the ones to operate. (Filipino practitioner 31)

Protracted interviews, repeated interrogation, and detention without charge

Reports by practitioners and suspects in the Philippines of the average duration of interviews revealed that they were protracted, 12 hours on average; however, suspect interviews in Indonesia and Sri Lanka often lasted multiple days, with many sessions. Repeated interviews were feasible because the law permitted the detention of suspects for lengthy periods. In the Philippines, some suspects were detained without charge for as long as ten years.

Records of interview

A key outcome of a law enforcement interview is the record of interview, which is often the basis for either release or continued detention of a suspect for criminal prosecution. Increasingly, police interviews with suspects are electronically video- and/or audio-recorded (Ibusuki, 2015). Empirical evidence has established consensus by police, prosecutors, defense lawyers and judges that mandatory electronic recording of police interviews curtails police misconduct in interviews, and deters oppressive and coercive conduct, such as verbal threats, assaults, and involuntary confessions (Dixon, 2007). Procedures to create a contemporaneous electronic record of interview or written records that closely track the question-answer sequence (de Keijser *et al.*, 2012) comprise best practice to advance fairness both to suspects and police, leaving less room for speculation and doubt as to what transpired in the interview and the quality of the proffered evidence (Sivasubramaniam *et al.*, 2014).

Currently, in Indonesia, the Philippines, and Sri Lanka there is no requirement to video-record or audio-record suspect interviews, although some individual practitioners made their own for their personal use:

> First you have to prepare the room … and the next thing, there should be recording in the rooms. (Indonesian practitioner 7)

Typically, handwritten notes taken by one or more interviewing officers across one or more interviews are compiled into a single typed Interrogation Report or Deposition. This retrospective summary does not reflect the question and answer sequence or convey verbatim answers by a suspect, or provide insight into the interview procedures. Official "interviews" to charge a suspect, at which time the suspect is asked to sign the Interrogation Report in the presence of the suspect's legal representative, are typically scheduled after a series of police–suspect interrogations that may persist for days. Even where mandatory video-recording is introduced, informal or "pre-record" police–suspect exchanges may persist unless these procedures are standardized (Dixon, 2007).

Confessions coerced by physical torture and abuse

Reports of confessions induced by physical torture were obtained from terrorism suspects in all three countries. A number of Filipino suspects described torture at the hands of Army interrogators. One suspect reported that he was rarely given food or drink over a period of nine days, and was physically abused.

> I was tied with a rope and they were pulling me backwards while I was crawling. What I almost could not endure was the electrocution … my body was suffering from inflammation and swelling … They dragged me outside the house to lie under the heat of the sun … My eyes were almost closed due to beatings … One of them said, "What we are doing is no longer right." (Filipino suspect 76)

Others were beaten to induce a confession:

> They beat us with a wooden baseball bat and the butt of a rifle. They did not beat us on the head, but all over our bodies, including our abdomen and legs … When they were not satisfied with our answers, they beat us. They wanted us to respond with answers they wanted to hear. (Filipino suspect 69)

> If I would not answer what they wanted, they would hurt me. I thought they would kill me, because they had been beating me since my arrest. They beat me on my back and on the stomach. Sometimes I fell down and they would make me sit again … I was just surprised that every time they disliked my answer, they kicked me and punched me. I almost tried to commit suicide. (Filipino suspect 73)

One Indonesian suspect reported extreme physical and psychological torture:

> I was blindfolded and beaten up by officers who placed two pistols, one in each ear, and they shot the gun upwards. Then I was taken to a mountain where I was forced to confess. I was beaten up and then pushed to thorny bushes. I was put in an interrogation room and interrogated there for 36 hours. The room was air conditioned to a very low temperature. I was freezing … I wasn't allowed to sleep … I was beaten about five times and electrocuted seven times. After I was electrocuted, I was taken to a sink and my face was drowned. (Indonesian suspect 21)

Suspects pointed out that they provided unreliable information to interrogators to avoid further discomfort:

> If [practitioners] use physical contact, or torture, then people will say anything. (Filipino suspect 69)

> I was taken to another room specialized to torture people. Each time, after I was electrocuted, I was taken to a basin and my face was held underwater. The police told me it was a treatment to recover from the electric shock … I was asked if I had any knowledge of the bombing plan. I changed my answer because I was electric shocked. I made it up. I told them that I knew of the plan. (Indonesian suspect 17)

Suspects and police further acknowledged that physically coercive methods were damaging to police–community relations, and incited counter-productive retaliation:

> Firstly, they have to be professionals in their job. Secondly, do not insult ideology. [The arresting officers'] arrogance and use of excessive force is reported to the media, and it just incites anger, hatred and revenge against

> police. That's why police are being killed or shot to death now in Indonesia. (Indonesian suspect 24)

> We need to maintain that good relationship. So, for example, even though the suspect already has his punishment, and is inside the prison, we still can use him as our informant. The most important thing is that the suspect doesn't hate the police. (Indonesian practitioner 9)

Coercive practices may lead detainees to withdraw involuntary confessions at a later date. One practitioner stated:

> Successful interrogation is where the objective is achieved, and where the suspect does not withdraw their statement when they are brought to court. (Indonesian practitioner 6)

Interview training in Indonesia, the Philippines, and Sri Lanka

Most practitioners in Indonesia, the Philippines, and Sri Lanka learned their interviewing skills on the job and favored practical instruction over classroom lectures. Other had attended training courses overseas, e.g. from the Royal Canadian Mounted Police, or in India and the United States of America. Training has been provided in Indonesia by ex-US special forces personnel, CIA, FBI, and the US Secret Service. Since 2003, the Jakarta Center for Law Enforcement Cooperation at the Indonesian National Police Academy has received substantial funding from the Australian Federal Police, who provide investigative training, as do the UK Metropolitan Police. Thus practitioners in Indonesia have been influenced by both US accusatory style approaches and Australian and British interview techniques applying an information-gathering approach. Filipino practitioners have been trained by the Joint US Mutual Assistance Group and US Joint Special Operations Task Force. Thus Filipino interviewers too are influenced by US accusatory styles and only more recently UK information-gathering models. Some senior Sri Lankan practitioners reported attending training courses in the USA. In addition, the Australian Federal Police provide training as well as resources such as intelligence, vehicles and surveillance equipment to their Sri Lankan counterparts (Loewensten, 2014). Given these historical influences, it is perhaps unsurprising that qualitative analyses of descriptions provided by practitioners in these countries of the techniques that they use revealed reliance on a range of coercive and non-coercive interview strategies.

Implications for research, policy, and practice

Few law enforcement agencies have resources adequate to conduct their own research into interviewing practices, thus they tend to rely on local or international academic researchers for this information. Access by external foreign researchers to police practitioners poses linguistic, logistic, and institutional barriers, and may yield less comprehensive outcomes. Research collaboration by local practitioners and academics is preferable.

Criticisms of interview and interrogation practices in Indonesia, the Philippines, and Sri Lanka center on physically coercive techniques that include reports of torture and the absence of electronic recording procedures to increase the transparency and accountability of interview procedures and the quality of the reported outcomes. Given these contextual issues, the foregoing examination of contemporary practices revealing an emphasis by professional interviewers on non-coercive social strategies is more potent. Strong practitioner and suspect support emerged for the effectiveness in high-stakes interviews of procedurally fair, non-coercive strategies (Goodman-Delahunty *et al.*, 2013) such as rapport-building and social persuasion (Goodman-Delahunty *et al.*, 2014). This consensus confirmed a practitioner shift away from coercive, accusatory practices towards reliance on non-coercive social strategies in policing contexts across diverse legal systems and cultures. The innovative programs on deradicalization and rehabilitation interviewing drew on the same expertise and strategies. Systematic evaluations of those programs are needed.

Policy-makers in Indonesia, the Philippines, and Sri Lanka can be heartened by the widespread acknowledgment by seasoned practitioners in those communities that social interview strategies elicited reliable evidence, including inculpatory admissions, and that these strategies fully comply with international best practices and standards respectful of suspects' human rights.

Acknowledgements

Funded by the US Department of Justice Federal Bureau of Investigation High Value Interrogation Group Grant J-FBI-10-009 through the Center of Law and Human Behavior at the University of Texas at El Paso Grants 26-3002-4125 and 26-3002-4130. Research assistance was provided by Alexandra Lonergan and Melissa Martin.

References

Alison, L. J., Alison, E., Noone, G., Elntib, S., and Christiansen, P. (2013) "Why tough tactics fail and rapport gets results: observing rapport-based interpersonal techniques (ORBIT) to generate useful information from terrorists," *Psychology, Public Policy, and Law*,19 (4): 411–31.

Ball, J. (2007) "Rethinking intelligence to integrate counter terrorism into the local law enforcement mission," March. Retrieved from http://www.dtic.mil/cgi-bin/GetTRDoc?AD=ADA467414.

Cialdini, R. B. (2001) "The science of persuasion," *Scientific American*, 284 (2): 76–81.

Cordell, M. (2012) "Our money helps kill, intimidate and torture," *New Matilda*, 23 March. Retrieved from https://newmatilda.com/2012/03/23/our-money-helps-indonesia-kill-intimidate-and-torture.

Dalgaard-Nielsen, A. (2013) "Promoting exit from violent extremism: themes and approaches," *Studies in Conflict and Terrorism*, 36: 99–115.

de Keijser, J., Malsch, M., Kranendonk, R., and de Gruijter, M. (2012) "Written records of police interrogation: differential registration as a determinant of statement credibility and interrogation quality," *Psychology, Crime and Law*, 18 (7): 613–29.

Dhami, M. K., Goodman-Delahunty, J., and Martschuk, N. (2014) *Rapport and Trust as a Key to Deradicalization*. Poster presentation at the Annual Conference of the European Association of Psychology-Law, St Petersburg, Russia.

Dixon, D. (2007) *Interrogating Images: Audio-visually Recorded Police Questioning of Suspects*. Sydney: Sydney Institute of Criminology.

Fitzpatrick, P. (2008) *Law as Resistance: Modernism, Imperialism, Legalism*. London: Ashgate.

Global Counter-Terrorism Forum (2012) *Rome Memorandum on Good Practices for Rehabilitation and Reintegration of Violent Extremist Offenders*. Retrieved July 2013 from: http://www.thegctf.org/documents/10295/19359/Rome+Memorandum+on+Good+Practices+for+Rehabilitation+and+Reintegration+of+Violent+Extremist+Offenders.

Goodman-Delahunty, J. and Howes, L. M. (2014) "Social persuasion to develop rapport in high stakes interviews: qualitative analyses of Asian-Pacific practices," *Policing and Society: An International Journal of Research and Policy*. Retrieved from: http://www.tandfonline.com/doi/full/10.1080/10439463.2014.942848.

Goodman-Delahunty, J., Martschuk, N., and Dhami, M. K. (2014) "Interviewing high value detainees: securing cooperation and disclosures," *Applied Cognitive Psychology*, 28: 883–97.

Goodman-Delahunty, J., O'Brien, K., and Gumbert-Jourjon, T. (2013) 'Police professionalism in suspect interviews: cross-cultural endorsement of procedural justice," *Journal of the Institute of Justice and International Studies*,13: 65–82.

Gunaratna, R. (2011) "Terrorist rehabilitation: a global imperative," *Journal of Policing, Intelligence and Counter Terrorism*, 6 (1): 65–82.

Gunaratna, R. (2013) "Countering extremism and building social resilience through community engagement," in R. Gunaratna, J. Jerard, and S. M. Nasir (eds), *Countering Extremism: Building Social Resilience Through Community Engagement*. London: Imperial College Press, pp. 1–19.

Hampson, F. O., Sevon, L., and Wieruszewski, R. (2009) *The Implementation of Certain Human Rights Conventions in Sri Lanka: Final Report*, 30 September. Retrieved from: http://reliefweb.int/report/sri-lanka/implementation-certain-human-rights-conventions-sri-lanka-final-report.

Hedayah and the International Centre for Counter-Terrorism (ICCT) (2013) *Building on the GCTF's Rome Memorandum: Additional Guidance on the Role of Psychologists/Psychology in Rehabilitation and Reintegration Programs*. Retrieved from http://www.icct.nl/download/file/Hedayah-ICCT%20Psychology%20Good%20Practices.pdf.

Holmberg, U. and Christianson, S. (2002) "Murderers' and sexual offenders' experiences of police interviews and their inclination to admit or deny crimes," *Behavioral Sciences and the Law*, 20: 31–45.

Howie, E. (2013) Sri Lankan boat migration to Australia: Motivations and dilemmas. Economic and Political Weekly. http://www.epw.in/authors/emily-howie

Ibusuki, M. (2015) Comparative study of interview recording law: A concept for analysis of the legal framework. Presentation at the Eighth Annual Conference of the International Investigative Interviewing Research Group, Geelong, Australia.

International Crisis Group (2007) *"Deradicalization" and Indonesian Prisons*, Asia Report 142. Brussels: ICG.

Johnston, A. K. (2009) "Assessing the Effectiveness of Deradicalization Programs on Islamist Extremists. Unpublished Master's thesis, Naval Postgraduate School, Monterey, California.

Jones, C. R. (2014) "Are prisons really schools for terrorism? Challenging the rhetoric on prison radicalization," *Punishment and Society*, 16: 74–103.

Jones, C. R. and Morales, R. S. (2012) "Integration versus segregation: a preliminary examination of Philippine correctional facilities for de-radicalization," *Studies in Conflict and Terrorism*, 35: 211–28.

Kelly, C. E., Miller, J. C., Kleinman, S. M., and Redlich, A. (2013) "A taxonomy of interrogation methods," *Psychology, Public Policy, and Law*, 19 (2): 165–78.

Loewenstein, A. (2014, July) When it comes to persecution, we've given Sri Lanka plenty of help. http://www.theguardian.com/commentisfree/2014/jul/16/when-it-comes-to-persecution-weve-given-sri-lanka-plenty-of-help

Moston, S. J., Stephenson, G. M., and Williamson, T. M. (1992) "The effects of case characteristics on suspect behaviour during police questioning," *British Journal of Criminology*, 32 (1): 23–40.

Neumann, P. R. (2010) *Prisons and Terrorism: Radicalisation and De-radicalisation in 15 Countries*. London: International Centre for the Study of Radicalisation and Political Violence. Retrieved from: http://icsr.info/wp-content/uploads/2012/10/1277699166 PrisonsandTerrorismRadicalisationandDeradicalisationin15Countries.pdf.

Oktofani, E. (2012) *Cooking Up a Clean New Life*, 24 November, Khabar Southeast Asia. Retrieved from: http://khabarsoutheastasia.com/en_GB/articles/apwi/articles/features/2012/11/24/feature-02.

Porter, L. E. and Kebbell, M. R. (2011) "Radicalization in Australia: examining Australia's convicted terrorists," *Psychiatry, Psychology and Law*, 18: 212–31.

Priamarizki, A. (2013) *Counter-terrorism in Indonesia: The End of Special Detachment 88*? Retrieved from: http://legatuspropraetor.wordpress.com/2013/04/11/counter-terrorism-in-indonesia-the-end-of-special-detachment-88/.

Sivasubramaniam, D., Goodman-Delahunty, J., Martin, M., and Fraser, M. (2014) "Protecting human rights in Australian investigative interviews: The role of recording and interview duration limits," *Australian Journal of Human Rights*, 20 (2): 107–32.

Sooka, Y., The Bar Human Rights Committee of England and Wales and the International Truth and Justice Project, Sri Lanka. (2014) *An unfinished war: Torture and sexual violence in Sri Lanka 2009-2014*. http://srilankabrief.org/2014/03/report-torture-and-sexual-violence-in-sri-lanka-2009-2014/

Thomsen, M. H. (2012) *Deradicalisation – Targeted Intervention: Report on Danish Pilot Experience with Deradicalisation and Prevention of Extremism*. Helsingør: Mhtconsult. Retrieved from: http://www.sm.dk/data/Dokumentertilpublikationer/Publikationer%202012/Afradikalisering_og_malrettet_intervention/Analyserapport_uk.pdf.

Watson, J. C., Steckley, P. L., and McMullen, E. J. (2014) "The role of empathy in promoting change," *Psychotherapy Research*, 24 (3): 286–8.

Weilnböck, H. (2012) *Anti Hate Crime and Deradicalisation Interventions – in Prison and Community: The Results of Recent Good Practice Studies in Germany and Internationally*. Berlin: Violence Prevention Network. Retrieved from: http://www.niacro.co.uk/filestore/documents/hate_crime_project_papers/09_Anti_Hate_Crime_and_Deradicalisation_Interventions.pdf.

White, G., Mazerolle, L., Porter, M. D., and Chalk, P. (2014) "Modelling the effectiveness of counter-terrorism interventions," *Trends and Issues in Crime and Criminal Justice*, 475: 1–7.

3 Iran – the interrogation of suspects

Nargess Tavassolian, Mohammad Hedayati-Kakhki, Alexandra R. Harrington and Kamiar Alaei

Introduction

This chapter examines Iranian legal practices relating to the interrogation of criminal suspects. It charts the development of these practices across Iranian legal history before discussing the procedural aspects of interrogations. These practices are extensive and require a nuanced understanding of the levels of law applicable in such circumstances. Additionally, the chapter provides insights into the training given to those investigation professionals in the Iranian criminal justice system.

From the outset, it must be noted that Iranian law relies heavily on Islamic law, or *Shari'a*. Like other Islamic countries, it carries the responsibility – as denoted in the Qur'an – of codifying and applying Shari'a in society (Entessar, 1988: 95).[1] In other words, by virtue of the mere basis of Islamic government, new laws may not be created by the state, just enacted. Further, it is essential to note that the Iranian legal system operates on two separate aspects of civil and criminal legal systems.

To provide context to this chapter, there are several additional points to be borne in mind. Crimes under Islamic law are broken into four categories based on their punishments: (1) *hadd* (pl. *hudud*) – crimes that have punishment for which the grounds for, type, amount, and conditions of execution are specified in holy *Shari'a*; (2) *ta'zir* – crimes for which the amount and type are not specified in *Shari'a*; (3) *qisas* – intentional bodily crimes; and (4) *diyya* – whether fixed or unfixed, a monetary amount under holy *Shari'a* which is determined by law and shall be paid for unintentional bodily crimes against life, limbs, and abilities or for intentional crimes when for whatever reason *qisas* is not applicable (Islamic Penal Code, 2013).[2] These different categories of crimes influence the manner in which suspects are treated. Certain crimes prompt pre-trial detention while others do not. Further, the classification of a crime influences the kind and number of witnesses necessary to make a case. While retribution and restitution are important considerations in Iranian law, Islamic law does favour forgiveness above all else, as it is deemed pleasing to God (Entessar, 1988). However, retribution is only deemed acceptable for *qisas* crimes, which include murder, manslaughter, mutilation, and battery. The family of the victim (in cases where the victim is dead, otherwise this is the right of the victim and not his/her family) may choose to inflict injury on the perpetrator that is of equal injury to that of the victim's injury (Entessar, 1998).

Historical development

The development of practices relating to the interrogation of suspects in Iran must be set in the historical context of a larger Persian civilization that is more than 3,000 years old. Cyrus the Great (576–530 BC) developed an empire comprising a civilization of diverse religions, cultures, and languages based on equality and tolerance. He is acknowledged as the author of the first Declaration of Human Rights, almost two millennia before the Magna Carta (ABC 2013). The justice system during this era is known as one in which freedom of the citizens was respected, slavery was forbidden, and people of different languages and cultures were granted equal rights and equal religious expression under the law (Haas, 2008). The Declaration of Human Rights safeguarded individuals from abuses by the state and those who delegated authority, protecting people against arbitrary arrest, torture, and other unfair treatment.

During the seventh century, Islam began to spread to Persia as it was known at the time. During this time, the foundations of Islamic law or Shari'a, namely the Qur'an and Sunnah, formed the basis of law in this country, codifying the rights of individuals and providing guidelines for their treatment should they break the law. It is clearly expressed within the Qur'an that inalienable individual rights are to be respected and no one should be held responsible without an appropriate proof. Islam developed a comprehensive standard of proof including confession, witness testimony, evidence, and knowledge of the judge.

In the Middle Ages, Iran was ruled by two successive Islamic dynasties, the longest reigning being the Safavid (1501–1722), during which time there was a mass conversion to Shi'a-ism, the second largest school of thought within Islam after Sunnism. The essential tenets of Shi'a beliefs resulted in a steady development of a powerful class of Shi'a clergy who exerted their influence, particularly in the area of law and justice. Relevant to the practice of the interrogation of suspects, during this era a secondary body of regulation developed which provided the framework necessary to address societal breaches not expressly mentioned in the Qur'an. They include consensus of the jurists (*Ijma*), analogy (*Qiyas*), independent reasoning (*Ijtihad*), and local tradition (*Urf*). All these secondary sources, in addition to what is stated within the Qur'an and the teachings of the Prophet Mohammad (Sunnah), were the basis for the treatment of a suspect facing interrogation and trial. It should be noted that, since the beginning of Islamic rule in Persia, both a religious and a traditional judiciary coexisted. The division was made in that the customary court applied the traditional *Urfi* law whereas the religious court used Islamic law as the basis of their judgements. Religious authorities predominantly dealt with torts, especially if they related to family law matters (*Encyclopedia Iranica*). It is important to note, however, that customary law was only enforceable so long as it was not in direct contradiction with the principles of Islamic *Shari'a* law.

During the post-Safavid period, the influence of the religious judiciary became less evident. Not until the mid-to-late nineteenth century did the Iranian judicial system begin to reform in the modern sense. During the Qajar dynasty and in particular under the leadership of Nasser al-Din Shah (1831–96), a number of western-influenced reforms were introduced including within the judiciary. The lack of uniformity between traditional (*Urfi*) and Islamic (*Shari'a*) courts and the sphere of their jurisdictions were specifically questioned. There were also challenges to the role and power of the clergy as well as the importance of circumstantial evidence within proceedings. The pressure for judicial reform intensified during the 1905–9 Constitutional Revolution. Following this troubled time, the country developed a codified legal system adopted from the European legal codes with a heavy influence from the French civil system of law. The modifications made to the Constitution in 1907 took into account the long-standing religious influence in the country's legal system by providing for a two-tiered structure – secular and religious – with a central office established to decide which cases went to the *Shari'a* courts. They repeated the ban against judicial torture, restricted executions to hangings and firing squads, and promised to respect the independence of the judiciary and the rights of the accused when standing trial.

Further attempts at reform of Iran's legal structures and the treatment of suspects began in 1910 but did not lead to substantive change until Reza Shah came to power in 1925. He began to completely reshape the traditional Iranian criminal justice system, introducing a series of new laws shifting the emphasis from Islamic traditional roots toward a western modern legal practice (Shahidullah, 2012). During this era, a modern Prosecutor's Office was established (1939), which mirrored the similar French institution. The definition of a suspect, the rights of the accused, and the methods of interrogation, the types of questions posed, the manner in which evidence is collected and the general structure of the Prosecutor's Office were almost identical to that practiced in France (Madelung and Daftary, 2007).

The Iranian Revolution in 1979 ended the experiment of liberalism in the country as manifested in the Constitution of 1906–7. A new Constitution was almost immediately introduced and Islam was declared the sole source of law in the country. The impact on criminal law was significant, as a new Islamic Penal Code[3] replaced the previous rights-based system redefining the types of crimes and introducing a new set of corresponding Islamic punishments.[4] It is clear from this development that the rights of suspects deteriorated substantially during the post-revolutionary period.

The structure of the Iranian criminal justice system and its impact on suspects

As both the interrogation of suspects and the treatment they receive are conducted by the Iranian judiciary, it is crucial to have an understanding of the procedural, operational, and hierarchical framework of the Iranian court system. It is also important to define the words 'suspect' and 'interrogation' as understood within Iran. By definition, an individual believed to be guilty of a crime or offence is regarded as a suspect. A mere suspicion, even when there is no concrete evidence of guilt, will also fall within the scope of being a suspect.

Entering into private property (e.g. dwellings, places of business, storage, etc.) for the purposes of criminal investigation must be done only through a court order. In the same manner, questioning suspected individuals, and searching the objects in non-obvious crimes, must be based on a court order (Art. 55, Criminal Procedure Code, 2014).[5] The judicial authorities must fashion the court order precisely and avoid sanctioning the inspection of irrelevant places or the questioning of non-suspicious individuals (Art. 56, Criminal Procedure Code).

According to Art. 32[6] of the Iranian Constitution no one may be detained or arrested unless certain, well-defined circumstances exist. In case of arrest, the accused is guaranteed distinct and specific rights that police and detention officers (that the accused may come in contact with prior to trial) are obliged to observe. Both parties to a lawsuit have the right in all courts of law to an attorney, and if they are unable to appoint one due to financial constraints, arrangements must be made to provide them with legal counsel for the most serious crimes (Rules 1–3, Act of Civil Rights and Legitimate Freedoms 2004).

Presumption of innocence

The presumption of innocence is enshrined within the Iranian Constitution. Article 37 stipulates that, "Innocence is to be presumed, and no one is to be held guilty of a charge unless his or her guilt has been established by a competent court." Despite this legal guarantee, in practice, interrogations are often conducted with a presumption of guilt and are the process by which information and confessions are extracted from suspects (Freedom from Torture Report, 2013). For example, in some cases, the accused or defendant was subjected to torture during the first few days of interrogation (Raeisi, 2010).

Furthermore, questions raised during interrogation must be clear, useful and related to the charges at hand. Curiosity regarding family and personal secrets and investigation of past irrelevant issues or conduct should be prohibited (Sub-articles 1–9, Statute of Respecting Legitimate Freedoms and Protecting Citizens' Rights 2004).[7] In practice, interrogators have not carefully implemented these principles and sometimes they have strayed into questioning about the accused's private life in order to convince the accused that his/her life is under the control and complete observation of the interrogators (Bahari, 2011).

Pre-trial investigations

In each regional district of the Prosecutor Office, a number of investigatory judges called the interrogators (*bazpors*) and secondary interrogators (*dadyar*) work under the supervision of the Deputy Prosecutor. These judges lead the investigation by managing its direction, for instance by specifying questions to ask at the suspect's interrogation or when investigating the witnesses, as well as providing guidance to law enforcement officials on how to gather relevant incriminating evidence. If the subject is required to appear before the investigating authorities, the initial mechanism utilized is the issuance of a summons.

Summoning the accused for the interrogation

Summoning the accused in a criminal investigation must be performed through a subpoena issued by the judicial authorities (Rule 1, Act of Civil Rights and Legitimate Liberties, 2004). It is necessary that the complete name of the accused be mentioned in the formal subpoena, alongside the exact details about the place and the time of that summons, and the legal consequences of absence for questioning (Arts. 169–70, Criminal Procedure Code).

The reasons for the issuance of the summons must be clearly cited in the subpoena, except in those situations where the judicial authority believes there are serious concerns for the reputation of the accused (before trial), or violation of public morals and public safety. In such circumstances, the reasons for the summons will not be mentioned in the subpoena; however, the accused can ask the judicial authorities about those reasons. In addition, the time interval between serving the subpoena and presence of the accused before the investigator should not be less than five days (Arts. 170–1, Criminal Procedure Code).

At the Prosecutor's Office, the investigatory judge should first ask the suspect to confirm his/her identity and address. He will also warn the suspect to be cautious about his/her statements and will inform the suspect about the accusation and its reasons. He will then start the interrogation. It should be noted that the preliminary interrogation should be confidential except in cases defined by law (Art. 91, Criminal Procedure Code).

Interrogation of the suspect

Interrogations should be distinguished from interviews, which is the approach when there is no evidence of guilt but the subject is merely a suspect who may have committed a crime or may be in possession of information that may assist in the discovery of an offence. When embarking upon the initial investigation of criminal matters, the authority responsible for its conduct and process is the Public and Revolutionary Prosecutor's Office. The system used in criminal justice within Iran is the inquisitorial system. Within this system, the judiciary plays a role in establishing the case and is actively involved in determining the facts, as opposed to an adversarial system where the role of the court is solely that of an impartial adjudicator.[8]

The questions asked during the interrogation should be clear and relate directly to the subject matter of the case. Compulsive and deceptive questions are prohibited and if the subject refuses to provide answers to the questions this refusal will be documented. All responses to the questions must be recorded as they are exactly expressed without any modification, distortion or change. Educated suspects could write their answers themselves (Art. 129, Criminal Procedure Code).

Protections against torture in investigations and interrogations[9]

Any form of torture to secure a confession or extract information is prohibited as per the Iranian Constitution (Arts. 22 and 38).[10] Any confession or evidence taken by force is null and void (Shahidullah, 2012: 426). The issue of the prohibition on torture has also been dealt with in the Islamic Penal Code and the Criminal Procedure Code.[11] The IPC considers the physical abuse of detainees as a crime and stipulates that if "Employees of the judiciary and non-judiciary branches of the government force a suspect to confess through the use of physical harassment or any form of retaliation, they would be liable to a sentence of between six months and three years imprisonment" (Art. 578, Islamic Penal Code).

Confidentiality of the investigation

Preliminary interrogation should be confidential except in cases defined by law (Art. 91, Criminal Procedure Code). Interrogation in some categories of crimes, such as sex crimes, requires specific circumstances, for instance "any kind of investigation or prosecution for adultery, sodomy, and indecent related crimes is prohibited and nobody should be investigated for these issues except in cases that the crime is publicly visible or it has a plaintiff. In these cases, the prosecution and investigation will be limited to the complaint or circumstances evident only by a trial judge (Art. 102, Criminal Procedure Code).

The suspect's right to remain silent

One of the most important rights of an individual accused of a crime is the right to remain silent. This means that the defendant has the right to be silent and to refuse to answer the questions. In such situations, the court officials have no right to force him to speak, and they must only mention the accused's silence during the interrogation and apply other methods for discovering the truth. The importance of the right to silence is even greater in cases where the accused has not yet had access to his/her lawyer, or the accused is unfamiliar with his/her rights. Based on some rules of the former Criminal Procedure Code for Public and Revolutionary Courts (1999), it would be argued that legislators and judges implicitly accepted this right, so that the judges and investigators were obliged to respect it during the initial investigations. Notwithstanding, the new Criminal Procedure Code (2014) has explicitly recognized the right to silence in Art. 197. Accordingly, if the accused refuses to respond or sign the statement, that refusal must be mentioned in the court reports.

The suspect's right to an attorney

Suspects can have a lawyer at the investigation stage. Having access to a lawyer during the interrogation process is one of the requirements for a fair trial.[12] Furthermore, "depriving a litigant from having a lawyer in trial is illegal and those judges who did so will be faced with disciplinary sanctions" (Art. 2, Act of Choosing a Lawyer by the Litigants, 1991). According to Art. 3 of the aforementioned Act, defense attorneys must have enjoyed the professional respect and the immunity that is necessary for carrying out their representations. However, in practice, lawyers almost always have been faced with many obstacles in having access to the materials of the cases, especially in serious crimes or political accusations, as the initial investigations have been perceived as a confidential step in the Iranian judicial system.

The lawyer cannot interfere with the interrogation but rather can assist the judge by providing documentary evidence and defending their client based on the relevant provisions of law after the initial investigation is completed. The law allows the investigatory judge to disallow the presence of the lawyers or restrict it until a certain stage of the proceedings in investigations regarding crimes against national security and morality offences (Art. 35, Constitution; Art. 128, Criminal Procedure Code). For example, those accused of organized crimes, offenses against the national security, robbery, narcotic trafficking, and crimes that will be punished with harsh corporal penalties, such as execution, amputation, or life imprisonment, and paying the complete or one-third of the blood money (i.e. *diyya*) cannot meet with their lawyers in the first week of their detainment (Arts. 48 and 302, Criminal Procedure Code). Unfortunately, almost all of the conscientious/political accused have been systematically deprived of their fundamental rights through the above exception, while the ordinary accused usually do not enjoy their legitimate rights during the investigations.

The suspect's right to a public defender

As Art. 190 prescribes, "in crimes for which the legal punishment is retribution, execution, stoning or a life sentence, and if the accused does not introduce his or her attorney during the initial investigations, assigning a public defender is a must for the court." According to Art. 347, "the accused can ask the court to appoint him or her a defense lawyer on the first trial session. If the accused is unable to afford a lawyer, the court will provide the accused with legal counsel, and will pay that lawyer."

Moreover, with crimes for which the legal punishment is execution, life imprisonment, or mutilation, and those crimes that will be punished with paying the complete or one-third of the blood money (*diyya*), the trial session would not be held without the presence of the defense lawyers (Art. 348, Criminal Procedure Code).

Procedures for crimes discovered by law enforcement

For the sake of completeness, there is a separate procedure used when a law enforcement authority (i.e. disciplinary forces/police or other similar bodies) discovers a crime. In this instance, they would be responsible for the investigation and acquisition of evidence on their own initiative without the need for prior permission from the Prosecutor's Office. They may interrogate and detain the individual on their own authority but are restricted to a 24-hour detention unless judicial permission can be secured to extend this time (from the Prosecutor's Office). The authorized entities include the police (who work under the direction of the Ministry of the Interior and the judiciary), the security forces (who are part of the Ministry of Intelligence and Information), and the Basij.[13]

The role of the investigatory judge

At the end of the investigation, if the investigatory judge is satisfied that sufficient information has been gathered to establish the guilt of the suspect and that there are otherwise reasonable prospects of success, he drafts a Bill of Indictment, addressed to the court and formally charging the accused. The indictment should specify the personal information of the defendant, a brief description of the criminal act committed as well as basic information on those acts constituting justification for the charges faced. In addition, the indictment would highlight the Articles breached by the defendant's behavior and request the court to proceed with adjudication on the defendant's liability on the basis of these provisions.

Acting as an organizer and leader of the pre-trial investigation, but before the indictment is drafted, the investigatory judge should also issue a preliminary finding of guilt (*Gharar-e Mojremiat*), which is not a 'conviction' but rather a professional determination at that stage. The Prosecutor or the Deputy Prosecutor of the district should approve this decision, and it is only after this approval is granted will the Bill of Indictment be issued. If sufficient evidence is actually gathered to proceed with the Bill of Indictment, then the case, along with the decision of the Prosecutor's Office, will be sent to the Criminal court/Revolutionary court administration. The administration will then assign a particular court branch to the case, which would then proceed to list the case for trial.

Gaps in professional personnel training

The initial investigation plays a vital role not only in deliberating the fate of accused individuals, but also in the realization of victims' rights and establishing justice[14] (Khalatbari, 1964). Within the Iranian criminal justice system, the initial investigation has been confined to the legal measures of the judicial officer or the research judge, who is responsible for collecting tangible evidence either against the accused individual or in his or her favor, issuing criminal security warrants to prevent the accused from absconding, hiding, or distributing evidence, as well as commenting about the guilt and/or innocence of the suspect (Ashori, 2000; Akhondi, 2006).

In cases of both pre-trial detention as well as post-penal detention, prison officers are or may be untrained in the proper handling of inmates. Often, these individuals are fulfilling compulsory military service and also have not received training in the proper handling of prisoners and pre-trial detainees. In the latter case, prison officers are in direct contact with the accused on a daily basis and when transferring prisoners, and have a greater opportunity to perpetrate violations of an accused's rights.

The only mentionable criteria for interrogation are the usefulness of questions for the investigators. In this situation, torture, despite its legal prohibition, has been used frequently in the law enforcement detention centers (Amnesty International Report 2014). In addition, some practices, such as covering the eyes while the accused individual has been chained hand and foot, cannot be excused according to both the constitutional obligations of the government and its dedication to the international human rights conventions[15] (Moazenzadegan, 2007; Goldust, 2007; Khaleghi, 2008). The Criminal Procedure Code (Arts. 53 and 60) does not stipulate the specific time and length of interrogations. Only Art. 183 of the Criminal Procedure Code asserts that arraignment is prohibited during the night, except for urgent issues based on the decision of the investigator.

As sources have noted, "according to the Articles 168[16] and 195[17] of the Criminal Procedure Code and the commentary notes of the Iranian Judiciary Branch, there must be a probable cause and reliable evidence to charge a defendant with a crime." Moreover, as Langeroudi (1980) argued, the rights of the accused[18] must be considered and be respected according to Islamic law. In this manner, the arraignment must be clear and quick to prevent any potential endangering of the presumption of innocence (Ardabili Mosavi, 1988). Accused women should be interrogated by female judicial officers, while only skilled investigators should question immature individuals within the juvenile justice system (Arts. 42 and 285, Criminal Procedure Code, 2014). Despite these facts, the confrontation between investigators, as the delegates of the dominant authority of the government, and the accused individual only repeats the sequence of citation–arrest–interrogation–trial–conviction in the Iranian criminal justice system (Shamloo Ahmadi, 2004; Yaghobi, 2003; Mohajeri, 2002).

Conclusion

Iran has developed a thoroughly modern, comprehensive legal system where the rights of suspects when arrested and during interrogation by law enforcement officials are theoretically safeguarded. However, whether these laws are implemented in practice continues to be questioned due to the existence of a number of credible human rights reports that contain various examples of these rules having been abused. This has been known to include extension of detention time limits and pressures exhorted on those who have been detained to obtain confessions, as well as denial of access to medical attention, denial of access to a lawyer, and arbitrary arrest.

Iranian laws do provide for the rights of the accused and pertinent legal guarantees during a criminal investigation; however, in practice, many of these rules have not been respected, especially in regard to conscientious/political prisoners, which seems to have happened intentionally rather than through mistake.

The Iranian judicial system has routinely applied the inquisitorial system during the preliminary stages of criminal investigations. Given the lack of sufficient attention to scientific techniques for investigating crime, there are serious concerns with regard to the strict enforcement of rules and legal guarantees in this system.

Acknowledgements

This chapter could not have been completed without the authorship of Nargess Tavassolian, Mohammad Hedayati-Kakhki, Alexandra Harrington, and Kamiar Alaei, who each offered their decades of collective academic and professional experience to explain and contextualize the background and current practices of the Iranian criminal justice system with respect to the treatment of suspects. Mehrnoosh Karimi Andu, Reza Raeesi, and Nakissa Jahanbani each also contributed to the writing, research, and translation necessary for this chapter.

Notes

1. Islamic law is known as the law of God or the *Shari'a*, which literally translates to mean "the way" (which, as revealed to the Prophet Muhammad, is the sum of God's will) (Mir-Hosseini, 2006). Classically, Islam draws no distinction between religious and secular life. Hence, *Shari'a* covers not only religious rituals, but also many aspects of day-to-day life, politics, economics, banking, business or contract law, and social issues. The term *Shari'a* itself, derives from the verb *shara'a*, which connects to the idea of spiritual law and the system of divine law. *Shari'a* has certain laws that are regarded as divinely ordained, concrete, and timeless for all relevant situations (i.e. the ban against drinking liquor as an intoxicant).

   Shari'a is based on four primary sources: (1) the Qur'an; (2) the *hadith* or tradition; (3) *ijma'* or consensus of jurists; and (4) *'aql* or reasoning (Entessar, 1988: 94). The Qur'an is the foundational source of law for all *Shari'a*; however, Shi'a *Shari'a* also places a great deal of weight on the considerations and views of the Imams in the formation of its legal system (Entessar, 1988: 94).

   Hadith, translated as "the tradition," refers to the statements, deeds, and sayings of the Prophet and the Imams recorded and codified by their companions (Entessar,1988: 94). Both *ijma'* and *'aql* are considered as secondary sources of Shi'a law, with the former delineating the views of the Shi'a scholars who were close companions of the Imams and the latter describing judgements based on pure and practical reason from which religious law can be inferred (Entessar, 1988: 94).

   Islamic jurisprudence is called *fiqh* (meaning "understanding") and refers to the inferences about Islamic rules drawn by scholars from the principles divined from Shari'a. *Fiqh* (described by Mir-Hosseini (2006) as that which is discerned and extracted from the sacred sources of Islam, i.e. the Qur'an and the *hadith*) is divided into two parts: the study of the sources and methodology (*usul fiqh*, "roots of the law") and the practical rules (*furu fiqh*, "branches of the law"). Legal scholars hope that Shari'a and *fiqh* are in harmony at all times, but in any given case cannot be sure.

   Shari'a is "sacred, universal, and eternal," while *fiqh* is that as subjectively interpreted and, like other forms of jurisprudence, can subsequently change over time (Mir-Hosseini, 2006). A final consideration is that *fiqh* is frequently, but falsely, likened to *Shari'a* by legal specialists, politicians, academics, and in popular Muslim discourses, and "often with ideological intent; that is, what Islamists and others assert to be a *Shari'a* mandate (hence divine and infallible)" (Mir-Hosseini,, 2006: 632).

2. The Iranian penal code upholds the four major categories of crime in Islamic law: *hudud*, *qisas*, *ta'zir*, and *diyyat*. *Hudud* crimes include theft, robbery, adultery, drinking alcohol, and rebellion. In Islamic law, adultery is classified as intercourse that could result in the creation of offspring (Reza, 2013: 21). Punishments for *hudud* crimes are enumerated in the Qur'an, and range from stoning to bodily mutilation to execution.

   Qisas crimes include murder, manslaughter, and mutilation. These offenses are regarded as acts against the victim. It is left to the discretion of the victim's family whether retributive injury should be inflicted on the perpetrator that is exactly equal to that inflicted on the victim (Entessar, 1988: 98). Despite the legalization of retribution and vendettas, the Qur'an and Iranian penal code recommend forgiveness as it is deemed pleasing to God (Entessar, 1988: 98).

   Ta'zir crimes are not otherwise specified in the Qur'an or *hadith*. Punishments for these crimes range from fines to seizure of property and public flogging. The judge is burdened with determining an appropriate punishment considering the temporal culture and public interest of the community (Entessar, 1988: 98).

   Diyyat, or blood money, delineates a form of compensation (i.e. reparation) rather than a category of punishment. In lieu of *qisas* (i.e. retribution), the victim's family may elect to seek reparations from the perpetrator. The Iranian penal code has codified *diyyat* allocations for numerous crimes (Entessar, 1988: 98).
3. Immediately after the 1979 Revolution, there was no Islamic criminal law. The Islamic Penal Code (IPC) is an important component of Islamic criminal law, as are the procedures enumerated in the Criminal Procedure Code. The first IPC was passed on 22 May 1982, and was implemented on 15 December 1982. The second IPC was passed in 1991. A new section on *ta'zir* crimes was added to that code in 1996. The newest version of the IPC was enacted and later enforced in 2013.
4. Additionally, a number of new crimes were introduced based on *Shari'a* law such as prohibitions on drinking alcohol and sex outside marriage. Additionally, corporal punishments including lashes and the amputation of limbs returned to the criminal justice system as a day-to-day method of punishment.
5. This legislation is formally titled as the "Criminal Code of Procedure in Public and Revolutionary Courts." Different authors and academic traditions refer to it in slightly different terms. For instance, Asli (2006) refers to it as the "Procedure Act of General and Revolutionary Courts in Penal Matters," shorted to "Criminal Procedure Act." Herein, this legislation will be referred to as the "Criminal Procedure Code" and will be regarded in its most recent iteration that was enacted and later enforced in 2014. If a previous version of the Code is referred to, it will be cited to include the year of its enforcement.
6. Ratified in December 1979 and revised in 1989.
7. This statute has only one article and 15 sub-articles.
8. The remit of the state-appointed Prosecutor's Office is to undertake the pre-trial investigation of an offence, issuing a Bill of Indictment and transferring the matter to the Criminal Division of the Public Court system if a case fulfills the criterion of having a successful prospect of securing a conviction. If the case falls within the jurisdiction of the Revolutionary Court, this judicial body would conduct the investigation through their allocated branches of the Prosecutor's Office.
9. Although Iran has not joined the UN Convention against Torture, the prohibition of torture has been addressed in its Constitution (Arts. 22 and 38) as well as other Iranian legislation.
10. Article 22 states "the dignity, life, property, rights, residence, and occupation of the individual are inviolate, except in cases sanctioned by law." Article 38 directly emphasizes the prohibition of torture. It states: "All forms of torture for the purpose of extracting confession or acquiring information are forbidden. Compulsion of individuals to testify, confess, or take an oath is not permissible; and any testimony, confession, or oath obtained under duress is devoid of value and credence. Violation of this article is liable to punishment in accordance with the law."

11. Based on Article 60 of the Criminal Procedure Code, "coercion or duress of accused person or using derogatory words; or misleading, deceptive or off-topic questions are prohibited during interrogation; therefore, response to these types of questions, or statements under the coercion or duress is not valid. Date, time and duration of interrogation should be mentioned in the interrogation forms and documented by accused's signature or fingerprint."
12. This right has been purported in different laws such as Iran's Constitution, the Criminal Procedure Code (2014), and the Act of Civil Rights and Legitimate Freedoms (2004).
13. A voluntary militia authorized by the judiciary to have arrest powers.
14. Article 90 of the Criminal Procedure Code states: "The initial investigations involve a set of measures that are required to detect a crime and to preserve its proof and evidence, and to try the accused from the beginning of a case until it is taken to the judicial authority."
15. The Constitution of the Islamic Republic of Iran notes some of these rights, for example Art. 38 (see note 10 above). Further, Art. 39 also asserts that: "All affronts to the dignity and repute of persons arrested, detained, imprisoned, or banished in accordance with the law, whatever form they may take, are forbidden and liable to punishment." The punishment mentioned would be based on Art. 578 of the new Islamic Penal Code (2013). However, this article covers only physical and not spiritual tortures.
16. "The judge should not summon or arrest a person, unless there are valid reasons for summoning or arrest, thus, the interrogation of suspect individuals must be according to valid reasons and evidences."
17. "The judicial officer should first notify the accused to be cautious about his statements. Then, he will explain the subject of the accusation and its reasons clearly. The judicial officer will announce to the accused that his cooperation with police could introduce a lower level of culpability, then he will start the investigation. The questions shall be clear and useful. Empathic, deceptive, reluctant and compulsive questions are prohibited." In practice, judicial officers do not warn the accused individuals orally because in the headings of formal interrogation letters, there is a written warning about statements by the accused. However, in the new code of criminal procedure, breach of this duty is subject to specified legal punishments. There is an identical problem with respect to mentioning the right of having access to a lawyer during the investigation (Art. 190, Criminal Procedure Code).
18. In different judicial systems, various rights have been affirmed for accused individuals, including the right to silence and the right to clear arraignment. Within the Iranian criminal justice system, only the right to silence has been approved implicitly (Art. 197, Criminal Procedure Code).

References

ABC News: "Before Constitution, Magna Carta, the Cyrus Cylinder Was Model of Tolerance." Retrieved from: http://cyruscylinder2013.com/2013/03/abc-news-magna-carta-cyrus-cyliner/ (last accessed 27 November 2014).

Abdul Hashem, Y. (2003) *The Investigation of Crimes on Judicial Trials*. Tehran: Ferdowsi.

Act of Choosing a Lawyer by the Litigants of the Islamic Republic of Iran (1991).

Act of Civil Rights and Legitimate Freedoms (2004).

Akhondi, M. (2006) *The Regulations of Penal Prosecution, Vol. 5*. Tehran: Majd Publishing.

Ali, K. (2008) *Ayin dadrasi keyfari* [*Criminal Procedure Law*]. Tehran: Shahr-e Danesh.

Ali, M. (2002) *The Trial Procedure*. Tehran: Fekr sazan.

Amnesty International (2014) *Torture in 2014: 30 Years of Broken Promises*. Retrieved from: http://www.amnestyusa.org/sites/default/files/act400042014en.pdf.

Ardabili Mosavi, S. A. (1988) *Fiqh Al-Ghaza*. Qom: Amir Al-Momenin Publications.

Arsalan, K. (1964) "Sherkat-e vakil dar tahghighat-e bazporsi" ["The presence of defense attorney in the interrogations"], *Magazine of the Iranian Bar Association*, 92.

Ashori, M. (2000) *Criminal Procedure Law, Vol. II*. Tehran: Samt Publications.

Asli, M. R. (2006) "Iranian criminal justice system in light of international standards relating to victims?" *European Journal of Crime, Criminal Law, and Criminal Justice*, 14: 185–207.

Bahari, M. (2011) *Then They Came for Me*. New York: Random House.

Constitution of the Islamic Republic of Iran (1979). Available at: http://www.refworld.org/docid/3ae6b56710.html (accessed 14 December 2015).

Criminal Code of Procedure for Public and Revolutionary Court (1999) Available at: http://www.ghavanin.ir/detail.asp?id=11610.

Criminal Code of Procedure for Public and Revolutionary Courts (2014) Available at: http://www.shenasname.ir/didgah/2329-aeen.html.

Encyclopaedia Iranica, "Judicial and Legal Systems iv. Judicial System from the Advent of Islam Through the 19th Century." Available at: http://www.iranicaonline.org/articles/judicial-and-legal-systems-iv-judicial-system-from-the-advent-of-islam-through-the-19th-century.

Entessar, N. (1988) "Criminal law and the legal system in revolutionary Iran," *Boston College Third World Law Journal*, 81: 91–102. Retrieved from: http://lawdigitalcommons.bc.edu/twlj/vol8/iss1/8.

Freedom from Torture Report (2013) "We will make you regret everything." Available at: http://www.freedomfromtorture.org/sites/default/files/documents/iran%20report_A4%20-%20FINAL%20web.pdf (last accessed 20 November 2014).

Goldust, R. A. (2007) *Principles of Criminal Procedure Law*. Tehran: Jangal Publications.

Haas, M. (2008) *International Human Rights: A Comprehensive Introduction*. London: Routledge.

Hasan Ali, M. (2007) "The legal guarantees of accused rights in primarily investigations and interrogation," *Magazine of Law and Policy Research*, 28: 301–30. Available at: http://www.sid.ir/fa/VEWSSID/J_pdf/74013892811.pdf.

IHRDC, Criminal Code of Procedures for Public and Revolutionary Court (1999). Available at: http://www.iranhrdc.org/english/human-rights-documents/iranian-codes/1000000026-english-translation-of-the-islamic-republic-of-irans-criminal-code-of-procedure-for-public-and-revolutionary-courts.html#.VGqntuNb2pE.link.

Islamic Penal Code of the Islamic Republic of Iran (2013)

Jafar, M. L. (1980) *The Encyclopedia of Islamic Law: Comparative and Scientific Study, 1*. Tehran: Ganj-e Danesh.

Khalatbari, A. (1964) "The presence of the defense attorney in interrogations," *Iranian Bar Association Journal*, 92.

Khaleghi, A. (2008) *Criminal Procedure Law*. Tehran: Shahr-e Danesh Publications.

Langeroudi, M. (1980) *The Encyclopedia of Islamic Law: Comparative and Scientific Study, 1*. Tehran: Ganj-e Danesh Publications.

Madelung, W. and Daftary, F. (2007) "Interrogators (bazpors)," in W. Madelung and F. Daftary (eds), *Encyclopaedia Islamica*. Leiden: Brill Academic. Available at: http://referenceworks.brillonline.com/browse/encyclopaedia-islamica.

Mahmood, A. (2006) *The Regulations of Penal Prosecution, Vol. 5*. Tehran: Majd.

Michael, H. (2012) *International Human Rights: A Comprehensive Introduction*. London: Routledge.

Mir-Hosseini, Z. (2006) "Muslim women's quest for equality: between Islamic law and feminism," *Critical Inquiry*, 32: 629–45.

Moazenzadegan, H. (2007) "The legal guarantees of the accused's rights in primary investigations and interrogations," *Law and Policy Research Journal*, 28: 301–30. Retrieved from: http://www.sid.ir/fa/VEWSSID/J_pdf/74013892811.pdf.

Mohajeri, A. (2002) *The Trial Procedures, Vol. 1*. Tehran: Fekr Sazan Publications.

Nader, E. (1988) "Criminal law and the legal system in revolutionary Iran," *Boston College Third World Law Journal*, 81: 91–102. Available at http://lawdigitalcommons.bc.edu/twlj/vol8/iss1/8.

Raeisi, G. (2010) "Respecting Human Dignity During Preliminary Investigation." Dissertation, Tehran University.

Rajab-Ali, G. (2007) *Koliyat Ayin dadrasi keyfari* [*The Principles of Criminal Procedure Law*]. Tehran: Jangal.

Reza, S. (2013) "Due process in Islamic criminal law," *George Washington International Law Review*, 46: 1–27.

Sadiq, R. (2013) "Due process in Islamic criminal law," *George Washington International Law Review*, 46: 1–27.

Shahidullah, S. M. (2012) *Comparative Criminal Justice Systems*. Burlington, MA: Jones & Bartlett Learning.

Shamloo Ahmadi, M. H. (2004) *Prosecution and Initial Investigation, Vol. I*. Isfahan: Dadyar Publications.

Statute of Respecting Legitimate Freedoms and Protecting Citizens' Rights (2004).

Yaghobi, A. H. (2003) *The Investigation of Crimes on Judicial Trials, Vol. VI*. Tehran: Ferdowsi Publications.

4 Investigative interviews with alleged suspects in Israel

It's all about age

Carmit Katz

Introduction

Exploring interview practices with suspects in Israel revealed the tremendous differences that exist between interview practices with children under the age of 14, with children above the age of 14, young people and adults. Children under the age of 14 in Israel are protected by a unique law created in 1955, the Law of Evidence Revision (Protection of Children). This law requires all children who are suspects to be interviewed by a special practitioner ('a child forensic interviewer') and that this interviewer be the only one who can approach the children. Organizationally, the child forensic interviewer is part of the welfare office, specifically the Service of Investigative Interviews. Additional legislation that is highly important for the understanding of the practices is that the age of criminal responsibility in Israel is 12 years, which means that regardless of the crime, if the suspect is under the age of 12, s/he cannot be criminally charged.

This law is not applicable to children above the age of 14 who are interviewed by a special unit in the police called the 'youth investigators'. The aim of this special unit is to interview and manage the criminal cases of youth in Israel. It is important to note that these interviews are not recorded, although documentation of it is usually carried out by the youth investigators. Moreover, it is important to stress that there is no standardised practice for interviewing accused youth in Israel and that no published studies were carried out on forensic interviewing among this population. Above the age of 18, young people and adults are interviewed by police officers trained to be investigators. In a similar way to forensic investigations with youth, the documentation of the interviews is carried out by the police officers, with no standardised best practice for interviewing and no published research. When suspects are accused following matters of security the investigation takes place by a special service in Israel, but no published information can be found on that area.

It is important to stress that the differences in legislation are not merely organisational. The child forensic interviewers are social workers in response to the notion that a child cannot be solely a perpetrator and that any child in this age group who was involved in the alleged incident is an 'at-risk' child. In contrast, youth or police investigators are dedicated to law enforcement and therefore represent the perspective of crime detection. This difference creates an enormous gap in practices, which might be a result of the resources dedicated to it. It is extremely important to stress that the area of forensic investigation with suspects in Israel is an understudied one, with no published information of the practices of youth and police investigators and sparse research with respect to forensic investigations with accused children.

The development of interview practices for alleged suspects in Israel

The practice for interviewing children who are suspects in alleged sexual assault cases up to the age of 14 is the NICHD (National Institute for Child Health and Human Development) Protocol. The use of this Protocol reflects the notion in Israel that children, even when forensically interviewed as suspects, are assumed to be victims and are treated correspondingly. As children up to the age of 12 have no criminal responsibility, they are interviewed in exactly the same way as alleged victims of abuse.

The NICHD Protocol (Lamb *et al.*, 2008; Orbach *et al.*, 2000) is fully structured and covers all phases of the investigative interview. In the introductory phase, the interviewers introduce themselves, clarify the children's task (the need to describe the events experienced truthfully and in detail) and explain the ground rules and expectations (i.e. the child can and should say 'I don't remember', 'I don't know', 'I don't understand' or correct the interviewer when appropriate). The rapport-building phase consists of two sections. The first is a structured, open-ended section designed to encourage children to provide personally meaningful information. In the second section, children are prompted to detail one recently experienced event to practise the retrieval of episodic memory and further develop a rapport with the interviewer. In addition to its rapport-building function, this phase of the interview is designed to simulate both the open-ended investigative strategies and techniques used in the substantive phase and the related patterns of interaction between interviewers and children while demonstrating to the children the specific level of detail expected of them.

In a transitional phase between the pre-substantive and substantive portions of the interview, open-ended prompts are used to identify the target event(s) under investigation. If the child does not disclose anything in response to the open-ended prompts, the interviewer proceeds to gradually narrow the prompts, referring to available information about previous disclosures, physical marks or other evidence as needed. When an allegation is being made by the child, the forensic interviewer will further elaborate on this allegation using open-ended prompts (e.g. 'Tell me more about it') followed by focused prompts (e.g. 'Where was it?') and is instructed to avoid any suggestive questioning (e.g. 'I am guessing you were scared, right?').

The aim of the following case study is to illustrate a forensic investigation with a child younger than 12 years of age.

Illustrative case study of a forensic investigation with an accused child younger than 12 years of age

Y is a ten-year-old child who was referred for forensic investigation following a complaint from his neighbours that he sexually abused their seven-year-old son. According to their complaint, Y touched their son's penis and forced him to kiss their dog's sexual organ. Y was interviewed in the child forensic interviewer's office; his parents accompanied him to her office and waited for him outside the room. Y entered the room with no difficulties and cooperated with the interviewer.

The interviewer started with an introduction, practised the communication rules with him and then moved to the rapport-building phase. Y was very cooperative, answered all of the open-ended invitations directed to him and provided personal information about the activities he loved, things that happened to him at school and an event in which he played football with his friends. The forensic interviewer proceeded to the allegation phase, in which she asked him a set of questions trying to determine if he was a victim of any sexual act. The following interaction between the forensic interviewer and the child emphasises the tension between interviewing the child as an alleged victim and interviewing him as a suspect:

Interviewer: 'As I told you before, I came here today to talk to you about things that have happened to you. Do you know why I want to talk to you today?'
Child: 'No.'
Interviewer: 'Did anyone hurt you?'
Child: 'I was fighting with my friends and one of them kicked me.'
Interviewer: 'Did anyone touch you?'
Child: 'When they punched me?'
Interviewer: 'Did someone touch your intimate body parts?'
Child: 'No.'
Interviewer: 'Ok. I also wanted to ask you if you've seen movies with sexual content?'
Child: 'What do you mean, "sexual content"?'
Interviewer: 'Have you seen movies with naked people?'
Child: 'Naked? No.'
Interviewer: 'Have you seen something like this on the computer?'
Child: 'No.'
Interviewer: 'Ok, did you touch someone else's intimate body parts?'
Child: 'No.'
Interviewer: 'Did you ask someone to kiss his dog?'
Child: 'Yes, one day I got back from school and I saw this boy and he really got me upset because he laughed at me, so I pushed him to kiss his dog.'

The child provided an allegation concerning the alleged incident and elaborated on what happened before he started touching and assaulting the boy and on the interaction between them. The interviewer, with the use of open-ended prompts, invited him to further elaborate his narratives, and the child cooperated and elaborated on the incident. Then the interviewer, again, made an intensive effort to understand how Y got these ideas:

Interviewer: 'I am not here to accuse you in anything; I just want to understand how you got the idea of doing this to him?'
Child: 'I don't know, he got me upset so it came to my head, and don't say that I did it to someone else.'
Interviewer: 'Has anyone done something like this to you?'
Child: 'No.'
Interviewer: 'Has anyone ever told you to kiss a dog?'
Child: 'No.'
Interviewer: 'Have you ever seen something like this in a movie or on a computer?'
Child: 'No.'

This illustrative case emphasises how challenging forensic interviews with child suspects can be and how the interviewer needs to hold in his mind two contradictory positions towards the child, one with the child as an alleged victim and the other with him as a suspect. It is important to stress that in this type of investigation, namely with children under the age of 12, the forensic interviewer does not need to report his conclusions to the police, only to the welfare system for evaluation and therapeutic planning. In comparison, for children above the age of 12, police involvement is evident in the practice and creates a unique challenge for the child forensic interviewer, as illustrated by the following case study.

Illustrative case study of a forensic investigation with an accused child aged 12½

M is a 12½-year-old boy who was referred to forensic investigation following a complaint made to the police that he sexually assaulted his teacher. The report claimed that he entered the teacher's room, closed the door and took off his pants. He then masturbated in front of her and told her that she is hot and beautiful. M arrived at the office of the child forensic interviewer and entered the room by himself. This case emphasises the adaptations made to the NICHD Protocol for interviewing suspects at the ages of 12 to 14. The first stage is still an introduction, but it integrates a formal warning to the child:

> *'You do not have to tell me anything; according to the law, anyone who is a suspect of abuse can choose not to talk.*
>
> *'If you decide to talk to me, I will have to transfer your testimony to the police for further investigation. If a trial is initiated, everything you are saying to me today can be used against you in court.*

'If you decide not to tell me anything, it may harm you, as it may lead to an absence of your testimony in the presence of others' testimonies and evidence against you.

'In addition, it is important for you to know that, based on our experience, the legal procedures are easier if you tell us exactly what happened so we can provide you with the right treatment.

'Have you understood everything I have told you?'

Once the child indicates that he understands this warning, the interviewer begins with the communication rules and rapport-building phase according to the NICHD Protocol. Next, he introduces the child to the nature of the complaint:

Interviewer: 'Ok, so you know why I came here today. I want you to tell me everything that happened with your teacher as best as you can.'

Child: 'I went into her room and accidentally closed the door, and suddenly my pants fell down by accident.'

The interviewer presented M with open-ended prompts to encourage him to elaborate his narrative. M insisted that it was all a mistake with no intention:

Child: 'The pants just fell off, maybe they were too big … my underwear just fell off, maybe it was too big … my penis was erect because I was embarrassed that my clothes fell off … I touched my penis because it itched.'

After a while, the forensic interviewer started to confront M:

Interviewer: 'How is it possible that both your pants and underwear got down? … She says you were smiling at her while closing the door, indicating that she cannot leave the room. How do you explain this? … '

M was reluctant to take any responsibility for the incident, repeating:

Child: 'I swear to God, you have to believe me, I wasn't mean anything, it was an accident because my clothes were too big.'

The investigation ended when the forensic interviewer asked the child if he was a victim to something like this in his life. When M said no, the interviewer told him that if he wanted to discuss anything further with the interviewer, the child's mother had the interviewer's phone number. This case study further emphasises the tension that forensic interviewers of children who are suspects face in their practice. Even when investigating children over the age of 12 who have criminal responsibility, the interviewer's fundamental stance is that the child is at risk.

The challenges faced by child forensic interviewers have increased in the last two years with the enactment of special legislation stating that people (of all ages) with disabilities who are suspects of alleged incidents are also to be interviewed by child forensic interviewers. This legislation was passed without providing preparation for child forensic interviewers, who now need to conduct these interviews using the practice they adhere to, the NICHD Protocol. The following case study illustrates this challenge.

Illustrative case study of forensic investigation with an accused person with a disability

N is a 40-year-old man diagnosed with moderate retardation. N was referred from the police to a forensic interviewer following a complaint that he sexually abused several boys by taking off his clothes, masturbating in front of them and trying to take off their clothes. N arrived to the forensic interview with his father, and the interview took place in the forensic interviewer's office. The interview structure was similar to that for a child of 12 to 14 years of age. The interview started with a warning from the police and then moved to practising the communication rules and rapport-building, followed by the allegation phase, when the complainant was introduced to the allegations against him.

Interviewer: 'So, we have here a complaint from several kids who claim that you did something to them.'
N: 'I regret doing this; I did not mean to do something bad. I love kids. I just wanted to play with them.'

The interviewer presented N with open-ended prompts to elaborate on the incidents; however, two main difficulties arose during the interview. The first problem concerned N's difficulty with providing answers in response to open-ended prompts. Once the interviewer detected these difficulties, he presented N with focused and closed questions, and N provided additional information. However, the second difficulty was that N could not differentiate in his narratives between different incidents with different children. Instead, N provided generic details with respect to all of the alleged incidents but admitted fully to everything in the complaint.

Interviewer: 'Tell me about one time that you took off a child's clothes.'
N: 'I was running after them.'
Interviewer: 'And then what happened?'
N: 'What?'
Interviewer: 'What you did then?'
N: 'I took off my clothes and touched my penis and started running after them, trying to touch their penises.'

The challenges raised in this case study require further exploration to enhance the practices of child forensic interviewers when investigating children and adults diagnosed with developmental and intellectual disabilities. Based on these three case studies, Table 4.1 elaborates on the similarities and differences in interview practices.

Table 4.1 Comparison of key similarities and differences in child forensic interviewer practices when interviewing children under the age of 12, children aged 12–14 and children and adults with disabilities

Similarities and differences	*Forensic investigation with child under the age of 12*	*Forensic investigation with child aged 12–14*	*Forensic investigation with people diagnosed with developmental and intellectual disabilities*
Beginning of the interview	Communication rules and rapport-building	Warning from the police and then communication rules and rapport-building	Warning from the police and then communication rules and rapport-building
Allegation phase	Questions mainly targeting the child as a victim first, followed by specific questions about the alleged incident	Questions targeting the alleged incident first, followed by specific questions on the possibility of being a victim	Questions targeting the alleged incident
Confrontations	No confrontation. The interviewer addresses the child as an alleged victim	Confrontation when needed based on the complaint	Confrontation when needed based on the complaint

The fact that children as suspects receive the same interview practices as children as victims and witnesses is also evident in the training mechanisms for child forensic interviewers, in which no unique course targets the interviewing of child suspects. The child forensic interviewers mainly receive training on the use of the NICHD Protocol. Clearly, additional efforts are needed to enhance interview practices and training with suspects. This lack of attention is evident within research as well, as only one study has been performed in Israel describing the investigative interviews of suspects to date (Hershkowitz *et al.*, 2004). That study presented analyses with 72 alleged perpetrators of the ages of 9–14 (mean age of 12). The main findings concerned the number of details elicited in response to different types of prompts. Overall, the number of details did not vary with age or whether the children fully or partially admitted the allegations. With respect to the contribution of the different prompt types to the children's narratives, it was found that more information was elicited using invitations rather than closed, option-posing or suggestive prompts. The researchers concluded that the use of open-ended prompts is recommended for forensic investigations with alleged perpetrators despite the basic reluctance in their testimonies.

Implications for research, policy and practice

Exploring forensic interview practices with alleged suspects in Israel reveals several key issues that need to be addressed. The first relates to the gap in practices that are mainly generated by the suspect's age. As was previously elaborated, children under the age of 14 in Israel are protected by special law, and interviewed by social workers who use the most accepted best practice worldwide, the NICHD Protocol. The perception of children in Israel can be explained by its cultural context. In Israel, there are several cultural groups that tend to be highly conservative: the Arabs and the Orthodox Jews. Both groups are considered collectivist societies, where the family seeks wholeness at any price (Ben-Arieh and Haj-Yahia, 2006; Leshem and Roer-Strier, 2003). Moreover, children in Israel and in the Jewish religion are considered to be highly important and a key aspect in keeping the safety of the family, which might help explain the gap in legislation.

Putting the focus on the differences in practices, it is also important to stress that there is a lack of transparency of interview practices. For forensic interviews with children and people with disabilities, all of the investigations are video-recorded. However, there is no transparency or any evaluation of forensic interviewers conducted by youth investigators and police officers. It might be that this lack of transparency might explain the lack of research in that area. Studies should explore forensic interviews with suspects in Israel, in order to promote best practice in that area.

It is important to stress that the child forensic interviewers had been providing continuous feedback with respect to the need to adapt their practical guidelines (NICHD Protocol) to better suit forensic investigations with suspects. There is also a call from the field to make adaptations to the practical guidelines for interviewing children and people with disabilities who are being interviewed as suspects. Further research is clearly needed in that area.

The current chapter emphasises that forensic investigations with suspects in Israel is an understudied area that needs to be further explored in order to enhance practices for forensic interviews with suspects and promote the justice that can be achieved for this population.

References

Ben-Arieh, A. and Haj-Yahia, M. M. (2006) 'The geography of child maltreatment in Israel: findings from a national data set of cases reported to the social services', *Child Abuse and Neglect*, 30: 991–1003.

Hershkowitz, I., Horowitz, D., Lamb, M. E., Orbach, Y. and Sternberg, K. J. (2004) *Child Abuse and Neglect*, 28: 423–38.

Lamb, M. E., Hershkowitz, I., Orbach, Y. and Esplin, P. (2008) *Tell Me What Happened: Structured Investigative Interviews of Child Victims and Witnesses*. Hoboken, NJ: Wiley.

Leshem, E. and Roer-Strier, D. (eds) (2003) *Cultural Difference as a Challenge for Human Services*. Jerusalem: Magnes Press (in Hebrew).

Orbach, Y., Hershkowitz, I., Lamb, M. E., Sternberg, K. J., Esplin, P. W. and Horowitz, D. (2000) 'Assessing the value of structured protocols for forensic interviews of alleged child abuse victims', *Child Abuse and Neglect*, 24: 733–52.

5 Current practice in interviews with suspects in Japan

Taeko Wachi and Kazumi Watanabe[1]

Introduction

In Japan,[2] approximately 293,100 police personnel are employed, of which 7,700 are personnel working for the National Police Agency (NPA) (2,100 police officers, 900 imperial guards, and 4,700 civilians), and 285,400 are prefectural police personnel (257,100 police officers and 28,300 civilians) (NPA, 2014). However, according to a white paper produced by the Japanese National Police Agency (2008), approximately 10,000 police officers will retire each year between 2006 and 2015, meaning that approximately 40 percent of the force will need to be replaced in this period. The same white paper (NPA, 2008) also argued that the Japanese police force urgently needed experienced officers to share their skills with younger officers, particularly their interviewing skills. According to the survey of detectives, as many as 78 percent of the 1,431 detectives believed that interrogation techniques and skills must be passed on from the older to the younger generation (NPA, 2008).

However, the Japanese police force only recently began providing national, systematic training courses specializing in interviewing techniques.[3] In fact, police officers have generally learned these techniques simply by observing experienced officers' interviews, listening to previous cases from experienced officers, hearing about various cases from their colleagues, and through on-the-job-training. However, the context of widespread recent retirement described above has deprived young officers of the opportunity to even attend and observe interrogations conducted by experienced officers. Thus both the Japanese police force as a whole and individual police officers are very concerned about their reduced knowledge of interviewing techniques.

Thus the situation surrounding interrogation is rapidly changing. The first section of this chapter explores the current changes in regulations concerning interrogations. In the second section, we review recent studies conducted in Japan. The third section explains current Japanese practices (including good and emerging practices), as well as the training process. Finally, implications for research and practice are discussed.

Here, before discussion of the Japanese situation, we explain the term *torishirabe*, namely the Japanese interrogation or interview. Since the introduction of the PEACE approach, the term *investigative interviewing* has been used instead of *interrogation* in England and Wales (Milne and Bull, 1999). The former focuses not on eliciting a confession from a suspect, but on gathering information from him/her (Soukara *et al.*, 2009). However, it is unclear whether this definition can be applied to Japanese interviewing or *torishirabe*. Therefore the terms *investigative interviewing* and *interrogation* are used throughout this chapter.

History of current interrogation practices

The role of interrogation in criminal investigation

The present Japanese law of criminal procedure was greatly influenced by US law and has been in force since 1949 (Taguchi, 2009). The main purpose of criminal procedure, as governed by the Code of Criminal Procedure (1948), is "to reveal the true facts of cases and to apply and realize criminal laws and regulations quickly and appropriately, while ensuring the maintenance of public welfare and the guarantee of the fundamental human rights of individuals" (Art. 1). According to this article, interrogation aims to reveal facts while ensuring the strict protection of fundamental human rights through due process.

In 2010, the chairman of the National Public Safety Commission[4] at the time argued that interrogation played a much more important role in Japanese criminal investigation than in other countries, and that there were many cases where it would have been impossible either to find out the truth or to arrest offenders without confessions (Shigematsu, 2013). In Japan, powerful investigation methods such as wiretapping for a wide range of crimes,[5] which are used in other countries, are prohibited, which limits our ability to collect evidence (Shigematsu, 2012b). Therefore confessions, alongside trials, have long been the most important pieces of evidence in Japanese criminal investigations.

According to Ueno and Matsui (2012), the role of the Japanese interrogation can be summarized under the following five points. The first role is to obtain the suspects' account (whether it is admission or denial of the crime) and to discover facts about the incident under investigation from the suspects. During interrogation, police officers obtain suspects' accounts, verify their accounts by further investigation, determine whether crimes occurred, and assess whether or not the suspects are guilty. In this way, Japanese police interviews aim not only to obtain confessions, but to find out when suspects are innocent (Kan, 2012).

Second, interrogations reveal the subjective aspects of criminal acts. Under Japanese law, prosecutors should explore subjective aspects of alleged offences, such as criminal motives, deliberate intentions, and accomplices.

The third role of interrogation is to reveal facts about the case from offenders. In Japan, crime victims and their families have a strong desire for offenders to talk about their criminal motives and to explain their criminal acts (Cabinet Office, 2014). For example, in one murder case, the bereaved family said that they could not accept the death of their daughter unless they understood why the offender killed her (cited in Ueno and Matsui, 2012). Such statements from the bereaved families are frequently reported by the media. In addition, the public also want the offenders to speak the truth in these cases. Interrogation meets this public interest by helping offenders give accounts of their criminal cases in detail.

The fourth role is to obtain information about criminal organizations. During the interrogation of members of criminal organizations, interrogators obtain information not only about each criminal act, but also the criminal organizations involved, in order to identify organized crime or/and eliminate criminal organizations.

Fifth, interrogation contributes to the reformation and rehabilitation of offenders and prevents them from committing repeat offenses. While revealing the truth, offenders sometimes need to overcome their fear of future sentencing, face their guilt, and show remorse and repentance, which provides them with opportunities for improvement and rehabilitation[6] (Ueno and Matsui, 2012).

Thus Japanese interrogation has played several roles in criminal investigation. However, Ueno and Matsui (2012) have argued that interrogation in other countries is more likely to focus on obtaining the suspects' accounts, and less likely to consider other roles, such as the second to fifth roles listed above.

Changing regulations concerning interrogation

The Japanese police system has recently undergone rapid change regarding interrogation practices and policies. In 2001, the Justice System Reform Council submitted a written opinion regarding the reform of the judicial system[7] to the Cabinet. As per Tsuyuki (2009), this written opinion proposed memorializing the details of interrogations of suspects in writing to ensure the propriety of interrogations within the broader introduction of a citizen judge system. In line with this recommendation, the Japanese police began creating written reports of the details of each interrogation, including the date, time, and location of the interrogation, names of the interrogators, and whether the suspect statement was written (Tsuyuki, 2009). Thus the policy aiming to ensure the propriety of interrogations had been implemented in association with the reform of the judicial system.

However, in 2007, two miscarriages of justice occurred, known as the *Himi* case[8] and the *Shibushi* case.[9] Severe criticism resulted, leading the National Police Agency to announce the "Policy on Ensuring Propriety of Examination in Police Investigations" in 2008 (Shigematsu, 2008, 2012b). The policy stressed the importance of strengthening supervision during interrogations and limiting the duration of interrogations (Shigematsu, 2008). In order to implement this policy, "Supervisory Regulations for Ensuring Propriety of Examination on Suspects" were enacted and portions of the Criminal Investigation Code (1957) were amended (Akutsu, 2008).

The citizen judge system was introduced in Japan in May 2009. In order to bolster the credibility of defendants' confessions effectively and efficiently in trials under citizen judges (Shigematsu, 2013), five prefectures began recording interrogations electronically on an experimental basis in September 2008. From April 2009, these practices were tentatively expanded across Japan. In these instances, the final stage of suspects' confessions, incorporating statements that include a brief summary and the core elements of each criminal matter, was recorded for those cases that were tried under the citizen judge system (Shigematsu, 2013).

Another miscarriage of justice case, known as the *Ashikaga* case,[10] occurred in 2010; this again led to mounting public criticism of the police investigation system. By considering these situations and seeking to implement the electronic recording of interrogations without a decline in public safety, the chairman of the National Public Safety Commission held a study group from 2010 to 2012 to discuss the future of criminal investigation and interrogation, including expanding tests of the practice of electronically recording interrogations (Kan, 2012; Shigematsu, 2013).

The National Police Agency officially announced the "Program to Advance Investigation Methods and Interrogations" to implement the recommendations made by the above study group in March 2012 (Shigematsu, 2012a, 2013). This program included the expansion of the practice of electronically recording interrogations. In April 2012, police forces across Japan began recording parts of interrogations of suspects denying wrongdoing or remaining silent, in addition to suspects who had confessed, in cases tried under the citizen judge system. Furthermore, electronic recording was expanded to record various stages, such as the beginning, middle, and/or last part(s) of a series of interrogations as well as the interrogation of suspects with intellectual disabilities from May 2012 (Kan *et al.*, 2012; Shigematsu, 2013).

As part of this program, further efforts were then introduced to ensure the propriety of suspect interrogations and to enhance interrogation techniques by considering the practices of other countries and making use of findings from psychological research (Shigematsu, 2012a, 2013). In particular, the National Police Agency aims to increase the extent to which police officers learn from scientifically based findings in the field of psychology. It also attempts to provide police officers with systematic, practical training tailored to Japanese police practices and based on psychological findings, instead of the previous tradition of on-the-job training as a primary means of learning investigative interviewing techniques (Shigematsu, 2012a). Shigematsu (2013) stressed the importance of studying Japanese police interrogations from various perspectives, such as offenders' perceptions, in order to learn more about police interrogation in Japan.

In December 2012, a basic training manual for investigative interviewing was published by the National Police Agency (see the section entitled, "Good Practice"). In May 2013, a new center was also launched at the National Police Academy. This center was established to provide national training for police officers across Japan, as well as to conduct psychological research related to the development of effective training and to evaluate the impact of training programs. In July 2013, this new center provided a national full-scale training course in investigative interviewing, with approximately ten senior police officers in attendance. Since then, the center has provided six eight-day training courses with senior police officers at the National Police Academy annually, which include lectures about psychological findings related to interviews, practice interviews, and debriefing (see the section entitled "Training" later in this chapter).

Thus the circumstances surrounding Japanese interrogation have been changing rapidly. In particular, senior police officials at the National Police Agency have begun to realize the importance of psychological knowledge when conducting interrogations appropriately. However, few studies of interrogation have been conducted in Japan. As argued by Shigematsu (2013), simply importing the interviewing methodology from other countries is not useful; the findings from studies of Japanese police practices will help provide training that is appropriately tailored to the Japanese police force.

Relevant literature conducted in the Japanese context

Most psychological studies on suspects' confessions have been conducted in Western countries; thus their results may not generalize to countries where cultures and policing practices differ. The difference between Japanese and Western laws may affect the roles that police interviews play in suspects' confessions. However, there have been a small number of empirical studies conducted on Japanese interrogation. Watanabe and his colleagues examined Japanese interrogation in the 1990s (e.g. Watanabe and Yokota, 1999), but these studies only focused on cases of murder or theft, and sample sizes were small; the more systematic, large-scale studies recently conducted by our team are reviewed here. The following studies investigated the interviewing styles most likely to elicit confessions from guilty suspects in Japan; self-report questionnaires were administered to Japanese police officers, prisoners, and the general public.

In order to examine common investigative interviewing techniques used for interrogating serious offenders and the relationships between interviewing styles and confessions, surveys were conducted of interrogators assigned to serious crimes (Wachi *et al.*, 2014). In this study, an extensive questionnaire was completed by 276 police officers responsible for interviewing suspects who had committed serious crimes such as murder, robbery, arson, rape, indecent assault, or kidnapping. In order to collect data from police officers all over Japan, we allocated a certain number of participants from each prefecture in proportion to the number of offenders arrested for the above crimes in 2006. Their responses regarding interview techniques were factor-analysed. As a result, the interview techniques were classified into five factors as follows: Presentation of Evidence, Confrontation, Active Listening, Rapport-Building, and Discussion of the Crime. Presentation of Evidence was related to the use of evidence in the interrogation; Confrontation included techniques in which interrogators confronted suspects; Active Listening included techniques related to the police officers listening closely to the suspects' accounts; Rapport-Building included techniques in which the police officers tried to build trusting relationships with the suspects; and Discussion of the Crime included techniques that involved directly talking about the crime. Based on these five factors, four interviewing styles were identified, as follows: Evidence-focused, Confrontational, Relationship-focused, and Undifferentiated.

When interrogators employed a Relationship-focused interviewing style, which stresses Active Listening, Rapport Building, and Discussion of the Crime, suspects were more likely to make full confessions; in contrast, suspects were more likely to make partial confessions when interrogators employed an Evidence-focused style which stresses the Presentation of Evidence and Active Listening (Wachi *et al.*, 2014).

A subsequent study (Wachi *et al.*, under review) focused on prisoners' opinions of the interrogations they had experienced. A total of 291 adult male inmates who had been convicted of murder, robbery, arson, rape, indecent assault, or kidnapping completed self-report questionnaires. Using the five factors obtained in Wachi *et al.* (2014), four interview styles were identified: Evidence-confrontational, Relationship-focused, Undifferentiated-high, and Undifferentiated-low. The effects of the interview styles were different depending on the prisoners' previous decisions: if they had decided to confess prior to interrogation, the interview style was not associated with the nature of their confession. However, if they had not decided to confess (or had decided to deny), they were more likely to make full confessions when they experienced either Undifferentiated-high or Relationship-focused interviews. In Undifferentiated-high interviews, the police officers employed all of the techniques examined in this study; they listened closely to the suspects' accounts, attempted to build good relationships, and discussed the crimes the suspect had committed, while also presenting evidence and confronting suspects. In Relationship-focused interviews, the police officers listened attentively to the offenders' accounts, tried to build good relationships, and discussed the crimes directly.

In another study, Wachi (2013) examined the opinions of Japanese adult university students about interrogation techniques using the same five factors evident in the recent studies conducted among police officers (Wachi *et al.*, 2014) and prisoners (Wachi *et al.*, under review). Wachi's (2013) study showed that participants regarded Active Listening, which was most likely to elicit true confessions from guilty suspects and least likely to elicit false confessions from innocent suspects, as the most preferable technique. Wachi and Lamb (2013) conducted an online survey among the adult general public using the same items describing interrogation techniques and replicated the above findings. These studies have important implications for identifying the most appropriate interrogation techniques to ensure that confessions can be admitted under the citizen judge system.

Current practice and training

Current practice

The National Police Agency conducted a survey to examine Japanese interrogation patterns (NPA, 2011). The survey examined the interviewing methods for 397 suspects who had been detained and notified of the final decisions in their cases (excluding traffic offenses) by the prosecutors during February in 2011.

The sample included 26 individuals suspected of felonious offences, 90 suspected of larceny offences, and 47 suspected of white-collar offences.

The mean number of days, duration, and number of interrogations for the cases were 5.7 days, 15 hours 15 minutes, and 10.1 times, respectively. The sample included felonious cases, for which the mean number of days, duration, and number of interrogations (9.2 days, 25 hours 25 minutes, and 18.2 times respectively) were greater than for other offenses (e.g. 5.5 days, 16 hours 7 minutes, and 9.5 times for larceny offenses, and 7.5 days, 20 hours 4 minutes, and 12.2 times for white-collar offenses).

With regard to suspects' confessions, 57 (14.4 percent) of the suspects had denied the allegations against them until the final decision by the prosecutors. A total of 279 suspects (70.3 percent) confessed on the first day of interrogation, and 61 suspects (15.3 percent) confessed on or after the second day of interrogation. Specifically, 65.4 percent of those suspected of felonies confessed, compared to 92.2 percent for theft and 87.2 percent for white-collar crimes. Thus those suspected of serious crimes were less likely to confess.

The Wachi *et al.* (2014) study, discussed in the previous section, examined the common interviewing techniques used for interrogating serious offenders. The police officers reported that the following interviewing techniques were most frequently used:

- "taking a resolute attitude toward the suspect"
- "respecting the suspect as a human being"
- "attempting to persuade the suspect to think about the meaning of the crime committed"
- "appealing to the suspect's conscience"
- "attending closely to the suspect's words."

In comparison, in the survey conducted among prisoners (Wachi *et al.*, under review), the most commonly used techniques reported by the prisoners were "respecting you as a human being," "listening to your life stories, such as personal history," "emphasizing the serious nature of the crime you have committed," "listening closely to your words," and "being friendly to you." Thus the most frequently used techniques involved listening to the prisoners' stories and treating them humanely.

As such, both police officers and prisoners agreed that "respecting the suspect as a human being" was a commonly used technique for interviewing serious criminals in Japan; however, the prisoners reported positive techniques, such as listening to their account, more frequently.

Good practice

In December 2012, the "Basic Manual for Interrogation" was published, as mentioned above. This manual, developed in collaboration with psychologists (authors), was the first attempt to provide a uniform manual for the entire

Japanese police force. It focuses primarily on how to interview witnesses and cooperative suspects in such a way as to obtain extensive, accurate information from them without contaminating their memories and damaging the credibility of the suspects' confessions. In order to create this manual, the police officials and lead psychologist (the first author) working for the National Police Agency visited Australia and the UK to obtain information about their current interrogation practices and training programs, especially PEACE training (including the cognitive interview). Thus this manual incorporates psychological findings that had already been applied to police practices in Western countries. The manual is mainly composed of two chapters. The first chapter is based on the psychology of memory, cognitive interview, and false confessions, while the second chapter explains the questioning styles, such as open questions (free report, 5WH questions), closed questions (multiple choice and yes-no questions), and leading questions, as well as how to use (or avoid) them in actual interrogations.

Since the manual was published, these techniques have been taught as part of training courses (described later) and lectures for police officers across Japan in order to implement them in everyday practice.

Emerging practice

As discussed in the previous section, the Japanese police force has been electronically recording portions of interrogations on an experimental basis since 2008. The National Police Agency reported trends regarding electronic recording between 1 April 2012 and 31 March 2013 (NPA, 2013). Since the electronic recording of cases tried under the citizen judge system was expanded in April 2012, the number of recorded cases has increased by approximately 100 to 200 per month. In addition, approximately 77 percent of all cases tried under the citizen judge system (2,637 for a year) were recorded. Of the recorded cases, 32 percent involved robbery (causing injury), 26 percent murder, and 11 percent arson. During the same period, there were 178 cases in which the suspects refused to be recorded, compared to 39 cases between 1 April 2011 and 31 March 2012. Between 1 April 2012 and 31 March 2013, pre-trial discovery was conducted in 256 cases, whereas video-recorded evidence was examined at trial (i.e. by playing a DVD) only twice (NPA, 2013).

On 30 April 2014, the Ministry of Justice submitted a proposal to the Special Committee of the Legislative Council, which is the advisory panel to the Ministry of Justice, recommending that the electronic recording of the entire interrogation of suspected offenders be mandated in principle (Ministry of Justice, 2014). According to the proposal, cases subject to trial by citizen judges, such as murder, robbery, rape, and arson cases, are to be recorded electronically by the police (Ministry of Justice, 2014). The Special Committee finalized the proposal in summer 2014. The Ministry then submitted the relevant bills to the Diet, and the debate on the bills started at a plenary session of the House of Representatives in May 2015. Thus the Japanese system of electronic recording has changed drastically.

Training

In May 2013, a new training center was established at the National Police Academy. The role of the new "Research and Training Center for Investigative Interview and Interrogation Techniques" is to provide training for police officers, to conduct research on the development of new training mechanisms, and to evaluate the impact of training programs. New national full-scale training courses were introduced at this center in July 2013. Since it opened its doors, this training center has provided six training courses annually for chief inspectors and inspectors from prefectural police headquarters, who supervise interrogations conducted by front-line police officers across their prefectures. Each course lasts eight days and is attended by approximately ten police officers. During the course, participating police officers learn the psychology of interviewing using the new manual, published in 2012, with a particular focus on the psychology of memory, false confessions, and questioning styles, and put their new knowledge into practice through role playing, which consists of mock interrogations of witnesses and suspects followed by group discussions. Each trainee also brings a video-recorded interrogation conducted in their prefectures and discusses its strengths and weaknesses. The center also provides a seven-day version of the training at regional police headquarters, where it is attended by the inspectors. The curriculum of this training course is very similar to that of the course at the National Police Academy. These training courses are provided by the staff at the National Police Academy's Research and Training Center.

Thus Japanese training practices have been rapidly expanding in recent years. By following the recommendations of the study group organized by the chairman of the National Public Safety Commission discussed above, the new training courses stress the importance of integrating psychological knowledge into interrogations, which is ground-breaking for the Japanese police force.

Implications for research and practice

Only a small number of empirical studies on Japanese interrogations have been conducted. Most studies have consisted of self-reported surveys, and there have been no observational studies of the actual interrogation practices in Japan. Since the Japanese police force began electronically recording portions of actual interrogations on an experimental basis, studies of these video-recorded interrogations are needed in order to examine actual interrogation practices and interactions between interrogators and suspects. Furthermore, the interrogations examined at trial must be studied in order to determine the type of interrogations that are considered admissible by citizen judges, although only a very limited number is available at present. Lastly, we need to evaluate the training programs and improve upon them based on the evaluation results.

In order to support the development of evidence-based practice, we, as researchers, should provide the psychological findings that the police need. For example, the police force wants to know which interrogation techniques are effective for repeat offenders, mafia members, and psychopathic offenders, who have rarely been studied either in Japan or other countries. Because the context surrounding interrogations is rapidly changing, researchers should be sensitive to the police force's needs and advance their research to provide useful information to the police force.

Notes

1. The statements of facts and opinions in this paper are solely those of the authors. These statements do not reflect the official position of the Japanese government.
2. Japan has been a member of INTERPOL since 1952, and the National Central Bureau (NCB) of Japan is located within the National Police Agency (NPA) (Interpol, 2014).
3. The National Police Agency began national full-scale training programs in July 2013. See the section entitled, "Training."
4. The NPA operates under the purview of the National Public Safety Commission, which ensure the neutrality of the police system (NPA, 2012).
5. Wiretapping can be used only for specific forms of organised crime in Japan (Ueno and Matsui, 2012).
6. Some scholars have argued that it is not permissible to call on suspects to reflect on their past conduct when they have not been convicted, but others have argued that the effect of offenders' remorse as an outcome of interrogation should not be dismissed (Daijinkenkyukai, 2012).
7. The reform of the judicial system included the introduction of a citizen judge (*Saiban-in*) system. "The Law concerning Participation of *Saiban-in* in Criminal Trials" was announced in 2004 and has been in force since 2009 (Ministry of Justice, 2004). After the five-year period of preparation for the new system, the first trial with citizen judges was held on 3 August 2009 at the Tokyo District Court.
8. In the *Himi* case, Mr X was convicted of two rapes in 2002 and was sentenced to three years in prison. He was released in 2005. However, the real rapist was arrested and prosecuted in 2007. After this, the public prosecutor's office appealed for a retrial of Mr X and the court handed down a not guilty verdict (Shigematsu, 2012b).
9. In 2003, 15 people were arrested for violating the Public Offices Election Law. Twelve of the 15 people were prosecuted. In as many as 54 trials, all defendants denied the allegations. They were finally acquitted in 2007 (Shigematsu, 2012b).
10. Mr Y was arrested for the murder of a four-year-old girl in 1991 based on his confession and DNA evidence. In 2000, he was sentenced to indefinite imprisonment. However, in 2009, the evidence that the DNA left at the crime scene did not match Mr Y's DNA was provided to the Tokyo High Court. In 2010, he was found not guilty at a retrial (Shigematsu, 2012b).

References

Akutsu, M. (2008) "'Higisya torishirabe tekiseika notameno kantoku ni kansuru kiroku' oyobi 'hanzaisousakihan no ichibu wo kaiseisuru kisoku' no seitei ni tsuite" ["'Regulations of Supervision for Ensuring Propriety of Examination on Suspects' and 'Amendment of the Criminal Investigation Code'"], *Journal of Police Science*, 61 (6): 63–97.

Cabinet Office, Japan (2014) *Measures for Crime Victims*. Retrieved from: http://www8.cao.go.jp/hanzai/whitepaper/w-2014/pdf/zenbun/pdf/1s5s1_01.pdf.

Daijinkenkyukai (2012) *Sosasyuho torishirabe no kodoka wo hakarutameno kenkyukai: saisyu hokoku* [*Final Report of the Study Group for Sophisticating Investigation*

Methods and Interrogations]. Retrieved from: http://www.npa.go.jp/shintyaku/keiki/saisyuu.pdf.

Interpol (2014) *Japan*. Retrieved from: http://www.interpol.int/Member-countries/AsiaSouth-Pacific/Japan.

Kan, J. (2012) "Sousasyuho torishirabe no kodoka wo hakarutameno kenkyukai niyoru saisyuhokokuni tsuite" ["Final report of the study group for sophisticating investigation methods and interrogations"], *Journal of Police Science*, 65 (7): 21–46.

Kan, J., Tsutsumi, H., Ogasawara, M., and Katano, S. (2012) "Keisatsu ni okeru torishirabe no rokuon rokuga no shiko no kakuzyu ni tsuite" ["The expansion of the trial scheme for electronic recording of police interrogations in Japan"], *Journal of Police Science*, 65 (7): 47–72.

Milne, R. and Bull, R. (1999) *Investigative Interviewing: Psychology and Practice*. Chichester: John Wiley & Sons.

Ministry of Justice (2004) *White Paper on Crime*. Tokyo: Ministry of Justice.

Ministry of Justice (2014) *Jimutokyoku shian* [*Proposal by the Head Office*]. Retrieved from: http://www.moj.go.jp/content/000122699.pdf.

National Police Agency (NPA) (2008) *White Paper on Police*. Tokyo: National Police Agency.

National Police Agency (NPA) (2011) *Keisatsu niokeru torishirabe no zitsujo ni tsuite* [*Current Situations About Police Interrogations*]. Retrieved from: http://www.npa.go.jp/sousa/kikaku/20111020_kekka.pdf.

National Police Agency (NPA) (2012) *White Paper on Police*. Tokyo: National Police Agency.

National Police Agency (NPA) (2013) *Keisatsu niokeru torishirabe no rokuon rokuga no shiko no kensyo ni tsuite* [*Evaluation of the Trials of Electronic Recording of Police Interrogations*]. Retrived from: http://www.npa.go.jp/sousa/kikaku/record/1-2.pdf.

National Police Agency (NPA) (2014) *Police of Japan 2014*. Retrevied from: http://www.npa.go.jp/english/kokusai/2014POJcontents.htm.

Shigematsu, H. (2008) "Keisatsu niokeru torishirabe tekiseikashishin ni tsuite" ["Policy on ensuring propriety of examination in police investigations"], *Journal of Police Science*, 61 (6): 18–62.

Shigematsu, H. (2012a) "Sousasyuho torishirabe no kodoka purogramu no sakutei ni tsuite" ["The National Police Agency's program for sophisticating investigation methods and interrogations"], *Journal of Police Science*, 65 (7): 1–20.

Shigematsu, H. (2012b) "Higisyatorishirabe womeguru saikin no doko to kongo no arikata (1)" ["The interrogations of suspects (1): recent movement and framework in the future"], *Journal of Police Science*, 65 (12): 1–24.

Shigematsu, H. (2013) "Higisyatorishirabe womeguru saikin no doko to kongo no arikata (2)" ["The interrogations of suspects (2): recent movement and framework in the future"]. *Journal of Police Science*, 66 (1): 48–115.

Soukara, S., Bull, R., Vrij, A., Turner, M., and Cherryman, J. (2009) "What really happens in police interviews of suspects? Tactics and confessions," *Psychology, Crime and Law*, 15: 493–506.

Taguchi, M. (2009) *Keiji sosyo hou* [*Law of Criminal Procedure*], 5th edn. Tokyo: Koubundou.

Tsuyuki, Y. (2009) *Keisatsukan no tameno keijishihoseido kaikaku kaisetsu* [*The Commentary of the Reform of the Criminal Justice System for Police Officers*], 2nd edn. Tokyo: Tachibana syobo.

Ueno, M. and Matsui, Y. (2012) "Syogaikoku niokeru keijishihoseido no tyosakenkyu: Sokatsu" ["Criminal justice system in foreign countries: summary"], *Journal of Police Science*, 65 (1): 120–39.

Wachi, T. (2013) "Torishirabe nitaisuru daigakusei no iken" ["University students' opinions on interrogations"], *Acta Criminologiae et Medicinae Legalis Japonica*, 79: 44–54.

Wachi, T. and Lamb, M. (2013) *Public Opinions of Japanese Interrogation Techniques and Their Effect on Penalties*. Paper presented at the 6th Annual Conference of the International Investigative Interviewing Research Group, Maastricht.

Wachi, T., Watanabe, K., Yokota, K., Otsuka, Y., Kuraishi, H., and Lamb, M. (2014) "Police interviewing styles and confessions in Japan," *Psychology, Crime and Law*, 20: 673–94.

Wachi, T., Watanabe, K., Yokota, K., Otsuka, Y., and Lamb, M. (under review) "Japanese interrogation techniques from prisoners' perspectives."

Watanabe, S. and Yokota, K. (1999) "Hininhigisyano zikyoniitaru shinri: hininno shinri" ["Psychological factors that facilitate denying suspects to confess: psychology of denial"], *Reports of the National Research Institute of Police Science*, 39: 136–43.

Australia

6 Interviewing suspects in Australia and New Zealand

Amanda Cain, Nina J. Westera and Mark Kebbell

Introduction

Since the early 2000s Australia and New Zealand have undergone substantial reforms to police practice for interviewing suspects. To understand these reforms it is important to first know about the context of these countries. Australia is a vast continent made up of six States and two Territories with 23.4 million inhabitants and 47,000 police officers. Most of the population is located in the metropolitan areas of these regions, with others living in remote areas that can be difficult to access (Australian Institute of Criminology, 2006). Each State or Territory has its own criminal justice system and police service, with the Australian Federal Police providing an inter-jurisdictional and international crime response. In contrast, New Zealand is a small country with 4.4 million inhabitants and one police organisation that operates under a single governance structure with just over 12,000 employees (New Zealand Police Annual Report, 2014). The English colonised these countries in the late 1700s (Australia) and early-to-mid 1800s (New Zealand), and hence the legal system and policing approaches are similar to those of England and Wales. A police commissioner governs each police service and is accountable to that jurisdiction's government, but acts as an independent body for law enforcement decisions. Many of the contemporary investigative interviewing practices in these countries have also been adapted from the approaches used in England and Wales.

In this chapter we will examine New Zealand suspect interviewing practices before going on to examine Australian practices. We chose this order because more is documented about New Zealand's reforms and these comprehensive changes to suspect interviewing practice occurred prior to many similar reforms in Australian jurisdictions. But first, we examine the legal context in both countries.

The legal context of suspect interviewing

The legal requirements for interviewing suspects in Australian and New Zealand legislation are derived from the English common law system (Findlay *et al.*, 2009). A suspect is presumed innocent until proven guilty. If a suspect is charged with an offence, unless he or she pleads guilty, an adversarial criminal trial will be held either before a judge alone or, usually in more serious cases, before a jury. There are legal protections for the suspect that were originally derived from the English Judges' Rules, which provided guidelines for a judge to consider when deciding if the suspect's statement (interview) is admissible as evidence. In all Australian jurisdictions and in New Zealand someone suspected of an offence has the right to silence and to seek advice from a lawyer, and to be informed of these rights. In practice, although many suspects may consult with a lawyer, this is usually done over the telephone and it is rare for defence counsel to be present during the interview of a suspect (although this is more likely to occur with allegations of serious offending).

Australian jurisdictions can detain a suspect for questioning for set time periods that vary depending on the jurisdiction (e.g. in Queensland police can hold a suspect for up to eight hours, with up to four hours of questioning permitted during that time (Findlay *et al*., 2009)). A unique aspect of the New Zealand legislation is that suspects cannot be detained for investigative purposes but, once arrested, are required to be brought before the courts as soon as reasonably practicable (New Zealand Bill of Rights Act 1990). This restricts the police's ability to interview a suspect over long periods of time and in multiple phases when a suspect is not willing to remain with the police.

The video recording of suspect interviews has been common practice in some Australian jurisdictions and in New Zealand since the early 1990s (Schollum, 2005). New Zealand Police self-initiated the introduction of video recording of suspects' interviews through policy (Schollum, 2005), but this is now reflected in the Practice Note on Police Questioning (see section 30(6), New Zealand Evidence Act 2006). This states the preferred way to interview suspects is on video unless not practicable or the suspect elects not to. (There is a similar requirement in all Australian jurisdictions.) In New Zealand this interview is often played in its entirety (or with only minor editing) to the fact-finder (whether judge or jury).

A review of investigative interviewing practices in New Zealand

The most documented reforms to police practice with regard to interviewing suspects in Australia and New Zealand took place in New Zealand in 2004 when their Police Executive commissioned a comprehensive review of police investigative interviewing practices (the 'Review' (Schollum, 2006b)). The primary drive for the Review was the recognition by police that practice could benefit from developments in the academic literature and international practice. Mary Schollum, a civilian member of the New Zealand Police, was tasked with leading the Review, which was comprehensive and had three outcomes – a literature review, an evaluation of current police practice and a recommendations report. The Review examined both suspect and witness interviewing practice, but we will limit the discussion to the focus of the current chapter, suspect interviewing.

The first phase of the Review examined the academic literature and police policy around the world to identify international best practice in investigative interviewing and decide what approach New Zealand Police should adopt in the future (Schollum, 2005). A strength of Schollum's approach was to cover a broad range of organisational factors to identify the best fit for New Zealand Police practice – the organisational strategy towards interviewing; interview methods; the ethical principles underlying the methods used; interviewer training; and interviewing technology and facilities.

The Review identified two main approaches to suspect interviewing that varied in terms of their primary purpose (Schollum, 2005). The first is an accusatory approach to interviewing that involves police interviewing a suspect for the primary purpose of obtaining a confession. For example, the 'Reid technique', commonly used in North America, encourages the interviewer to use of a variety of methods to psychologically induce a suspect into confessing to a crime (Inbau *et al.*, 1986; Inbau *et al.*, 2005). The second approach is the information-gathering approach to interviewing that involves police interviewing a suspect with the primary purpose of gathering information from the suspect about the crime. An example of this is the conversation management approach, commonly used in England and Wales, which encourages the interviewer to gather as much information as possible about a suspect's version of events and relevant to the investigation. This approach also encourages suspects to give explanations for any contradictions between his or her account and other evidence (Shepherd, 2007).

In the literature review, Schollum highlighted the limitations to 'accusatory' interview methods including a heightened risk of false confessions (see Meissner *et al.*, 2012). These findings were supported by experiences in other countries where accusatory methods were identified as a major factor contributing to miscarriages of justice (see Gudjonsson, 2003). The literature review also placed an emphasis on the importance of an ethical approach to interviewing – treating the suspect fairly and with respect to promote cooperation.

The literature review also identified the importance of adopting a broad organisational strategy to embed investigative interviewing practices (Schollum, 2005). Schollum described in detail the strategy used in England and Wales with the adoption of the 'PEACE' approach to investigative interviewing. (PEACE refers to the suggested phases of all investigative interviews: Planning and preparation, Engage and explain, Account, Closure and Evaluation (see Clarke and Milne, 2001).) Nevertheless, an evaluation of 'PEACE' by Clarke and Milne (2001) found this approach did not meet expectations in practice and they recommended increased supervisory support for interviewers, assessment of interviewers and a four-tier approach to interviewing to encourage the progressive development of skills. In England and Wales they also developed a leadership group and a national strategy to embed investigative interviewing practice at an organisational level.

The second phase of the Review used a mixed methods approach to examine actual policy and practice in the New Zealand Police (Schollum, 2006a). This review found policy and training for suspect interviewing was primarily about ensuring officers complied with legal requirements and could operate the video-interview equipment. Although 'PEACE' had been adopted by NZ Police formally, in practice there were inadequate opportunities for skill development for interviewers of suspects or guidance on how to elicit information from a suspect during the interview (e.g. questioning methods, how to structure the interview).

In a survey by Schollum of 279 NZ police officers, officers reported they were confident in conducting video interviews (79 per cent were either 'confident' or 'very confident'). But, only 58 per cent of the Criminal Investigation Branch (CIB) officers and 21 per cent of front-line uniform officers reported video recording their interviews with suspects (Schollum, 2006a). One hundred and eighty-three video recorded suspect interviews were randomly selected from each station in the country and measured against the conversation management model within the PEACE interviewing framework. An analysis found in 45 per cent of these interviews the interviewer was rated as performing poorly by a panel of assessors (both academics and police). Officers were weakest at eliciting a suspect's account, questioning and closing the interview.

The recommendations in New Zealand

In the final phase of the Review (Schollum, 2006b) made 24 recommendations for the governance, resourcing, policies, standards, training and assessment of investigative interviewing to bring the New Zealand Police towards evidence-based practice. The recommendations were largely modelled on the 'PEACE' approach, with refinements to cater for the lessons learned in England and Wales (for example from Clarke and Milne, 2001). The first recommendations were implemented in late 2007 with the establishment of a three-person team (the Investigative Interviewing Unit, including the author NW who was responsible for policy, guidance, standards and training), who reported to the National Crime Manager. This team was responsible for the governance and implementation of a national strategy for investigative interviewing.

From 2007 to 2011 the team implemented nearly all the remaining recommendations. Ten ethical principles were adopted to underpin all interviewing practices that promoted an information-gathering approach rather than an accusatory approach to interviewing (see Schollum, 2006b). This approach was considered more ethical and provided a better fit with current New Zealand legislation. Some of the methods used in the accusatory approach could be perceived by the courts as oppressive and unfair, such as misleading the suspect about the nature of the evidence, and could lead to the interviewing being ruled inadmissible and disciplinary action against the interviewing officer.

The primary interviewing model adopted for suspects was conversation management. The introduction of this method was considered to give a structure for officers to elicit an account from a suspect during the interview, an area of weakness found in the Review. The 'Investigative Interviewing Doctrine' and 'Investigative Interviewing Suspect Guide' were developed, peer-reviewed and published to provide official guidance for investigators on these procedures and related policy (New Zealand Police, 2007, 2008a).

The conversation management approach involves giving more of a structure to planning and preparing for the interview through a focused review of the information available from the investigation and knowing how to structure the interview to elicit information relevant to these issues. The main steps to the interview are to build rapport with the suspect, explain the interview process and legal rights, elicit a detailed account from the suspect about his or her version of events, cover any topics important to the investigation, challenge the suspect on any inconsistencies between his or her account and the evidence, and close the interview (see Clarke and Milne, 2001, for a more detailed description). Within this process are the skills of questioning, active listening, using appropriate nonverbal communication, summarising, asking the suspect to draw a sketch plan and having a flexible structure to the process.

Conversation management was originally developed by practitioners in consultation with influential scholars in this field such as Ray Bull and Eric Shepherd (Bull, 2013; Shepherd, 2007), but has remained untested until recently. A number of studies now suggest the use of these methods increases the likelihood of gaining a comprehensive account from the suspect and detecting if he or she is being deceitful (e.g. Dando *et al.*, 2015; Hartwig *et al.*, 2005; Meissner *et al.*, 2012; Walsh and Bull, 2010).

Building on this foundation, the New Zealand Police progressively implemented the first three levels of a four-level hierarchical training framework for interviewers (Level 1: Foundation; Level 2: Advanced; Level 3: Specialist Suspect; Level 4: Advisory[1]). To help deliver this programme, three full-time national investigative interviewing trainer positions were established at the Royal New Zealand Police College. An underlying principle of the programme was to use evidence-based methods for learning the knowledge and skills of interviewing (e.g. Ericsson *et al.*, 1993; Hattie *et al.*, 1996; Hattie and Timperley, 2007; Powell *et al.*, 2005), a principle that was applied to varying degrees depending on organisational resourcing priorities.

Each level of interviewing has national standards and involves learning the knowledge foundation for the methods and attending a face-to-face training programme that incorporates skills practice with expert feedback (New Zealand Police, 2008b). Once the training is completed, participants enter into an ongoing learning and workplace assessment programme to become accredited at that level. This process involves submitting evidence of field interviews and completing a self-reflective evaluation of the interviews to designated assessors. The purpose of this process is to create national consistency in standards and provide the interviewers with expert feedback for skill development. The assessor evaluates each interview and the self-reflection document against national standards and provides an assessment of competency and feedback about how to improve practice. Interviewers who are 'not yet competent' develop a plan with the trainer to address issues arising and must then submit a further recording for evaluation. Although the same in broad structure, the specifics of each level's competency programme vary with increased intensity at higher levels.

The competency program

Level 1: Foundation suspect interviewing

Level 1: Foundation interviewing aims to equip all officers with the skills to conduct interviews with witnesses and suspects for priority and volume crime (New Zealand Police, 2008b). The success of a pilot of the training provided impetus in districts to provide the training to all sworn officers below the rank of Inspector from 2007 to 2011. Due to an absence of expertise in New Zealand, trainers were contracted from England (on three occasions) to train the New Zealand trainers, who were nominated by each of the twelve districts in the New Zealand Police. The training package was developed by NW with the help of a learning developer based on learning materials from England.

In this initial implementation, 7,500 employees received the Level 1 training. The training course includes learning knowledge about memory and communication, and two days are spent learning the skills to interview suspects. The training course was typically held over five days with twelve participants and two trainers. The participant's supervisor usually conducted the workplace assessment of two video interviews. From 2009 Level 1 was embedded in recruit training and delivered by the national trainers, so all new recruits are now trained in this level.

During the national implementation of Level 1, the New Zealand Police evaluated how the interviewing model was being used at a practice level (Cunningham, 2010). The research, conducted in the period leading up to 2010, analysed the opinions of 677 police interviewers throughout New Zealand of varying ranks and also conducted a variety of focus groups from staff among this sample. At the time 81 per cent of all district staff had completed Level One PEACE training. Only 9 per cent, however, had successfully completed the subsequent accreditation process. Officers perceived that PEACE had led to better planning and preparation of interviews, better structure during interviews and an increase in video-recorded interviews. But officers' responses to the survey suggest they struggled to understand the relevance of the assessment process and that many supervisors did not have the skills or make the time to conduct the assessments. While this study provided some insight into how police officers felt the PEACE framework was aiding interviewing, it again only offered subjective reports from officers themselves and gave little insight into what was happening in the interviewing room.

Level 2: Advanced suspect interviewing

In 2009 the Level 2: Advanced interviewing was implemented to provide those in an investigatory role with the skills to conduct interviews with witnesses and suspects to serious crime. Priority to attend the training is given to investigators, especially those who have been nominated to progress to a specialist level of interviewing. In Level 2, interviewers learn to apply conversation management across more complex scenarios (e.g. youth suspects, interviewing with a lawyer present). The training is typically delivered by two national trainers over five days with twelve participants, and followed by workplace assessment similar to Level 1. In an attempt to overcome the shortcomings of the Level workplace assessment around assessor skills and motivation, Level 2 trainers conducted the assessments. This learning programme has not yet become a part of the detective training programme as originally intended, but many of the districts are training officers already in the Criminal Investigation Branch.

Level 3: Specialist Suspect interviewing

In 2012, the Level 3: Specialist Suspect interviewing was implemented to develop a national pool of interviewers for suspects of major crime (e.g. homicide, sexual assault, other serious violence, aggravated robbery). There is currently a national pool of over 50 specialist interviewers. Each region selected participants (often also detective trained) to attend a ten-day residential national interviewer training course. The training was developed by the New Zealand national trainer (who had attended the Tier 3 Suspect training in West Yorkshire) with NW and an educationalist. Gary Shaw, who was the national lead for interviewing in England and Wales, was consulted on the development and led the first training with the national trainer. This training is now delivered by the national trainer, and with the assistance of an accredited Level 3 Suspect interviewer. The eight participants learn about the psychological and investigative basis of the interview methods and practise the skills and receive feedback from the trainers.

A review of investigative interviewing practices in Australia

Similar to New Zealand, suspect interviewing practices in most Australian States and Territories have undergone considerable reform over the last decade. In some jurisdictions these changes were initiated by police simply to improve practice, while in others miscarriages of justice have contributed to driving change. For example, in Western Australia a coercive confession that resulted in a false conviction (*Mallard* v. *The Queen*, 2005) put pressure on Western Australian Police to reform suspect interviewing. This pressure was increased when a coercive confession of Dante Arthurs to a sexual offence against a child was ruled as inadmissible. This allowed him to go free and untreated and enabled him to go on to kill a young girl, Sofia Rodriguez-Urrutia Shu. Western Australia Police detectives investigating the murder then coerced another confession from Arthurs that was ruled as inadmissible (*Arthurs* v. *The State of Western Australia*, 2007). In other jurisdictions it has been suggested that there has been a more relaxed attitude towards coercive confessions. For instance, Moston (2009) says that when coercive practices, such as beating suspects, were revealed by an Office of Police Integrity investigation by Victoria Police there was little public concern and little change in suspect-interviewing in Victoria.

The division of jurisdictions means that there is an assortment of approaches to interviewing suspects across Australia. Every jurisdiction, except for one, was represented at a workshop hosted by Queensland Police Service in 2011. Each presented on the current situation in their own jurisdiction with discussions indicating that nearly every jurisdiction had adopted the English and Welsh 'PEACE' approach to witness interviewing. The degree to which each organisation had implemented this approach varied. Some had just adopted the broad framework and integrated it into detective training while others had adopted a more a comprehensive approach. But there was seldom evidence of broader organisational reform that went beyond training and guidance to include governance and resourcing. This is somewhat surprising as front-line police officers overwhelmingly endorse interviewing as important (Hill and Moston, 2011). For instance, in a survey of 2,769 Queensland police officers, over half said that investigative interviewing was 'very important' (58.1 per cent), with an additional third (33.6 per cent) rating it as 'important'.

The adoption of the 'PEACE' approach means there is considerable overlap between New Zealand and Australian jurisdictions. For example, Queensland Police has undergone comprehensive changes to investigative interviewing. After reviewing interviewing practices around the same time as New Zealand, they have nearly completed implementing a similar four-level competency framework based on the 'PEACE' approach. As a result, both services have worked closely together and, because Queensland Police's implementation started slightly later, New Zealand has shared much of its guidance and learning products and trained some of their trainers. These services have also shared the costs of bringing consultants from England to help with training local trainers. Queensland Police have shared their learning products and trained members of other Australian police services (e.g. Northern Territory, Western Australia). Although this has come about in an ad hoc way, this sharing of resources means there is some consistency across the jurisdictions in terms of practice, but each organisation has implemented it differently. Most other jurisdictions have recently undergone, or are currently undergoing, reforms of suspect interviewing practices, but we are unable to give a detailed account of each jurisdiction within the limits of this book chapter. For example, Victoria Police Service has recently implemented a programme for interviewing suspected sex offenders and the Australian Federal Police are in the process of implementing extensive reforms to interviewing practice based on the 'PEACE' approach.

Whatever the case, the Australian and New Zealand Policing Advisory Agency (ANZPAA), which includes representatives of each police commissioner, has now developed standards for interviewing across both countries. These standards recommend the 'PEACE' approach to interviewing suspects.

Implications for research and practice

Suspect interviewing is taken seriously in New Zealand with regard to ethics, compliance with the legislation, training and supervision. Similar patterns are present or emerging in nearly all parts of Australia. Many of these reforms are evidence-based. For those jurisdictions where less comprehensive changes have been made, it is difficult to know what is happening without any evaluation. Prior evidence about the difficulty in learning suspect interviewing skills does, however, suggest there is likely to be a great deal of discrepancy between policy and reality (see, for example, Clarke and Milne, 2001).

The effectiveness of the 'PEACE' approach to interviewing suspects needs to be evaluated. The only evaluation of this was conducted by Clarke and Milne in 2001, which suggested the approach was under-delivering what was expected. Since then, there have been numerous reforms, such as the implementation of the tiered approach and the assessment of interview performance. Until a proper evaluation is conducted it is not possible to know if these expensive reforms are producing improvements in practice. For example, Griffiths *et al.* (2011) suggest interviewers who received advanced levels of suspect interview training do demonstrate a higher level of skill, but still struggle with the more complex parts of the interview process (e.g. how to challenge a suspect). More evaluative research of this type is required so police can determine how to implement practice in the most cost-effective way.

More research is required from scholars to further develop the evidence-base to meet the needs of police practice. Research into suspect interviewing practice is growing, but there is a need to examine the common scenarios police deal with in their day-to-day work and determine how, if at all, interviewing practices can be adapted to meet operational needs. Offenders are often more likely to have difficulties in verbal language, have had a limited education and be illiterate (Gudjonsson, 2003), and interview settings often provoke high anxiety (Kebbell *et al.*, 2006). Complex tasks, such as understanding legal rights that often contain technical legal jargon, may be difficult for many suspects. With the international call for more ethical interviewing (e.g. Kebbell *et al.*, 2006; Poyser and Milne, 2011) it is likely that courts will begin to be more stringent around this in the future, particularly in cases where a suspect is deemed vulnerable (Napier and Adams, 2002).

How best to elicit an account from different types of interviewees also requires more research. For example, little is known about whether interview practices should be adapted to interview adolescents or the indigenous people of Australia (Aboriginal people and Torres Strait Islanders) and New Zealand (Maori). Many suspects are also likely to be vulnerable for other reasons such as suffering from a mental disorder or intellectual impairment. These vulnerable groups are most at risk when it comes to making false confessions, but there is little research on how to deal with these different types of groups. The evidence-base is growing for how best to interview suspected sex offenders, but less is known about suspects of other types of crime (Oxburgh *et al.*, 2012; Read *et al.*, 2009). There is some evidence, for example, that a different approach may be required with some murderers when compared to sex offenders (Holmberg and Christianson, 2002).

In conclusion, there is a great deal that is positive in New Zealand and Australia with regards suspect interviewing. While the pace of change may vary from jurisdiction to jurisdiction, it is in the right direction in terms of what the scientific evidence suggests. The fact that front-line police recognise the critical importance of suspect interviews and have been exposed to evidence-based approaches and are positive about it should mean that progress should be maintained.

Note

1. Level 4 has not yet been implemented.

References

Arthurs v. *The State of Western Australia* (2007) WASC 209 (31 August 2007).

Australian Institute of Criminology (2006) *Composition of Australia's Police Services as at 30 June 2006*. Canberra. Retrieved on 5 May 2014 from: http://www.aic.gov.au/statistics/criminaljustice/police_services.html.

Bull, R. (2013) 'When in interviews to disclose information to suspects and to challenge them?', in R. Bull (ed.), *Investigation Interviewing*. New York: Springer, pp. 67–181.

Clarke, C. and Milne, R. (2001) *National Evaluation of the PEACE Investigative Interviewing Course*, Police Research Award Scheme Report No. PRAS/149. Institute of Criminal Justice Studies, University of Portsmouth.

Cunningham, S. (2010) *Evaluation of the Implementation of Investigative Interviewing Training and Assessment*. Wellington: New Zealand Police.

Dando, C., Bull, R., Ormerod, T. and Sandham, A. (2015) 'Interviewing suspects: using information tactically to increase cognitive demand and detect deception', *Legal and Criminological Psychology*, 20: 114–28.

Ericsson, K. A., Krampe, R. T. and Tesch-Römer, C. (1993) 'The role of deliberate practice in the acquisition of expert performance', *Psychological Review*, 100 (3): 363–406.

Findlay, M., Odgers, S. and Yeo, S. (2009) *Australian Criminal Justice*. Melbourne: Oxford University Press.

Griffiths, A., Milne, B. and Cherryman, J. (2011) 'A question of control? The formulation of suspect and witness interview question strategies by advanced interviewers', *International Journal of Police Science and Management*, 13 (3): 255–67.

Gudjonsson, G. H. (2003) *The Psychology of Interrogations and Confessions: A Handbook*. Chichester: Wiley.

Hartwig, M., Granhag, P. A., Stromwall, L. A. and Vrij, A. (2005) 'Detecting deception via strategic disclosure of evidence', *Law and Human Behavior*, 29 (4): 469–84.

Hattie, J. and Timperley, H. (2007) 'The power of feedback', *Review of Educational Research*, 70 (1): 81–112.

Hattie, J., Biggs, J. and Purdie, N. (1996) 'Effects of learning skills interventions on student learning: a meta-analysis', *Review of Educational Research*, 66 (2): 99–136.

Hill, J. A. and Moston, S. (2011) 'Police perceptions of investigative interviewing: training needs and operational practices in Australia', *British Journal of Forensic Practice*, 13: 72–83.

Holmberg, U. and Christianson, S. (2002) 'Murderers' and sexual offenders' experiences of police interviews and their inclination to admit or deny crimes', *Behavioral Sciences and the Law*, 20: 31–45.

Inbau, F. E., Reid, J. E. and Buckley, J. P. (1986) *Criminal Interrogation and Confessions*, 3rd edn. Baltimore, MD: Williams & Wilkins.

Inbau, F. E., Reid, J. E., Buckley, J. P. and Jayne, B. C. (2005) *Essentials of the Reid Technique: Criminal Interrogations and Confessions*. Sudbury: Jones & Bartlett.

Kebbell, M. R., Hurren, E. and Mazerolle, P. (2006) *An Investigation into the Effective and Ethical Interviewing of Suspected Sex Offenders*, Trends and Issues in Crime and Criminal Justice No. 327. Canberra: Australian Institute of Criminology.

Mallard v. *The Queen* (2005) HCA 68.

Meissner, C. A., Redlich, A. D., Bhatt, S. and Brandon, S. (2012) *Interview and Interrogation Methods and Their Effects on True and False Confessions*, Campbell Systematic Reviews No. 13.

Moston, S. (2009) 'Investigative interviewing in Australia', in B. Milne, S. Savage and T. Williamson (eds), *International Developments in Investigative Interviewing*. Cullompton: Willan.

Napier, M. R., and Adams, S. H. (2002) 'Criminal confessions: overcoming the challenges', *FBI Law Enforcement Bulletin*, 71: 9–15.

New Zealand Police (2007) *Investigative Interviewing Doctrine*. Wellington: NZP.

New Zealand Police (2008a) *Witness Guide*. Wellington: NZP.

New Zealand Police (2008b) *Investigative Interviewing: Accreditation Policy*. Wellington: NZP.

New Zealand Police (2014) *Annual Report: NZ Police 2013/1014*. Wellington: NZP.

Oxburgh, G. E., Ost, J. and Cherryman, J. (2012) 'Police interviews with suspected child sex offenders: does use of empathy and question type influence the amount of investigation relevant information obtained?', *Psychology, Crime and Law*, 18 (3): 259–73.

Powell, M. B., Fisher, R. P. and Wright, R. (2005) 'Investigative interviewing', in N. Brewer and K. Williams (eds.), *Psychology and Law: An Empirical Perspective*. New York: Guilford, pp. 11–42.

Poyser, S. and Milne, R. (2011) 'Miscarriages of justice: a call for continued research focusing on reforming the investigative process', *British Journal of Forensic Practice*, 13: 61–71.

Read, J. M., Powell, M. B., Kebbell, M. R. and Milne, R. (2009) 'Investigative interviewing of suspected sex offenders: a review of what constitues best practice', *International Journal of Police Science and Management*, 11: 442–59.

Schollum, M. (2005) *Investigative Interviewing: The Literature*. Wellington: NZP.

Schollum, M. (2006a) *Investigative Interviewing: The Current Situation*. Wellington: NZP.

Schollum, M. (2006b) *Investigative Interviewing: The Recommendations*. Wellington: NZP.

Shepherd, E. (2007) *Investigative Interviewing: The Conversation Management Approach*. Oxford: Oxford University Press.

Walsh, D. and Bull, R. (2010) 'What really is effective in interviews with suspects? A study comparing interviewing skills against interviewing outcomes', *Legal and Criminological Psychology*, 15: 305–21.

Europe

7 Interviewing suspects in Belgium

Miet Vanderhallen, Alexandra de Jong and Geert Vervaeke

Introduction

Unlike other countries such as England and Wales and the Netherlands, Belgian legislation focuses mainly on police interviewing in general. The same goes for the interview model, which forms the basis of most training programmes, being applicable to victims and witnesses as well as suspects. Next to this general approach there are several specific points of attention when interviewing suspects.

Notwithstanding Belgian legislation on police interviewing being applicable to both Flanders and Wallonia, differences in theories, training and practices might occur between training programmes and practices in these regions.

When looking at the Belgian police structure, this diversity does not come as a surprise. Until 2001 the police consisted of three separate police services: (1) the gendarmerie, a national police force; (2) the judicial police attached to the public prosecutor's service; and (3) the municipal police (Enhus and Ponsaers, 2005). Due to several judicial failures in the 1980s and 1990s, and especially the *Dutroux* case,[1] major reforms of police services have taken place. The lack of cooperation between the different police forces, seen as partly responsible for the dramatic cases, resulted in an 'integrated police', structured on two levels: the federal and local police,[2] consisting of 194 police regions. The federal level comprises the commissionership-general and 27 federal judicial police units, paralleling the geographical judicial structure. From 1 June 2014 onwards, these decentralised units have been reduced to 14[3] following judicial reform. Between the two levels, junctions have been built structurally to facilitate integrated functioning (Verstraeten, 2005), although the various police units have kept a substantial autonomy in policy and practice, with consequences for the field of training.

Another factor that can contribute to the diversity in training and practice can be found in a traditional absence of research interest in police interviewing in Belgium, although there has been some research (see below). This lack of scientific attention might have stimulated police officers to gain insights abroad. For many years Canada and the United States served as a source of inspiration without much critical reflection, so that examples of interview techniques were embedded in divergent judicial systems. This led to the implementation of and support for divergent techniques from a more accusatory approach on the one hand and an information-gathering approach on the other (Van De Plas, 2007). In the last two decades, an increased comprehension of potential risks related to certain manipulative techniques has led to additional efforts to further strengthen the information-gathering strategies instead of confession-oriented ones.

Despite the lack of scientific research attention, in recent years, Belgian practice has increasingly adopted an evidence-based approach of police interviewing in general, also inspired by English practices and research results since the implementation of PEACE. However, various techniques coming from more accusatorial interview styles seem still to be in use (Bockstaele, 2008a; Ponsaers *et al.*, 2001; Vanderhallen, 2007). This could be an indication of practitioners, academics and instructors not working in unison, not only between but also within these groups.

Finally, the diversity and lack of uniformity might be a result of the structure of the police academies. Next to the federal police school and the regional police academies related to the provinces, the national school for senior officers as well as the national detective's school provide a variety of training on interviewing at a federal level. Regardless of some basic formal guidelines, these academies possess substantial autonomy in developing their educational programmes.

Training[4]

In line with the Belgian police and police academies structured on a federal and decentralised level, the provision of training is fragmentary. For example, training courses differ in the extent to which they focus on the interviewing of suspects. Few courses focus solely on the suspect interview. The majority of courses cover the interviewing of victims and witnesses as well as suspects in separate modules. As this chapter concerns the investigative interviewing of suspects, only the latter will be discussed.

Training programmes

Training programmes on interviewing are offered within the Belgian police academies as well as externally, the latter being organised by private organisations or on the initiative of a local police service, which engages non-police officers for specific training. Training offered within the Belgian police academies are referred to as formal training programmes.

Formal programmes: three categories

Formal training programmes can be classified into three categories: basic training, functional training and advanced training.

Basic training – notwithstanding the concept 'basic' – is provided at different levels depending on the specialised skills and knowledge required for a certain position or rank that come under three management levels: basic level, middle level and ranking officer management level. For each level a specific course has to be completed entailing a module on interviewing. Training at basic and middle management level is offered by the police academies of nine provinces, as well as by the three abovementioned federal academies. The latter also provide basic training at ranking officer level.

The category of *functional training* comprises courses required when police officers want to advance to a certain position on a horizontal level. With a view to interview training, the functional judicial course is of relevance. A criminal investigator (inspector or chief inspector) is obligated to take this course in which he receives additional and in-depth training on forensic investigative methods, crime analysis and interview techniques. The National detective's school specialises in providing training regarding these topics, while the federal police school and the national school for senior officers provide functional training on other topics.

The third category of *advanced training* aims at skills and knowledge maintenance, and specialisation in specific topics, including police interviewing. Therefore, police officers are required to acquire a number of education points on a yearly basis by following advanced courses on a variety of subjects. There are various advanced courses regarding different aspects of the investigative interview, offered at both federal and regional police academies. However, some special, more in-depth courses are solely available at the federal academies.

Table 7.1 provides an overview of the training programmes and courses in Belgium that either directly focus on or involve certain aspects of the suspect interview. The list of training programmes within the category of advanced training is illustrative and provides a random selection from different police academies in order to demonstrate the diversity of aspects which are covered in training. The underscored courses refer to courses that contain a component of or mainly concern the suspect interview.

The aim of the courses is to increase the knowledge on interviewing and to teach new or improve current skills. At the basic management level, however, the bare minimum of interview training is provided as officers at this level do not question witnesses, victims or suspects often, and when they do, it is solely in regard to minor offences. As responsibilities increase within the police hierarchy, so too does the depth of the required training, resulting in extensive knowledge and specialised skills at ranking officer level.

Under the heading of advanced training, the federal police school and several regional police academies recently introduced a follow-up course on interview coaching, resulting from a study by Smets (2012). This study showed that follow-up by means of individual coaching improves interpersonal interview competencies. The identification of these interview competencies were based upon an earlier study by De Fruyt *et al.* (2006).

For all courses, officers have to meet a set of basic requirements, for instance the completion of basic training at management level. Often no further selection of participants takes place. Moreover, it is not standard procedure to evaluate participants at the end of the course, nor is supervision[5] in the field. It is therefore not only difficult to assess participants' progress and their level of skills and

Table 7.1 Overview of training programmes

Training categories	*Level*	*Programmes*	*Content regarding the investigative interview*
Basic	Basic management	Agent (554 hours)	Basic interview techniques
		Inspector (506 hours)	Basic interview techniques for interview with victims or witnesses of minor crimes, and written record
	Middle management	Chief inspector (754 hours)	Various (special) interview techniques (hypnoses and polygraph), *interview of adult victims, witnesses and suspects, interview of juvenile victims and suspects*, audio-visual interviewing, and written record
	Ranking officer	Commissioner (1,100 hours)	Module interview/line-up within the functional judicial course (see below)
Functional		*Functional judicial course* (320 hours): module interview/line-up (34 hours)	Various interview techniques, memory, lie detection, audio-visual interviewing and Salduz interviewing
		Functional training behaviour analysis (240 hours)	Profiling in serious cases, behaviour analysis, risk analysis, coaching of police interviews
		Functional training polygraph (385 hours)	Theories on computerised polygraphs, interrogation and statement analysis
		Courses	
Advanced		*Refresher basic interview techniques* (8 hours)	Basic skills and proper conduct of interviewing witness, victim or suspect
		Interview techniques (32 hours)	Interview techniques, communication skills, victim/witness and suspect interview
		Lie detection (verbal and non-verbal signals) during questioning (16 hours)	Current developments in lie detection, verbal and non-verbal signals of lying, Behaviour Observation Questions (BOQs), and Scientific Content Analysis (SCAN)
		Investigative interview techniques (60 hours)	Communication techniques, preparation interview, interview of victims, witnesses and suspects, special interview techniques, and written record

(Continued)

Table 7.1 Overview of training programmes (Continued)

Training categories	*Level*	*Programmes*	*Content regarding the investigative interview*
		Audio-visual interview adult suspects (56 hours)	Legal framework, preparation, Behaviour Observation Questions (BOQs), principles of interview model for adult victims, witnesses and suspects, operating equipment
		Introduction to the polygraph (12 hours)	Basic principles, operation, legal framework and the course of the interview
		Interview sexual offenders (18 hours)	Theoretical aspects of sexual offending, the influence of stereotypes and emotion of the police officer during interrogation and investigation
		Mental disorders and police attitudes (12 hours)	Common pathologies and the interpretation of statements
		Audio-visual interview juvenile suspects (33 hours)	Legal framework and communication strategies
		Salduz interview (28 hours)	Concept and legislation, preparation and conduct *Salduz* interview, best practices
		Interview coach (104 hours)	Systematic coaching of interpersonal interview skills

knowledge, but studies show that to sustain a change in attitudes and an improvement in skills, training should be followed by expert supervision (e.g. Clarke *et al.*, 2011; Crawshaw *et al.*, 1998; Powell *et al.*, 2005; Price and Roberts, 2011). Continuous supervision has been shown to improve the previously acquired knowledge on how to accurately apply components of structured interview protocols (e.g. Lamb *et al.*, 2000; Powell and Steinberg, 2012).

Finally, police services autonomously install specific training projects. For example, internal coaching projects in which colleagues discuss interviews among themselves is one such project.

External training programmes

In addition to the formal training programmes offered by police academies there is a series of so-called external programmes. This category covers concurrent initiatives to the formal programmes offered by police academies. These external programmes can be initiated by the police or by other public or private institutions.

Some local police services have developed their own initiatives to improve knowledge and skills regarding suspect interviewing, for example by external supervision projects (Vanderhallen *et al.*, 2013). Local police services engage experts to provide tailor-made training, for example regarding interviewing of different types of suspects. Furthermore, several courses on interview training have also been introduced within the private sector. For instance, there are courses on the interrogation of psychopaths (Politeia) as well as on Scientific Content Analysis[6] (Centre for Police Studies).

Content, materials and instructors

With regard to the content of the formal training programmes, variation is the keyword. If we look at the training programmes which (mainly) focus on suspect interviewing, for example, the general course on investigative interview techniques and the course concerning the audio-visual interviewing of adult suspects are quite different in orientation. The first covers the basic interview strategy and communication techniques that result from this strategy, while the second recommends the use of controversial interview techniques (see section on 'Legislation and current practices on suspect interviewing' below). This has also to do with the lack of a uniform viewpoint on interviewing suspects and lack of training materials.

Uniform course materials are only available for basic training programmes. These materials served as the basis for two handbooks on interviewing for practitioners (Bockstaele, 2008a, 2008b). Police academies and academy teachers are not obligated to use these materials and may develop their own. However, the basic interview strategy does usually form the basis of the majority of the interview courses (Volckaert, 2005). As a consequence of this independence regarding the interpretation of training programmes, working styles equally differ. The latter at times results in contrasting proportions of theory and practice between similar training programmes in basic training, for example. The majority of training programmes pay attention to include exercises as well as role plays, which is, according to Powell *et al.* (2005), one of the key elements of effective training.

As regards the selection of the instructors, there are no official qualification requirements, allowing academies to choose whoever they deem qualified. It is therefore even more difficult to measure and compare the quality of the training programmes offered by the different academies.

From 2008 onwards, the national detective's school and some regional police academies introduced interview courses taught by two instructors, one academic expert and one field expert. By means of a heterogeneous didactic team, both theory and practice can be integrated in training. Collaboration with the academic field to jointly develop training programmes is a newer trend. At the regional police academy in Limburg, for instance, a skills training programme with regard to the *Salduz* interview (see below) is offered as a result of collaboration with several universities and experienced police officers.

The most recent innovation concerns joint training, in which interview training is attended by both lawyers and police officers in order to learn from each other. Research shows that this type of training is appreciated by both professional groups and not only just in Belgium (Blackstock *et al.*, 2014; Vanderhallen *et al.*, 2014).

Training programmes summary

The interview training offered in Belgium shows a lack of uniformity in terms of the available programmes, course content and material, as well as instructors. Furthermore, even though the courses do include the suspect interview, there is no advanced training that specialises in the interrogation of suspects as a whole, leading to a fragmentary curriculum. When examining the content of the courses, diversity is found in ideas and techniques that do not always coincide. Hence, police officers might be confronted with contradictions regarding their approach to suspect interviewing. Coordination, efficiency and a successive structure in interview training are indispensable, though in Belgium they are ingredients that are lacking for a sound curriculum on interviewing suspects.

Legislation and current practices on suspect interviewing

Changes in interviewing practice do not only originate from a top-down regulatory function. Although interview practice is regulated by a judicial framework, this guidance was limited for a prolonged time. New regulatory initiatives often arise from incidents (such as the *Dutroux* case) or case law (such as *Salduz*). However, sometimes initiatives from practice can lead to a regulatory necessity as well, which can be seen as a bottom-up approach.

Legislation in a historical perspective

For decades specific legislation on police interviewing was also very limited. An initial legislative reform of the rudimentary framework with regard to interviewing was introduced in 1998 with the so-called law 'Franchimont'.[7] This law is considered a specific legal basis for the police interview in general and deals with, among other aspects, the interview of victims, witnesses and suspects. New rules concerning the start of the interview were implemented, of which a subtle version of the caution ('what you say might be used in court') was one of the important innovations. Once more, a general view on interviewing is chosen since these legal rules apply to all interviewees.

In 2002 legislation on audio-visual interviewing was implemented,[8] by means of which the audio-visual recording of interviews at a distance (for example video-conferencing) is regulated. In contrast with other regulations, this legislation was initiated from practice. After implementing guidelines on audio-visual interviews of suspects[9] and a corresponding training programme at the national school of criminal investigation, there was a need for regulation (Bockstaele, 2002).

Over the last several years, suspect interviewing has received a lot of attention due to the *Salduz* ECHR case law. The implementation of the so-called *Salduz* law on 1 January 2012 is considered the most thorough development in police interviewing.[10] Next to legislation, the board of prosecutors-general issued binding guidelines in order to facilitate and optimise police practice in accordance with these new rulings. The main modification relates to the implementation of legal assistance and information on suspect's rights. With regard to the first interview, arrested suspects have the right to a confidential consultation with a lawyer who can be present during the interview as well.[11] Interviewers are obliged to inform all suspects not only about the right to legal assistance but, among other matters, about the right to remain silent and the right not to incriminate themselves. Although not only focusing on suspects, the *Salduz* law establishes the largest changes with respect to the status of the suspect. Hence this law had quite an impact on police officers. Responses ranged from 'resistance' to taking on an 'opportunity' to increase interview quality. Nonetheless, resistance and insecurity were found to be the most common feelings (Vanderhallen *et al*., 2014). With a view to uniformity, a national course explaining the new procedures and practice was initiated in 2011–12, and a new module on *Salduz* interviewing was embedded in existing training programmes. In addition, some police academies offer separate training programmes on interviewing and legal assistance.

Recently, as a result of the *Salduz* law, a new practice proceeded from police services aimed at recording suspect interviews audio-visually, in terms of a sole recording of the interview and not in terms of a video-interview (i.e. without written record that has to be signed, in a monitoring room and so on). This practice reflects earlier guidelines from the board of prosecutors-general[12] and is also formulated in the Police Guidebook on the application of the *Salduz* law (Allaerts, 2012). However, at the moment only a few police services appear to be able to record interviews due to lack of equipment, adapted interview rooms, etc.

Currently, after a thorough evaluation of the (implementation of the) *Salduz* law, an adjustment is in preparation in order to amplify legal assistance in Belgium.

Interview model and techniques: a theoretical exploration

Concurrent to the preparation of the law Franchimont, a working group with members from the three former police services developed a new interview model in 1999 (Van De Plas, 2007). In line with the reform of the legislation (law Franchimont), this 'Basic Interview Technique' envisages both the interviewing of victims and witnesses as well as suspects (Van De Plas, 2000). This interview model was approved for educational purposes by the board of prosecutors-general and serves as the basis for many training programmes.

The Basic Interview Technique was first published in 2000 (Van De Plas, 2000) and reflected an orientation towards an information gathering interview style with an emphasis on interview instead of interrogation. The second edition in 2007 reinforced a more evidence-based approach providing in addition possible theoretical mechanisms and empirical evidence in the fields of observation, memory and confirmation bias (Van De Plas, 2007).

Content-wise, the Basic Interview Technique is similar to the PEACE model.[13] In terms of structure, the Belgian model consists of three phases: preparation, execution and evaluation (Van De Plas, 2007). The preparation phase (related to Planning and Preparation) consists of the mental preparation (e.g. knowledge of the case file, aim …) and tangible preparation (e.g. location, materials …). The execution entails a flowchart comprising five steps: introduction (relates to Engage and Explain), free recall (Account), questioning (Account), paraphrased recording of the written statement and closure (Closure). The evaluation phase reflects both an impact as well as a process evaluation.

The Basic Interview Technique concerns a general framework for interviewing and solely focuses on general techniques such as basic communication skills and neutral confrontations, for example to introduce evidence or to point at discrepancies in the statement. This might be the reason why during training various other techniques, more related to the obtaining of confessions, are promoted for interviewing suspects in particular. In this regard, more controversial techniques (for example, rationalisation, minimisation, projection) are regularly described in the professional literature and taught in various training programmes throughout the three categories of formal training and beyond (Bockstaele, 2008a).

Hence, notwithstanding the implementation of a standardised interview model (the Basic Interview Technique), various specific interview techniques ranging from basic communication skills to techniques aimed at changing attitudes towards confessions can be found in the literature on interviewing in Belgium.

Neither the installation of two working groups (consisting both of interview experts, magistrates and academics) nor the appointment of an interview coordinator could fill the gap between these divergent attitudes and theoretical views.

Interviewing in practice

Given the diversity in training and applied theories, it is interesting to look at Belgian police interview practice. Given the limited extent to which interviews are audio-visually recorded, a direct examination is for the most part lacking. What happens in the interview room is thus not only partially enlightened in empirical studies, but insights are often derived from surveys and interviews and thus provide practitioners' perceptions. Only a minority of research observed (video-recorded) suspect interviews.

Over the last two decades, only a few comprehensive studies have specifically examined police interviewing practice and shed light on interview practice in general or suspect interviewing in particular.[14]

A study in 2001 (Ponsaers *et al.*, 2001) concerned a survey on interview techniques among 360 interviewers. The majority of the interviewers indicated 'gathering verifiable information' as the goal of the interview. When asked about their use of 105 interview techniques, some remarkable findings were found in light of the aim of gathering information. With regard to the introduction of evidence in interviewing, about 28 per cent of the interviewers mention they frequently refer to evidence which was actually perceived as uncertain and approximately

9 per cent refer to evidence that does not exist. Notwithstanding the shift to a more information gathering interview style, 37 per cent of the interviewers displayed their conviction of guilt towards the suspect on a frequent basis.

In 2007 a study on the role of the working alliance in 126 police interviews was conducted through questionnaires filled in by police interviewers and interviewees (Vanderhallen *et al.*, 2011). Findings show that suspects perceive the interview style (see Holmberg, 2004) as more dominant in comparison to victims and witnesses, although interviewers don't report a difference. The working alliance is also perceived less effective with suspects in comparison to victims and witnesses whereas interviewers again do not report differences. This contrast in perception between interviewee and interviewer is also found with regard to the status of the interviewee. Instead of 46.8 per cent of interviewees being indicated as a suspect by the interviewer, only 31.7 per cent of the interviewees perceived themselves as a suspect suggesting that suspects – among other explanations – might not always be aware of their status. However, a good working alliance was found to predict higher satisfaction with interviewers on both the outcome and proceedings of the suspect interview.

A final study concerns the evaluation of the Salduz law in which quantitative and qualitative data were gathered. Findings show that the implementation of legal assistance is characterised by some difficulties but the number of incidents is rather low and decreases after some time (Penne *et al.*, 2013). For example, the study showed difficulties regarding the timing of interviewing (during night time), the role of the lawyer during the interview (passive versus active), waiting time for the lawyer to arrive at the police station (causing delay in the criminal investigation) and when a lawyer did show up.

These studies indicate that a number of Belgian interviewers still seem to adopt a dominant interview style and that the working alliance with the suspect can be improved.

In addition to research examining interview practice, some studies focused on specific aspects surrounding the police interview. In this regard, Smets (2012) looked into a new interview training approach of individual coaching which showed improvement of interview competencies in interviewing with 52 per cent of the participants. Another experimental study handled the peculiar position of interpreters in video-conferencing, comparing different methods (Balogh and Hertog, 2012). This Belgian study was conducted under the heading of a larger European project, AVIDICUS. The study showed that face-to-face interpreting is most desirable for the parties involved, but if a suspect is interviewed at a distance, the interpreter sitting with the police instead of with the suspect is preferred.

Currently, three studies are still ongoing in which (videotapes of) real interviews are being observed. Two studies examine interviews of juvenile suspects to provide insights on interviews with vulnerable suspects.[15] A final study focuses on the evidential evaluation of suspects' statements by judges (Tersago, in preparation). In this study interviews in the presence of a lawyer are analysed in terms of interview style and technique in relation to the lawyer's interventions.

Current practice discussed in terms of evidence and support

As there is little research on suspect interviewing in Belgium, training and practice in the last decade has often been based on international research reflecting an evidence-based tendency in Belgium. This tendency is reflected in the increased collaboration between academics and practitioners. One example of collaboration can be found in the delivery of training by heterogeneous didactic teams (see above). Moreover, follow-up initiatives such as coaching and supervision have been introduced as a result of empirical findings (Smets, 2012; Dommicent *et al.*, 2008). The most recent example is the publication of a practitioner's guide on suspect interviewing in which academics and practitioners from various countries together describe relevant topics such as development of rapport, inappropriate pressure, interviewing in the presence of a lawyer, stimulation of cooperation and strategic use of evidence (Schellingen and Scholten, 2014). However, since research does not fully clarify which specific techniques are efficient and which are a potential risk for false confessions, some techniques and practices are under discussion, resulting in training programmes recommending controversial techniques and other programmes leaving these techniques out. Some clues are missing in general, for example on the efficacy of the preparation of the interview: how helpful are different methods of preparation to obtain accurate information? Another under-researched general topic is the introduction of evidence to obtain accurate statements: should it be strategic, gradual or late? With regard to other topics, operationalisation of accepted practice is insufficient. Although there is strong agreement on the importance of building rapport, questions arise on how to build rapport and whether maintaining rapport is always relevant (Vanderhallen and Vervaeke, 2014). Research shows that rapport maintenance is important for the result of the interview but interviewers need to improve on maintaining rapport (Walsh and Bull, 2012). In practice, however, there is uncertainty on how to use mirroring and self-disclosure in this regard. Similar questions are raised on the extent to which free recall is needed: extensively or not? And after an introduction with more 'personal' questions to what extent is the interviewer allowed to interrupt the free recall, for example by echoing, and so on.

However, other techniques are subject to the most controversy and might even lead to controversial practices, for instance the rationalisation/minimisation/projection technique, the Behaviour Observation Questions (BOQ) and Scientific Content Analysis (SCAN). With regard to minimisation, scientific research shows that this technique increases the risk of false confessions (e.g. Kassin and Kiechel, 1996; Russano *et al.*, 2005). Therefore, the professional literature suggests a non-directive minimisation approach by the interviewer only when there is a strong presumption of the suspect's guilt in order to facilitate the suspect to talk about what happened (Bockstaele, 2008b). However, this approach has not been tested via Belgian research as yet.

Similarly, Behaviour Observation Questions are not empirically tested as such, but research on the Behaviour Analysis Interview (BAI) – which is in line with the BOQ's – show that the assumptions are often not justified (e.g. Kassin and Fong, 1999; Vrij *et al.*, 2006). In Belgium, it is argued that BOQs are not used on the basis of these assumptions, but only in order to stimulate cooperation from the suspect. The question whether this is an effective strategy remains unanswered.

As regards SCAN, available research (e.g. Nahari *et al.*, 2012) shows that there are major problems with reliability and validity but Belgium is one of the countries in which training in this method continues to be organised.

There is disagreement on the use of these techniques, not only between academics and professionals but among professionals as well. Techniques such as maximisation and persuasion are being used in a minority of interviews (Ponsaers *et al.*, 2001; Tersago, in preparation). Similar techniques seem to be used in interviews with juvenile suspects (Tersago, in preparation). To conclude, in Belgian practice, interviewing suspects is more or less characterised by the use of accepted, unclear and controversial techniques.

Implications for research, policy and practice

In England and Wales, a large-scale study by Clarke and Milne (2001) showed that training does not necessarily improve the quality of all suspect interviews, but suggested that the use of certain techniques such as minimisation decreased or even disappeared. These findings were confirmed by later research (Griffiths and Milne, 2006; Walsh and Bull, 2010). Thus clarity and uniformity on which techniques to use in practice should already have been installed throughout training programmes. Nonetheless, this is only a condition and not a guarantee and police policy should be adjusted as well.

In contrast with England and Wales and the Netherlands, Belgium until now had not been confronted with controversial cases in which miscarriages of justice were detected. Such cases in other countries have become an incentive for fundamental reforms of the criminal investigation process as a whole and suspect interviewing in particular. This might be an alternative explanation for why Belgian interview practice is still characterised with accusatory as well as information-gathering interview techniques, reflecting a rather laborious shift towards a thorough search for the truth and voluntary confessions. This observation suggests a need for uniformity. Diversity in techniques is proper practice but techniques should be evidence-based and in line with an information-gathering interview style. Therefore more insights not only in daily practice but also in interview techniques which are diagnostic for accurate and voluntary statements are needed.

Acknowledgements

The authors thank the regional police academy Limburg (PLOT) for providing insight into the structure of training in Belgium and analysis of courses involving interview training. We also thank the national detective's school for providing general insights as well as in-depth views and course materials.

Notes

1. The *Dutroux* case concerns a series of abductions, rapes and murders of young girls in 1995 and 1996 for which Marc Dutroux was sentenced to lifelong imprisonment in 2004. The Belgian people criticised the lack of collaboration between the different police forces and the lack of quality of judges – who until then were appointed by politicians. Belgians held the failing police and justice system responsible for the death of the girls. This case was also the direct reason for the Belgian police reform which structured the police on two levels (federal and local) in 1998.
2. Wet 7 december 1998 tot organisatie van een geïntegreerde politiedienst, gestructureerd op twee niveaus [Law Integrated Police], *Government Gazette*, 5 January 1999.
3. http://www.polfed-fedpol.be/org/org_dgj_pilierjudiciaire_nl.php (15 May 2014).
4. The training overview is based upon information from official websites of the Belgian police and the various police academies and documentation from the national criminal investigation school and the police academy of Limburg (PLOT). In addition, interviews with the educational coordinators of both police academies were held in order to sketch the current educational landscape on (suspect) interviewing.
5. Supervision in this chapter refers to a type of coaching in which coaches can be both internal (police) and external (academic) experts.
6. Scientific Content Analysis (SCAN) is a lie detection tool developed by Sapir Avinoam (http://www.isiscan.com).
7. Wet 12 maart 1998 tot verbetering van de strafrechtsbedeling in het stadium van het opsporingsonderzoek en het gerechtelijk onderzoek [Law on the Improvement of Criminal Investigation], *Government Gazette*, 2 April 1998.
8. Wet 2 augustus 2002 over het afnemen van verklaringen met behulp van audiovisuele media [Law on Audiovisual Recorded Interviewing], *Government Gazette*, 12 September 2012.
9. This audio-visual suspect interview does not refer to a traditional suspect interview which is recorded, but to the special interview in which interviewers do not write a statement but the whole interview is audio-visually recorded and transcribed afterwards. Additionally, expert colleagues can be present in the monitoring room to –if necessary and convenient – advise the interviewer(s).
10. Wet 13 augustus 2011 tot wijziging van het Wetboek van Strafvordering en van de wet van 20 juli 1990 betreffende de voorlopige hechtenis, om aan elkeen die wordt verhoord en aan elkeen wiens vrijheid wordt benomen rechten te verlenen, waaronder het recht om een advocaat te raadplegen en door hem te worden bijgestaan [Law to Provide Rights to Arrested Suspects Among Others the Right to Legal Assistance – Salduz Law]), *Government Gazette*, 5 September 2011.
11. The right to legal assistance is also applied to interviews within the 24 hours following arrest, and subsequent interviews in case of an extension of the arrest to 48 hours.
12. These guidelines are taken down in the circular letter COL 8/2011 which preceded the *Salduz* law.
13. PEACE stands for: Planning and preparation, Explain and engage, Account, Closure and Evaluation.
14. Following these studies many Masters' theses looked into different aspects of interview practice but given the often limited data collection these small-scale studies are not included.
15. One study compares Belgian practice with that of the United States and is being conducted at the Free University Brussels (VUB). The other is an international study funded by the European Union (JUST/2011/JPEN/AG/2909), conducted in five countries and coordinated by Maastricht University.

References

Allaerts, D. (2012) 'De leidraad voor de politie bij de toepassing van de Salduzwet' ['The guidance for police when applying the Salduz law'], in F. Goossens, H. Berkmoes, A. Duchatelet and F. Hutsebaut (eds), *De Salduzregeling. Theorie en praktijk, vandaag en morgen*. Brussel: Politeia, pp. 95–106.

Balogh, K. and Hertog, E. (2012) 'AVIDICUS comparative studies – part II: traditional, videoconference and remote interpreting in police interviews', in S. Braun and J. Taylor (eds), *Videoconference and Remote Interpreting in Criminal Proceedings*. Guildford: University of Surrey, pp. 119–36.

Blackstock, J., Cape, E., Hodgson, J., Ogorodova, A., Spronken, T. and Vanderhallen, M. (2014) *Inside Police Custody. Training Framework on the Provision of Suspect's Rights*. Antwerp: Intersentia.

Bockstaele, M. (2002) 'Het videoverhoor van volwassenen' ['Video-recorded interviewing of adults'], in P. Ponsaers (ed.), *Vernieuwing in de recherche*. Antwerp: Maklu, pp. 47–84.

Bockstaele, M. (2008a) *Handboek verhoren 1* [*Handbook of Police Interviewing 1*]. Antwerp: Maklu.

Bockstaele, M. (2008b) *Handboek verhoren 2* [*Handbook on Police Interviewing 2*]. Antwerp: Maklu.

Clarke, C. and Milne, R. (2001) *National Evaluation of the PEACE Investigative Interviewing Course*, Report no. PRAS/149. London: Home Office.

Clarke, C., Milne, R. and Bull, R. (2011) 'Interviewing suspects of crime: the impact of PEACE training, supervision and the presence of a legal advisor', *Journal of Investigative Psychology Offender Profiling*, 8: 149–62.

Crawshaw, R., Devlin, B. and Williamson, T. (1998) *Human Rights and Policing: Standards for Good Behaviour and a Strategy for Change*. Den Haag: Kluwer International.

De Fruyt, F., Bockstaele, M., Taris, R. and Van Hiel, A. (2006) 'Police interview competencies: assessment and associated traits', *European Journal of Personality*, 20: 567–84.

Dommicent J., Vanderhallen, M., de Wiest, H., Bastiaens, M., van de Plas, M. and Vervaeke, G. (2008) 'Interviewing children in Belgium: an evaluation of practices', *Police Journal*, 81 (3): 248–61.

Enhus, E. and Ponsaers, P. (2005) 'Onmacht tot cultuurverandering. Politiehervorming in België' ['Incapacity to change culture. Police reform in Belgium'], *Tijdschrift voor Criminologie*, 47 (4): 345–54.

Griffiths, A. and Milne, R. (2006) 'Will it all end in tiers?', in T. Williamson (ed.), *Investigative Interviewing: Research Rights and Regulation*. Cullompton: Willan, pp. 167–89.

Holmberg, U. (2004) *Police Interviews with Victims and Suspects of Violent Sexual Crimes: Interviewee's Experiences and Outcomes*. Stockholm: Stockholm University, Department of Psychology.

Kassin, S. M. and Fong, C. T. (1999) 'I'm innocent! Effects of training on judgments of truth and deception in the interrogation room', *Law and Human Behavior*, 23: 499–516.

Kassin, S. M. and Kiechel, K. L. (1996) 'The social psychology of false confessions. Compliance, internalization and confabulation', *American Psychological Society*, 7 (3): 125–8.

Lamb, M. E., Sternberg, K. J., Orbach, Y., Hershkowitz, I., Horowitz, D. and Esplin, P. W. (2000) 'Is ongoing feedback necessary to maintain the quality of investigative interviews with allegedly abused children?', *Applied Developmental Science*, 6 (3): 114–25.

Nahari, G., Vrij, A. and Fisher, R. (2012) 'Does the truth come out in the writing? SCAN as a lie detection tool', *Law and Human Behavior*, 36: 68–76.

Penne, H., Raes, A., Deveux, E., Deladriere, A., De Keulenaer, S., Franssens, M. and Decramer, K. (2013) *Evaluatie Salduz wet. Eindrapport* [*Evaluation Salduz Law: Final Report*]. Brussel: Dienst voor het Strafrechtelijk beleid.

Ponsaers, P., Mulkers, J. and Stoop, R. (2001) *De ondervraging: analyse van een politietechniek* [*Questioning: Analysis of a Police Technique*]. Antwerp: Maklu.

Powell, M. B. and Steinberg, R. (2012) 'Overcoming barriers to best practice interviewing', *II-RP*, 4 (1): 5–9.

Powell, M. B., Fisher, R. P. and Wright, R. (2005) 'Investigative interviewing', in N. Brewer and K. Williams (eds), *Psychology and Law: An Empirical Perspective*. New York: Guilford Press, pp. 11–42.

Price, H. L. and Roberts, K. P. (2011) 'The effects of an intensive training and feedback program on police and social workers' investigative interviews of children', *Canadian Journal of Behavioral Science*, 43 (3): 235–44.

Russano, M. B., Meissner, C. A., Narchet, F. M. and Kassin, S. M. (2005) 'Investigating true and false confessions within a novel experimental paradigm', *American Psychological Society*, 16 (6): 481–6.

Schellingen, R. and Scholten, N. (2014) *Het verdachtenverhoor: meer dan het stellen van vragen* [*The Suspect Interview: More Than Asking Questions*]. Mechelen: Kluwer.

Smets, L. (2012) *Police Investigative Interviewing. A New Training Approach*, Reeks Politiestudies no. 3. Antwerp: Maklu.

Tersago, P. (in preparation) 'De bewijswaarde van verdachtenverklaringen' ['Evidential Value of Suspect Statements']. Antwerp: Antwerp University.

Van De Plas, M. (2000) *Handboek politieverhoor. Basistechnieken* [*Handbook on Police Interview: Basic Techniques*]. Brussel: Politeia.

Van De Plas, M. (2007) *Handboek politieverhoor. Basistechnieken* [*Handbook on Police Interview: Basic Techniques*]. Brussel: Politeia.

Vanderhallen, M. (2007) 'De werkalliantie in het politieverhoor' ['The working alliance in police interviews']. Unpublished PhD dissertation. Leuven: Catholic University of Leuven.

Vanderhallen, M. and Vervaeke, G. (2014) 'De ontwikkeling van een werkrelatie met een verdachte' ['Development of rapport with suspects'], in R. Schellingen and N. Scholten (eds), *Het verdachtenverhoor: meer dan het stellen van vragen* [*The Suspect Interview: More Than Asking Questions*]. Mechelen: Kluwer, pp. 111–34.

Vanderhallen, M., Vervaeke, G. and Holmberg, U. (2011) 'Witness and suspect perceptions of working alliance and interviewing style', *Journal of Investigative Psychology and Offender Profiling*, 8 (2): 110–30.

Vanderhallen, M., Vervaeke, G., Mulleners, F. and Michaux, E. (2013) 'Experiences from training and supervision in real (video-recorded) suspect interviews in Belgium: pitfalls and opportunities', *II-RP Journal*, 5 (1): 36–45.

Vanderhallen, M., de Jong, A., Nelen, H. and Spronken, T. (2014) *Toga's in de verhoorkamer. De invloed van rechtsbijstand op het politieverhoor* [*The Toga in the Interview Room. The Influence of Legal Assistance on Police Interviewing*]. The Hague: Boom Lemma Uitgevers.

Verstraeten, R. (2005) *Handboek strafvordering* [*Handbook of Criminal Procedure*]. Antwerp: Maklu.

Volckaert, M. (2005) 'Verhoor in de basisopleiding voor inspecteur van politie' ['Interview in the Basic Training for Inspectors']. Unpublished dissertation. Leuven: Catholic University of Leuven.

Vrij, A., Mann, S. and Fisher, R. (2006) 'An empirical test of the behavior analysis interview', *Law and Human Behavior*, 30: 329–45.

Walsh, D. and Bull, R. (2010) 'What really is effective in interviews with suspects? A study comparing interview skills against interviewing outcomes', *Legal and Criminological Psychology*, 15: 305–21.

Walsh, D., and Bull, R. (2012) 'Examining rapport in investigative interviews with suspects: does its building and maintenance work?', *Journal of Police and Criminal Psychology*, 27: 73–84.

Wet 7 December 1998 tot organisatie van een geïntegreerde politiedienst, gestructureerd op twee niveaus [Law Integrated Police], *Government Gazette*, 5 January 1999.

Wet 12 maart 1998 tot verbetering van de strafrechtsbedeling in het stadium van het opsporingsonderzoek en het gerechtelijk onderzoek [Law Improvement of Criminal Investigation], *Government Gazette*, 2 April 1998.

Wet 2 augustus 2002 over het afnemen van verklaringen met behulp van audiovisuele media [Law Audio-Visual Recorded Interviewing], *Government Gazette*, 12 September 2012.

Wet 13 augustus 2011 tot wijziging van het Wetboek van Strafvordering en van de wet van 20 juli 1990 betreffende de voorlopige hechtenis, om aan elkeen die wordt verhoord en aan elkeen wiens vrijheid wordt benomen rechten te verlenen, waaronder het recht om een advocaat te raadplegen en door hem te worden bijgestaan [Law to Provide Rights to Arrested Suspects Among Others the Right to Legal Assistance – Salduz Law], *Government Gazette*, 5 September 2011.

8 Interviewing suspects in England and Wales

Colin Clarke and Rebecca Milne

Introduction

Prior to the introduction of the PEACE model of interviewing victims, witnesses and suspects in 1993, police officers in England and Wales (in Britain) received little or no instruction in this aspect of their work. Interview techniques were usually passed from one officer to another, sometimes by officers who received specialist training in the military, which resulted in a range of techniques that seemed to produce confessions (McKenzie, 1992). However, these techniques often included some form of coercion despite psychologists' beliefs that they were unproductive (Hassler, 1930; Peixoto, 1934). Indeed, in a study for the Royal Commission on Criminal Procedure that was published in 1981, Irving (1980) found police used a variety of manipulative and persuasive tactics to obtain confessions. On the other hand, Walkley (1983), at that time a serving British police officer, surveyed detectives' views on the use of force when conducting interviews and found that over half believed police officers should not use force, with 10 per cent admitting to having used force to obtain a confession. What people say they do and actually do is not always one and the same.

The police in Britain have a long history of working with academics, primarily psychologists, to develop their interviewing practice. To address the concerns noted above, ACPO and the Home Office (the government department responsible for the police), in the early 1990s, put together a team of experienced detectives to develop new interview training for the police. PEACE was born, based on a then recent literature review by psychologists (see Bull, 2014, for further information) and the newly developed principles of investigative interviewing (HO Circular No. 22, 1992), PEACE being a mnemonic (Planning and preparation, Engage and explain, Account, Closure and Evaluation) for an interviewing framework and associated training course. PEACE has been fully explained elsewhere (see Griffiths and Milne, 2006; Milne *et al.*, 2008). Following a positive trial and evaluation of the PEACE training course (McGurk *et al.*, 1993) all police officers in Britain were issued with two booklets delivering guidance on PEACE interviewing: *A Guide to Interviewing* and *The Interviewer's Rule Book* (CPTU, 1992a and 1992b).

These developments were driven by Tom Williamson who was (at that time) a senior police officer, active researcher and champion for the ethical interviewing of suspects by police (Moston *et al.*, 1992; Williamson *et al.*, 2009). Williamson was one of an early group of police officers who also conducted applied research into various aspects of police practice, particularly in relation to investigative interviewing. Subsequently a strong tradition of practitioner researchers has developed among police officers throughout Britain, many of who will be referenced in the following discussion (e.g. Clarke, Griffiths, O'Neill). The benefits of this includes a deep understanding of the practice of conducting real-life interviews together with unrivalled access to police officers and field interviews with suspects, thus enabling ecologically valid studies to be conducted in the field.

Introducing PEACE signalled two important changes in the interviewing of suspects in Britain. Firstly, the police service began the widest-ranging training programme initially to train all police officers with under five years service (later this was extended to all officers) to use the PEACE framework for interviewing suspects, victims and witnesses. Secondly, underpinning the PEACE model is an ethical approach to interviewing, which concerned replacing the term interrogation with investigative interviewing in an attempt to change the mindsets of serving officers, among others, with the ethos of interviewing changing in focus from obtaining a confession to gathering and testing evidence. However, within five years a number of studies by police officers were finding that PEACE training might not be having the positive impact reported by McGurk *et al.* (1993).

In 2001 the authors reported on a three-year study of PEACE interview training in England and Wales in Clarke and Milne (2001). The findings from this work suggested there had been little improvement in the way that those suspected of crime (suspects) were interviewed and that the supervision of such interviews was patchy despite the earlier recommendations of Stockdale (1993). Stockdale argued that, despite the resource demands, the supervision of investigative interviews is important for maintaining and improving interview quality, which will not be achieved by training 'supervisors and managers [alone] but will require both organisational and cultural change' (Stockdale, 1993: v). As a result of this work Clarke and Milne suggested that officers were being expected to learn too much on the PEACE course and advised the use of a tiered approach to training interviewers, a developmental approach to interview training across an investigative interviewer's career span. This advice has been wholeheartedly adopted by the Association of Chief Police Officers (ACPO) in Britain (ACPO, 2005) and in many other countries (e.g. Australia, New Zealand). It is now over a decade since the above report and this chapter provides an opportunity for the authors to examine the current research and practice of interviewing suspects in Britain. It will be interesting to examine the question: How far have we come? Our primary focus will be on research and practices in the twenty-first century, primarily post-2001.

Our own analysis of field interviews found that trained officers conducted significantly longer interviews than their untrained colleagues (Clarke *et al.*, 2011). But did this result in interviews of a higher standard than seen in the past (e.g. Baldwin, 1992)? The results were mixed. On the positive side we found some evidence that interviewers (1) were improving their interview planning; (2) had improved their compliance with the legal requirements when interviewing suspects; (3) were using a more logical structure across the interview; (4) interrupted less; (5) used fewer leading questions; and (6) encouraged suspects to provide their account of events. Overall, a clear change in approach to a more ethical style of interviewing was identified across the sample. However, there were indications that interview planning was lacking and, despite the improvement in compliance with legal requirements, interviewers persisted with poor explanations of the interview purpose. Interviewers failed to explore, summarise or challenge aspects of the suspect's account, while their communication remained dominated by the use of closed questions. In short, there was little evidence of either Conversation Management (Shepherd and Griffiths, 2013) or the Cognitive Interview (Fisher and Geiselman, 1992) styles of interview (an integral part of PEACE training) across the sample of interviews. Instead, interviewers were gathering information in a rigid manner, using their skills and pattern of questions 'to dominate the interview and keep the interviewee on topic' (Clarke and Milne, 2001). As a result we recommended that:

- refresher training should be used to target communication skills;
- the need to summarise a suspect's account at the end of an interview should be included in an aide-memoire card;
- supervision should be targeted at topics covered during refresher training;
- a tiered approach to interview training should be developed across England and Wales; and
- a nationally agreed policy on the supervision of interviews should be implemented.

In light of our report ACPO implemented many of our recommendations, particularly in relation to the tiered approach for developing interview skills (ACPO, 2005). However, a separate and nationally agreed policy for the supervision of investigative interviews was not adopted. Instead, the service integrated interview supervision within the Professionalising the Investigation Programme (PIP). Thus, such supervision was implicit rather than explicit. That is, it was integrated within the wider supervision of the investigative process rather than being specific supervision by those with a detailed knowledge of investigative interviewing and PEACE. Therefore we must ask what has happened since the introduction of these initiatives? Indeed, this is an important question as many countries have adopted PEACE, or a variation of it, in an effort to professionalise investigative interviewing in their own countries (e.g. Norway, Australia).

Unfortunately there remain surprisingly few studies of actual interviews with suspects in Britain. Walsh and Milne (2008) and Walsh and Bull (2010) examined field interviews with suspects conducted by fraud investigators, some of whom were PEACE trained and the remainder who were not. Using a similar methodology to our national evaluation they found limited performance improvement after training. Griffiths and Milne (2006) evaluated pre- and post-field interviews of detectives who had undertaken a three-week advanced interview course (Tier 3) for interviewing suspects, which experienced detectives reported as being 'equally (if not more) important than experience' (Soukara *et al.*, 2002: 109). Advanced training was found to improve both technical (i.e. compliance with legal requirements) and social communication aspects of interviewing (i.e. rapport building, topic development). Nevertheless, after a year Griffiths and Milne found that the more complex interviewing behaviours concerning social communication (e.g. rapport) began to degrade. Soukara *et al.* (2002) and Soukara *et al.*, (2009) reported a series of studies which examined field interviews to determine the 'tactics' used during interviews with suspects and these findings will be discussed across this chapter. Oxburgh and colleagues conducted a series of studies to examine emotional content, empathy and question use in interviews with those suspected of serious crime. Rather than examine interviews in relation to PEACE, Oxburgh *et al.* (2012) considered what constitutes quality in respect of an investigative interview and concluded 'a good quality interview should be one in which a humane (or empathic) interviewing style is used, and appropriate (or productive) questions are asked' (Oxburgh *et al.*, 2010: 262).

Oxburgh *et al.* (2006), in an examination of interviews with suspected sex offenders, found (contrary to their expectations) that interviewers, who had not themselves interviewed the victim, used more negative emotional words when interviewing the suspect than those who had first both interviewed the victim and then proceeded to interview the suspect. They conjectured that having interviewed the victim, interviewers believe they have all the knowledge or understand the need to be impartial. The UK guide for investigative interviewing (Centrex, 2004) suggests interviewers develop empathy but does not define or provide guidance on how this should be achieved. Indeed, the literature provides little clarity as to what empathy is (Oxburgh *et al.*, 2015), so the lack of empathy in interviews should not be surprising. In their survey of police officers' perceptions of empathy for those suspected of committing serious crimes, Oxburgh *et al.* (2015) found that just under half (43 per cent) of respondents would not show or found it difficult to show empathy to suspects in serious cases. Examination of interview transcripts (Oxburgh *et al.*, 2010) and actual interviews (Oxburgh *et al.*, 2014) have so far found no link between empathy and the quantity of Investigation Relevant Information or IRI (i.e. what happened, how the crime was committed, persons involved, when and where the crime took place, and any items used in the commission of the offence) (Oxburgh *et al.*, 2010: 263). However, the use of more appropriate questions resulted in significantly more IRI being obtained (Oxburgh *et al.*, 2010; Oxburgh *et al.*, 2014). Appropriate questions were more likely to be asked in empathic interviews and were also more likely to be found in interviews with those suspected of child sexual abuse (Oxburgh *et al.*, 2014). The latter point suggests that question use might be a function of offence type. On the other hand, international studies have found suspects are more likely to provide information when the interviewer demonstrates a humane and open-minded approach (Holmberg and Christianson, 2002; Read *et al.*, 2014), something that police officers may find hard to do.

Finally, Leahy-Harland *et al.* (in preparation a and b) examined the opening and closing phase of the interview (Leahy-Harland *et al.*, in preparation a), question use, suspects' responses and interruptions (Leahy-Harland *et al.*, in preparation b) in interviews with those suspected of serious crime. These studies show that research has tended to focus on advanced interviewing, i.e. interviews related to serious crime, in terms of training and practice. Together there has also been a move towards examining interviewing practices in terms of the IRI obtained and different features of the interview, including empathy and tactics. The findings from these and other relevant studies will now be considered in relation to each phase of the PEACE interview.

Planning and preparation

When surveyed police officers acknowledge the importance of pre-interview preparation (Soukara *et al.*, 2002), although planning has been rated as less important or evident in other studies (O'Neill and Milne, 2014). Conversely, Soukara *et al.* (2002) found that 40 per cent of detectives believed the presence of 'good evidence' (our quotes) lessened the need for preparation – though it could be argued that the identification of 'good evidence' is in itself evidence of planning and preparation (O'Neill and Milne, 2014). However, what interviewers say they do does not always translate into practice.

In our original 2001 report we highlighted the difficulties of evaluating 'Planning and preparation' from an audio recording. Since then, Walsh and Bull (2010) have cogently argued that planning skills can be assessed when experienced assessors rate the quality and breadth of the interviewers' understanding of the suspected offence(s) and exhibit knowledge of the legal points to be proved. Walsh and Bull also suggest that good preparation is demonstrated through the consideration of any potential defence mitigation (legitimate or otherwise) and has prepared contingency responses to these, also ensuring that the evidence and exhibits are to hand (having given forethought to their order of disclosure). Good planning is also reckoned to be evident through the assessed quality of the tactics and strategies that are manifest during questioning (Walsh and Bull, 2010). Using this method Walsh and Milne (2008) found less evidence of planning and preparation than in our study with the sample mean suggesting planning and preparation was not fit for purpose. Nevertheless, for those who did spend time planning and preparing, there was some association with obtaining a comprehensive account. Walsh and Bull (2010) found that good planning and preparation skills were associated with overall interview quality and a better likelihood of obtaining a confession or comprehensive account. This research underpins the importance of this phase of the interview.

Engage and explain

The 'Engage and explain' phase is where the interviewer sets the tone for the interview and begins to use their all-important social and communication skills (Soukara *et al.*, 2002; O'Neill and Milne, 2014). During this phase interviewers must comply with various legal requirements including informing the suspect of their right of silence (the caution), right to legal advice, etc. (see Leahy-Harland *et al.*, in preparation a) as well as explaining the purpose and format of the interview. The conduct of interviews with suspects in Britain is determined by the Police and Criminal Evidence Act 1986 and associated codes of practice (Code C: Home Office, 2008; Code E: Home Office, 2010). In our 2001 evaluation we assessed 13 elements relating to legal requirements and five procedural elements of this phase, including rapport. We found that interviewers generally complied with the legal requirements (as did Leahy-Harland *et al.*, in preparation a), usually by providing the information from an aide-memoire card, but they had difficulty explaining the purpose and processes of the interview. On the other hand, Walsh and Bull (2010) question the manner in which the caution is usually presented in a single block of information, and suggest that presenting the caution in this manner does not aid comprehension. Indeed, they found that only 16 per cent of interviewers thoroughly checked a suspect's understanding of the caution, which is particularly problematic for the vulnerable suspect (Richards and Milne, in preparation).

The groundwork for building and maintaining rapport with the suspect starts during this phase of the interview and in recent years a growing international literature has highlighted our improved understanding of the constituent parts of rapport. While we originally described rapport as 'a professional relationship with the interviewee' (Clarke and Milne, 2001: 36), Tickle-Degnen and Rosenthal's (1990) theoretical model has since become a commonly accepted framework for rapport (e.g. Walsh and Bull, 2012; Abbe and Brandon, 2013, Holmberg and Madsen, 2014). This consists of mutual attention, positivity and coordination. However, Walsh and Milne (2008) continued to find PEACE training had minimal impact during the 'Engage and explain' phase. Of the seven competencies examined, trained interviewers only performed at the PEACE standard (i.e. rated 3 on the 5-point scale, which Clarke and Milne (2001) deemed the minimum acceptable standard for PEACE) when presenting the caution, which was done significantly more appropriately than untrained interviewers. Importantly, little rapport building was conducted at this time or throughout the interview. In a subsequent study Walsh and Bull (2010) found that two-thirds of the overall assessment of this phase could be accounted for by the behavioural competencies of building rapport, explaining the interview purpose, and checking the suspects' understanding of the caution, although these continued to be performed below the PEACE standard. Nevertheless, rapport building was found to significantly impact upon the overall quality of the interview and the interview outcome, showing the importance of rapport as to its effect upon the overall quality of the interview.

Walsh and Bull (2012) examined interviews with suspects conducted by fraud investigators (who were not police officers) for any association between rapport building, interview quality and interview outcome, plus the influence that maintaining rapport had on interview quality and outcome. The authors examined 25 rapport-building behaviours across the 'Engage and explain', 'Account' and 'Closure' phases of the interview, together with general interviewer behaviours.

During the 'Engage and explain' phase a significant difference was found for rapport building between those rated at or above the PEACE standard and those rated below the standard. In addition, those rated at or above the PEACE standard took significantly more time to conduct this phase than those rated below par. However, rapport building during this phase was not related to the overall interview outcome. Interviewers' rapport behaviours during the 'Account' phase was generally found to be poor with numerous missed opportunities identified, although a strong association was found between overall interview quality and those interviews where rapport building was rated at or above the PEACE standard during the 'Account' phase. Overall, 70 per cent of interviewers were identified as needing further training in rapport building, although poor rapport was improved in the account phase for 40 per cent of the interviews. Interviewers classed as satisfactory or skilled for rapport maintenance also demonstrated skilled or highly skilled general behaviours (i.e. showing equality signs, displaying calmness and empathy).

Our original evaluation found little rapport building during the 'Engage and explain' phase when interviewers generally failed to explain the interview purpose, how the interview would be conducted or ensure the suspect understood the caution. Walsh and Bull (2012) suggest the latter activities provide opportunities for developing rapport, and interviewers have a poor understanding of how such activities help develop rapport and a shared understanding between the suspect and interviewer. Instead interviewers focus on the administrative and legal aspects of interviews with suspects, thus failing to fulfil Tickle-Degnen and Rosenthall's (1990) criteria for rapport: mutual attention, positivity and coordination.

Account

It is during this phase that suspects should be provided an opportunity to give their account of events, which the interviewer can then clarify and/or challenge depending upon other evidence in their possession. Linguistic research demonstrates how the 'Account' phase is used to negotiate a shared account of 'the facts' (Johnson, 2008, original quotes) in a format that is acceptable to the judiciary (Johnson, 2006).

PEACE provides two interview models for conducting this phase of the interview: Conversation Management (CM) and the Cognitive Interview (CI), the latter usually being used for cooperative suspects. Nevertheless, CM is the principle model used when interviewing suspects in Britain and during the past decade a more coherent description of the model has emerged (Milne and Bull, 1999; Shepherd and Griffiths, 2013). Nevertheless, only one empirical study has been conducted on the efficacy of CM (Clifford and George, 1996), which compared the effects of training police investigators to use the CI, CM or CI + CM (the PEACE approach) with a control group when interviewing witnesses. Clifford and George found that only interviewers in the CI group gained significantly more information from the real-life witnesses in comparison with the control group. Interestingly the CI + CM group did not fare as well as the CI group on its own.

Our evaluation (Clarke and Milne, 2001) found good use of CM in 23 per cent of the sample although there was no evidence of CM in 30 per cent of interviews. Evidence of the CI was identified in only six interviews mainly concerning assaults. A good effort was made to encourage suspects to provide an account in 42 per cent of cases, although there was little exploration of that account and explorations that did occur generally lacked structure or logical sequence. Challenges to the suspects' account were identified in 66 per cent of interviews of which 19 per cent were deemed to be conducted in a professional manner and with evidence while communication skills, e.g. active listening, dealing with difficulty were deemed to be conducted at or above the PEACE standard. Finally, using a five-point ascending assessment scale (where a score of 5 related highly skilled performance) questioning skills overall were rated as being just below the PEACE standard (i.e. a score of 3; mean = 2.8). From a count of question types Clarke and Milne found a 'good' use of open questions (mean = 13.1) and few leading questions (mean = 3.8), although closed questions (mean = 15.4) remained the primary question type. (For an explanation of these question types, see Oxburgh *et al.* (2010).)

An integral part of interviews with suspects is the probing of points needed to prove the offence(s) under investigation, finding a motive for committing the offence(s) and asking whether the suspect has committed the offence. We found that 76 per cent of interviewers asked whether the suspect had committed the offence, whereas the points to prove were rated at just below PEACE standard and only 30 per cent of interviews were probed in a comprehensive manner. Exploring the suspect's motive was rated at below PEACE standard overall with only 25 per cent of motives being explored in a comprehensive manner. Thus the majority of interviews were below standard, i.e. not fit for purpose.

Subsequently Walsh and Milne (2008) have found that trained interviewers were significantly more likely than their untrained colleagues to encourage the provision of a suspect's version of events, develop topics for further exploration, explore the information, use pauses and silences, and deal with difficulty more appropriately. However, in line with our evaluation, there was little evidence found in this sample either of probing the points to prove an offence, finding the suspect's motive or summarising. Moreover, Griffiths *et al.* (2006) found that even advanced (Tier 3) interviewers find it difficult to maintain over a period of time complex skills such as developing topics.

Questioning is a key skill for any interviewer to master. Research has constantly shown that open-ended questions are superior for gaining maximum quantity and quality of information from all types of interviewee with victims and suspects (Powell and Guadagno, 2008; Oxburgh *et al.*, 2010) and reducing the risk of underestimating suspects' language limitations (Read *et al.*, 2009). As such, evaluating the use of different types of question across an investigative interview is a consistent feature of experimental and applied research. However, researchers often use different descriptions for the same question type, a situation recently addressed from a psychological and linguistic perspective by Oxburgh *et al.* (2010). They highlighted the variety of sources from which question definitions are derived; researchers, police trainers, and government departments; each discipline concentrating on different functions of the question type. The psychological perspective tends to focus on information retrieval, ethics and deception whereas linguists consider interviews as speech events for which the context, actors, norms, outcomes, etc. must be taken into account (see Newbury and Johnson, 2006; Johnson, 2008).

Research has, nevertheless, consistently shown that trained interviewers use more open and appropriate closed questions (appropriate referring to those questions asking for confirmation of information already provided) and fewer leading questions or statements than before the introduction of PEACE (or training); however, inappropriate closed questions (i.e. where open question should have been asked) continue to dominate the interviews (Walsh and Milne, 2008). Griffiths and Milne (2006) propose that question use should be considered in relation to context rather than as a simple count of questions or percentage of question type in relation to utterances. To this end Griffiths (2008) developed the Griffiths Question Map (GQM) to facilitate the mapping and coding of eight types of questions in two broad categories: (1) productive; and (2) non-productive questions. Griffiths and Milne (2006) demonstrated how the GQM enables the visualisation of question use as a chronology across the interview, as recurring patterns and interview phases, thus facilitating a context-driven analysis of question use. Newbury and Johnson (2006) consider the function of police questions from a linguistic perspective, using two categories at the macro level: confirmation-seeking and information-seeking. They argue that information-seeking questions can be further classified based on the amount of information requested, whereas confirmatory questions can be differentiated according to the degree in which they coerce the suspect to agree. Regardless of the classification of questions, research needs to start examining how to enable practitioners to use open questions. Yii *et al.* (2014) have started this process with two innovative studies that set out to develop interviewers' knowledge of open questions using a training design that combines the presentation of knowledge with practical coding and question-generation exercises and a mock interview. They found the ability to identify open questions was a good indicator of open question use in the mock interview. This training approach is consistent with the literature on acquiring expert performance and the role of deliberate practice in specific aspects of a topic or task (Ericsson *et al.*, 1993).

The final area of assessment that Clarke and Milne (2001) conducted for this phase of the interview concerned interviewers' characteristics; these were assessed as being above the PEACE standard for clarity and confidence, at the PEACE level for open-mindedness, but having little evidence of flexibility. Walsh and Milne (2008) found there were no differences in interviewers' characteristics dependent on training, though both trained and untrained interviewers met the PEACE standard across the interviews. There was also a continuing assumption of guilt among interviewers. Interestingly, Walsh and Bull (2010) identified communication skills and flexibility as the primary predictors of quality (i.e. at or above PEACE standard) during this phase. These findings are consistent with the importance that police officers attribute to social/communication skills in determining the outcome of interviews (Soukara *et al.*, 2002). Overall, Walsh and Bull (2010) found that most interviewers assessed as having limited skills in the 'Account' phase were rated as poorer interviewers generally, whereas more skilled performance of the competencies in this phase were associated with comprehensive accounts or confessions. Walsh and Bull (2010: 317) conjectured that skilled performance during the 'Account' phase 'may be highly influential in deciding the interview's outcome'. The issue of interviewers' individual differences is taken up again later.

Tactics

The coherent challenging of a suspect's account of events requires careful planning or a strategy, i.e. a tactic. The use of tactics has received little attention since the PEACE model was introduced in Britain, in part because of a perceived connection with coercive interviewer behaviours but also because of the association with gaining a confession rather than obtaining a suspect's account. However, a series of studies (Soukara *et al.*, 2002; Soukara *et al.*, 2009; Bull and Soukara, 2010) has examined the use of tactics in PEACE interviews. A survey of detectives identified disclosure of evidence as their primary tactic (Soukara *et al.*, 2002), which was subsequently supported with an analysis of field interviews (Soukara *et al.*, 2009). However, an international survey of police interviewers found a lack of understanding concerning the most appropriate time to disclose evidence, particularly in the area of forensic evidence (Smith and Bull, 2013). Indeed, Smith and Bull identify a need for training in forensic awareness and appropriate strategies of disclosing evidence dependent upon the situation (Walsh, Milne and Bull, in press).

The use of other tactics depends upon the type and seriousness of the offence and/or the suspect's character and behaviour (Soukara *et al.*, 2002). Their evaluation of field interviews also identified (1) disclosure of evidence, (2) open questions, (3) leading questions and (iv) repetitive questioning as tactics used to some extent across the sample (Soukara *et al.*, 2009: 500). Disclosing evidence and providing a different perspective can be used to encourage the suspect to re-contextualise an event and negotiate a shared understanding of the suspect's action (Johnson, 2008). Soukara *et al.* (2009) found no evidence of unethical tactics – minimisation, intimidation or situational futility – which is to be expected after the implementation of the Police and Criminal Evidence Act 1984, judicial guidance and training. They also investigated the association between tactic use and confessions, finding that interviewers used fewer open questions and disclosed less evidence in interviews where the suspect confessed than in interviews where they did not. Additionally, interviewers were found to put more emphasis on contradicting a suspect's account and challenging the account when the suspect was not moving their account from denial to confession. Overall, the primary differences between confession and non-confession interviews were the increased use of emphasising contradictions, repetitive questioning and challenging a suspect's account in non-confession interviews. This has an element of common sense in that interviewers are more likely to rigorously test denials to ensure, as much as possible, they are true ones when a suspect does not provide or provides a different account of events. Soukara *et al.* (2002) go on to emphasise that these findings are consistent with the current ethos of ethical interviewing in Britain, especially as they found little evidence of unethical tactics such as intimidation, maximisation/minimisation and situational futility.

The use of tactics in interviews with suspects is not limited to the interviewer – suspects can and do use tactics. There is little research in this area. However, Newbury and Johnson (2007) provide a fascinating linguistic analysis of police interviews with the serial murderer Harold Shipman. The authors demonstrate how this intelligent and articulate man resists the interviewer using the tactics of 'contest, correction, avoidance and refusal' (p. 214) and note that Shipman tries to present himself as cooperative (a key feature of rapport) by avoiding outright resistance or uncooperative behaviour. For example, instead of answering a confirmatory question by saying 'yes' he responded 'if you say'. On the other hand, when Shipman was challenged using expert evidence, the pathologist's findings, he generalised medical opinion using nouns and pronouns, and avoided using the pathologist's name, or the words 'I' and 'findings'. Similarly, Johnson (2008) demonstrated how Shipman minimised his actions by suggesting he was protecting his brother. These and tactics like them should be integrated into the training of forensic interviewers and further research.

Closure

This phase provides an opportunity for interviewers to summarise their understanding of the interview, provide an opportunity for the suspect to add, alter or correct their account, and give information about what will happen next. Summarising the interview provides an opportunity for suspects to identify any misunderstandings the interviewer may have, hence the reason for providing an opportunity to add, alter or correct their account. Indeed, this can lead to the resumption or return to the 'Account' phase. However, legal advisors in Britain can and do object to this practice, because of perceived issues with the interviewer's memory and resultant accuracy of the summary. We found this phase to be poorly conducted and below the PEACE standard. Subsequent studies have continued to find that interviewers conduct this phase of the interview inadequately (Walsh and Milne, 2008; Walsh and Bull, 2012; Leahy-Harland *et al.*, in preparation a). That is, these studies find that interview closure is below the PEACE standard irrespective of training, despite many of these tasks being provided via an aide-memoire card (Walsh and Milne, 2008). Although, Walsh and Bull (2010) identified differences, dependent on training, across the assessed behaviours for the 'Closure' phase, they suggest that these findings should be viewed with caution. It seems that 'Closure' is always missed or rushed and has not benefited from the focused research afforded other areas of the interview process. Concerns strengthened by the finding that 'the average duration of this [Closure] phase was under two minutes, with over eighty per cent lasting less than a minute' (Walsh and Bull, 2012: 80).

Evaluation

'Evaluation' is the phase of a PEACE interview that has received little or no examination, and to our knowledge there is no empirical research for this phase of PEACE interviews. Evaluation was integrated into PEACE to emphasise the importance for interviewers to be reflective practitioners (Schön, 1984) by reflecting on their performance during the interview and identifying aspects of the interview that went well and those aspects they might have done differently, together with an evaluation of the probative value of the information obtained/not obtained. These topics are touched upon within PEACE training but are not fully explored. This could be problematic in relation to the probative value of the information obtained/not obtained as recent work has highlighted weaknesses in interviewers' understanding of the probative value and use of forensic evidence (Smith and Bull, 2013). Indeed, in our assessment of a Behaviourally Anchored Rating Scale (BARS) (Clarke, 2005) we found some assessors, as well as interviewers, had a poor understanding of the caution and legal points required to prove an offence (see also Powell *et al.*, 2005).

The final element of this phase concerns the evaluation of interviews by supervisors to aid staff development and as a quality control measure. There is considerable literature on the importance of workplace supervision for the transference of learning and this has been acknowledged since the introduction of PEACE (Stockdale, 1993; Clarke and Milne, 2001; Powell *et al.*, 2010). Indeed, as previously mentioned, the importance of supervising interviews was the topic of one of our recommendations. Walsh and Milne (2008) made a similar recommendation with regard to fraud investigators. While our recommendation was acted upon by integrating the supervision of interviews within the PIP programme, anecdotal evidence suggests that this has not worked, in part because training in the supervision of interviews is not widely offered to police supervisors in Britain, a situation compounded by the recent economic climate and resultant cuts to public spending, with a consequent reduction in the training budgets of most police organisations across Britain. While there is international research into the positive impact of expert feedback/supervision on investigative interviews (Orbach *et al.*, 2000; Powell *et al.*, 2005; Powell *et al.*, 2010; Price and Roberts, 2011) and in non- forensic settings such as healthcare (Uitterhoeve *et al.*, 2010), this type of support is expensive. Indeed, in a recent survey of police officers who interview children, less than half indicated they received any feedback, and most feedback that was provided related to the case rather than interview quality (La Rooy *et al.*, 2011).

Applied research into the effect of workplace supervision for investigative interviews is sparse in Britain. Our original evaluation (Clarke and Milne, 2001) resulted in mixed findings. The introduction of a supervision policy (whether fully implemented or not) appeared to offer some improvements in practice. On the other hand, our pilot evaluation of a BARS found limited consistency when supervisors assessed the same interviews using a scale providing clear behavioural exemplars. Heaven *et al.* (2006) report a study in healthcare which found clinical supervision had a limited impact on the transfer of communication skills to the workplace, although they suggest this might be due to the study's short, four-week time frame and suggest a longer (18-month) period might be more acceptable. These findings clearly identify the need for further research into the best methods for scaffolding the transference of good interview practice into the workplace (see above, Yii *et al.*, 2014). In view of the need for cost-effective solutions such research must encompass the use of new technologies for assessing forensic interviews. Such technologies are already being developed for children (Yii *et al.*, 2014), people with communication difficulties (Tanaka *et al.*, 2013) and the analysis of interviews with suspects to aid the development of interview training (Akker *et al.*, 2013).

Interviewer characteristics

Received wisdom and surveys of police detectives (Soukara *et al.*, 2002) suggest that an interviewer's characteristics have an impact on the outcome of all forensic interviews. We included a coarse measure of interviewer characteristics in our original study and, as indicated previously, found the samples were generally rated as being confident and open-minded in contrast to Baldwin's original (1992) findings of feebleness and ineptitude.

In a recent overview of the literature on what is known about the characteristics that contribute to being a good interviewer Bull (2013) concluded that there is good international consensus on the necessary skills and abilities. However, research attempting to measure these differences has inconsistent findings. In an examination of police investigators from Britain (O'Neill, 2012; O'Neill and Milne, 2014), no differences were found between high and low performers and mean scores on the five-factor model of personality using the NEO PI-R, intellectual capacity using Raven's Standard Progressive Matrices or empathy assessed with the Interpersonal Reactivity Index. On the other hand, in the USA, Ono *et al.* (2011) report a study involving the performance of federal law enforcement officers during training was found to be related to conscientiousness: further discussion of the latter findings is beyond the scope of this chapter. Nevertheless we believe the characteristics of good interviewers will become an increasingly important factor for the future development of investigative interviewers. Further research needs to start examining the question: can everyone interview?

Conclusion

Overall, Walsh and Milne (2008) conclude that despite the poor transference of PEACE training, a noticeably ethical approach to interviewing has been visible across the sample, though 'only in simpler less resistant interviews was improved interviewing particularly evident' (p. 54). Notably, Walsh and Bull (2010) found that interviewers who attained the PEACE standard were significantly more likely to obtain a full comprehensive account or confession. Nevertheless, Griffiths (2008) found that even advanced interviewers' skills showed some decline one year after receiving their training, particularly in the complex skills, such as question use and development of topics; refresher training is key. On a positive note, research into police interviewing in Britain has enhanced our understanding of rapport building, the different challenges of interviewing those suspected of specific types of crime and the fickle influences of individual differences on interviewers' performance. Walsh and Milne (2008) posit several possible explanations for poor skills transference, such as the notion that a five-day PEACE course contains too much content (Cherryman, 2000) and interviewers return to their original interviewing habits/style on return to their workplace, possibly due to the lack of interviewing supervision within the organisation. Griffiths and Milne (2006) argue for continued training and supervision. Another explanation is that the design of PEACE training does not sufficiently incorporate the principles for training complex cognitive tasks (Paas and van Gog, 2009). Yii *et al.* (2014) have begun to demonstrate this with their focused practice studies concerning the development of skills and knowledge relating to open questions. A model of learning consistent with the idea of deliberate practice from the development of expertise literature is required (Ericsson *et al.*, 1993; Ward *et al.*, 2007).

Nevertheless, despite the improvement in knowledge and practice over the past ten years, we need to continue to inform interviewers' ability to gather IRI: 'There is no room to relax and we must always "stay ahead of the game"' (Oxburgh and Dando, 2011: 141).

References

Abbe, A. and Brandon, S. E. (2013) 'The role of rapport in investigative interviewing: a review', *Journal of Investigative Psychology and Offender Profiling*, 10 (3): 237–49.

Akker, R., Bruijnes, M., Peters, R. and Krikke, T. (2013) 'Interpersonal stance in police interviews: content analysis', *Computational Linguistics in the Netherlands*, 3: 193–216.

Association of Chief Police Officers, Central Police Training and Development Authority (Centrex) (2005) *Practice Advice on Core Investigative Doctrine*. Camborne: National Centre for Policing Excellence.

Baldwin, J. (1992) *Video Taping Police Interviews with Suspects – An Evaluation*, Police Research Series Paper 1. London: Home Office.

Bordin, E. S. (1994) 'Theory and research on the therapeutic working alliance: new directions', in A.O. Horvath and L. S. Greenberg (eds), *The Working Alliance: Theory, Research and Practice*. Chichester: John Wiley & Sons, pp. 13–37.

Bull, R. (2013) 'What is "believed" or actually "known" about characteristics that may contribute to being a good/effective interviewer?', *Investigative Interviewing Research and Practice*, 5 (2): 128–43.

Bull, R. (2014) 'When in interviews to disclose information to suspects and to challenge them?', in R. Bull (ed.), *Investigative Interviewing*. New York: Springer, pp. 167–82.

Bull, R. and Soukara, S. (2010) 'Four studies of what really happens in police interviews', in G. D. Lassiter and C. A. Meisner (eds), *Police Interrogations and False Confessions: Current Research, Practice, and Policy Recommendations*. Washington, DC: American Psychological Association, pp. 81–95.

Central Police Training and Development Authority (Centrex) (2004) *Practical Guide to Investigative Interviewing*. London: Central Police Training and Development Authority.

Cherryman, J. (2000) *Police Investigative Interviewing: Skills Analysis and Concordance of Evaluations*. Doctoral thesis, University of Portsmouth, UK.

Clarke, C. (2005) *A National Evaluation of PEACE Investigative Interviewing*. Doctoral thesis, University of Portsmouth, UK.

Clarke, C. and Milne, R. (2001) *National Evaluation of PEACE Investigative Interviewing Course*, Report No. PRAS/149. London: Home Office.

Clarke, C., Milne, R. and Bull, R. (2011) 'Interviewing suspects of crime: the impact of PEACE training, supervision and the presence of a legal advisor', *Journal of Investigative Psychology and Offender Profiling*, 8: 149–62.

Clifford, B. and George, R. (1996) 'A field evaluation of training in three methods of witness victim investigative interviewing', *Psychology Crime and Law*, 2 (3): 231–48.

CPTU (1992a) *A Guide to Interviewing*. Harrogate: Central Planning and Training Unit.

CPTU (1992b) *Interviewer's Rule Book*. Harrogate: Central Planning and Training Unit.

Ericsson, K., Krampe, R. and Tesch-Romer, C. (1993) 'The role of deliberate practice in the acquisition of expert performance', *Psychological Review*, 100 (3): 363–406.

Fisher, R. P. and Geiselman, R. E. (1992) *Memory-Enhancing Techniques for Investigative Interviewing: The Cognitive Interview*. Springfield, IL: Charles C. Thomas.

Griffiths, A. and Milne, R. (2006) 'Will it all end in tiers? Police interviews with suspects in Britain', in T. Williamson (ed.), *Investigative Interviewing: Rights, Research, Regulation*. Cullompton: Willan, pp. 167–89.

Griffiths, A. and Milne, R. (2008) 'The Griffiths Question Map (GQM): A Training Manual'. Unpublished.

Hassler, A. (1930) *Föreläsningar över den Svenska kriminalprocessen*. Stockholm: A. B. Nordiska Bokhandeln i Distribution; cited in U. Holmberg (2004) *Police Interviews with Victims and Suspects of Violent and Sexual Crimes: Interviewee's Experiences and Interview Outcomes*. Doctoral thesis, University of Stockholm, Sweden.

Heaven, C., Clegg, J. and Maguire, P. (2006) 'Transfer of communication skills training from workshop to workplace: the impact of clinical supervision', *Patient Education and Counseling*, 60 (3): 313–25.

Holmberg, U. and Christianson, S. (2002) 'Murderers' and sexual offenders' experience of police interviews and their inclination to admit or deny crimes', *Behavioral Sciences and the Law*, 20: 31–45.

Holmberg, U. and Madsen, K. (2014) 'Rapport operationalized as a humanitarian interview in investigative interview settings', *Psychiatry Psychology and Law*, 21: 591–610.

Home Office (1992) *Principles of Investigative Interviewing*, Circular No. 22. London: Home Office.

Home Office (2008). *PACE Code C: Code of Practice for the Detention, Treatment and Questioning of Persons by Police Officers*. London: Home Office.

Home Office (2010) *PACE Code E: Code of Practice on Audio Recording Interviews with Suspects*. London: Home Office.

Horvath, C. W. (1995) 'Biological origins of communicator style', *Communication Quarterly*, 43 (4): 394–407.

Irving, B. (1980) *Police Interrogation. A Case Study of Current Practice. Study Number 2. Royal Commission on Criminal Procedure*. London: HMSO.

Johnson, A. (2006) 'Police questioning', *Encyclopedia of Language and Linguistics*, 2: 661–72.

Johnson, A. (2008) '"From where we're sat ": negotiating narrative transformation through interaction in police interviews with suspects', *Text and Talk – An Interdisciplinary Journal of Language and Discourse Communication Studies*, 28: 327–49.

La Rooy, D., Lamb, M. E. and Memon, A. (2011) 'Forensic interviews with children in Scotland: a survey of interview practices among police', *Journal of Police and Criminal Psychology*, 26: 26–34.

Leahy-Harland, S., Bull, R. and Milne, R. (in preparation a) 'Getting the basics right: examining the use of the special warning and the opening and closing stages of real-life suspect interviews'.

Leahy-Harland, S., Bull, R. and Milne, R. (in preparation b) 'Police questioning in real-life serious crime suspect interviews'.

McGurk, B. J., Carr, M. J., and McGurk, D. (1993) *Investigative Interviewing Courses for Police Officers: An Evaluation*, Police Research Series Paper 4. London: Police Research Group, Home Office.

McKenzie, I. (1992) *Torture, Tactics and Technology: The Past, Present and Future of Police–Suspect Interactions*. Paper presented at the Conference on the Police Questioning of Suspects. Westminster, London, 11 December.

Milne, R. and Bull, R. (1999) *Investigative Interviewing: Psychology and Practice*. Chichester: John Wiley & Sons.

Milne, B., Shaw, G. and Bull, R. (2008) 'Investigative interviewing: the role of research', in D. Carson, R. Milne, F. Pakes, K. Shalev and A. Shawyer (eds), *Applying Psychology to Criminal Justice*. New York: John Wiley & Sons, pp. 65–80.

Moston, S., Stephenson, G. M. and Williamson, T. M. (1992) 'The effects of case characteristics on suspect behaviour during police questioning', *British Journal of Criminology*, 32 (1): 23–40.

Newbury, P. and Johnson, A. (2006) 'Suspects' resistance to constraining and coercive questioning strategies in the police interview', *International Journal of Speech, Language and the Law*, 13: 213–40.

O'Neill, M. (2012) *What Makes a Successful Volume Crime Investigator?* Doctoral dissertation, University of Portsmouth, UK.

O'Neill, M. and Milne, R. (2014) 'Success within criminal investigations: is communication still a key component?', in R. Bull (ed.), *Investigative Interviewing*. New York: Springer, pp. 123–46.

Ono, M., Sachau, D., Deal, W., Englert, D. and Taylor, M. (2011) 'Cognitive ability, emotional intelligence, and the "Big Five" personality dimensions as predictors of criminal investigator performance', *Criminal Justice and Behavior*, 38: 471–91; cited in R. Bull (2013) 'What is "believed" or actually "known" about characteristics that may contribute to being a good/effective interviewer?', *Investigative Interviewing Research and Practice*, 5 (2): 128–43.

Orbach, Y., Hershkowitz, I., Lamb, M. E., Sternberg, K. J., Esplin, P. W. and Horowitz, D. (2000) 'Assessing the value of structured protocols for forensic interviews of alleged child abuse victims', *Child Abuse and Neglect*, 24 (6): 733–52.

Oxburgh, G. E. and Dando, C. J. (2011) 'Psychology and interviewing: what direction now in our quest for reliable information?', *British Journal of Forensic Practice*, 13: 135–44.

Oxburgh, G., Myklebust, T. and Grant, T. (2010) 'The question of question types in police interviews: a review of the literature from a psychological and linguistic perspective', *International Journal of Speech, Language and the Law*, 17: 45–66.

Oxburgh, G., Ost, J. and Cherryman, J. (2012) 'Police interviews with suspected child sex offenders: does use of empathy and question type influence the amount of investigation relevant information obtained?', *Psychology, Crime and Law*, 18: 259–73.

Oxburgh, G. E., Williamson, T. and Ost, J. (2006) 'Police officers' use of negative emotional language during child sexual abuse investigations', *International Journal of Investigative Psychology and Offender Profiling*, 3: 35–45.

Oxburgh, G., Ost, J., Morris, P. and Cherryman, J. (2015) 'Police officers' perceptions of interviews in cases of sexual offences and murder involving children and adult victims', *Police Practice and Research: An International Journal*, 16: 36–50.

Paas, F. and van Gog, T. (2009) 'Principles for designing effective and efficient training of complex cognitive skills', *Reviews of Human Factors and Ergonomics*, 5: 166–94.

Peixoto, A. (1934) 'The interrogation and confessions in the judiciary process', *Revista de Criminologia Buenos Aires*, 21: 383–95; cited in U. Hulmberg (2004) *Police Interviews with Victims and Suspects of Violent and Sexual Crimes: Interviewee's Experiences and Interview Outcomes*. Doctoral thesis, University of Stockholm Sweden.

Powell, M. and Guadagno, B. (2008) 'An examination of the limitations in investigative interviewers' use of open-ended questions', *Psychiatry, Psychology and Law*, 15 (3): 382–95.

Powell, M., Wright, R. and Clark, S. (2010) 'Improving the competency of police officers in conducting investigative interviews with children', *Police Practice and Research: An International Journal*, 11: 211–26.

Powell, M., Fisher, R., Wright, R., Neil, B. and Williams, K. (2005) 'Investigative interviewing', in N. Brewer and K. D. Kipling (eds), *Psychology and Law: An Empirical Perspective*. New York: Guildford Press, pp. 11–42.

Price, H. L. and Roberts, K. P. (2011) 'The effects of an intensive training and feedback program on police and social workers'' investigative interviews of children', *Canadian Journal of Behavioural Science/Revue Canadienne des Sciences du Comportement*, 43: 235–44.

Read, J. M., Powell, M. B., Kebbell, M. R. and Milne, R. (2009) 'Investigative interviewing of suspected sex offenders: a review of what constitutes best practice', *International Journal of Police Science and Management*, 11: 442–59.

Read, J., Powell, M., Kebbell, M., Milne, B. and Steinberg, R. (2014) 'Evaluating police interviewing practices with suspects in child sexual abuse cases', *Policing and Society*, 24 (5): 523–44.

Richards, J. and Milne, R. (in preparation) 'Do people from the higher end of the autism spectrum understand the police caution?', *Autism*.

Schön, D. A. (1984) *The Reflective Practitioner: How Professionals Think in Action*. New York: Basic Books.

Shepherd, E. and Griffiths, A. (2013) *Investigative Interviewing: The Conversation Management Approach*, 2nd edn. Oxford: Oxford University Press.

Smith, L. and Bull, R. (2013) 'Exploring the disclosure of forensic evidence in police interviews with suspects', *Journal of Police and Criminal Psychology*, 29: 81–6.

Soukara, S., Bull, R. and Vrij, A. (2002) 'Police detectives' aims regarding their interviews with suspects: any change at the turn of the millennium', *International Journal of Police Science and Management*, 4 (2): 101–14.

Soukara, S., Bull, R., Vrij, A., Turner, M. and Cherryman, J. (2009) 'What really happens in police interviews of suspects? Tactics and confessions', *Psychology Crime and Law*, 15: 493–506.

Stockdale, J. (1993) *Management and Supervision of Police Interviews*, Police Research Series Paper 4. London: Home Office.

Tanaka, H., Sakti, S., Neubig, G., Toda, T. and Nakamura, S. (2013) 'NOCOA: a computer-based training tool for social and communication skills that exploits non-verbal behaviors', *Journal of Information and Systems in Education*, 12: 19–26.

Tickle-Degnen, L. and Rosenthal, R. (2009) 'The nature of rapport and its nonverbal correlates', *Psychological Inquiry: An International Journal for the Advancement of Psychological Theory*, 1: 285–93.

Uitterhoeve, R. J., Bensing, J. M., Grol, R. P., Demulder, P. H. M. and van Achterberg, T. (2010) 'The effect of communication skills training on patient outcomes in cancer care: a systematic review of the literature', *European Journal of Cancer Care*, 19: 442–57.

Walkley, J. (1983) 'Police Interrogation: A Study of the Psychology, Theory and Practice of Police Interrogations and the Implications for Police Training'. Unpublished MSc dissertation, Cranfield Institute of Technology.

Walsh, D. and Bull, R. (2010) 'What really is effective in interviews with suspects? A study comparing interviewing skills against interviewing outcomes', *Legal and Criminological Psychology*, 15: 305–21.

Walsh, D. and Bull, R. (2012) 'Examining rapport in investigative interviews with suspects: does its building and maintenance work?', *Journal of Police and Criminal Psychology*, 27: 73–84.

Walsh, D. and Bull, R. (2015) 'Interviewing suspects: examining the association between skills, questioning, evidence disclosure, and interview outcomes', *Psychology Crime and Law,* 21, 661–80.

Walsh, D. and Milne, R. (2008) 'Keeping the PEACE? A study of investigative interviewing practices in the public sector', *Legal and Criminological Psychology*, 13 (1): 39–57.

Walsh, D., Milne, R. and Bull, R. (in press) 'One way or another? Criminal investigators' beliefs regarding the disclosure of evidence in interviews with suspects in England and Wales', *Journal of Police and Criminal Psychology*.

Ward, P., Hodges, N. J., Starkes, J. L. and Williams, M. A. (2007) 'The road to excellence: deliberate practice and the development of expertise', *High Ability Studies*, 18: 119–53.

Williamson, T., Milne, B. and Savage, S. (eds) (2009) *International Developments in Investigative Interviewing*. Cullompton: Willan.

Yii, S. L. B., Powell, M. B. and Guadagno, B. (2014) 'The association between investigative interviewers' knowledge of question type and adherence to best-practice interviewing', *Legal and Criminological Psychology*, 19: 270–81.

9 Interviews with suspects in Estonia

Raivo Öpik and Kristjan Kask

Introduction

Since the restoration of independence of the Republic of Estonia from the Soviet Union in 1991 there has been much development in criminal proceedings. Up to 2004 the pre-trial procedure and judicial proceedings were carried out under the Code of Criminal Practice. This was based on the Code of Criminal Process which was in force during the Estonian Socialist Soviet Republic but changed and corrected after declaring independence to conform to the principles of the state based on the rule of law. However, the Code was inquisitorial whereby the judicial proceedings were carried out mainly based on the criminal file from the pre-trial procedure in which, for example, the statement of the suspect was viewed as independent evidence.

In the reform of the criminal proceedings in 2004 the previous style of proceedings changed to adversarial with the aim to ensure that no one should be declared guilty whose guilt is yet to be proven. The reform changed the role of the suspect's statement during the pre-trial procedure – it is now no longer separate evidence (Kangur, 2008) and thus the purpose of interviewing suspects is now more focused upon the circumstances of the crime and is reliant upon any evidence gathered. Based on the change in the legal regulation and procedure, the tactics employed by investigators when interviewing suspects have been also influenced by the new methods used in training investigators and their experiences within the new framework of criminal procedure.

In this chapter current interviewing practices with suspects in Estonia are introduced. First a historical review is given along with a description of current interviewing practices followed by an overview of some relevant literature concerning current practices. After that the investigators' training in Estonia is described. Finally, the implications for research, policy and practice are given.

A historical overview of interviewing suspects in Estonia

In criminal proceedings the statements of suspects are among the most used types of evidence, thus great attention was targeted on the tactics and rules in interviewing, including the personal characteristics of the interviewer, from the beginning of Estonia's independence. (Estonia was an independent republic from 1918 to 1939.) August Liit, the author of several books on policing, wrote in 1927:

> The art of interviewing is not available to every person in a similar way. Different features are important – practical experiences, ability to evaluate a person's character quickly and accurately, natural way of communicating, logics, serious interest towards the case and complete impartiality. (Liit, 1927: 10)

Liit added that ineffective interviewers were those who discouraged suspects from talking by monopolising the interview, failing to either listen or adapt their style to that of the suspect. The rules of interviewing at that time were stated in the Law of Criminal Proceedings (LCP) according to which the suspect is interviewed by a court investigator conducting the pre-trial procedures. The police were responsible for the investigation and did not interview anyone as a suspect. When developing the LCP it was decided that the police cannot be given permission to interview because in making an accusation the police needed to understand the law to be sure that an offence had actually been committed. This would be beyond the jurisdiction of the police as it demands a good judicial education and knowledge of the substantive law (Matto, 1934). However, the fact that the police did not charge anyone did not mean that the police did not have the right to interview the accused. Räägo (1937) has explained that the investigation does not always have a formal 'suspect' and, as such, any person may be in this ambiguous role during the investigation and pre-trial procedure up to the formulation of regulation of LCP § 168, at which point in the investigation the person can be interviewed by the police as an accused.

As a general rule the police did not have the right to force someone to participate in an interview. Paragraph 60 was soon added to the LCP which stated that if someone is suspected of a crime then the police can bring that person to interview using force. The interview was supposed to take place immediately and after being interviewed the suspect should have been released unless arrested (Märdi, 1943). Attention was directed to establishing the rights of suspects and police officers were given guidance in that regard. Several notices of best practice were published in the police journal at that time. The suspect had a right to know of which act he/she was suspected and this information was to be introduced clearly to the suspect to prevent false confessions, especially when the evidence was weak (Liit, 1924). The suspect was not interviewed under oath and although the statement given without an oath was punishable according to the LCP § 141, this did not involve the suspect (Pae, 1942).

In the literature it was also discussed how the interviewer can prompt the suspect to confess, without contravening their right to silence. It was stated that 'confession from the pure soul can give purification and thus diminish the deserved punishment' (Liit, 1927). Based on that, if interviewers used those methods which were not declared unsuitable by law, then the investigator could help the suspect to make a confession easier and no blame would follow afterwards. However, investigators were to refrain from undertaking tactics which clearly breached the law (such as lying about possessing evidence when such evidence was not to hand) (Lindmets, 1992).

Furthermore, issues such as how suspects work to the detriment of the interview were discussed in the literature, for example simulating sickness before or during the interview. Liit (1927) suggested that a suspect's sudden or acute sickness, mental illness or epilepsy, fainting or impaired hearing could occur during an interview. It was also mentioned (Kahkra, 1935) that a suspect's complete silence almost never occurs. More often suspects would provide an (either true or false) alibi.

Liit (1927) targeted attention on topics which are relevant even now. For example, when the suspect makes a confession the interviewer should let the suspect first talk freely and then start asking questions about motives and evidence; also the statement could contain some details which can only be known to the suspect. Interview protocol should not only contain the words of the suspect but also the correct meaning of the words. Liit (1924) noted: 'The credibility of the protocol can be evaluated by the comments of the interviewer about the specifics of the interviewee and his/her behaviour.'

During the Soviet occupation of 1945–91 suspect interviewing was regulated first by the Code of Criminal Process of the Russian Soviet Socialist Republic. In 1961 the Code of Criminal Process of the Estonian SSR was applied according to which (§ 102 section 1) the suspect was a person who was detained on suspicion of committing a crime or towards whom, before presenting the accusation, preventive measures were applied. Section 6 of the same paragraph stated that the suspect will be interviewed under the rules of interviewing an accused. The Code also stated that the suspect has the right to know of what crime he/she is suspected but as the law did not specify when this should be declared then such knowledge can be given either at the beginning or at any time during the course of the interview (Lindmäe, 1972: 80–2), depending on the tactics to be used by the interviewer.

In the literature, tactical recommendations were also given concerning interviewing suspects, where firm and calm communication should be used along with open-mindedness (Karachev, 1969). In the 1950s and 1960s in the literature the tactics used in foreign countries were disapproved of (e.g. where the interviewer justifies the behaviour of the suspect and feels overly compassionate) (Luzgin and Minkovsky, 1959)). In the 1980s these attitudes were changed and in the literature new tactical methods were mentioned such as increasing contradictions, presenting evidence, increasing the attitude that admission of guilt is approved of in the pre-trial procedure, emotionally influencing the suspect and providing a 'legend' (e.g. the suspect's explanation of what happened) (Lindmäe, 1981).

Description of current practice

Different issues influence the interviewing of suspects, for example his/her specific status in the proceedings (e.g. specific rights and obligations in the procedure) as well as the investigators' knowledge and experience in using different tactical methods and combinations (see also Krüger, 2008). The suspect's status in the proceedings can be achieved in two ways according to the Code of Criminal Procedure (CCP) § 33, firstly if the person has been detained on suspicion of a criminal offence, or, alternatively, if there is sufficient basis to suspect the commission of a criminal offence.

The aim of interviewing a suspect in the pre-trial procedure is to find new evidence or to use the statements as evidence (which rarely happens as suspects are known to change their statements by the time they are in court and, as such, these new statements are given more weight than the originals). The tactics used in the interview depends on the circumstances, evidence and also the severity of the crime. The effectiveness of the interview can depend on the preparation (i.e. collecting personal data about the suspect). If the suspect is arrested shortly after committing the crime, then he/she is supposed to be interviewed within a set time (usually 48 hours, although there can rarely be time to do a preliminary collection of data about the person). However, such detention can be prolonged up to six months if there is a chance that the person may commit more crimes or circumvent criminal proceedings.

First, the suspect's personal data is collected and his/her rights and obligations are introduced. Thereafter, the suspects is questioned in the attempt to solicit information about the suspect's personality, life, values, attitudes towards the crime(s), any other persons involved and the criminal proceedings. This information may allow the investigator to forecast how to proceed with the interview concerning tactics.

Then the suspect is provided (CCP § 34 section 1) with the content of the accusation (which enables him/her to defend him/herself). The content should be introduced before giving statements. Sometimes all the circumstances which support the accusation are not clear at the time of the interview. Thus the investigator should not present all the evidence available but only enough for the suspect to defend him/herself. Then the rights and obligations are introduced – the investigator should make sure that the suspect understands these issues correctly. It should be mentioned that he/she has a right not to say anything but, on the other hand, he/she has a right to be interviewed to refute the accusation of which he/she is accused. It should be mentioned that when the suspect gives statements then these can be used against him (Kergandberg and Pikamäe, 2013). The suspect also has the right to the presence of a counsel (hired by the suspect or appointed by the investigator with the aid of the state – for further information concerning this aspect, see Ginter and Soo, 2012).

Next, the suspect is asked whether he/she committed the crime(s) of which he/she is accused and then the suspect is invited to provide their own account as to what happened in the form of free recall. (This can also be in the form of a written statement.) As the suspect has a right not to give statements it is pointed out that this is a chance to explain the circumstances and to disprove the evidence. The answer to this invitation indicates to the investigator which tactics to use further – typically the suspect can be cooperative or the interview is confrontational with weak (or strong) resistance. In general, lack of cooperation (for example resistance) is interpreted by the investigators that the suspect has something to hide.

In a cooperative situation the suspect may well supply truthful statements admitting their involvement in the crime. However, a confrontational situation may also occur where the suspect provides weak resistance by only partly admitting their involvement in the crime or trying to provide an account that, for example, places them in a better light. From the authors' knowledge, this position, when chosen by the suspect, is usually when the involvement in a crime cannot be denied or it is presumed by the suspect that the investigator has incriminating evidence. However, in those circumstances where the evidence is less strong or the facts have not been established then suspects may provide wholly false statements. In such a confrontational situation with strong resistance the suspect may well completely deny involvement in the crime, presenting either a false alibi or statement, or may even not give any statement at all. This may happen in a situation where there are no witnesses or the punishment for the crime is more severe.

In practice, the situation in an interview is not constant but can change. Most interviews are believed to be conducted in a conflict situation. For example, in a study in the Eastern Prefecture involving property crimes, 90 per cent of the interviews were conducted in such a manner that in one-third of the cases there was a refusal to give statements (Link, 2013). Giving false statements is, however, not punishable in Estonia (except where such statements incriminate others).

To motivate the person to still give statements, a different combination of tactics are used such as persuasion, insinuation, giving examples of the scenario (that suggest what happened) or showing that the suspect is lying (for example, by contrasting the given story with the evidence held). If the suspect decides to give a statement then usually free recall is used first and then questions are asked. In practice, however, this is not always followed (Kriisa, 2013). As a rule free recall is not interrupted; this is done only when the free recall is too general and not stating facts about the content of the accusation. It is proposed then to make the free recall more specific. When the suspect finishes he/she is then asked whether he/she wishes to add something to the free recall.

Tactically, the interview should be organised in such a manner that the suspect him/herself reveals information about the circumstances. All the facts known only to the suspect should encourage him/her to speak out, i.e. to use active listening. The investigator evaluates the credibility of the free recall (whether there are internal contradictions, i.e. the recall itself, or external contradictions, i.e. when compared to evidence known to the investigator). Then the investigator should decide whether the contradictions are due to mistakes (when the aim is to find out the factors influencing them and decrease their effect) or lying (suspect swayed to give truthful statements).

In cases in which the suspect is presenting a false statement (i.e. the evidence strongly points to the suspect being likely guilty), the problem in practice is how to overcome the suspect's lies. Based on the evidence and the behaviour of the suspect, two different options are known by the authors to be used.

First, the free recall is interrupted and the suspect is forced to tell the truth. This can be done when there is enough evidence to present. Another method can be also used, i.e. to let the suspect talk, to put the statement they have given in writing and then encourage the suspect to tell the truth by presenting evidence. This latter method can be more difficult since the suspect has already committed himself/herself to a story in his/her original account. As such, he/she would have to, in such circumstances, acknowledge that this original account was false, something which the suspect may find difficult to admit.

The main tactical methods of interviewing in a confrontational situation are:

- explaining the juridical consequences of giving a truthful statement (it is explained to the suspect that providing a truthful statement can be regarded as a mitigating circumstance decreasing the length of the sentence);
- eliminating the motives to give false statements (if false statements are given because the suspect is afraid to be imprisoned then it is explained that the court can apply other sanctions such as a conditional sentence, if applicable);
- indicating the meaningless of the selected position (the methods, for example using DNA expertise, which can be used to prove his/her statements are incorrect are explained to the suspect);
- providing an apparently logical analysis of the discrepancies given in the suspect's account;
- providing a 'legend' (for example, introducing mitigating circumstances as to why people commit these type of crimes and if the suspect begins to confess then the statement is not corrected or contradicted during the interview despite the inconsistencies);
- using discrepancies between accomplices in order to get more truthful statements;
- demonstrating what the investigators know about the case;
- asking control questions to control facts (i.e. asking questions from a suspect to control whether he/she responds to the question in a similar way as was stated earlier in the interview and, if not, then confronting the suspect with it); and
- presenting evidence. Only evidence which is felt to be accurate is presented but factual information about the circumstances which can be known only to the suspect is not presented. The evidence is disclosed from light to more grave (or vice versa) and is usually presented incrementally and not in sum. The suspect's statement is then summarised in the written protocol.

Literature of current practice

In this section the results of the relevant studies from the Academy of Security Sciences and the University of Tartu are introduced. Kärner (2011) has studied the legal aspects of interviewing suspects in pre-trial procedures. He found that CCP is effective in establishing the basic rights of the suspect during interviewing. Problems in his study were found to arise more in the practice where these legal issues are applied by investigators and the possibility of using these rights can vary. He noted that video-recording the interviewing process can help to solve this issue; however, it can have an effect on the quality of the interviewing.

Latin (2012) examined the tactics of confrontation and their use in the pre-trial procedure by means of questionnaires and court case analyses. He found that the more experienced investigator the better the quality of the confrontation; however, sometimes preparation was rarely conducted which resulted in the interviews being of poor quality. Investigators did not present evidence and the wording of the questions was poor – often the same questions were repeated again and again. Latin concluded that in half of cases the confrontation ends with the resolution of major contradictions and suggests that interviewers should invest more time in preparing how best to undertake confronting the suspect.

Link (2013) examined the preparation and tactics of interviewing suspect in conflict situation by investigators and observing the real interviews with suspects in the Eastern Prefecture. She found that in 90 per cent of the interviews, confrontational style was present, while more detailed preparation is done when the suspect is interviewed in more difficult cases. Her study found that those interviews, which began with small talk; achieved better psychological contact with the suspect and, such early discussions helped to choose the best tactics by the investigators, for example when and how to present evidence to the suspect. Link also noted that if the suspect is known to the investigator then the investigator should contact the previous interviewer to gain knowledge of the person to be better prepared for the interview.

Kriisa (2013) studied the special treatment of suspects who were minors in the pre-trial procedure with questionnaires to the investigators. The investigators used similar tactics as with adults, such as conducting small talk at the beginning of an interview. It was found that the investigators had difficulty in overcoming resistance by using pauses during the course of the interview. It was also found that some investigators tried to presume why the juvenile suspect is not talking. Kriisa concluded that specialised investigators are needed who knew more about developmental psychology, for example how to ask developmentally appropriate questions. In another study concerning the interviewing of young people, Õilsalu (2006) found that only 16 per cent of investigators interviewing minor suspects have had special education in how to interview minors. A need for special rooms was recommended, as was training in the necessary skills required for communicating effectively with a minor.

Laine (2003) examined the use of video-recording in the interview and concluded that recording may help to control the statements and prevent any accusations that the investigators use excessive force in obtaining confessions. Kulla (2007) researched the layout of the interviewing room in the Northern Prefecture. It was found that the rooms were equipped mainly with security reasons in mind which may not help to achieve good quality rapport with the suspect. It was suggested that the furniture should be portable to rearrange the room based on the interview. Kulla found that most rooms were small, meant for two persons, thus larger rooms are needed. It was also found in this study that the rooms should be better ventilated, while a reduction in background noise (from, say, computers) would be needed.

Öpik (in preparation) has analysed 60 mock suspect interviews conducted by police officers while undergoing training, noting that often free recall is not allowed and interviewers tend to proceed directly to the intensive use of the question–answer format. Those answers viewed as less certain were interrupted with another question by interviewers who tended to formulate an action plan based on a single investigative hypothesis but not on other possible scenarios. In sum, these studies indicate that although the legislative side is well established shortcomings arise in applying the law and regulations in practice, i.e. whether the investigator has enough time and has been trained appropriately to conduct the procedure according to law.

Training of investigators

The teaching of suspect interviewing consists of three aspects: legal regulation, psychological aspects (as an interview is a means of communication between people); and tactical aspects. In Estonia, these skills are taught at the Department of Law at the University of Tartu and in the Academy of Security Sciences. As the main aim of the university is to prepare lawyers, then mainly the legal regulation of interviewing is taught, as well as the general principles of psychology and the tactics of interviewing.

The Academy of Security Sciences is an applied higher education institution and its aim is to provide students not only with the theoretical knowledge but also with skills and experiences for their future jobs. This is intended to enable students to begin work after they graduate at a good professional level. Therefore suspect interviewing skills are taught in greater depth. There are several subjects where the tactics and methods of interviewing are taught along with the communication skills and how to behave according to the law in different situations. However, this does not mean that the theoretical background is not taught and attention is directed only to practical skills.

In the general curriculum, subjects such as psychology are covered first. Thereafter more specialised subjects are taught (punitive law; introducing and establishing proof in the legislative proceedings of offences; methodology in forensic science). Then the specialist course (tactics of establishing proof) is taught, where interviewing skills are also taught and practised. The curriculum is based on the methods used in the FBI Academy and the ICITAP (International Criminal Investigative Training Assistance Program) (http://www.justice.gov/criminal/icitap/) interviewing methods.

The theoretical part of the course is based on teaching from a general to a more specific level. That is, firstly there is coverage of the general psychological and tactical bases of interviewing followed by a more detailed overview that includes the various stages in legal proceedings, including interviewing suspects (that is, specific tactical methods and their combinations). In practical training, special attention is targeted to developing such intellectual and psychological features in trainees which are necessary for investigating different crimes (for example, crimes against the person). Training with video feedback is used both in basic education and in further adult education to solve correctly 'untypical' and psychologically difficult situations. Practical training is conducted based on the data of solving an 'example case' in two formats.

First, there is a seminar in the format of group work where the trainees discuss the legal, psychological and tactical aspects of the interview and then form an interviewing plan. One task is analysing the primary data to estimate different interviewing situations and to form algorithms in solving these. During the seminar it is discussed with trainers why the trainees planned to use the chosen tactics. The lecturer targets attention to probable problems which may emerge from such planning, as well as the advantages of their use, but in general it is not said whether the decision is correct or not – this is revealed once a mock interview has been conducted. As such, students are not led but learn from the experience of the mock interview.

The second part of this training involves video-based training as a role play where the students conduct the interview which they prepared in the seminar. The practice takes place in a specially built mock interview room. In the room there are only the participants of the interview based on the case (that is, interviewer(s), suspect, legal advisor and, if necessary, an interpreter). The person in the role of investigator sets up the layout of the room. In the room there are four cameras which the educator can direct. There is also a radio connection between the lecturer and the suspect to give suggestions as to how to behave (when to lie or tell the truth, when to make the situation emotionally or tactically difficult). The other trainees can also remotely observe the situation in real time.

Once the interview has been conducted it is discussed whether the interview aims were achieved and which emotions and difficulties arose. First, both the interviewer and the mock suspect are encouraged to reveal how they feel themselves (to decrease any tension after coming out from the interview). The mock suspect is also asked how he/she felt in the role, revealing whether it was it difficult or easy to manipulate the interviewer and how the interviewer's behaviour had an impact on them.

Once this stage has been completed the following topics are discussed with the interviewer. Firstly, whether the interview took place according to plan and whether the goal was achieved is discussed in terms of what was difficult or unexpected and which details were not asked (and why the interviewer thought this happened). Next, a speculative discussion takes place to consider what could have possibly happened if those missing elements had been included and, were the same interview to take place again, what would be done differently. Also discussed is the connection of this task to the real world (i.e. what did the cadet learn from this mock interview that they can take forward to practice). Finally, a general discussion is held where all students can ask questions of the participants. The lecturer does not criticise after the task but directs the discussion and presents general notions and suggestions at the end. During the discussion the recording of the interview is viewed which helps the interviewer to see what he/she did not notice during the interview (non-verbal signals, discrepancies in the speech, awkward wording, etc.) (see Öpik, 2009).

This programme is used in educating trainees in their basic training but also in further adult education at two levels (i.e. beginners and advanced). This curriculum is not only used in the Academy of Security Sciences but also in educating border guards, investigators in the Tax and Customs Board, military police officers and other specialists in investigation bureaus who interview suspects or persons in matters of misdemeanour.

Implications for research, policy and practice

From the legal point of view there has been less discussion in Estonia concerning at which point suspicion is strong enough that the person can be treated as a suspect. So far this question has been analysed from the perspective that the person should be protected from the state to avoid becoming a suspect too easily. Less attention has been focused on those persons not treated as a suspect, where such legal protection (e.g. the right to remain silent) is not given as it is with those treated as suspects.

The law also does not state clearly that the suspect has as equal a right as the witness to provide statements in written form. This should be made more explicit because according to the adversarial justice system the sides should have equal opportunities, and the suspect could quickly provide an explanation about what happened.

There is also no universal view as to how broad the boundaries regarding the acceptance of false statements should be. For example, when the suspect during interviews or confrontation says something which clearly contradicts witness or victim statements then in what circumstances would it be allowed as the statement of a suspect and in which circumstances would it be punishable by the law as creating a false accusation?

There is still almost no research on how suspect interviews take place in Estonia. One reason for this is that there remains restricted access to such interviews. More research should be conducted in this regard and this research should include to what extent, if any, the suspect is influenced by such matters as non-verbal communication (including spatial distance between an investigator and the suspect, body language of investigators, etc.) and how certain factors (e.g. ethnicity or age) affect the possibility of achieving reliable statements in the interview. Also, these studies should examine which strategies the investigators should use and how effective these are in obtaining reliable statements. In conclusion, scientific research in interviewing suspects in Estonia is still in its infancy although the first steps have been taken.

References

Code of Criminal Procedure – RT I, 04.10.2013, 4 (in Estonian).

Ginter, J. and Soo, A. (2012) 'The right of the suspect to counsel in pre-trial criminal proceedings, its content, and the extent of application', *Juridica International*, 19: 170–8.

Kahkra, L. (1935) 'Tunnistajad kriminaalprotsessis' ['Witnesses in criminal process'], *Eesti Politsei*, 4: 632.

Kangur, A. (2008) 'Millal saab isiku kohtust väljapooltehtud avaldus olla tõendiks kohtumenetluses?' ['When does the statement done outside the court become evidence in criminal proceedings?'], *Juridica*, 1: 11–23.

Karachev, K. M. (1969) *Osnovnye processualnye i krimialisticeskie polozenija doprosa obvinjaemogo* [*Major Procedural and Criminal Provisions of Interrogation of the Accused*]. Alma-Ata: [publisher unknown].

Kärner, M. (2011) *Kahtlustatava ülekuulamine kohtueelses menetluses.* [*Interviewing Suspects in Pre-trial Procedure*]. Bachelor thesis, University of Tartu, Tallinn.

Kergandberg, E. and Pikamäe, P. (2013) *Kriminaalmenetluse seadustik. Kommenteeritud väljaanne.* [*Code of Criminal Procedure: Comments*]. Tallinn: Juura.

Kriisa, P. (2013) *Alaealise kahtlustatava ülekuulamise erisused kohtueelses menetluses.* [*The Specialties of Interviewing Minor Suspects in Pre-trial Procedure*]. Bachelor thesis, Academy of Security Sciences, Tallinn.

Krüger, U. (2008) *Ülekuulamine kohtueelses menetluses: Õiguslikud aspektid* [*Interrogation in the Pre-trial Procedure: Juridical Aspects*]. Tallinn: Sisekaitseakadeemia.

Kulla, I. (2007) *Ruumi mõju ülekuulamisele Põhja Politseiprefektuuri näitel* [*The Effect of the Interviewing Room on the Interrogation in Northern Police Prefecture*]. Bachelor thesis, Academy of Security Sciences, Tallinn.

Laine, I. (2003) *Videosalvestus uurimistoimingutes [Videorecording Criminal Investigation Activities*]. Bachelor thesis, Academy of Security Sciences, Tallinn.

Latin, V. (2012) *Vastastamise taktika, tulemuste hindamine ning kasutamine kriminaalmenetluses* [*Tactics of Confrontation, Evaluating Its Results and Use in Criminal Proceedings*]. Bachelor thesis, Academy of Security Sciences, Tallinn.

Liit, A. (1924) 'Kuritegude jälgimine' ['Following crimes'], *Eesti Politseileht*, 32: 517.

Liit, A. (1927) *Kuritegude jälgimine* [*Following Crimes*]. Tallinn: Siseministeeriumi Administratiiw-ala kirjastus.

Lindmäe, H. (1972) *Uurimistaktika* [*Tactics of Investigation*]. Tartu State University.

Lindmäe, H. (1981) *Uurimistaktika* [*Tactics of Investigation*]. Tartu State University.

Lindmets, H. (1992) *Uurimistaktika käsitlus Eesti Politsei kutseajakirjas* [*Investigation Tactics in the Journal of the Estonian Police*]. Academic thesis, University of Tartu, Tartu.

Link, J. (2013) *Kahtlustatava ülekuulamise ettevalmistus ja taktika konfliktses olukorras.* [*The Preparation and Tactics of Preparation of Interviewing Suspects in a Conflict Situation*]. Bachelor thesis, Academy of Security Sciences, Tallinn.

Luzgin, I. M. and Minkovsky, G. M. (1959) *Obzor inostrannoj literatury po kriminalistike* [*Study of Foreign Literature of Forensic Science Vol. 2*]. Moscow: [publisher unknown].

Märdi, A. (1943) *Politseiline juurdlus* [*Police Investigation*]. Academic thesis, University of Tartu.

Matto, K. (1934) *Kriminaalkohtupidamise seadustik: kommentaaridega* [*Law of Criminal Procedure: With Comments*]. Tallinn: Ühiselu.

Õilsalu, K. (2006) *Alaealiste ülekuulamine kriminaalmenetluses, selle psühholoogilised erisused.* [*Interviewing Minors in Criminal Investigation and Its Psychological Differences*]. Bachelor thesis, Academy of Security Sciences, Tallinn.

Öpik, R. (2009) Тренинговые программы по подготовкек расследовнию преступлений исползуемые в Академии Эстонии ['Training programmes for preparation for crime investigation used in the Academy of the Ministry of the Interior of the Republic of

Estonia'], *Criminalistics and Forensic Examination: Science, Studies, Practice*. Vilnius: Lietuvos teismo ekspertizes centras.

Öpik, R. (in preparation) *An Analysis of the Quality of Mock Suspect Interviews in Estonia*.

Pae, V. (1942) *Valetunnistus* [*False Confession*]. Academic thesis, University of Tartu.

Penal Code – RT I, 04.04.2012, 1 (in Estonian).

Räägo, R. (1937) *Kriminaalprotsessi õpperaamat* [*Textbook in Criminal Process*]. Tartu: Akadeemilise Kooperatiivi kirjastus.

10 Interviewing suspects in France

Samuel Demarchi and Laurent Delhalle

Introduction

Whatever the nation of origin, representations of interrogations in television series, movies, and books often transmit an image of investigators engaging in a frank and direct interaction with a suspect. They articulate various feelings and emotions, modulate the pressure, and act in a manner appearing more intuitive than prepared. It also appears that the investigator's goal is a clear quest for confessions; the confrontation is augmented by drama. These are obviously fictional interpretations.

A historically anchored empirical view of interrogations and confessions

In France, although we regularly hear police officials and lead investigators argue that a confession cannot be viewed in isolation, it remains in practice and in the Code of Criminal Procedure (Art. 428) that only a single item of proof, comparable with others, and bearing neither more nor less weight, is sufficient for conviction.

A parallel can also be made for the control of an interrogation. Except for the legislative framework recalling that this procedure must respect basic principles of human dignity, and exercise the basic rights of the defense (along with filming the interview), no text exists concerning the organization of the control and rollout of suspect interrogations. According to the law, in the context of an interrogation, a Judiciary Police Officer is only responsible for his choice of methods and for his acts of investigation. The most important point is that the techniques used by the investigators are transmitted by their peers, etc. – "the more empiricism, the better." However, many studies emphasize the need for methodical, organized and planned interviews (e.g. Cherryman and Bull, 2000; Clark and Milne, 2001), guided by adequate training. To our knowledge, within the French university system there is not a single scientific program examining the evaluation, audit, comprehension, modification, and/or improvement of interrogation methods. However, police officers can read several recent books in the French language from foreign authors, mainly from Canada (Guéniat and Fabio, 2013; St-Yves, 2014;

St-Yves and Collins, 2011; St-Yves and Landry, 2004; St-Yves and Tanguay, 2007). Other non-scientific publications are also available (Clément, 2004; Portelli and Clément, 2002).

Nevertheless, it must be noted that the French *Gendarmerie Nationale* recently introduced the ProGREAI method (see description below), dedicated to an understanding-based interrogatory procedure and active listening techniques during the interrogation. Today, future *gendarmes* receive initial ProGREAI training followed by ongoing follow-up sessions organized with control of each interview according to this method. But to date, there has been no experimental evaluation of its efficiency.

Filling the gap

The lack of evaluative programs is critical and underlines France's failure to adopt standardized general procedures in the field of suspect interviews, for which investigators should be trained. However, for several years a few confidential reports have recommended abandoning technique-based practical empiricism for tested methodologies. This evolution is also guided by the evolution of the crime, the legal environment, and the perception of the interrogation.

Currently, and for ten years prior, the French *Gendarmerie* has recommended using several distinctly different methods and techniques to structure a suspect interview. First, an investigator must adopt a framework of reasoning called the "Tactical Method of Reasoning" (TMR), inspired by military methodology. TMR aims to highlight those elements that are likely to directly influence the course of an investigation. The guide lists the stages to be checked and the points studied, but the method cannot be a single procedure with merely a checklist of important aspects of the investigative process. It must be viewed as an overarching guiding principle for the analysis of the criminal case, an aid in the synthesis and decision process in order to enable the investigator to answer simple summarizing questions such as: What is this about? What type of question is the suspect going to ask me? Where? When? Why? What? What with? Against whom? etc. TMR is also recommended to effectively manage the strategy of an interrogation. This corresponds to St-Yves *et al.*'s (2004) five recommendations:

1. *Maintain objectivity*. A declaration, a testimony, a report expert, a legal file, a photograph, etc. can influence impressions against which the investigator must try to fight. Objectivity can be respected by avoiding prejudices, by putting distance between their own manner of acting and the suspected person, and by avoiding the confirmation of assumptions by the use of "methodological doubt" (Rosenthal, 2000; Rosenthal and Rosnow, 2009).
2. *Build a relationship*. The investigator has to find an equilibrium between the wishes and wills of the heard person and his/her own will. In this power play, he or she must remain attentive to the words being used, unvoiced comments, verbal and non-verbal behaviors, emotions, etc. He or she must also know how to remain silent to listen better and collect information, and to use

silence as a technique which places the suspected person in an uncomfortable position, encouraging them to speak (Guéniat and Benoît, 2013).

3. *"To adopt active listening"* (Rogers, 1959). To encourage verbal expression by the use, for example, of visual or verbal prompts (nod of the head, "hum, hum"), by reformulating the speech of the suspect, by speaking about his emotions, or using open questions.
4. *Be professional.* The officer has to control his position of authority to facilitate communication, but he or she must also be careful not to be submerged by the legal requirements which structure the rules of police custody. For better communication, it is recommended to spend at least a few minutes getting to know the suspect.
5. *Know how to conclude.* The police officer has to confirm that all the main aspects were reviewed, that the suspected persons could express themselves as wished, and inform them of the continuation of the interview (next procedural stage).

In addition to these general recommendations, the *Gendarmerie* expressed the will to structure the interview of the suspects. After having consulted international experts and gaining knowledge of the various practices, particularly from the United Kingdom and North America, a general process of collection of the talks, interviews, and interrogations (*Processus Général de Recueil des Entretiens, Auditions et Interrogatoires*, or ProGREAI) was developed. It is a framework of information structured around three fundamental stages: Preparation, Control of Interview, and Assessments. Apart from these stages, the framework is flexible. It must be adapted to the characteristics of the case being treated, the penal procedure, and the legal framework.

This method presents several similarities with the PEACE procedure used by the British investigation services. In 1992, the British Home Office and an association of police officers financed a feasibility study concerning the installation of the audio-visual recording of suspects (Baldwin, 1992). This study, beyond its primary goal, highlighted several defective practices during the interview of the suspected person. The main weaknesses were an obvious lack of preparation, the absence of a precise and definitive method, and a strong presumption of culpability. From such elements, the British Home Office required the forces to respect a general framework of interview when speaking to a suspect. It aims at countering the "at all cost" confession point of view, and at setting up a procedure of a neutral investigation instead of an accusatory procedure.

PEACE comprises seven general principles which must be applied – as soon as possible – to all the heard people, whether they are a witness or a suspect (Home Office Circular, 1992). Several of these principles were considered in the ProGREAI and TMR procedures which are indicated below by an asterisk (*). First, the interview must be conducted with a true open-mind (*). Then, information obtained must be checked and tested systematically, and compared with information and the elements previously obtained in order to determine what can and what must reasonably be confirmed (*). Moreover, during the interview, the police officer must respect the characteristics of the heard person, as with those of the case in progress (*). In addition, the officer does not have to be satisfied with the first answer given; insistent or persistent questioning is not considered abusive (*). As a corollary, even if the suspect exerts his or her right to silence, the investigator has the right to ask questions (*), just like the investigator is free to ask all the questions which make it possible to establish the truth, unless the heard people are abused or mistreated children (*). Lastly, vulnerable people, whatever their status (witness, victim, or suspect) must be interviewed under particular conditions. Per the Criminal Procedure Code section on procedural constraint, in contrast to suspects, victims and witnesses cannot be detained.

Beyond this general framework, the British Home Office also defined a specific control of the investigation interview, the PEACE model, which comprises five stages. These five stages have, in turn, been incorporated into the three steps of ProGREAI (see Table 10.1).

The ProGREAI Method

Preparations

The interview must be carefully prepared before all other actions. This is an individual or a collective work of synthesis and thought. The interview strategy has to be defined at this time. It should rest on the facts and the validation/elimination of assumptions. The investigators must call on the TMR technique to identify grey areas which will be the objects of questions put to the suspect. The person who will lead the interview must take care to suppress (or reduce) all potential disturbing elements (e.g. phone calls, etc.).

The interview

This is the most important phase of the interview. The investigator will alternate non-accusatory periods (general approach), then offensive periods without being accusatory (specific approach, e.g. asking for more details, searching for behavioral reactions), then accusatory periods.

At the beginning, the investigator has to explain the objectives to lay the foundation for the future interaction. Then the investigator approaches the legal facts.

Table 10.1 Steps of the ProGREAI method according to the stages of the PEACE method

PEACE	*ProGREAI*		
	Planning	*Interview*	*Assessments*
Planning & preparation	*		
Engage & explain		*	
Account		*	
Closure		*	
Evaluation			*

It is a non-accusatory period only concerning the criminal facts. The investigator has to evaluate the credibility of the heard person and the conformity of their declarations to the hypotheses, and all known elements extracted from the preparatory investigation process. The investigator will encourage the suspect to deliver their own version of the facts and should not stop the speech, even in the case of a proven lie. The investigator will then begin a dialogue by taking the suspect's version again and asking for more details. It is not a confrontation, but a search for information based on the former declarations, whether true or not. At this time, the investigator can use "trigger" questions without pauses, in order to obtain behavioral reactions which could be related to the motivation (drive), the affects, and the consciousness of the act. These questions must be prepared in advance to lead the suspect towards the truth, while making it possible to eliminate certain assumptions.

Finally an accusatory phase takes place, where the investigator will imply to the suspect that he/she was involved in the crime. The investigator will use "trap" questions which are meant to generate doubt and destabilize the defendant. They are related to facts (testimonies, prints, etc.), insinuating the possible existence of accusatory evidence which does not call for any answer. After a break, the confrontation between the suspect and the officer begins. The latter will specify with determination that he/she (the investigator) is thinking that he/she (the suspect) is the criminal, while allowing the suspect the opportunity to propose an alternative version. The investigator also mentions possible motives for the crime, and asks the suspect to clarify them if he/she wishes. The aim of this stage is to generate psychological discomfort, bringing the truth out of the person (not necessarily to obtain a confession).

The last stage of the interview follows the recommendations of the last phase of TMR, which also corresponds to the recommendations of the National Crime Faculty (NCF) (2000). It is necessary to systematically explain to the suspect what will occur following the interview, to answer all the questions as clearly as possible, and to prepare for the next step in the criminal case.

Assessments

After the interview, it is imperative to consider new information with all the known elements, giving priority to the facts, the heard person, and the investigator, in accordance with the British PEACE practice. Investigators also have to analyze successes and failures in terms of obtaining information, and to assess their relevance and credibility. Lastly, the investigator has to carry out self-evaluation about his "performance," all of which are sources of improvement and training. The NCF suggests that this self-evaluation should be done in the presence of a colleague or a superior (NCF, 1996).

The ProGREAI method constitutes a real step forward in terms of the organization and optimization of suspect interviewing (an anonymous source claims: "ProGREAI is a state of mind before being a technique"). However, the evolution of the legal framework tends towards the increased presence of defense during the interview, which requires adaptations: for the moment, the police officer is the "director" of the interrogation process. But, with a lawyer during the process, the application of the ProGREAI rules could be called into question, and it will be the very nature of the interrogation process by police officers – namely the search for evidence, not the accusation per se – that will be modified.

Conclusion

Recent decades have been marked by an unprecedented desire of the people in charge of the investigation services to obtain more effective interviewing methods and techniques for suspected persons in France, as well as in many other countries. The ProGREAI method can be considered a step forward because it structures the interview, which is completely contrary to the empiricism observed before its adoption.

However, because investigators are only responsible for the methods and tools they use, they must be trained throughout their career, in particular for the evolution of, and fidelity to, the ProGREAI method. In addition, it is appropriate to encourage collaborations between investigation services, research organizations, and universities in order to create and propose new methods, to identify the optimal or noxious practices, or to adapt the methods to the French inquisitorial legislative framework.

References

Baldwin, J. (1992) *Video-taping of Police Interviews with Suspects – An Evaluation*, Police Research Series Paper No. 1. London: Home Office.

Bull, R. and Cherryman, J. (1995) *Helping to Identify Skills Gaps in Specialist Investigative Interviewing: Literature Review*. London: Home Office.

Bull, R. and Cherryman, J. (1996) *Helping to Identify Skills Gaps in Specialist Investigative Interviewing: Enhancement of Professional Skills*. London: Home Office, Police Department.

Cherryman, J. and Bull, R. (2000) "Reflections on investigative interviewing," in F. Leishman, B. Loveday, and S. Savage (eds), *Core Issues in Policing*, 2nd edn. London: Longman.

Clarke, C. and Milne, R. (2001) *National Evaluation of the PEACE Investigative Interviewing Course*. London: Home Office.

Clément, S. (2004) *L'Entretien judiciaire*. Paris: Institut des hautes études de sécurité intérieure, Direction Générale de la Gendarmerie Nationale, centre de prospective.

Guéniat, O. and Benoît, F. (2013) *Les secrets des interrogatoires et des interviews*. Lausanne: Presses polytechniques et universitaires romandes.

Home Office Circular (1992) *Principles of Investigative Interviewing*. London: Home Office.

National Crime Faculty (2000) *A Practical Guide to Investigative Interviewing*. Bramshill: National Crime Faculty, National Police Training.

Portelli, S. and Clément, S. (2002) *L'Interrogatoire*. Paris: Sofiac.

Rogers, C. R. (1959) "A theory of therapy, personality, and interpersonal relationships as developed in the client-centered framework," in S. Koch (ed.), *Psychology: The Study of a Science. Vol. 3: Formulations of the Person and the Social Contexts*. New York: McGraw-Hill, pp. 184–256.

Rosenthal, R. (2000) "Expectancy effects," in A. E. Kazdin (ed.), *Encyclopedia of Psychology*. Washington, DC: American Psychological Association, pp. 294–6.

Rosenthal, R. and Rosnow, R. L. (2009) *Artifacts in Behavioral Research: Robert Rosenthal and Ralph L. Rosnow's Classic Books*. Oxford: Oxford University Press.

St-Yves, M. (2014) *L'Entrevue d'enquête: l'essentiel*. Montréal: Yvon Blais.

St-Yves, M. and Collins, P. (2011) *Psychologie de l'intervention policière en situation de crise*. Montréal: Yvon Blais.

St-Yves, M. and Landry, J. (eds) (2004) *Psychology of Investigative Interviewing: From Research to Practice*. Cowansville, Quebec: Editions Yvon Blais.

St-Yves, M. and Tanguay M. (2007) *Psychologie de l'enquête criminelle – La recherche de la vérité*. Montréal: Yvon Blais.

St-Yves, M., Tanguay, M. and Crépault, D. (2004) "La psychologie de la relation: cinq règles de base," *Psychologie des entrevues d'enquête: de la recherche à la pratique*. Cowansville, Québec: Yvon Blais, pp. 135–53.

11 Investigative interviewing of suspects in Germany

Defining what not to do

Renate Volbert and Bianca Baker

Introduction

The legal framework for the investigative interviewing of suspects in Germany is designed to enable the police to obtain relevant information on the crime under investigation while, at the same time, allowing suspects to defend themselves from any accusations made against them. This confronts police officers with the difficult task of establishing an interview setting that will ensure that suspects can exercise their procedural rights while simultaneously enabling the police to collect evidence against them (Mohr *et al.*, 2006). The legal requirements for this mainly describe what police officers have to avoid rather than specifically explaining how they should conduct these interviews. Nevertheless, police officers are expected to follow an information-gathering interview approach while motivating suspects to give statements and make confessions without, however, eliciting false confessions. Little is known about how this is done in practice, because research in this area in Germany is limited.

Legal background

Witness versus suspect

The first question is at what point does somebody become suspicious enough to be interviewed as a suspect? The Code of Criminal Procedure distinguishes only between witnesses and suspects. The actual regulations for interviewing a suspicious person are dictated by the verdicts of the Federal Supreme Court in Germany. Witnesses (who are required by law to provide truthful information during interviewing) are normally called in to contribute information that will help to solve a crime and not because they are considered to be the perpetrator. However, persons can still be considered as witnesses when there is a minimal suspicion of their involvement in a crime. If this suspicion is substantiated during the course of the investigation, witnesses become suspects, and investigators are then legally required to treat them as suspects and abide by the corresponding laws. If their status changes from witness to suspect, suspects must then be informed of this change in status and of their rights as a suspect. Their previous testimony then has no probative value and cannot be used against them. Remarks made by suspects when they had the status of a witness can be used against them only if they repeat them during their questioning as suspects (although the remarks do still remain on file). In addition, all individuals who have a complaint filed against them have to be treated as suspects, regardless of what evidence exists.

Police agenda in suspect investigative interviewing

The primary goal of the German Code of Criminal Procedure (Strafprozessordnung (StPO)) is to offer suspects an opportunity to prove their innocence. The law states specifically that the investigative interview should be designed to give accused persons an opportunity to dispel the present grounds for suspicion and to assert the facts that speak in their favor (§136 II StPO).

The suspect is entitled to be heard

In §163a of the Code of Criminal Procedure it is stipulated that a suspect interview must be conducted before the conclusion of an investigation, if the suspect is willing to make a statement (unless the investigation results in termination). There are no restrictions in terms of the time of the interview, which allows for tactical considerations about when best to conduct the interview.

Rights of the suspect

The law requires that suspects be informed of the charges against them at the commencement of the first investigative interview (§136 StPO).

Suspects are not obliged to present themselves to the police, but they are obliged to appear at the public prosecution office or the court if summoned.

The law grants suspects the right to respond to the charges or to remain silent, and suspects can choose to exercise this right even during an interview. If the suspects choose to exercise their right to remain silent, the law prohibits any assumptions being made about this and it being held against them in court. However, should suspects remain silent on particular questions during interviewing, this can be employed against them.

Suspects have the right to legal representation and consultation. This right implies the freedom to have a lawyer of their choosing. It also implies that the consultation may take place before or during the police interview. Nonetheless, this does not necessarily imply that the lawyer is permitted to be present during the police interview.

Suspects have the right to request evidence to be taken in their defense (§136 StPO) as long as the requested evidence is relevant to the case against them.

Suspects must be informed of their rights at their first police interview. If suspects have not been informed about their right to remain silent, or if it is determined at a later time that this right has not been understood, the information gathered during the interview cannot be used unless suspects explicitly consent to its use after having been informed of their right to have this information withheld. Nonetheless, information offered spontaneously by suspects can be used against them as long as this was not given in response to questions asked by the police. Further questions about such spontaneous remarks may be asked, but again only after suspects have been informed of and understood their rights. If suspects have requested a consultation with a lawyer but this request has been denied, the statement and questioning cannot be employed. In addition there are no specific provisions for vulnerable suspects such as suspects under the age of 18, mentally ill or intellectually disabled suspects.

Prohibited methods of interviewing

Prohibited means and methods of interrogation are listed under §136a in the Code of Criminal Procedure. Specifically this paragraph states:

(1) The freedom of suspects to make decisions and to manifest their will shall not be impaired by ill treatment, induced fatigue, physical interference, administration of drugs, torment, deception, or hypnosis. Coercion may be applied only as far as this is permitted by criminal law. Threatening the suspect with measures not permitted under its provisions or holding out the prospect of an advantage not envisaged by statute shall be prohibited.
(2) Measures that impair the memory of suspects or their ability to understand shall not be permitted.
(3) The prohibition under subsections (1) and (2) shall apply irrespective of the suspect's consent. Statements obtained in breach of this prohibition shall not be used, even if the suspect consents to their use.

However, the boundaries between permitted and prohibited methods of interviewing are not always clear-cut. For example, the provision of incorrect facts falls under the prohibited methods of interviewing, whereas the use of so-called criminal trickery and the posing of trick questions or dispensing of ambiguous statements is allowed (Meyer-Goßner, 2011).

Interrogation practice

Although there are many specific regulations on how an investigative interview should *not* proceed, there are relatively few requirements on how it should be conducted. The legal framework suggests clearly that an interview should follow an information-gathering rather than an accusatory approach. However, it is often lamented that German textbooks on investigative interviews are confined mostly to describing the formal requirements regarding the legal inviolability of an interrogation (Habschick, 2010). There are no binding recommendations on how to conduct an investigative interview, no uniform training is provided, and currently there is no significant debate on this issue in Germany.

Nevertheless, basic trends can be described. Although this is not a legal requirement, the German literature on investigative interviewing generally recommends eliciting a free narrative and utilizing a funnel-shaped survey strategy in which a free report is given first that is followed eventually by the asking of more specific questions (e.g. Brockmann and Chedor, 1999; Habschick, 2010; Hermanutz *et al.*, 2005; Stüllenberg, 1992). There are also systematic training programs based on the PEACE model (see Milne and Bull, 1999) that have been implemented in at least some regions of Germany (Berresheim and Capellmann, 2013; Berresheim and Weber, 2003; Klein *et al.*, 2005; Weber and Berresheim, 2001).

While there seems to be consensus on the use of open questioning with a cooperative suspect, it is less clear how police officers should proceed when the suspect does not cooperate from the onset. A lack of cooperation is constituted by either (1) a lack of willingness to make any statement at all or (2) providing false or only partially truthful information.

Mohr *et al.* (2006) have criticized that the PEACE approach lacks a discussion on how to increase suspects' motivation to volunteer information when they have the right to remain silent. They reason that police officers succeed in extracting information from suspects only if they are able to build up a relationship with them that results in the suspect feeling an obligation to cooperate.

Other authors emphasize the importance of personal utility maximization. Brockmann and Chedor (1999) argue that the behavior of a suspect during an interview is the outcome of an interplay between personal motives and the incentives provided by the interviewers. When interviewers understand the needs and goals of the suspect, they can use incentives to foster a suspect's motivation to make a statement. There may be very different reasons for a refusal to testify. If suspects weigh the evidence as insufficient, the presentation of additional existing evidence together with the information that a confession could reduce a sentence may well increase their willingness to testify. However, if the suspect is ashamed of his act, a confrontation with incriminating evidence may have no such effect. In this case, expressing sympathy and understanding is considered a better strategy to motivate a suspect to testify.

Berresheim and Capellmann (2013) have proposed that investigative interviews with an uncooperative suspect should be conducted no differently than interviews with a cooperative suspect. They recommend informing suspects of their rights and about the potential benefits of the interview itself. Benefits for the innocent may comprise the opportunity to contribute exculpatory information. For guilty suspects, the benefits of cooperating in the interview may comprise a possible mitigation of the sentence after a confession. The authors further recommend that information that possibly provokes statement resistance in the form of a refusal to testify or denial should be identified in advance and should be held back as long as possible. Even then, it should not be mentioned directly in order to maintain the cooperation of the suspect. Instead, interviewers should address other topics that permit conclusions on the information that is actually relevant to the case. It is only after this that they should switch to direct inquiries or confront suspects with existing evidence. Direct inquiries should only be made early on in an interview when there is particularly strong evidence against the suspect. Other authors suggest particular interrogation techniques for examining a non-cooperative suspect such as the "zigzag method." This is an interviewing method based on a rapid succession of questions on different topics that has been shown to make persisting in lying more difficult (Hermanutz *et al.*, 2005).

A major point that requires more clarification is that it is generally accepted that an investigative interview should offer the suspect the opportunity to give full and truthful information about the relevant facts rather than being confession-oriented (Brockmann and Chedor, 1999). For example, promoting willingness to give a statement should be explicitly distinguished from promoting readiness to confess, by which wrongly accused suspects may see themselves as being cornered into giving a false confession. Willingness to make a statement is a content-neutral interview goal. Its aim is to increase the participation of suspects and their willingness to volunteer information, instead of focusing prematurely on the outcome of the interview. However, the boundaries between willingness to make a statement and willingness to confess are obviously easily blurred. Even Mohr *et al.* (2006), who distinguish explicitly between the two concepts, sometimes use both terms interchangeably. Given that the boundaries between these two terms are often blurred in the literature, it can be assumed that they are also often blurred in practice.

Thus police officials often express their wish for a technique that will raise the number of confessions. This may also be a reason why there have been various initiatives in the past to implement the confession-oriented Reid technique (Inbau *et al.*, 2011) in Germany, even though use of the technique has been consistently dissuaded in German literature on police interviews and does not comply with the German legal framework (Weber and Berresheim, 2001).

Documenting suspect interviews

Electronic recordings of interviews are not obligatory in Germany; their course must be documented in writing. Nonetheless, the relevant legal guidelines are formulated in ways permitting a relatively broad degree of freedom in their application. For example, the guidelines state the following:

> For *significant parts* of the interview, the *recommendation* is to document the questions and replies *as far as possible* word for word. If the suspect makes a confession, the details of the offense should be reported as far as possible in the suspect's own words. It should be ensured that the record contains those circumstances of an offense that only the offender may know. (Richtlinien für das Strafverfahren und das Bussgeldverfahren [Guidelines for Criminal and Summary Proceedings], Abschnitt 45, emphasis added)

As a safeguard, suspects are given the record to read after the interrogation. They are then asked to make any necessary corrections before confirming that the record is correct by signing it on every page. However, it is assumed that more than 14 per cent of the German working-age population can be classified as functionally illiterate (possibly able to read individual sentences, but unable to take in information adequately from a simple text) (Grotlüschen and Riekmann, 2012). This makes it necessary to ask whether this procedure is really a sufficient corrective.

In practice, the legal requirements are implemented in quite different ways. Sometimes, interviews are summarized in the third person ("The suspect reported that he …"). At other times, they are recorded in a question-and-answer format. However, because these records are not based on sound recordings, the reported questions and answers do not necessarily mirror the exact course of the interview. Sometimes they are documented in the form of a free narrative in the first person. However, the possibility that free narratives are reformulated by the interrogating police officer cannot be ruled out, and phrases such as "Upon questioning by the officer, I declare … ." are often found.

The police interview literature also reveals no uniform, systematic recommendations on how to record an interview. For example, whereas Hermanutz *et al.* (2005) and Brockmann and Chedor (1999) recommend video or audio recordings, at least for complex interviews, other authors propose that documentation should be performed only after the interview has taken place. Mohr *et al.* (2006) recommend, for example: "After the facts have been discussed in the so-called preliminary interview … the minutes of the interrogation are taken. It is necessary that the whole information is recapitulated gradually and put in text form."

However, summarized records may produce a misleading picture. They may incorrectly suggest that detailed information and offender knowledge have been expressed by the suspect, even when the suspect has only admitted to the charges. Moreover, records with a question-and-answer format that nonetheless do not present the course of the interview verbatim may lead to the false impression that interviewing under pressure can be ruled out.

Banscherus (1977) empirically examined the quality of records on the basis of 27 mock interviews conducted by police officers. He concluded that records are influenced strongly by efforts to make the texts "bulletproof." The records he analyzed contained many omissions and modifications of the original statement. Particularly experienced officers tended to modify information to fit their assumptions about events. If the information fits their assumptions, they would enter it in the record; if it did not fit, they would often modify or even omit it. Although parts of the records matched neither the answers given nor the course of the interviews, they were still confirmed by the interviewee's signature. Despite the fact that it is many years since Banscherus conducted his study, there have been no fundamental changes to the conditions for documenting suspect interviews in Germany since then. This is a critical issue, because the documentation of police interviews makes a major contribution to court proceedings. The prosecution base their decisions primarily on the files, and these include the record of the suspect interview. Judges also form their first impression on the basis of what is documented in the files. Even if judges carry out their own questioning in the trial, they tend to assess suspects' credibility by comparing their testimony in court with the record of their statement to the police.

Finally, Klein *et al.* (2005) point out that the need for simultaneous documentation of the information obtained is difficult to reconcile with effective forms of communication during the interview.

Empirical findings

There is little systematic empirical research on police interviews in Germany, and the existing studies are mainly quite dated. However, several studies have dealt with suspects' willingness to confess. These show a somewhat inconsistent picture. Compared to international studies (e.g. Moston and Stephenson, 2009), some German studies reveal very high confession rates. In retrospective interviews with 56 incarcerated male adolescents, Kraheck-Brägelmann (1997) found that 45 per cent made a full and 50 per cent a partial confession. Bippert (2013) analyzed the files of 106 male defendants who were convicted of homicide offenses, and found that 55 per cent made a full and 28 per cent a partial confession during the course of the whole proceeding. When solely police interviews were considered, then 48 per cent of all suspects made a confession at the beginning of the investigative interview, 19 per cent confessed during the course of the police interview and 33 per cent did not confess. However, these studies analyzed non-representative samples and only cases which were further prosecuted. A review of *all* 743 suspects (irrespective of whether the cases were further prosecuted or not) from *one* police department across the span of one year showed that 35 per cent confessed, 15 per cent denied the alleged offence, and 50 per cent did not make a statement (Kroll, 2012). Klein *et al.* (2005) studied suspect interviews in a participant observation of 23 randomly selected suspect hearings and a subsequent survey of police officers. Based on their results and the literature, the authors concluded that about 60 per cent of defendants who appear for questioning at the police station and approximately 75 per cent of those who provide information to the police make a confession. However, because most of these studies used small samples and/or specific groups of accused (e.g. adolescents, homicide offenses) and some studies refer to all cases reported to the police while others refer only to cases which were further prosecuted or convicted, their results can hardly be generalized.

According to both Bippert (2013) and Kroll (2012), young age, a low criminal record, and low pre-conviction rates seem to be predictors of confession readiness (see also Klein *et al.*, 2005). This is in line with international studies (Pearse *et al.*, 1998; Teplin *et al.*, 2002; Viljoen *et al.*, 2005). Bippert's (2003) analysis of records showing a high number of confessions at the beginning of the police interrogation together with Kraheck-Brägelmann's (1997) analysis revealing how adolescents stated that they mainly confessed because they feared they would otherwise worsen their situation, suggest that interrogation techniques may be less important for obtaining a confession than is often assumed. This is underlined by Kroll (2012) who reported that confessions are given mainly in the presence of strong evidence. Klein *et al.* (2005), however, found that a positive interviewing environment was the second most powerful predictor of obtaining a confession (see also Walsh and Bull, 2012).

Conclusion

The legal framework in Germany contains numerous requirements regarding the interviewing of suspects. However, the emphasis is placed far more on what not to do during an interview. Because the Code of Criminal Procedure states explicitly that police interviews should give suspects the opportunity to dispel the evidence against them, it is clear that the legal framing conditions suggest an information-gathering approach. However, there are no specific rules about how such an approach should be realized. Published guidelines on police interrogations consistently recommend an open survey strategy. Although they are not legally binding, these guidelines are referred to in the training of police officers. Indeed, there seems to be a clear consensus that this is the appropriate approach for interviewing cooperative suspects (these being suspects who make a statement and those who confess). However, there is less consensus regarding the treatment of suspects who are not willing to make a statement or deny the accusation made against them. The problem is that it is exactly these cases that represent the major challenge for police officers.

Thus, in practice, interviewing officers often call for strategies to motivate uncooperative suspects to make a statement or even a confession (Klein *et al.*, 2005). The German police interview literature also emphasizes that questioning can only follow an information-gathering approach when the suspect can be motivated to make a statement. Even if most authors add that the interview should be designed in a way that enhances the suspects' willingness to cooperate without pushing innocents to make a false confession, there is still a risk that a willingness to make a statement is not differentiated clearly from a willingness to confess. This is accentuated by the fact that the two terms are occasionally used synonymously even in publications that name this risk explicitly. The principal question underlying this discussion is what significance is attributed to the right to remain silent. When this right exists, but the police are expected to motivate suspects to waive it, then it is more of a disruptive factor rather than a right that is respected and taken particularly seriously. Indeed, up until now, there is still no explicit concurrence on whether incentives to give a statement should be employed, how they should be employed, and how to ensure that these incentives do not increase the risk of false confessions.

In this respect, police officers currently have to meet many expectations. They have to conduct information-gathering interviews, motivate suspects to make a statement and possibly a confession without eliciting false confessions by innocents, and simultaneously produce an appropriate documentation of the questions asked and the answers given. Little is known about how police officers in Germany deal with these expectations in practice, because there has been hardly any empirical research on how they carry out their suspect interviews.

References

Banscherus, J. (1977) *Polizeiliche Vernehmung: Formen, Verhalten, Protokollierung* [*Police Interviews: Forms, Behaviors, Documentation*]. Wiesbaden: Bundeskriminalamt.

Berresheim, A. and Capellmann, M. (2013) "Personen mit und ohne Aussagewiderstand. Taktische Kommunikation im Rahmen der Strukturierten Vernehmung" ["Persons with and without testimony resistance. Tactical communication in structured interviews"], *Kriminalistik*, 67 (2): 93–9.

Berresheim, A. and Weber, A. (2003) "Die Strukturierte Zeugenvernehmung und ihre Wirksamkeit" ["The structured interview and its effectiveness"], *Kriminalistik*, 57 (12): 757–70.

Bippert, M. (2013) "Das Aussage- und Geständnisverhalten von Beschuldigten in Verfahren aufgrund von Tötungsdelikten" ["Suspects' Willingness to Give a Statement and to Confess in Homicide Cases"]. Unpublished diploma thesis, Freie Universität Berlin, Germany.

Brockmann, C. and Chedor, R. (1999) *Vernehmung, Hilfen für den Praktiker* [*Police Interviewing. Practical Tips*]. Hilden: Verlag Deutsche Polizeiliteratur.

Grotlüschen, A. and Riekmann, W. (eds) (2012) *Funktionaler Analphabetismus in Deutschland*. Münster: Waxmann.

Habschik, K. (2010) *Erfolgreich vernehmen* [*Successful Interviewing*], 2nd rev. edn. Heidelberg: Kriminalistik Verlag.

Hermanutz, M., Litzcke, S., and Kroll, O. (2005) *Polizeiliche Vernehmung und Glaubhaftigkeit. Ein Trainingsleitfaden* [*Police Interviews and Credibility Assessment*]. Stuttgart: Richard Boorberg Verlag.

Inbau, F. E., Reid, J. E., Buckley, J. P., and Jayne, B. C. (2011) *Criminal Interrogations and Confessions*, 5th edn. Burlington, MA: Jones & Bartlett Learning.

Klein, F., Berresheim, A., and Weber, A. (2005) "Aussageverhalten von Beschuldigten und Konsequenzen für die Fortbildung" ["Suspects' willingness to give a statement and its consequence on interview training"], *Polizei und Wissenschaft*, 1: 2–15.

Kraheck-Brägelmann, S. (1997) "Geständnisbereitschaft und -motivation jugendlicher Straftäter im Zusammenhang der polizeilichen Vernehmung" ["Adolescent suspects' readiness to confess in police interviews"], in L. Greuel, Th. Fabian, and M. Stadler (eds), *Psychologie der Zeugenaussage. Ergebnisse der rechtspsychologischen Forschung*. Weinheim: Psychologie Verlags Union, pp. 287–301.

Kroll, O. (2012) *Wahre und falsche Geständnisse in Vernehmungen* [*True and False Confessions in Police Interviews*]. Stuttgart: Richard Boorberg Verlag.

Meyer-Goßner, L. (2011) *Strafprozeßordnung* (Beck'sche Kurzkommentare, Vol. 6, 54th edn) [Code of Criminal Procedure]. München: Beck.

Milne, R. and Bull, R. (1999) *Investigative Interviewing: Psychology and Practice*. Chichester: Wiley.

Mohr, M., Schimpel, F., and Schröer, N. (2006) *Die Beschuldigtenvernehmung* [*Interviewing Suspects*]. Hilden: Verlag Deutsche Polizeiliteratur.

Moston, S. and Stephenson, G. M. (2009) "Denial strategies in the interview room," in R. Bull and T. Williamson (eds), *Handbook of Investigative Psychology*. Chichester: Wiley-Blackwell, pp. 17–34.

Pearse, J., Gudjonsson, G. H., Clare, I. C. H., and Rutter, S. (1998) "Police interviewing and psychological vulnerabilities: predicting the likelihood of a confession," *Journal of Community and Applied Social Psychology*, 8 (1): 1–21.

Stüllenberg, H. (1992) "Die Vernehmung" ["Police interviews"], in W. Burghard and H.-W. Werner (eds), *Lehr- und Studienbriefe Kriminalistik Nr. 4*. Hilden: Verlag Deutsche Polizeiliteratur, pp. 3–61.

Teplin, L., Abram, K., McClelland, G., Dulcan M., and Mericle, A. (2002) "Psychiatric disorders in youth in juvenile detention," *Archives of General Psychiatry*, 59 (12): 1133–43.

Viljoen, J., Klaver, J., and Roesch, R. (2005) "Legal decisions of preadolescent and adolescent defendants: predictors of confessions, pleas, communication with attorneys, and appeals," *Law and Human Behavior*, 29 (3): 253–77.

Walsh, D. and Bull, R. (2012) "How do interviewers attempt to overcome suspects' denials," *Psychiatry, Psychology and Law*, 19: 151–68.

Weber, A. and Berresheim, A. (2001) "Polizeiliche Vernehmungen oder: Schon aus Erfahrung gut?" ["Police interviewing. Is experience enough?"], *Kriminalistik*, 55 (12): 785–96.

12 Criminal interrogation in Italy

Legal procedures and practices

Angelo Zappalà, Francesco Pompedda, Vittorio Maria Rossini and Massimo Scarabello

Introduction

Interviewing and interrogation practices depend upon the system of rules that govern trials and investigations. In a civil law system of rules (as opposed to a common law system), parliament develops and enacts statutes to regulate criminal procedure. In Italy in 1988, a new *Codice di procedura penale*[1] (Gazzetta Ufficiale, 1988) came into force, based upon the adversarial system and inspired by the Anglo-American system. An entirely new set of rules control interrogation and witness statements, but some aspects of the inquisitorial tradition still influence the way oral statements are collected during trial or pre-trial investigations.

Interview and interrogation practices: differences among legal systems, protagonists of the trial and different phases of the *iter processuale*

The pre-trial phase is aimed at gathering the evidence the case is built upon. Therefore this is a very delicate stage, in which interviewing and interrogation practices can play a key role and display significant consequences for the suspect's situation. As a result, these activities and the conduct of the actors involved are strictly ruled, in order both to pursue the need to gather evidence and to protect the suspect's procedural rights.

Prosecutor and police officers

Police officers are empowered to examine any person orally (including a suspect) who supposedly has information regarding the facts and circumstances of the case, and s/he should create a separate written record of the statement of each such person. The person so questioned shall be bound to answer all questions relating to such a case put to him/her, unless answering such questions could implicate them in a chargeable criminal offence. In this event, police officers must give the person some warning before the interrogation is continued. The person must be advised that:

- s/he has the right to remain silent, nonetheless the proceedings continue;
- anything s/he says can be used as evidence against them;
- if s/he accuses other people, s/he will be bound to answer the truth as a witness during the trial against those accused.

The examination of a person not yet formally investigated is also carried out by the police, without a lawyer, and may take place anywhere. As a rule, police questioning starts by establishing the identity of the subject and formalising the prosecution (showing the charges and the evidence). The police then check if s/he intends to respond. From this point, the interrogation can continue only if the suspect is assisted by his/her counsel. In this case, the Italian criminal procedure code provides interesting rules. The suspect, when questioned, must be free of all undue influence, both psychological and physical. S/he must be willing to provide information. Neither the police nor the prosecutor may use any methods or techniques that may influence the suspect's right to self-determination, or alter his/her memory or capability to evaluate facts. This right cannot be waived by the suspect under any circumstances, even if they so wished.

The rule implies that police officers cannot lie to the suspect letting them believe that they have gathered evidence against him/her. According to the Italian criminal procedure code, facts and evidence gathered against the suspect must be clearly stated, in order to let him/her choose the best and most effective line of defence. They cannot use hypnosis (or any other method) to force the suspect (or the witness) to remember what occurred.

In Italy, the use of lie detectors, such as a polygraph, is not admissible. However, a new tool (autobiographical IAT (aIAT)), was used to establish the credibility of subjects. The autobiographical IAT (Sartori *et al.*, 2008) is a modification of the Implicit Association Test (IAT) (Greenwald *et al.*, 1998) and has been developed to establish whether an autobiographical memory trace is encoded in the respondent's mind/brain (see http://aiat.psy.unipd.it/). aIAT is a computerised categorisation task. The test includes stimuli belonging to four categories, two of which are logical categories and are represented by sentences that are always true (e.g. 'I am sitting down') or always false (e.g. 'I am going to swim') for the respondent; two other categories are represented by alternative versions of an autobiographical event (e.g. 'I went to Turin for Christmas' or 'I went to Rome for Christmas'), only one of which is true. The true autobiographical event is detected because, in a combined block, it gives rise to faster reaction times when it shares the same motor response with true sentences (see Agosta and Sartori, 2013, for a review). In very few cases have similar techniques been used. In one case (still under appeal) an IAT test was used to test the credibility of a witness. In that case, the witness was also the victim of the crime, thus his credibility was extremely important to decide whether the crime was committed by the person indicted. The court convicted the suspect because the results of the test confirmed other evidence gathered during the investigation and trial.

In adversarial systems, under no circumstances is the suspect forced to confess. If s/he willingly confesses to a police officer or prosecutor, it will not necessarily lead to a conviction, but may be used as evidence at their trial. However, if the suspect later retracts the confession, or changes it, the original confession may no longer be used as evidence. The interrogations described above are of a specific question-and-answer model. Nonetheless, in the place and time the crime occurred, police can gather spontaneous declarations from the suspect. These statements cannot be used as evidence against him/her, but just for the purpose of carrying out investigations. In this occurrence, police cannot actively question the suspect until he appoints a counsel and is warned of the consequences of what he says.

Attorneys

In the Italian system, attorneys also have the ability to interview any persons that may know facts relevant to the case (including both the person accused of the crime and the victim of the crime) in the interests of their client. To do this, they must produce a written request for the person asking them to undertake an interview. Any individual that receives such a request may agree to be interviewed, but they are under no obligation to do so. If an individual declines to be interviewed, the requesting attorney can ask the judge or prosecutor to compel the individual to appear in order to be interviewed. The request from the attorney to the judge does not imply that the attorney will lose the right to interview the suspect personally. In both situations, a person being questioned is obligated to answer truthfully and is criminally liable for any false statement. It is better to highlight that, if the subject of the questioning is a person accused of the crime, the code requires that the interview must be conducted in the presence of the accused's legal counsel.

These investigative interviews are divided into two categories: formal and informal.

- The formal interview is distinguished from the informal because it implies that the interview must be recorded. The recording of the interview follows a number of rules: (1) the interview must be recorded in its entirety with nothing omitted; (2) it is not enough to produce a video recording; and (3) there must also be a written record and an audio-recording of the interview.
- The informal interview is used for general information-gathering. If an attorney wants to use information from an interview during the trial, it must be from a formal recorded session. It may be used at trial when a witness's oral testimony contradicts their statements made during the interview. It is strictly forbidden to omit parts of the interview if an informal interview is being used during the trial. Just as it must be recorded in its entirety, it must be used during the trial in its entirety.

Attorneys are under the same restrictions as the prosecutor and police officers with regard to interrogation methods. They may not do anything to coerce an individual to say certain things. A person being questioned must be able to answer questions without any outside influence as to the answers.

The trial stage

The contrast between adversarial and inquisitorial styles of conducting the criminal process becomes most evident at the trial stage. This fact determines differences in the way in which oral evidence is gathered and then used to prove the relevant facts. In inquisitorial systems, the trial is typically dominated by the presiding judge, who interrogates defendants, witnesses and experts. In adversarial systems, the judge's role is limited to presiding over the parties' presentation of the evidence. The advantages and disadvantages of both systems have long been the subject of scholarly debate. To some extent, the difference between the modes of trial is technical rather than substantive; as long as the courts, in addition to all parties concerned, have the right to question witnesses, the sequence of interrogation has no relevance.

However, there is one basic difference between adversarial and inquisitorial systems that relates back to the different definitions of the purpose of the process. The inquisitorial judge has the responsibility to ascertain that a complete account of the relevant facts is provided to the court; in this way the verdict can be based on 'the truth'. In the adversarial system, by contrast, the finder of fact decides on the factual basis and the judge decides reasoning on the facts that are presented by the parties (the adversaries). Neither the court nor the jury have the right to probe into the factual background or (in most systems) to introduce evidence on their own initiative. This influences the technique used to question witnesses or the suspect. Neither during preliminary investigation nor during the trial is a suspect bound to answer the truth, if s/he desires to answer questions. This is a consequence of the principle known as *nemo tenetur se detegere*, which means that nobody, in any way, must be forced to say something that could lead to a charge against him/her. In other words, the suspect could lie for what concerns his/her own responsibility, with no consequences at all. This important rule, together with the fact that there are no regulations, in this case, on how to ask questions, could be used by the lawyer of the indicted person for defence purposes, in the sense that it is possible that the lawyer suggests to the indicted what to say.

Training

In Italy, police officers or public prosecutors do not receive any specific training on techniques or strategies to conduct a criminal interrogation, even if it is one of the principal activities carried out by these professionals. In addition, there are no procedures or guidelines regarding the best way to conduct investigative interviews. It seems that there is a *standard interview* used by the majority of these professionals but that is not supported by any empirical findings. Also, the use of this kind of interview could be harmful, because it may lead the interviewers to use suggestive questions or behaviour and to misinterpret some non-verbal acts, using the outcome as proof.

Tactics and techniques used in Italy

In this section, we report a few tactics and techniques used by the police during interrogation in certain crimes. Although we will use the terms, tactics and techniques, in relation to police officers, we will indicate also the public prosecutor. In the absence of published research, we refer to our own experience and the material that we had to consider. The lack of official training in empirically validated interrogation techniques leads many police officers and public prosecutors to have a naive idea of the psychological mechanisms that arise during a criminal interrogation or an investigative interview. Even if, to our knowledge, systematic research into criminal interrogation in Italy has not been conducted, anecdotal and unpublished findings show a few typical techniques and common practices regarding what works during a criminal interrogation. For example, many officers believe that there are a number of patterns of non-verbal behaviour which suggest when a person is lying. Usually these beliefs come from reading and interpreting the work of Ekman (Ekman, 2014) on lie detection using micro expressions or epigons, which is very popular in Italy. The patterns of non-verbal behaviour that is believed to indicate one is lying are: (1) the avoidance of eye contact; (2) the smile; (3) the turn of the body; and (4) gesticulation and in general any sign of nervousness. The findings of research on non-verbal and verbal cues to deception and lie detection have been widely ignored (for a review see Vrij, 2008). The reason for this is the lack of professional courses regarding criminal interrogation (as we will see below in the section on 'Training') and the scant diffusion of the empirical research on this topic. So, the knowledge commonly held among police officers regarding the cues to lying is not based on any scientific literature.

At the same time, the adoption of a 'good cop/bad cop' technique is, from anecdotal evidence, commonplace. Although the use of this tactic is denied by police officers when asked about its utility, transcripts of criminal interrogations show that this is very common. Regarding the style of conversation during criminal interrogation, an analysis of a non-random selection of transcripts of unpublished criminal interrogations reveals how police officers do not frequently use open-ended questions while the suspect's statements are often interrupted by the police officers with the intent to induce confusion in the suspect and to make it difficult for him/her to create a false story. Regarding the use of evidence during interrogation, it should be noted that when police officers have evidence against the suspect, they usually present it at the beginning of the interrogation, regardless of the findings by Granhag *et al.* (2007) who collectively suggest that evidence available at the beginning of the interrogation should not be used. Anecdotal cases in Italy, in line with Stephenson and Moston's findings (1993, 1994) show that the availability of evidence affected the style of the interview used (i.e. when the evidence was valued as weak, police officers used the information-gathering strategy differently to when the evidence was valued as strong, when the interviewer used an accusatorial approach).

The most common technique in criminal interrogations consists of prolonging the duration of the interrogation. The main idea is that a person is always able to tell the truth even if s/he is very stressed while the fatigue induced by the stressful conditions makes it difficult to lie. The phenomenon of false confessions and the vast psychological literature surrounding this is basically ignored (see Kassin and Gudjonsson, 2004, for a review). Police officers believe that false confessions can be the product of a suspect's mental disorder or an intentional method of protecting someone. Police officers basically ignore, or they grossly underestimate, the phenomenon of false confessions as a way for the suspect to interrupt the stressful situation. However, it should be noted that it is not only police officers who underestimate false confessions; in Italy, the scientific literature on false confessions is also widely ignored among psychologists and psychiatrists.

Interrogation of suspects of sexual crimes

In the case of the interrogation of offenders suspected of committing a sexual offence against an adult woman, the tactics commonly used are the 'bad cop/good cop' routine where the 'bad cop' uses a macho style while the 'good cop' follows a few of the tactics used in the Reid technique of interrogation (Inbau *et al.*, 2011), in other words the tactics and techniques for the interrogation of suspects whose guilt is definite or reasonably certain. Police will sympathise with the subject by telling him/her that anyone else under similar conditions or circumstances might have done the same thing, or will reduce the subject's guilty feelings by minimising the moral seriousness of their offence, or will point out the possibility of exaggeration on the part of the accuser or victim or exaggerate the nature and seriousness of the offence itself. However, the attitude of the interviewer changes according to the statements made by the suspect. In fact, for suspects who deny the accusation but the interviewer believes in their guilt, the style of interview is characterised by confrontation, pressure and coercion while when the suspect admits their sex crime the interviewer is empathetic (Holmberg, 1996).

In the case of the interrogation of a person accused of a sexual offence against children, the interview style varies according to the gravity of the crime and the type of paedophile. First of all, it should be noted that not all the offenders who commit an offence against children are paedophiles – only around half of all people who commit a sexual offence against a child are so inclined (Seto, 2008). Even if police officers ignore this difference, the interrogation style changes according to whether the suspect is a child molester or a paedophile. Child molesters (i.e. people who whose primary sexual preference is oriented to adults but who may molest children) are generally interrogated by police officers in a brusque and confrontational way. For non-contact offenders (i.e. those that view child pornography material), the style of the interrogation is characterised by attempts to establish an empathic relationship with the suspect. For the suspected 'contact' paedophile offenders (whether penetrative or not) the style of the interrogation often begins in a 'smooth' and empathic way but quickly changes if the offender does not admit the crime. It should be noted that the scientific literature on the cognitive distortions in sexual offenders (e.g. all that the offenders think and tell themselves and others which allows them to justify their behaviour to themselves – see Abel *et al.*,1984, 1989; Pollock and Hashmall, 1991, Rogers and Dickey, 1991; Neidigha and Krop,1992; Bumby, 1996) appears to be either unknown or is widely ignored in Italy. Cognitive distortions include justifications, denials and the minimisation of the crime. Such knowledge, if known among police officers, would improve the quality of criminal interrogations with this kind of suspect.

Common criminality

The criminal interrogation of robbers, bank robbers and other common criminals are characterised by a lack of empathy by the interviewer, and generally lacks the phase in which rapport is established. The interrogation is in a confrontational and confession-seeking style in which the interrogator assumes dominance through a stream of questions in order to keep up pressure on the suspect.

Domestic violence

In cases of domestic violence, interrogation styles change case by case (i.e. according to the gravity of maltreatment, the amount of alleged maltreatment, the role of the victim, whether the suspect usually uses drugs or alcohol). When there is only one or two episodes of alleged maltreatment, the style of interrogation is in an information-gathering style (i.e. 'Okay then, tell me a little how things are going with your wife? What's wrong? We are here to understand what happened …'). If the suspect is alcohol-dependent and/or the number of episodes is more than two, the interrogation style is similar to that for the antisocial person: the interrogator does not appear to build rapport with the suspect and the interrogation is often conducted in a confrontational manner. In fact, it is to this area we now turn.

Interrogation of suspects of organised crime

It is well known that, for a long time in Italy, organised crime has plagued the politics, the economy and the everyday life of millions of people. At present in Italy, several local criminal organisations are operating (e.g. the Mafia, the Ndrangheta, the Camorra, to name only those best known) as well as new organisations from Europe and other continents. If we consider only the native criminal organisations, it should be noted that each organisation is typical of an Italian region (e.g. the Mafia in Sicily, the Ndrangheta in Calabria, the Camorra in Campania). The Italian criminal organisations are particularly structured characterised of a complex of networks and hundreds of members. Moreover, the members of these gangs are like the soldiers of an army related to each other by kinship or in terms of honour. Members swear loyalty to the organisation through rituals that resemble religious rites. In addition, each organisation speaks a different dialect and has its own rituals, organisation and hierarchy and its own anthropology. Police officers must have a range of skills from a knowledge of the dialect (the key to understanding and being understood) of the network nodes to an in-depth knowledge of the criminal psychology of the members of each particular organisation. In addition, the interrogator must display authority to attract the attention of the suspect. Unlike common criminals, it is easy to understand how members of these organisations are particularly hard to interrogate, such suspects having a long criminal career suffering from antisocial disorders and often psychopathic traits.

Future directions

In our opinion, in order to improve the quality of criminal interrogations, it is necessary to disseminate the findings of the empirical research into what works effectively among public prosecutors and police officers. Moreover, ('learning by doing' based) training courses should be provided to train by the professionals who routinely interrogate suspects.

Note

1. Set of rules specifically dedicated to direct all the phases of a criminal proceeding.

References

Abel, G. G., Becker, J. V. and Cunningham-Rathner, J. (1984) 'Complications, consent, and cognitions in sex between children and adults', *International Journal of Law and Psychiatry*, 7 (1): 89–103.

Abel, G. G., Gore, D. K., Holland, C. L. and Camp, N. (1989) 'The measurement of the cognitive distortions of child molesters', *Annals of Sex Research*, 2 (2): 135–52.

Agosta, S. and Sartori, G. (2013) 'The autobiographical IAT: a review', *Frontiers in Psychology*, 4: 519.

Bumby, K. M. (1996) 'Assessing the cognitive distortions of child molesters and rapists: developments and validation of the MOLEST and RAPE scales', *Sexual Abuse: A Journal of Research and Treatment*, 8: 37–54.

Ekman, P. (2014) *I volti della menzogna. Gli indizi dell'inganno nei rapporti interpersonali* [*The Faces of Lies: The Evidence of Deception in Relationships*). Florence: Giunti Editore.

Gazzetta Ufficiale Italiana (1988) *Decreto del presidente della repubblica 22 settembre 1988, n. 447*. Retrieved from: http://www.giustizia.lazio.it/appello.it/form_onoraria/circolari/Codice%20procedura%20penale%202011.pdf).

Granhag P. A., Strömwall, L. and Hartwig, M. (2007) 'The SUE-technique: the way to interview to detect deception', *Forensic Update*, 88: 25–9.

Greenwald, A. G., McGhee, D. E. and Schwartz, J. K. L. (1998) 'Measuring individual differences in implicit cognition: the Implicit Association Test', *Journal of Personality and Social Psychology*, 74: 1464–80.

Holmberg, U. (1996) *Sexualbrottsförövares upplevelser av polisförhör*, Report Series 1996:7. Kristianstad: Kristianstad University.

Holmberg, U. and Christianson, S.-Å. (2002) 'Murderers' and sexual offenders' experiences of police interviews and their inclination to admit or deny crimes', *Behavioral Sciences and the Law*, 20: 31–45.

Inbau, F. E., Reid, J. E., Buckley J. P. and Jayne, B. C. (2011) *Criminal Interrogation and Confessions*, 5th edn. Burlington, MA: Jones & Bartlett Learning.

Kassin, S. and Gudjonsson, G. (2004) 'The psychology of confession evidence: a review of the literature and issues. *Psychological Science in the Public Interest*, 5: 2.

Leo, R. A. (1992) 'From coercion to deception: the changing nature of police interrogation in America', *Crime, Law and Social Change*, 18: 35–59.

Leo, R. A. (1996) 'Criminal law: inside the interrogation room', *Journal of Criminal Law and Criminology*, 86 (2): 266–303.

Moston, S. and Engelberg, T. (1993) 'Police questioning techniques in tape recorded interviews with criminal suspects', *Policing and Society*, 3: 223–37.

Moston, S. and Stephenson, G. M. (1993) 'The changing face of police interrogation', *Journal of Community and Applied Social Psychology*, 3: 101–15.

Neidigh, L. and Krop, H. (1992) 'Cognitive distortions among child sexual offenders', *Journal of Sex Education and Therapy*, 18: 208–15.

Pollock, N. L. and Hashmall, J. M. (1991) 'The excuses of child molesters', *Behavioral Sciences and the Law*, 9 (1): 53–9.

Rogers, R. and Dickey, R. (1991) 'Denial and minimization among sex offenders', *Sexual Abuse: A Journal of Research and Treatment*, 4 (1): 49–63.

Sartori, G., Agosta, S., Zogmaister, C., Ferrara, S. D. and Castiello, U. (2008) 'How to accurately detect autobiographical events', *Psychological Science*, 19: 772–80.

Seto, M. C. (2008) *Understanding Pedophilia and Sexual Offending Against Children: Theory, Assessment, and Intervention.* Washington, DC: American Psychological Association.

Vrij, A. (2008) *Detecting Lies and Deceit: Pitfalls and Opportunities*, Wiley Series in the Psychology of Crime, Policing and Law. Chichester: Wiley.

13 The investigative interviewing of suspects in the Netherlands

Current practices and historical developments

Martijn van Beek and Jos Hoekendijk

Introduction

It is commonly agreed that contemporary criminal investigation techniques in the Netherlands commenced as a result of the aftermath of the Schiedam Park Murder in 2000. In this case the suspect Cees B. confessed to the police he had raped and killed a 10-year-old girl and also raped and attempted to kill an 11-year-old boy two months earlier in the Beatrixpark in the Dutch city of Schiedam. Cees B. withdrew his confession one day later, but in 2002 the Appeal Court in the Netherlands sentenced him to 18 years. However, in 2004 another man, Wik H., was found to be the real perpetrator. Although the Schiedam Park Murder was not the only miscarriage of justice in the Netherlands during the 1990s and first years of the new century, it is perhaps the most thoroughly reviewed one (e.g. Van Koppen *et al.*, 2010; Clément *et al.*, 2009; Posthumus, 2005; Van Koppen, 2003). The Schiedam case resulted in an improvement programme for the public prosecution service, the National Institute of Forensics and the police (Openbaar Ministerie, 2005).

In this chapter we will consecutively discuss: (1) the implications of this improvement programme for educating Dutch detectives in interviewing suspects; (2) recent developments concerning interviewing vulnerable suspects; (3) interview tools and strategies that Dutch interviewers are trained in; and (4) future directions.

Education

With regard to investigative interviewing the Dutch police committed itself to several of the guidelines that the improvement programme prescribed. These guidelines cover, among others, the need for training (at basic and expert levels) for being well-prepared for interviews, particularly in major cases, for documenting the aims and tactics of the interview and for coaching and (de-)briefing the interviewers. Since 2006 every police region has been obliged to have a protocol to ensure these issues. As an example of 'best practice' the improvement programme mentioned the 'Utrecht approach'. This refers to a training programme developed in 1999 by the Police Academy of the Netherlands for the Utrecht area police (personal communication, De Vries, 28 January 2014) which has become in the years since a standard for the national education of detectives in investigative interviewing. It resulted into two courses in order to train detectives to the highest possible interview level. In 2013 these courses merged into the current curriculum of Professional Training in Interviewing (PTI[1]).

The PTI is a programme that involves 320 hours of study in the following modules:

1. *Personal efficacy*: a module about self-reflection in order to improve learning (attitude) and in order to be aware of the possible effects of one's own behaviour during interviews.
2. *Enrichment evidence matrix*: a follow-up on the basic training of working with an evidence matrix. The matrix will be discussed later in this chapter.
3. *Person-oriented interview*: training in building rapport and discussing personal topics with the suspect (or witness).
4. *Enrichment case-oriented interview*: a follow-up on the basic training of discussing case-related topics with the suspect.
5. *Enrichment witness interviewing*: a follow-up on the basic training of witness interviewing.

   A *Integrating module 1*: integrating the knowledge and skills learned in modules 1 to 5 by preparing and performing an interview at one's own station, while being supervised by the tutor and classmates.

6. *Culture*: a training in (inter-)cultural aspects concerning suspect and witness interviewing.
7. *Psychopathology*: training in awareness about (possible) mental illnesses of witnesses and suspects.
8. *Third parties*: training in how to cooperate with third parties being present during interviews (i.e. lawyer, interpreter, psychologist).

   B *Integrating module 2*: integrating the knowledge and skills learned in modules 6, 7 and 8 by preparing and performing a supervised interview with factors concerning culture, psychopathology and/or a third party being present.

Starting in 2015 the curriculum will also include a module of coaching peer interviewers. PTI participants are required to undertake two examinations in order to successfully complete all modules. In modules 1–5 and A, participants have to prepare and perform an interview with both a witness and a suspect in a role-play setting, while in modules 6–8 and B, again in a role-play setting, they have to prepare and perform a suspect interview with a suspect having either a mental illness or a non-western cultural background. Participants can choose to follow the curriculum until the first exam and, if they wish, defer the second part to a later time.

Vulnerable suspects

Another case that has led to controversy in the Netherlands was the case of the 'Ice Cream Man'.[2] This case involved a man interviewed by the police, who believed he had concealed the dead body of a man reported being missing in order to obstruct the investigation as to the whereabouts of this victim. It took four years before the police found the body and in the meantime the suspect had suffered three cerebral haemorrhages. Parts of the taped police interview, showing a man having difficulties with concentration, thinking and speech, were broadcast on television in 2008 and led to questions being asked in the Dutch parliament about the interviewing methods being used with such a vulnerable man (Ministerie van Justitie, 2008). This debate resulted in a course being introduced called Interviewing Vulnerable Suspects (IVS[3]). The first training (224 hours) took place in 2012. It addresses the following issues:

- raising awareness about legal and ethical dilemmas considering (interviewing) vulnerable suspects;
- recognising signs of potential vulnerability, e.g. impaired intelligence or some psychiatric conditions, that may lead to increased risks of suggestibility and/or compliance;
- integrating information from relevant third parties surrounding the suspect into the preparation and performance of the interview, i.e. supervisors, counsellors, physicians or neurologists.

The IVS contains, among others, an internship (32 hours) in either the psychiatric/neurologic domain or the field of youth and/or cognitive impairments, common interviews with vulnerable people about their daily lives, for example, and suspect interviews in a role-play setting. Those participants on the IVS are examined in a role-play setting where they have to prepare and perform an interview with a vulnerable suspect. The training is open for those detectives who have successfully completed the PTI course and/or those who have successfully completed the training for interviewing vulnerable witnesses in sexual cases. (See Rispens and Van der Sleen (2015) for details about this training.)

Tools and strategies

Key factors in training and practice are the evidence matrix, initial contact, the person-oriented interview, the case-oriented interview and the generic model for interviewing witnesses. Apart from the witness model (see Rispens and Van der Sleen, 2015) the other topics will be discussed consecutively in this section.

Evidence matrix

The evidence matrix is a tool for the investigative team to assess the (potential) incriminating and exculpatory information available at the start of the interview (see Table 13.1). When working with evidence matrices, a matrix needs to be filed for the investigation. Table 13.1 is an example of such a matrix, where the investigation concerns a crime that may be either murder or manslaughter.

Table 13.1 Evidence matrix

*Murder (section 289 Criminal Code): anyone who intentionally and with premeditation takes the life of another person is guilty of murder and liable to life imprisonment or a term of imprisonment not exceeding thirty years of imprisonment or a fine of €67,000.**

Elements	*Meaning*	*Tactical clues*	*Aims*	*Incriminating or exculpatory*	*Action*
Anyone who intentionally with premeditation takes the life of another person					

*In Dutch: Hij die opzettelijk en met voorbedachten rade een ander van het leven berooft, wordt, als schuldig aan moord, gestraft met levenslange gevangenisstraf of tijdelijke van ten hoogste dertig jaren of geldboete van de vijfde categorie.

Source: Van Amelsvoort *et al.* (2012). Reproduced with kind permission both from Reed Business Information and Imke Rispens.

As shown in Table 13.1, an evidence matrix contains the Article of the Criminal Code the suspect is indicted of together with six columns. The first column ('Elements') shows the different elements that comprise the Article. According to the Dutch inquisitorial criminal justice system a judge can only prove the suspect guilty when there is enough evidence for each separate element. The second column ('Meaning') explains the meaning of the particular element. This can mostly be found in legal jurisprudence. Premeditation, for example, requires signs of the perpetrator being 'calm and deliberate' (just) before the act of the crime.[4] In the third column ('Tactical clues') the detective files the tactical clues considered to be potential pieces of evidence related to the corresponding elements of the Criminal Code Article.[5] This will allow him/her to assess whether there is incriminating information concerning the particular element or information that might exclude the suspect from having committed that element (which means he/she may be innocent or his/her crime may be a perpetration of another Article of the Criminal Code). Such methods might highlight that both incriminating and exculpatory information are missing at this point in the investigation (to be noted in the fifth column). This analysis allows the investigation team to establish aims for the ongoing investigation (these are written down in the fourth column: 'Aims'). It is important to note the matrix is dynamic by nature. It both guides and follows the ongoing investigations: every time an aim is met the result is a new incriminating or exculpatory tactical clue. In the sixth column ('Actions') the team can formulate the investigative actions that might be undertaken to collect the information needed to meet the aims. These actions cover the whole range of police investigative strategies and tactics, ranging from interviewing witnesses to wiretapping the suspect or to seek forensic advice from experts.

In an ideal situation, interviewing the suspect will take place only when all or most of the other possible actions are closed. At this point there are incriminating tactical clues available to challenge the suspect with during the interview and possible exculpatory clues are (apparently) falsified by the result of other investigative actions. The collected clues and the questions related to the still vacant aims serve the interviewer to prepare and conduct the interview. How this is done will be discussed later in this chapter when describing 'case-oriented interviews'.

Initial contact

'Initial contact' is the opening phase of every investigative interview (Van Amelsvoort *et al.*, 2015). It helps the interviewer to structure the subsequent interview and helps the interviewee to accommodate the interview situation (Van den Adel, 1997). The interviewer explains the reason for the interview and the legal process. Roles and positions are also explained and the interviewer makes sure the suspect thoroughly understands his/her legal rights. Other aims of this opening part of the interview are to check the willingness of the suspect to talk to the interviewer(s)[6] and to observe any signs of vulnerability, since knowing both of these elements are crucial factors in the choice of strategy in the 'case-oriented part' of the interview. A well performed initial contact can display to the suspect the meticulousness of the interviewer's approach, which many suspects may appreciate. This can provide a stimulus for a good cooperative relationship. It also offers the interviewer the opportunity to answer any questions the suspect might have, with the advantage that these issues then no longer form an obstacle during the interview.

Person-oriented interview

The 'person oriented interview' phase (POI) forms part of the interview as a whole and, in particular, it supplements the 'initial contact' phase. It provides insight through an analysis of the suspect. In practice, the POI generally precedes the 'case-oriented interview'. During the POI, there should be no discussion of the offence itself. The building up of pressure, due to challenging the suspect's statements with opposing tactical clues, is in principle absent. The POI is meant to lead to a dynamic, natural way of conversation. The POI can be subdivided into three phases (see Table 13.2). The interviewer introduces the 'person-orientated interview' by stating that he/she wants to talk about more personal topics first, to obtain a broader picture of the suspect. By discussing these person-related topics, several interview-strategic aims are met. First of all, building rapport. This is in line with the common opinion which suggests that building rapport is one of the success factors in interviewing (e.g. Abbe and Brandon, 2014; Vanderhallen *et al.*, 2011; Walsh and Bull, 2012) and that there appears to be a correlation between the perceived quality of the working relationship and the subject's willingness to talk (Vanderhallen *et al.*, 2014).

Dealing with topics which do not seem to be directly related to the case, at least in the suspect's eyes, might invite the suspect to enter into a dialogue and can add to the working relationship between interviewer and suspect. Moreover, it may well give the interviewer the opportunity to show his/her intentions, which should be trustworthy and neutral.

Additionally, the suspect can become accustomed to the interviewer and his/her style of questioning. On the other hand, the POI serves to collect information about

Table 13.2 The three phases of POI

Phase	*Activity*
Opening	Introduce the objective of the interview
Discuss person-related topics	Building rapport Complete information about the suspect Ascertain whether the suspect is willing to provide an account Additional elements: Observe behaviour of suspect in relation to possible signs of, for example, vulnerability, cooperation or resistance Generate tactical clues Normalise level of tension Improve willingness to talk
Closing	Explain further proceedings and introduce the 'case-oriented interview'

Source: Van Amelsvoort *et al.* (2015). Reproduced with kind permission from Reed Business Information.

the suspect, by discussing certain topics. These topics should be (indirectly) related to the crime, the possible motive(s) and/or the personality of the suspect. This is illustrated by Figure 13.1, which reflects a mind map of topics, objectives and possible bridges in a case of domestic violence. Note this mind map can be easily taken into the interview to help guide the interviewer. All topics in the mind map are related to the crime, the possible motive(s) and the personality of the suspect. Note this approach might be particularly effective in more emotional crimes, with strong relations between offence, motive and personality, as the case in Figure 13.1 is an example of. In general, aspects like character and attitudes might reflect stronger in the motive and/or the modus operandi when the offence is emotionally driven. Examples of this relationship between offence and emotional motive can be seen in some serial arsonists, who are often driven by inner conflicts and experiences of failure in daily life: setting fire then serves as a disturbed way of coping with stress (Schoenmakers *et al.*, 2010). The POI can be deployed in such cases to explore relevant themes from the suspect's perspective.

One of the techniques shown in the mind map in Figure 13.1 is called 'source encircling'. In this example the testimony of the victim contains significant tactical clues. Before challenging the suspect later on with these clues, it is tested how reliable the suspect claims the victim is. From the answers provided, the interviewer gains an impression of the value the tactical clues in the witness statement will have from the perspective of the suspect.

The POI can serve as an instrument to explore what topics the suspect is willing to talk about and on what topics he/she may be more reticent to discuss. It can also be a useful tool to help the suspect to explain his/her actions. de Ruiter and van Beek (2014) discuss this matter in greater detail. The POI might help the interviewer to explore which interview techniques to undertake and which to avoid. These indications serve as input for the following 'case-oriented interview' phase.

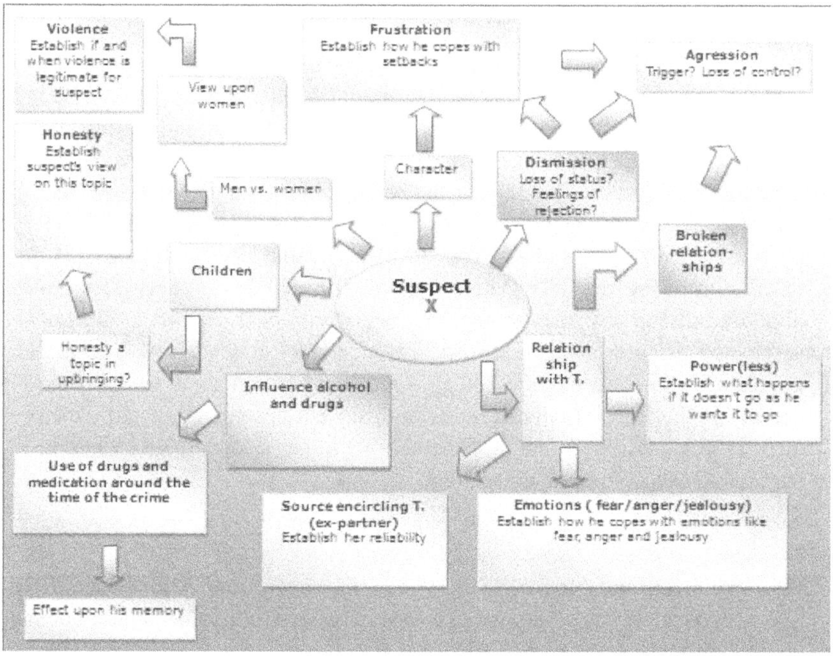

Figure 13.1 Mind map of a person-oriented interview plan with a suspect of domestic violence.

Reproduced with kind permission from Detective Senior Sergeant Mark Bisschops.

The POI originated from sex crime interviews, where the topic of sex itself might be difficult for the interviewee to talk about (even without being accused of having committed a crime in this matter). It allows an opportunity for the interviewer to show an understanding of any feelings of shame and unease held by the suspect, and can often help to normalise talking about the topic of the investigation, a known technique in psychotherapy and coaching for dealing with difficult topics (e.g. Visser, 2014).

After closing the POI the detective should think about the implications the collected information has upon the following 'case-oriented interview' phase, in order to allow considerations as to which (if any) adjustments are to be made either in the interview strategy or in the manner in which the interviewer approaches the suspect. Finally, the choice of topics in the POI creates an opportunity to upgrade tactical clues. An example of this is given in Box 13.1.

The 'case-oriented interview' phase

In order to conduct the 'case-oriented' phase of a suspect interview (COI) every Dutch detective is, at least at a basic level, trained in the General Interviewing Strategy (GIS). For in-depth discussions of the GIS model, see Clément *et al.*

Box 13.1 Upgrading tactical clues within the POI

A woman was suspected of poisoning her husband several years ago. In the POI the topics of education and work, among others, were discussed. She told the interviewer she had obtained a diploma as a nurse and, at the time her husband died, she had been working in healthcare for several years. She gave a comprehensive account of the responsibilities in her job. She also told what actions to take in case of a diversity of symptoms. Beforehand, an evidence matrix-based assessment of the available tactical clues indicated murder (Section 289 Dutch Code of Criminal Procedure) was probably too difficult to prove, so she was secondarily charged with neglect of assistance in mortal danger (Section 450 Dutch Code of Criminal procedure[7]). The result of the POI gave sufficient tactical clues to challenge her within the 'case-orientated interview', since it appeared the victim died after a three-day illness and no general practitioner was alarmed by her, in spite of all the symptoms present.

(2009), van Beek and Hoekendijk (2015), Hoekendijk and van Beek (2015) and Van der Sleen (2009). The model is also described in the Dutch interviewing manual (Van Amelsvoort *et al.*, 2015).

The GIS model has evolved from an exploratory field experiment in 1989 (Van Amelsvoort, personal communication, 10 February 2013). In this study (see Hoekendijk and van Beek, 2015) the Police Academy of the Netherlands selected and observed four detectives with good interview reputations, each performing four interviews with role-play actors who had committed some (staged) petty crimes. The actors were free to choose their strategy in committing the crime and also their interview 'counter'-strategy. They would receive a bonus on their wages if they were able to avoid being found out that they were the 'perpetrators'. Effective interview behaviour, operationalised in terms of collecting information in line with the 'ground truth' and without missing information or collecting false information, appeared in this experiment to be related with: (1) being able to build rapport; (2) disclosure of evidence in a neutral tone of voice; and (3) disclosure of evidence only after having ruled out possible alternatives that the suspect may give to provide alibis or excuses for the evidence that was available. These findings led to the idea that an effective interview would rely on the following principles:

- Make use of internal pressure (as opposed to all forms of external pressure).
- Try to minimise eventual reluctance to provide an account (build rapport).
- Try to upgrade tactical clues (rule out alternatives).
- Challenge the account (when necessary).

In the GIS model investigators are encouraged to ask sets of open-ended questions around tactical clues. These questions serve to explore or rule out possible alternative explanations for these clues (realistic alternatives as well as excuses from the suspect), and, as such, can upgrade the value of the clue. After each questioning set, the suspect can be challenged with the particular clue. By ranking the clues from light to heavy and by starting with questions about the lightest clue first, the eventual reluctance to provide an account is believed to be lowered. As a guide during the interview, the detective should prepare him/herself by writing down the strategy applied to this particular suspect in this particular investigation in an interview table. Examples of such a table can be found both in van Beek and Hoekendijk (2015) and Van der Sleen (2009). An example is provided in Box 13.2.

The GIS model fits into the current paramount paradigm of the humanitarian, information-gathering approaches. It is related to models like Conversation Management (Shepherd and Griffiths, 2013), Strategic Use of Evidence (SUE) (Granhag and Hartwig, 2008) and Tactical Use of Evidence (TUE) (Dando and Bull, 2011). Although the GIS model itself has never been tested in a structured way (even the explorative study cited earlier is unpublished), research conducted using models like SUE and TUE along the concept of internal pressure (see, although partly differentially operationalized, Horgan *et al.*, 2012) seems to suggest some support for its potential effectiveness. Nevertheless, the GIS model would benefit from further research, particularly where it differs from the other models. For example, the SUE and TUE models are more aimed at lie detection and are therefore constructed to amplify the difference between truth-tellers and liars, although it is acknowledged that the amount of consistency in the suspect's story could be a key factor in detecting whether the suspect is lying or telling the truth. Regardless, the GIS is more aimed at truth-finding and therefore is, in theory, constructed in a manner that should open the way for a lying, guilty suspect to stop lying and open up.

Although Dutch detectives have been trained in the model since the beginning in 1989, its use was only catalysed after the 2005 improvement programme. Nierop and Mooij (2000) cite two small studies in the late 1990s regarding the use of the GIS model. The first study, in 1997, found only 27 per cent of the

Box 13.2 Example of the GIS model

A witness saw a car similar to the suspect's car at the crime scene, just before the crime took place. In the interview the interviewer will ask the suspect first what methods of transportation he uses. The interviewer then collects fine-grained details about, for example, the car and the bike of the suspect. He also asks whether, and, if so, to whom and when the suspect lent out his car and bike. The suspect might state he has never done so. The value of the witness account is upgraded now. When the suspect tells the interviewer he recently did lend out his car to someone, the detective can start asking questions about this person and then might stop the interview to first start an investigation into this person.

participating detectives stated they had at least once made an interview table. The second study, in 1998, found that in the Utrecht area 56 per cent of the respondents claimed (elements of) the GIS model (are) is used in complex cases. Lack of time, lack of knowledge and lack of motivation were the reasons mentioned in the latter study for not undertaking the GIS model.

Forced by the guidelines from the 2005 improvement programme to provide better accounts for the interview methods used and accompanied by the rising numbers of extra trained detectives, the model gradually seem to have received more acceptance in practice. At least, this is the impression the Police Academy of the Netherlands holds, based upon its evaluative contacts with the Dutch National Police. Vanderhallen *et al.* (2014) partly confirm this: a focus group of twelve participants (two tutors of the Police Academy, an investigative psychologist, three team leaders, two of them being interviewers as well, and six detectives) did disagree about whether or not 'trickery' still occurred every now and then, but they all agreed the 2005 programme 'inaugurated a new era' for Dutch interviewing practices.

On the other hand, based upon observing 95 Dutch suspect interviews, Blackstock *et al.* (2014) conclude most of the observed officers appeared *not* to have been trained in the GIS, although they did employ some of the GIS techniques. (Note Blackstock *et al.* refer to GIS as 'SIM'.) Unfortunately, two of the four techniques observed and mentioned by Blackstock *et al.* are, strictly speaking, not part of the GIS (seeking to win trust and appeal to emotions) while some of the more important techniques of GIS (e.g. encircling questions) are not mentioned, so it remains unclear whether or not detectives actually made use of them during the observed interviews.

All together, these findings do stress the importance of a systematic study of the actual current use of GIS in Dutch suspect interviews. In the absence of this kind of study, one might assume, in line with international findings, that although the rudiments of a model might be expected to be undertaken in most interviews, actual methods may vary (e.g. Bull and Soukara, 2010) and even many trained investigators might undertake interviews unsatisfactorily (Walsh and Bull, 2010).

Future directions

In relation to the investigative interviewing of suspects at least four future directions can be identified. Firstly, as discussed earlier in this chapter, the GIS model has never been independently tested. A full understanding of what aspect of what model works best in what situation is required, particularly where the GIS differs from models like SUE and TUE. Nor is it quite clear what the actual use is of the model in Dutch interviewing practices.

Secondly, it needs to be further examined what the effects are of the presence of a lawyer. European regulations (following the *Salduz* ruling) have meant that the Dutch inquisitorial justice system gives the lawyer more rights to intervene in order to respect the human rights of the suspect (Blackstock *et al.*, 2014; Ministerie van Veiligheid en Justitie, 2014). These regulations concern the presence of a lawyer during suspect interviews, where the general opinion, although not (yet) supported by research (Blackstock *et al.*, 2014), is that an increasing amount of suspects will remain silent when questioned because of the lawyer being present. Detectives do wonder whether it is worthwhile investing time in preparing and conducting interviews when there may be a real chance that the suspect will remain silent in which case the interviewer will not elicit any information. Further, when a suspect interview is still to be conducted, will there be a shift from an information-gathering approach to a more negotiation-like approach? Vanderhallen *et al.* (2014) have investigated these matters and, among other conclusions based upon previous developments in England and Wales and Belgium (where the *Salduz* ruling is already implemented), have suggested that the interviewing of suspects in the Netherlands will not lose its importance, but will 'evolve to a strategic "joust" between interviewers and lawyers'. After this first phase of apparent mutual distrust, they predict a second phase where both parties will come to a position that better serves the public interest. Vanderhallen *et al.* therefore advise the Dutch Ministry of Justice to support and facilitate the police to undergo this process.

A third aspect to be examined is cultural diversity. As a consequence of factors such as globalisation and growing diversity in Dutch society more suspects of non-Dutch origin are being interviewed as suspects (KLPD, 2009). This does raise the question whether the assumptions underlying the Dutch interviewing practices will apply equally to foreign suspects. Research indicates that the effectiveness of strategies being used in investigative interviewing may be dependent on the suspect's culture. Beune *et al.* (2011) showed rational arguments were effective for eliciting information from suspects originating from cultures that use content-oriented, direct communication (roughly speaking western cultures), whereas there was a trend for suspects originating from cultures that use context-oriented, indirect communication (roughly speaking non-western cultures) to provide more information to an interviewer making use of relational interventions (like active listening). More research is needed for a better understanding of what strategies may increase this cultural fit during interviews.

Finally, the matter of how best to coach interviewers needs to be further examined. Investigative interviewing of suspects is a highly complex cognitive task (Shepherd and Kite, 1988) that requires a skilled combination (Bull, 2014) of both avoiding negative feedback and appropriate revelation of incriminating information. It is also dynamic in nature (De Fruyt *et al.*, 2006, cited in Smets and Rispens, 2014): no two interviews are alike. As may be expected from this, interviewers benefit not just from appropriate training, but also from continued coaching on the job (Smets and Rispens, 2014). Although several initiatives are currently taking place in Dutch practice in order to secure ongoing professionalism, the field may benefit from scientific research addressed to questions such as examining what (combination of) coaching techniques works best.

Conclusion

Summarising the above-mentioned notions about the interviewing of suspects in the Netherlands seems to lead to the following conclusion: after some miscarriages of justice, including false confessions, at least a growing awareness can be observed in the Netherlands concerning the importance of having well skilled interviewers working with models which fit into a humanitarian and information-gathering approach. Whether or not this has substantially improved the quality of suspect interviews in the last decade is still inconclusive, while in the meantime new challenges are also emerging on the horizon.

Acknowledgements

The authors wish to thank Adri van Amelsvoort (freelance senior advisor of the Dutch National Police), Mark Bisschops (Dutch National Police), Imke Rispens (Police Academy of the Netherlands), Monique Scholten (Reed Business Information), Arend de Vries (Police Academy of the Netherlands) and all those other people involved for their support in the writing of this chapter.

Notes

1. In Dutch: Professioneel Verhoor (PV).
2. Being the nickname of the suspect: a man who used to sell ice creams.
3. In Dutch: Verhoor Kwetsbare Verdachten (VKV).
4. In Dutch: kalm en rijp beraad.
5. A tactical clue is defined as a piece of information with a source that might link the suspect to the case (Van Amelsvoort *et al*., 2015). The Dutch police uses the concept of tactical clues instead of pieces of evidence due to the Dutch inquisitorial criminal justice system: whether or not this information is (finally) perceived to be evidence is decided in court.
6. In general, suspect interviews in moderate to major crimes in the Netherlands are conducted by two detectives.
7. In Dutch: 'Hij die, getuige van het ogenblikkelijk levensgevaar waarin een ander verkeert, nalaat deze die hulp te verlenen of te verschaffen die hij hem, zonder gevaar voor zichzelf of anderen redelijkerwijs te kunnen duchten, verlenen of verschaffen kan, wordt, indien de dood van de hulpbehoevende volgt, gestraft met hechtenis van ten hoogste drie maanden of geldboete van de tweede categorie.'

References

Abbe, A. and Brandon, S. E. (2014) 'Building and maintaining rapport in investigative interviews', *Police Practice and Research: An International Journal*, 15: 207–20.

Beune, K., Giebels, E., Adair, W. L., Fennis, B. M. and van der Zee, K. I. (2011) 'Strategic sequences in police interviews and the importance of order and cultural fit', *Criminal Justice and Behavior*, 38: 934–54.

Blackstock, J., Cape, E., Hodgson, J., Ogorodova, A. and Spronken, T. (2014) *Inside Police Custody: An Empirical Account of Suspects' Rights in Four Jurisdictions*. Cambridge: Intersentia.

Bull, R. (2014) 'When in interviews to disclose information to suspects and to challenge them?', in R. Bull (ed.), *Investigative interviewing*. New York: Springer.

Bull, R. and Soukara, S. (2010) 'Four studies of what really happens in police interviews', in G. D. Lassiter and C. A. Meissner (eds), *Police Interrogations and False Confessions:*

Current Research, Practice and Policy Recommendations. Washington, DC: American Psychological Association, pp. 81–95.

Clément, S., Van de Plas, M., Van den Eshof, P. and Nierop, N. (2009) 'Police interviewing in France, Belgium and The Netherlands: something is moving', in T. Williamson, B. Milne and S. P. Savage (eds), *International Developments in Investigative Interviewing*. Cullompton: Willan, pp. 66–91.

Dando, C. J. and Bull, R. (2011) 'Maximising opportunities to detect verbal deception: training police officers to interview tactically', *Journal of Investigative Psychology and Offender Profiling*, 8: 189–202.

de Ruiter, R. and van Beek, M. L. J. (2014) 'Het bevorderen van de verklaringsbereidheid', in R. Schellingen and N. Scholten (eds), *Het verdachtenverhoor: meer dan het stellen van vragen*. Mechelen: Kluwer, pp. 163–81.

Granhag, P. A. and Hartwig, M. (2008) 'A new theoretical perspective on deception detection: on the psychology of instrumental mind-reading', *Psychology, Crime and Law*, 14: 189–200.

Hoekendijk, J. W. and van Beek, M. L. J. (2015) 'The GIS-model: a Dutch approach to gather information in suspect interviews', *Investigative Interviewing: Research and Practice,* 7(1), 1–9.

Horgan, A. J., Russano, M. B., Meissner, C. A. and Evans, J. R. (2012) 'Minimization and maximization techniques: assessing the perceived consequences of confessing and confession diagnosticity', *Psychology, Crime and Law*, 18: 65–78.

KLPD (2009) Landelijk Verdachtenbeeld 2009. http://www.politie.nl/binaries/content/assets/politie/documenten-algemeen/publicaties-archief/2010_17_landelijk_verdachtenbeeld_2009.pdf.

Ministerie van Justitie (2008) *Beantwoording vragen over het verhoren van kwetsbare verdachten*. Retrieved from: http://www.rijksoverheid.nl/documenten-en-publicaties/kamerstukken/2008/02/25/antwoorden-kamervragen-inzake-het-verhoren-van-kwetsbare-verdachten.html.

Ministerie van Veiligheid en Justitie (2014) *Besluit inrichting en orde politieverhoor*. Retrieved from: http://www.rijksoverheid.nl/documenten-en-publicaties/besluiten/2014/02/13/besluit-inrichting-en-orde-politieverhoor.html.

Nierop, N. M. and Mooij, A. J. M. (2000) *Het verdachtenverhoor in bijzondere zaken: de relatie tussen opleiding en praktijk*. Zoetermeer: KLPD.

Openbaar Ministerie (2005) *Versterking opsporing en vervolging*. Retrieved from: http://www.om.nl/algemene_onderdelen/uitgebreid_zoeken/@143544/rapport_versterking/.

Posthumus, F. (2005) *Evaluatieonderzoek in de Schiedammer parkmoord*. Retrieved from: http://www.om.nl/algemene_onderdelen/uitgebreid_zoeken/@143611/evaluatieonderzoek/.

Rispens, I. and Van der Sleen, J. (2015) 'Interviewing witnesses in the Netherlands', in D. Walsh, G. E. Oxburgh, A. D. Redlich and T. Myklebust (eds), *International Developments and Practices in Investigative Interviewing and Interrogation: Vol. 1 Victims and Witnesses*. London: Routledge.

Schoenmakers, Y., Hoekendijk, J. W. and van der Kruk, R. (2010) *Het vuur aan de schenen: seriematige brandstichtingen in de opsporing, een criminaliteitskundig onderzoek*. Apeldoorn: Politieacademie.

Shepherd, E. and Griffiths, A. (2013) *Investigative Interviewing: The Conversation Management Approach*. Oxford: Oxford University Press.

Shepherd, E. and Kite, F. (1988) 'Training to interview', *Policing*, 4: 264–80.

Smets, L. and Rispens, I. (2014) 'Investigative interviewing and training: the investigative interviewer apprentice', in R. Bull (ed.), *Investigative Interviewing*. New York: Springer, pp. 147–65.

Van Amelsvoort, A., Rispens, I. and Grolman, H. (2012) *Handleiding Verhoor*, 5th edn. Amsterdam: Stapel & De Koning.

Van Amelsvoort, A., Rispens, I. and Grolman (2015) *Handleiding Verhoor*, 6th edn. Doetinchem: Reed Business.

van Beek, M. L. J. and Hoekendijk, J. W. (2015) 'The interview table: a toolbox-approach for suspect interviewing', *Investigative Interviewing: Research and Practice,* 7(1), 10–20.

Van den Adel, H. M. (1997) *Handleiding Verdachtenverhoor: Handhaving, controle en opsporing in de praktijk*. The Hague: Vuga.

Van der Sleen, J. (2009) 'A structured model for investigative interviewing of suspects', in R. Bull, T. Valentine and T. Williamson (eds), *Handbook of Psychology of Investigative Interviewing*. Chichester: Wiley, pp. 35–52.

Van Koppen, P. J. (2003) *De Schiedammer parkmoord: een rechtspychologische reconstructie*. Nijmegen: Ars Aequi.

Van Koppen, P. J., Merckelbach, H., Jelicic, M. and de Keijser, J. W. (2010) 'Over de rechtspychologie', in P. J. van Koppen, H. Merckelbach, M. Jelicic and J. W. de Keijser (eds), *Reizen met mijn Rechter: Pyschologie van het Recht*. Deventer: Kluwer, pp. 1–11.

Vanderhallen, M., Vervaeke, G. and Holmberg, U. (2011) 'Witness and suspect perceptions of working alliance and interviewing style', *Journal of Investigative Psychology and Offender Profiling*, 8: 110–30.

Vanderhallen, M., de Jong, A., Nelen, H. and Spronken, T. (2014) *Rechtsbijstand en de waarde van het verhoor: Een studie naar de te verwachten gevolgen op de verklaringsbereidheid en de opsporing en bewijsvoering in strafzaken van het verlenen van rechtsbijstand voorafgaand en tijdens het verhoor*. Retrieved from: http://wodc.nl/onderzoeksdatabase/verhoor-en-verklaring-in-relatie-tot-andere-opsporingsmiddelen.aspx.

Visser, C. (2014) *25 progressiegerichte technieken*. Retrieved from: http://progressiegerichtwerken.nl/25-progressiegerichte-technieken/.

Walsh, D. and Bull, R. (2010) 'Interviewing suspects of fraud: an analysis of interviewing skills', *Journal of Psychiatry and Law*, 38: 99–135.

Walsh, D. and Bull, R. (2012) 'Examining rapport in investigative interviews with suspects: does its building and maintenance work?', *Journal of Police and Criminal Psychology*, 27: 73–84.

14 Interviewing suspects of crime in Portugal

Carlos Eduardo Peixoto, Alexandra Seabra and António Castanho

Introduction

Gathering information is a key step in criminal investigation. This is particularly relevant in the investigation of complex crimes, where information collection will set the pace and direction of the investigation process. Also, information collected will unveil other types of evidence that will, or will not, corroborate what we know. In crimes where sometimes there is no other type of evidence, the statement will be even more of a determinant of the criminal investigation success. For that reason, psychological research has collected data and developed tools to understand and collect information in a more efficient way and with better quality (Gudjonsson, 2003; Kassin, 2008; Lassiter and Meissner, 2010; Milne and Bull, 1999; Shepherd, 2007; Shepherd and Griffiths, 2013).

In this chapter we describe how the issue of suspect interrogation is dealt with in Portugal, the existing research and police training and practice, and we point to future challenges and developments in the Portuguese context.

Interview and interrogation in the Portuguese judicial system

Portuguese law, more specifically, the Portuguese Criminal Procedure Code (PCPC) defines testimony as key evidence. Therefore rules and restrictions have been established to guarantee that testimonies are collected properly. In fact, the PCPC indicates that procedures that contaminate memory are not allowed (Art. 126º 1.b), specifying that the use of suggestive questioning is not admissible. Also, the use of any kind of coercion, physical or moral offense, or the promise of legal advantages are examples of strategies that are not admissible in a criminal investigation in Portugal.

The interrogation of suspects of crime, for both adults and children, should be, by rule, carried out by a public prosecutor (PP). Nevertheless, the PCPC states that the PP can delegate this procedure to the police who are in charge of the criminal investigation. In practice, the suspect's first interview is conducted by the police. This interview is only admissible in a trial, and only if the PP or judge ("juiz de instrução") is present to monitor it.

With respect to young offenders, even though a specific law regulates this kind of criminal investigation (Educational Custody Law (LTE)[1]) the same general principles are applied concerning interrogation. Nevertheless, due to the offenders' age and the nature of the offense, the LTE states that during the investigative interview, the young suspect could be assisted and supported by a social worker or a psychologist.

In Portugal there is a long tradition of collecting testimonies in written statements. This registration method, in our opinion, has been the cause of several difficulties in the administration of justice, particularly in the criminal investigation phase. First, producing a written statement has the problem of altering the dynamic of an interview. In Portugal, most of the time the written document is produced at the same time, so the interviewer has to stop several times to write what the interviewee has said. This procedure has negative consequences, for example in rapport building and maintaining a free-recall narrative. Other times, police officers produce the written document at the end of the interview, reading it and then asking the interviewee to validate it. In this case, the risk of producing wrong information is high due to possible difficulties in memory, by the interviewer and interviewee, of the exact information given. Second, a written statement, with consecutive stops and dictation, increases the interview duration and, therefore, the criminal investigation duration. Third, the use of a written statement also does not allow a proper evaluation of the interview because the real interaction between interviewer and interviewee cannot be observed. In a written statement, for example, there are no transcriptions of the interviewer's questions. Therefore this does not allow the opportunity for self-evaluation and to identify training issues. Nonetheless, in 2013, a revision of the PCPC allowed criminal investigators to use video recording in interviews with witnesses and suspects (Law no. 20/2013, 21 February). This could be a key step in the development of forensic interviews in the Portuguese judicial context. Research has pointed to the important role that video recording of interviews has in the development of interview skills (Milne and Bull, 1992) and for the prevention of false confessions (Kassin *et al.*, 2014; Lassiter *et al.*, 2010).

Research on interview and interrogation practices

Suspect interviewing has not generally been a research topic in Portuguese scientific literature. Although there are some guidelines about how to interview crime suspects (MAI, 2013; Maia, 2013), and some recommendations on how to interview offenders in the context of a psychological evaluation (Braga and Gonçalves, 2011; Gonçalves *et al.*, 2011; Gonçalves and Dias, 2011), empirical research addressing interview techniques and protocols with this specific group is lacking. However, there's a rising interest in psychological processes that influence investigative interviewing. Recently there has been an increasing body of studies about suggestibility in adults (Cruz and Pinho, 2014; Pires *et al.*, 2013a, 2013b, 2014).

Pires and colleagues, after validating for the Portuguese population the Gudjonsson Suggestibility Scales (GSS1 and GSS2) (Pires *et al.*, 2013a), observed, in a sample of 258 subjects from the general population, the influence of individuals' personality styles in their suggestibility levels (Pires *et al.*, 2013b). Particularly, they found that individuals who have a personality style characterized by conventionality, self-control, lack of spontaneity and seeking to please others have a greater risk of being suggestible. These findings are confirmed in the existing literature (Gudjonsson, 2003).

In another study, Pires and colleagues (2014) found that a sample of Portuguese inmates were more prone to suggestibility than a general population sample. In their analysis they point to lower memory capacity as a possible explanation for the heightened suggestibility. Also, even among inmates with Antisocial Personality Disorder, high levels of cooperation with the task were found, which could explain a proneness to suggestibility. This high level of collaboration, according to the authors, could have been elicited by the initial instruction that the execution of the task would not have any consequences on their situation.

Portuguese psychological research has also begun to focus on interview techniques used in police investigations. For example, Paulo *et al.* (2013) highlight the importance of the cognitive interview (CI) in the criminal investigation context, and advocate its use in Portugal. The cognitive interview was developed by psychologists Edward Geiselman and Ron Fisher in the 1980s. Their objective was to enhance accuracy and increase the quality of eyewitnesses' statements by applying what they called "generally accepted scientific principles of memory" (Fisher *et al.*, 1989: 722).

Memory has a key role in the CI. The task of reporting an event triggers memory functioning, so to understand the interview contents, it is important to understand the basic principles of cognition and memory. One of the basic principles highlighted by the CI is the role of encoding mechanisms in the retrieval moment. Based on Tulving's studies (e.g. Tulving and Thomson, 1973), the CI procedure indicates that the interview should recreate the context when the event was encoded in memory. Specifically, according to Fisher and collaborators (1989), the interview should reintroduce the emotional and cognitive states and the physical conditions of the target event. Context reinstatement is one of the key CI techniques, and its use has demonstrated an increase in the information obtained (Hershkowitz *et al.*, 2001; Memon *et al.*, 2010). Encoding context is also important when the CI indicates that the interviewer should ask the interviewee to identify sensorial dimensions of the event. For example, the interviewer could ask for a description of smells or sounds heard during the target event. The interviewee should also be asked to retrieve information using a different perspective to the target event. Therefore the interviewee will be asked to describe the event chronologically and backwards, and from the perspective of another person present at the event (Fisher and Geiselman,1992). The CI also highlights social dynamics present in the interview context. Rapport-building as a way to diminish the emotional distress of the interviewee and motivate statements has a central role (Fisher and Geiselman,1992). Also, the interviewee will be motivated to take control of the interview, because he is the only one that can provide information about the event. He is the event's expert. As a communication rule, the CI procedure requests that the interviewee tell everything about the event (Fisher and Geiselman,1992). The interviewee should make a free recall statement about the event, describing all the details, even those that seem less important (Holliday *et al.*, 2009).

Research has demonstrated that the CI, when compared with a structured interview, obtains more reliable information. These findings have been achieved in experimental studies (Memon *et al.*, 2010), and in field studies (Fisher *et al.*, 1989). In a meta-analysis, Memon and collaborators (2010) advise that there still are few studies that share important characteristics with real criminal cases, like long periods of time between the event and the interview. Memon and collaborators (2010) also point out that few studies use real forensic interviewers with consolidated experience in the application of the CI.

In the Ministry of Internal Affairs (MAI) Police Handbook for domestic violence (2013) the issue of interviewing suspects is mentioned. General recommendations, such as observation of the suspect's behavior and emotional state, or suggesting the use of the cognitive interview (Fisher and Geiselman, 1992), are made. Although a full description of the cognitive interview is made in the manual, summarizing some of the underlying research, explaining the steps, and giving examples of questions, the specificity of its use with suspects is not developed.

Maia (2013), a criminal investigator and police trainer, has recently written a full description of the interview and interrogation techniques used by several Portuguese police forces. He states that interviewing, even in the context of a criminal investigation, is a communication process. As such, the interview is a bidirectional flow of information between the interviewer and interviewee. Thus Maia (2013) highlights the importance of non-verbal behavior as a way of communicating with the interviewee. So the interviewer, according to this author, should manage properly and intentionally distance from the interviewee (what he calls 'proxemics') as a way to assure success of the communication process. Other competences that the interviewer has to manage are the way he uses and understands body language and movements to express and comprehend emotional states (kinetics and paralanguage).

In his paper, Maia (2013) indicates that an important challenge in a suspect interview is the interviewee's lack of motivation to engage in the communication process, in other words to give relevant and true information. So the interviewer will have to use several techniques to enhance interviewee motivation. The author suggests the use of questions about neutral topics as an ice-breaker, and also as the way to assess the interviewee's initial motivation and emotional state. To establish rapport, Maia (2013) advises the use of facilitators and echo wording to transmit his focus and interest in the interviewee's message. To guarantee that the information is properly understood, the interviewer also should use clarification and the refocusing of questions, and summaries. Maia (2013) claims that the interviewer also has to use, in a strategic way, information previously collected, for example the evidence collected in other interviews, and confront the interviewee with it. The author states that confronting the interviewee sometimes makes him reassess and change his statement, giving more accurate and truthful information afterwards.

In his paper, Maia (2013) delineates what he calls the "Inverted Triangle Interview Model", a three-stage interview. In the first stage, the interviewer should use open-ended questions to get the interviewee to make a general description of the facts under investigation. In the second stage, the interviewer, using more direct questions, proceeds to a confirmation process of the information obtained. In the final stage, the interviewer will confront the interviewee with other information that is not congruent with what he (the suspect) has already given. Maia (2013) states that the usefulness of this model has been shown over several years of criminal investigation experience.

From analysis of the ideas presented by Maia (2013) and the interview model, important aspects of interviewing such as body language, rapport and the funnel approach to questioning are addressed. Interviewing is in fact a communication process (Hargie, 2006), and for a successful criminal investigation, understanding and managing questioning and paralanguage to motivate the interviewee and elicit information are determinant (Milne and Bull, 1999). Also, a confrontation phase in the interview, where the interviewer unveils some of his knowledge about the facts, could be useful and, sometimes, motivates a confession (Gudjonsson, 2003; Kassin and Gudjonsson, 2004). Nevertheless, Maia's paper does not address important topics such as memory research and its influence in interviewing (e.g. Fisher and Geiselman, 1992), the psychology of true and false confessions (e.g. Lassiter and Meissner, 2010), or research-grounded interview protocols like the PEACE Model (e.g. Milne and Bull, 1999). In fact, he states that the interview model and the principles that he proposes are mainly defined by his large experience as a criminal investigator and interviewer, and do not address any empirical research.

Police training and current practices

The police, as a formal institution to investigate crime and maintain public safety, have been established in Portugal since the seventeenth century (Fernandes, 2012). It came about at a time when the Inquisition still had jurisdiction, despite a decreasing political and judicial power (Marcocci and Paiva, 2013). Nevertheless, the police practices, at that time, adopted some of the Inquisition's investigation techniques, especially the use of torture, to elicit information and achieve a confession.

In the nineteenth century, police work was organized into specialized police forces: one with the responsibility of guaranteeing public safety in major urban areas, one working under the supervision of the Ministry of Justice and developing criminal investigation work, and one as a national militarized police force (Branco, 2010). These three police organizations were the predecessors of the three major police forces in Portugal: the Public Safety Police (PSP), the Judiciary Police (PJ), and the Republican National Guard (GNR).

Up until 1974, for the greater part of the twentieth century Portugal was characterized as a regime under dictatorship. Even though there were some important improvements in police training and work, for example with the creation of the first police training centers, in this period, the use of violence and torture was accepted and seen as necessary by the regime. The creation of a political police

(Policia Internacional e de Defesa do Estado (PIDE)) demonstrated that every kind of coercive strategy was permitted to obtain information and confessions (Pimentel, 2007).

Only in the mid-1980s and 1990s of the last century, following a progressive democratization of political and judicial institutions, were internal and external mechanisms implemented to supervise police work, specifically to eradicate the use of excessive force and coercive interrogation techniques (Fernandes, 2012).

As mentioned, there are three major police forces in Portugal that have a duty in criminal investigation: the PSP, the GNR and the PJ. The PSP and GNR have a wide range of police roles, and are under the government of the Ministry of Internal Affairs. Their duties are diverse and include roles such as guaranteeing public safety, patrol work, and the investigation of crimes that are not exclusively the role of the PJ.

The PJ is dedicated exclusively to criminal investigation, mainly of complex crimes, and is under the government of the Ministry of Justice. Crimes such as drug trafficking, corruption, terrorism, kidnapping, sexual crimes (including the sexual abuse of children), criminal association, and homicide are reserved for this police force. The PJ also has a role as the Portuguese interface with international organizations such as INTERPOL and EUROPOL.

Interrogation and interview techniques are topics present in the training of every police force in Portugal, but are further developed in the training of police officers who have criminal investigation duties. For criminal investigators from the PSP and GNR, interview training consists of a module of eight 50-minute sessions including issues such as: the legal framework for the interview; human communication; interview and interrogatory techniques; and motivation techniques. The module also has practical training in interview techniques. Special criminal investigation teams, such as the Specific Victims Intervention and Support Team (NIAVE) at the GNR, receive an updated course in interviewing for the specific crimes they investigate (e.g. domestic violence). However, after completing initial training in these specific criminal investigations, no additional training, supervision or feedback is given regarding interview techniques.

The PJ provides more extensive training in interview and interrogation techniques. Issues such as memory functioning and processes and the use of interview protocols such as the cognitive interview and the PEACE Model are taught. Criminal investigators in the PJ also seem to have some unstructured and sporadic training, such as supervision of and feedback on their interview techniques. It must be noted that the long tradition of testimony in the form of a written statement and the recent mandatory requirement to use video and audio recording, did not create the conditions for supervision and feedback policies in terms of investigative interviewing (see below).

Implications for research, policy, and practice

Research about investigative interview and interrogation of suspects is at an early stage in Portugal. Although there is a growing interest by the psychological scientific community demonstrated by the publishing of several papers (e.g. Paulo *et al.*, 2014) around the theme, or about central psychological processes (e.g. suggestibility) (e.g. Pires *et al.*, 2013), little effect has been seen in police training and practice. Through these developments, research has failed to tackle important issues, for example false confessions and the interrogation of young offenders. We also recommend that more applied research should be undertaken, with a focus on real cases and on real police interviews, instead of relying on an exclusively experimental methodology.

Nevertheless, it has to be said that, as seen above, police organizations have been struggling with a heavy history and prejudice from public opinion, in particular associating them with violence and coercive methods. Only at the end of the twentieth century did police organizations in Portugal have the necessary conditions, political and financial, to make necessary reforms. For example, the development of police training schools arose, with one such school providing a higher education degree in police work. At the same time, the creation of special criminal investigation units for complex crimes (e.g. domestic violence in the GNR and PSP; sexual crimes in the PJ) were important developments in the police organizations.

Although it seems that police officers have a good standard preparation for the conduct of investigative interviews, there is no clear evidence of its application in the field. There is almost no research about police practices in investigative interviewing in the field and the probable internal analysis about this issue is confidential. Our impression from real case practice tells us that police officers have serious difficulties implementing interview training, and most of the time use unstructured strategies based on experience (Maia, 2013). Also, it seems that there is no supervision of or feedback on police officers' performance – if it exists, it is not regularly provided. As said above, the recently amended statutes that disallowed video recording, along with a long tradition of written statements, in our opinion, did not provide a good context in which to develop a self- and peer/supervisor evaluation dynamic with regard to investigative interviewing.

We foresee that the coming years are going to be a time of great development in investigative interview and interrogation practices, fueled by scientific interest, the dynamics of police organization, and the necessity for evidence-based tools to gather information in the context of more complex crimes. The specialization of police work in terms of the investigative interview is inevitable. So, the creation of investigative interview expert teams and a culture of monitoring interview quality are crucial to the development and increased efficacy of police work in Portugal.

Acknowledgement

Carlos E. Peixoto is supported by the Portuguese Science and Technology Foundation (FCT) (PTDC/MHC-PAP/4295/2012) and by the Operational Program for Competitive Factors (COMPETE) (CCOMP-01-0124-FEDER-029554).

Note

1. This law only concerns offenders between the ages of 12 and 16 years. Over 16 the offender is treated as an adult and the Portuguese Penal Code and Criminal Procedure is applied.

References

Braga, T. and Gonçalves, R. A. (2011) "Avaliação psicológica de jovens ofensores," in M. Matos, R. A. Gonçalves, and C. Machado (), *Manual de psicologia forense: Contextos, práticas e desafios*. Braga: Psiquilibrios, pp. 271–92.

Branco, C. (2010) *Guarda Nacional Republicana – Contradições e Ambiguidades*. Lisbon: Edições Sílabo.

Cruz, M. P. and Pinho, M. S. (2014) "Sugestionabilidade em pessoas idosas: Um estudo com a Escala de Sugestionabilidade de Gudjonsson (GSS 1)," *Análise Psicológica*, 32 (2): 199–213.

Fernandes, L. F. (2012) "In search of a police system: from quadrilheiros to a democratic police system," in D. Palmer, M. M. Berlin, and D. K. Das (eds), *Global Environment of Policing*. Boca Raton, FL: CRC Press, pp. 77–96.

Fisher, R. P. and Geiselman, R. E. (1992) *Memory-enhancing Techniques for Investigative Interviewing: The Cognitive Interview*. Springfield, IL: Charles C. Thomas.

Fisher, R. P., Geiselman, R. E., and Amador, M. (1989) "Field test of the cognitive interview: enhancing the recollection of actual victims and witnesses of crime," *Journal of Applied Psychology*, 74 (5): 722–7.

Gonçalves, R. A. and Dias, A. R. (2011) "Avaliação psicológica de agressores sexuais," in M. Matos, R. A. Gonçalves, and C. Machado (eds), *Manual de psicologia forense: Contextos, práticas e desafios*. Braga: Psiquilibrios, pp. 223–46.

Gonçalves, R. A., Cunha, O., and Dias, A. R. (2011) "Avaliação psicológica de agressores conjugais," in M. Matos, R. A. Gonçalves, and C. Machado (eds), *Manual de psicologia forense: Contextos, práticas e desafios*. Braga: Psiquilibrios, pp. 247–70.

Gudjonsson, G. H. (2003) *The Psychology of Interrogations and Confessions*. Chichester: John Wiley & Sons.

Hargie, O. (2006) *Handbook of Communication Skills*. New York: Routledge.

Hershkowitz, I., Orbach, Y., Lamb, M. E., Sternberg, K. J., and Horowitz, D. (2001) "The effects of mental context reinstatement on children's accounts of sexual abuse," *Applied Cognitive Psychology*, 15 (3): 235–48.

Holliday, R., Brainerd, C. J., Reyna, V. F., and Humphries, J. E. (2009) 'The cognitive interview: research and practice across the lifespan," in R. Bull, T. Valentine, and T. Williamson (eds), *Handbook of Psychology of Investigative Interviewing*. Chichester: Wiley-Blackwell, pp. 137–60.

Kassin, S. M. (2008) "False confessions causes, consequences, and implications for reform," *Current Directions in Psychological Science*, 17 (4): 249–53.

Kassin, S. M. and Gudjonsson, G. H. (2004) "The psychology of confessions: a review of the literature and issues," *Psychological Science in the Public Interest*, 5 (2): 33–67.

Kassin, S. M., Kukucka, J., Lawson, V. Z., and DeCarlo, J. (2014) "Does video recording alter the behavior of police during interrogation? A mock crime-and-investigation study," *Law and Human Behavior*, 38 (1): 73–83.

Lassiter, G. D. and Meissner, C. A. (eds) (2010) *Police Interrogations and False Confessions: Current Research, Practice, and Policy Recommendations*. Washington, DC: American Psychological Association.

Lassiter, G. D., Ware, L. J., Lindberg, M. J., and Ratcliff, J. J. (2010) "Videotaping custodial interrogations: toward a scientifically based policy," in G. D. Lassiter and C. A. Meissner (eds), *Police Interrogations and False Confessions: Current Research, Practice, and Policy Recommendations*. Washington, DC: American Psychological Association, pp. 143–60.

Maia, A. (2013) "Técnicas de entrevista e interrogatório em investigação criminal," *Revista do Ministério Público*, 135: 107–38.

Marcocci, G. and Paiva, J. P. (2013) *História da Inquisição Portuguesa 1526–1821*. Lisbon: A Esfera dos Livros.

Memon, A., Meissner, C. A., and Fraser, J. (2010) "The cognitive interview: a meta-analytic review and study space analysis of the past 25 years," *Psychology, Public Policy, and Law*, 16 (4): 340–72.

Milne, R., and Bull, R. (1999) *Investigative Interviewing: Psychology and Practice*. Chichester: Wiley.

Ministério da Administração Interna (MAI) (2013) *Manual de Policiamento da Violência Doméstica*. Lisbon: MAI.

Paulo, R. M., Albuquerque, P. B., and Bull, R. (2013) "The enhanced cognitive interview: towards a better use and understanding of this procedure," *International Journal of Police Science and Management*, 15 (3): 190–9.

Pimentel, I. F. (2007) *A História da PIDE*. Lisbon: Círculo de Leitores.

Pires, R., Silva, D. R., and Ferreira, A. S. (2013a) "Personality styles and suggestibility: a differential approach," *Personality and Individual Differences*, 55 (4): 381–6.

Pires, R., Silva, D. R., and Ferreira, A. S. (2013b) "Portuguese adaptation of the Gudjonsson Suggestibility Scales (GSS1 and GSS2): empirical findings," *Personality and Individual Differences*, 54 (2): 251–5.

Pires, R., Silva, D. R., and Ferreira, A. S. (2014) "The Portuguese adaptation of the Gudjonsson Suggestibility Scale (GSS1) in a sample of inmates," *International Journal of Law and Psychiatry*, 37 (3): 289–94.

Shepherd, E. (2007) *Investigative Interviewing: The Conversation Management Approach*. Oxford: Oxford University Press.

Shepherd, E. and Griffths, A. (2013) *Investigative Interviewing: The Conversation Management Approach*, 2nd edn. Oxford: Oxford University Press.

Tulving, E. and Thomson, D. M. (1973) "Encoding specificity and retrieval processes in episodic memory," *Psychological Review*, 80: 352–73.

15 Investigative interviewing of suspects in Scandinavia

Ivar A. Fahsing, Kristina Kepinska Jakobsen and Harriet Jakobsson Öhrn

Introduction

Scandinavia consists of Denmark, Sweden, and Norway which are all highly stable welfare societies with very low crime rates and high levels of transparency. Indeed, the three Scandinavian countries do generally have very much in common socially, politically, and culturally. This is true also when it comes to policing, legislation, and criminal investigation practices. When it comes to the practice of interviewing of suspects, however, there appears to be more dissimilarity than one should expect. After some serious public scandals of miscarriage of justice in Norway in the 1990s the Norwegian police service introduced a national program for investigative interviewing heavily influenced by the British process (Granhag *et al.*, 2014). Hence, confession-based interrogation techniques were identified, warned against publicly (Rachlew, 2003), and replaced with scientifically based methods like conversation management and strategic use of evidence (Fahsing and Rachlew, 2009). Interestingly, more than ten years later no similar process of change from within the police service has been identified in either Denmark or Sweden. The present chapter will seek to identify and explore some factors that might explain these apparent differences. It will be held that it is not due to the lack of available and relevant knowledge, nor public scandals in any of the three countries (Fahsing and Rachlew, 2009; Jakobsson Öhrn and Nyberg, 2009; Politiets videncenter, 2012).

Legislation and organization of criminal investigations

The legislation with regard to criminal law and criminal procedures law is quite similar across the region. Criminal investigations shall be characterized by so-called objectivity, which practically means that all circumstances both in favor of and against a suspect shall be explored. The investigators must also show discretion and not unnecessarily expose the suspect to suspicion. Investigations shall be conducted promptly for the sake of an effective clear-up of the crime, but also for the safety of the suspect. It is forbidden to use means such as false information, promises, and threats or force in order to elicit a confession or a particular statement. A record shall be kept of matters of importance to the investigation and interviews shall be written down straightaway. The interviewee is given the opportunity to check, adjust, and sign before the interview is filed. Sound and video recordings are not obligatory, but if used, they can be written down literally or in summary. In Sweden and Norway it is recommended that all interviews in serious crimes should be taped and the recordings saved, whereas in Denmark there are no such national guidelines. The rights to a fair trial and the presumption of innocence until proven guilty imply the duties to inform the suspect of the nature of the suspicion, the grounds for arrest and the right to free counsel. All this is done routinely in all of the three countries.

Concerning the right to silence all suspects in Denmark and Norway are routinely informed of this right prior to interview. Until recently this was not common practice in Sweden and it was not required by Swedish legislation before June 2014. Nowadays, suspects must be informed that they have the right to refrain from making any comment concerning the matter they are being questioned about. In all three countries the prosecution service is formally responsible for leading the preliminary investigation from the time when someone can reasonably be suspected of an offense. In Denmark and Norway parts of the prosecution service are integrated in the police organization, while in Sweden it is entirely separate. The way that the responsibility for practical investigations is organized in the daily service varies between the countries and sometimes even from case to case. The court procedure in the three countries is predominantly adversarial but with inquisitorial elements. Fact-finding is primarily the parties' responsibility, but the court can demand further investigation, although not outside of the formal charge put forward by the prosecution service. All evidence is presented orally and directly to the court.

When it comes to investigative methods, including interviewing, none of the countries have produced a specific national code of conduct based on available research and the principles of investigative interviewing; nevertheless these investigative methods can be relatively detailed and sound guidance is given in various forms of legislative documents. Traditionally though, much of the practical responsibility for how to go about the task has been left up to the individual officer. This might be due to an apparently a high level of public trust in the police service in general and therefore methods applied in police interviews have not traditionally been questioned in court – or elsewhere. However, some 18 years ago the public trust in the police was to be questioned in Norway following the dramatic murder case of a young woman on the west coast. This case and its subsequent implications will be discussed below.

Norway

The Norwegian police force suffered a major setback in 1997. A young man was acquitted by the Crown court for a murder to which he previously had confessed. The disputed confession was elicited by a detective who, at the time, was regarded as one of the best interviewers in Norway. He worked as a homicide detective at the National Norwegian Criminal Investigation Service, a unit whose professionalism had never been challenged in any serious way. Court-appointed forensic experts from England concluded that the style of interviewing seemed heavily influenced by the same philosophy underlying in the North American literature on interrogation where manipulation and various tricks were employed with one goal in mind: to obtain a confession.

The case revealed that the Norwegian police service had little formal expertise within the field of investigative interviewing and forensic psychology. As a consequence, the Norwegian police offered full sponsorship for two detectives, enabling them to undertake forensic MSc courses in England the following years. The first dissertation (Rachlew, 1999) was specifically designed as a white paper, facilitating the first, national investigative interviewing training program (KREATIV). Rachlew's dissertation documented that Norwegian police officers had little or no training in investigative interviewing. Their skills were based on experience and observational learning, placing them at the "survival level" identified in England and Wales approximately ten years earlier (Shepherd and Kite, 1988). Furthermore, the majority of the few texts available in Norwegian regarding investigative interviewing were written by police officers and classified as "police only" material. A subsequent review of these texts (Rachlew, 2003) confirmed the discouraging picture drawn up by the forensic experts in the murder trial. The texts, all written in an advisory form by experienced police officers at the time recognized as the most skillful interviewers in the nation, were dominated by a manipulative, confession-focused approach:

> You use your influence to "soften him up" from the very beginning … You control who he is allowed to have contact with, and in that way prevent him receiving psychological support from others. (Kripos, 1998)

It seems evident that the European Committee for the Prevention of Torture and Inhuman or Degrading Treatment or Punishment (CPT) never had access to these "secret" documents. Nevertheless, in the 1990s, the CPT repeatedly expressed concerns with suspect interviews in Norway. It was reported that "officers routinely seek to put pressure upon inmates subject to restrictions, by suggesting, that restrictions could be eased or lifted if they began to provide information which would assist the police investigation. A number of police officers with whom the delegation spoke indicated that these allegations were not unfounded" (CPT, 2000). Detained persons met by the CPT expressed the belief that "the purpose of restrictions was to exert psychological pressure on them, that restrictions were most common when the police had a weak case and that, even if it had not been explicitly stated by the police, restrictions would be eased or lifted in response to co-operation with the police" (CPT, 1997).

Based upon the experiences from England and Wales, a revision of practice was initiated from within the Norwegian police force. With support from Oslo police district, the National Norwegian Criminal Investigation Service and the Director of Public Prosecutions, a national, investigative interviewing training course was commissioned by the National University College in 2002, based on a pilot training program (KREATIV), heavily influenced by the British PEACE course (see Milne and Bull, 1999, and Shepherd and Griffiths, 2013, for an explanation of the PEACE model). Professor Ray Bull from England, Professor Pär-Anders Granhag from Sweden and DCI (retired) David Murthwaite (Merseyside Police, England) were brought to Norway to help train the trainers and initiate the program.

The trainers were recruited from within the police force and, since 2001, approximately 100 officers have completed the six-week trainers course, covering topics such as pedagogy, human rights, ethical interviewing, interview and communication skills (the PEACE model), eyewitness memory, cognitive interviewing, interview strategies, and false confessions.

In an attempt to prevent the problems identified by Milne and Bull (1999), who reported that some trainers in England had to train others in the model having only just completed a training course themselves, scholars were brought in. Hence, international scholars have assisted in the training of the trainers in Norway.

The trainers are encouraged to improvise and exemplify their lessons when delivering the course in the field. However, to ensure consistency and prevent another problem identified in England and Wales, where some areas were downplayed while others were overemphasized (Shaw, 2001), the Norwegian trainers are provided with a presentation package of 22 short but mandatory PowerPoint lessons. These are evaluated on a yearly basis by the trainers and updated by scholars in an attempt to keep KREATIV up to date with the scientific developments within the field. Again drawing upon experiences from England and Wales, managers were trained first to facilitate ownership, supervision and organisational changes (see Stockdale, 1993).

The KREATIV course is, in line with Baldwin's conclusions (1993), pitched at a "down-to-earth" level, free from any psychologically advanced techniques, and has now been delivered to almost two thousand detectives, NCOs, and members of the prosecution service. As is the original PEACE course, the KREATIV course is a five-day, intensive training program with mandatory reading of literature in advance. This program is now an integral part of basic police education for all Norwegian police officers – the Bachelor's program in Policing.

From 2013 KREATIV level 2 was introduced as a formal education program (10 ECTS[1]) further enhancing the underpinning knowledge and core methodological skills. An internal evaluation identified a further need for focusing on general skills rather than specific specialization in enclosed fields. A plan for such a development into a more specialized level 3 is under development.

Electronic recording of police interviews are becoming increasingly common in Norway. The Director of Public Prosecutions (Prosecutor General) has strongly recommended that the police to tape interviews of suspects and key witnesses in all serious cases.

Research

Interestingly, there is no research on what actually happens in police interviews with suspects in Norway. This stands in stark contrast to the evident process of change within the Norwegian police over the last 15 years. One reason for this might be that the necessary need for change and development was already documented and described in comprehensive expert testimonies in the Birgitte Tengs-case by Gisli Gudjonsson and Barrie Irving (see Gudjonsson, 2003) and detailed official inquiries, such as in the Fritz Moen case (Justisdepartementet, 2007). The situation in Norway has been seen as almost an analog to what happened in England and Wales ten years earlier and therefore most of the British research and advice was applied directly in the development and implementation of KREATIV. Although this was sufficient for starting up a process of change there is now an apparent need for: (1) a more detailed knowledge about what happens in police interviews after the introduction of KREATIV; and (2) how the concepts applied from laboratory research can be further developed and refined in practical settings.

Denmark

As was seen in Norway, Denmark has experienced several cases of miscarriage of justice. But in contrast to what has happened in other countries it has not led to as much attention from the media or the general public with regard to how the police conduct their interviews. This may well be the reason why the Danish police have not yet been forced to make changes in their interview concept.

While not all the details of relevant cases are known to the authors of this chapter the impression is, however, that at least one of the cases to some extent to be linked to the way the police interview was conducted. The suspect was a young mentally disabled person who confessed to a serious sex crime during police interviews. Two years later, a DNA test proved his innocence and another man was convicted for the crime. As a consequence of this case, the Director for Public Prosecutions developed new guidelines for the interviewing of persons with mental disabilities. The guidelines stress that the defense lawyer as a rule ought to be present during the interview to ensure that the suspect does not confess in order to satisfy the detective.

As described above in Norway, high-profile police officers have actively and publicly promoted a need for change. This has not been the case in Denmark. On the contrary, some high-profile detectives have promoted a traditional way of dealing with suspects in interviews. One example is the introduction of a modified version of the nine-step confession-oriented "Reid model" in the training courses that were in place from 2010 to 2015. Also, a retired well-known detective from the national homicide squad published a book in 2011 titled *He Made the Murderers Confess* (Christensen, 2011). In the book Christensen writes about his experiences with interviewing suspects and describes several confession-focused techniques. While the book is not used as part of the basic training curriculum, the author was until his retirement in 2012 often used as a teacher at training programs on investigation and interviewing. Likewise, another high-ranking officer still in service and also with a background in the national homicide squad has recently published a book about his career in which he openly states that his approach to interviewing suspects was to tell the suspect that the only way out of suspicion was to fully cooperate with the police and lay all details on the table (Isager-Nielsen, 2012). No emphasis was seemingly put on the presumption of innocence and the right to silence. On the other hand, in 2013, another retired high-profile chief inspector published a book in which he discussed the lack of research, education, and debate in the field of investigative interviews in Denmark. He recommended that the Danish Police replace the confession-focused approach with a more information-gathering approach (Bonnichsen, 2012).

In 2014, the basic police officer education was raised to the level of Bachelor's degree delivered by the national police academy. Interview training is part of students' 3 ECTS education in investigation. According to the syllabus, the approach is inspired by the Norwegian KREATIV model and the cognitive interview (Fisher and Geiselman, 1992). With regard to the interviewing of suspects, though, the approach has not yet been described as planning is still in process. Prior to the revision of the police officer education, training in interviewing suspects mainly focused on the rules governing police interviews and how to write down a formal statement. Training materials were compiled internally by police officers and hence were not based on research.

A one-week training course in interviewing was introduced in 2005 by the Police Academy in close collaboration with the national commissioner in Denmark and a psychologist with a Master's degree in investigative interviewing. In contrast to KREATIV the course focused solely on interviewing witnesses and victims. Hence a tactical model for suspect interviews such as the SUE technique (see Hartwig, 2005) was not introduced. The training courses involved some discussion of interviewing of suspects, depending on the trainers' personal opinions and experience in the field. In some of these training courses, a modified model of Reid's nine-step model was introduced. At other times, the focus was solely on cognitive interviewing techniques. The training course was meant to be followed up by a suspect interview training package – a plan, however, that has still not been realized. In 2010, the responsibility for conducting postgraduate training was decentralized to local police authorities and the central training program was terminated.

Following this delegation to the local police authorities the focus and length of the training practices seems to vary greatly. Some districts have included interviewing techniques in other training programs, spending two hours on this issue. Other local authorities have chosen to put in place a four-day training program. In 2014, the National Police Board initiated a project that is to explore the current situation and future training needs. Furthermore, the intention is to draw on experiences from other countries, especially from the UK and Norway. The project is expected to result in new training programs that are due in the imminent future.

As stated above, it is not mandatory to record interviews with adult suspects in Denmark. Recording is, however, permissible as long as the interviewee is informed that the recording is taking place. No general official policy on recording exists and the use of recording is not widespread.

Research

Suspect interview techniques have not been subject to systematic research in Denmark. The only known study was carried out for the Police Service in 2010 by one of the authors of the present chapter (Politiets Videncenter, 2012). Being the very first study of suspect interviews in Denmark, the aim was to establish better knowledge of the current practice. In line with previous studies from the UK (Baldwin, 1993; Clarke and Milne, 2001) little evidence was found of any clear methodological approach to the task. The interviewees were not given the opportunity to give their own free account. The interviewers mainly posed closed or leading questions with very few open questions. On the other hand, evidence of widespread use of confession-based techniques was not found. This study, however, is tainted by the fact that the researcher was not granted free access to all interviews. Hence the interviews in the study might not have been representative. The study was meant to be followed up by further research. These plans, however, were terminated by the Danish Police Knowledge and Research Center in 2012.

A description of the current situation with regard to the interviewing of suspects is difficult to give due to the lack of research, formal existing education programs and the pending status of the development projects. The Danish police have not been officially warned against a confession-oriented approach in suspect interviews, nor has a more information-gathering approach been promoted. It is the impression, however, that both approaches do exist. The newly established Bachelor's level education seems to have led to a recognized need for updated postgraduate training programs and guidelines.

Sweden

In March 2005 a woman was stabbed to death in her home. Her partner Tommie Karim called the police saying that he had seen a man with a blood-stained knife in their flat. The police found this improbable and Karim was arrested and detained in custody for nearly three months. Despite the fact that at the crime scene a blood smear from an unknown man was found mixed up with the victim's blood, the interviewers seemed to have already made up their minds and showed no interest in Karim's story. They repeatedly interrupted him, presented their own accusations as the truth and put strong emotional pressure on him. Karim remained the prime suspect for six months, until the actual killer committed another murder and in interviews admitted that he also killed Karim's partner. Karim identified the new suspect in a photo line-up as the man he had seen and his original story was eventually confirmed. The case was reported to the Swedish Parliamentary Ombudsman for contravening the principle of objectivity and use of forbidden means in order to elicit a confession. The Ombudsman did not find the interviews unlawful, but questioned the appropriateness of the methods (Fahsing and Rachlew, 2009; Jakobsson Öhrn and Nyberg, 2009).

In 1991 a man called Thomas Quick committed a violent robbery and was sentenced to secure psychiatric care. In therapy he confessed to having committed about thirty murders. The following legal process resulted in eight convictions of murder during the years 1994–2001. According to the courts' findings Quick's detailed accounts were supported by other facts and he was found guilty despite the lack of forensic evidence. The courts also considered Quick's earlier criminal record. He had a previous conviction for rape and had been diagnosed with suffering from a severe personality disorder with sexually deviant and sadistic behavior. His current psychiatrist affirmed that Quick still suffered from these disorders. Quick was described in the media as Sweden's worst serial killer. However, doubts about his guilt were raised and he was said to be a compulsive liar. In 2008 Quick withdrew his confessions during an interview with a journalist (SOU, 2015; Råstam, 2012). New legal processes in 2010–13 freed Quick from all charges. The prosecutors found contradictions in the material and pointed out that the gradual accuracy of Quick's statements could be a result of information from the media, suggestive therapy, and hints from the investigators. The Director of Public Prosecutions called the case a miscarriage of justice, unique in Swedish law history. In 2013 the government appointed a commission with instructions to examine the actions of the judicial system and the psychiatric care in order to find out if any structural shortcomings had occurred. Even though malpractice linked to the interviewing of suspects seems to have been an important factor in both of the above mentioned cases, no substantial changes in official guidelines or training programs regarding investigative interviewing have so far been proposed in Sweden.

The government commission was published in spring 2015 and it points out several fundamental weaknesses in how the so-called Thomas Quick (Sture Bergwall) investigations had not been loyal to the principles of objectivity and contradiction. Facts had been added, twisted, leaked or systematically held back both before the suspect and the courts. Consequently, the commission recommends the government to consider substantial changes in interview and general investigative methodology to ensure a better use of the principals of innocence, objectivity and contradiction both in criminal investigations and in court hearings (SOU, 2015). Substantial changes both in laws and procedures are therefore due in the near future. The general conclusions do seeming also apply to Norway since the Norwegian police and prosecution service was heavily involved in some of the investigations.

The Police Academy is responsible for the basic training of police officers and for the further national training of police officers (and civilian staff). Police training takes place at three locations: the National Police Academy in Solna, Stockholm, and the police programs at Umeå University (northern Sweden) and Linnaeus University (southern Sweden). The Swedish government has decided to keep the undergraduate format for basic training despite recommendations from official reports (SOU, 2008: 39). Two national courses in advanced interviewing have been carried out at the Swedish National Police Academy: a three-week course in 1996–2003 and a five-week course in 2004–11. The latest national course was inspired by research-based methods for investigative interviewing such as the PEACE model and the cognitive interview. These courses, however, have now been closed down due to budget cuts and the responsibility for such training has been handed over to the local police authorities.

In contrast to Norway and Denmark, Sweden has a long tradition of research in forensically applied social sciences the presentation of which is beyond the scope of this short chapter. Only an extract of some of the most relevant findings are therefore discussed below. Long before the debate surrounding suspect interviews arose in Norway Swedish research pointed out the dangers linked to communicative asymmetries and dominance of the police perspective in interviews with suspects. The suspects had the opportunity to tell their story, but it was found that the interviewers selectively encouraged some and ignored other information (Trankell, 1972; Jönsson, 1988). Similarly, in studies conducted by Holmberg and Christianson (2002) and Holmberg (2004) men convicted of murder or sexual offences reported their experiences of police interviews. Two kinds of attitudes were found: one was a dominant attitude in which the interviewer was perceived as aggressive and impatient; the other was described by the researchers as a humanitarian attitude, where the interviewer was perceived as cooperative and helpful. The dominant attitude was mainly associated with denial of crime, while the humanitarian attitude was significantly associated with admission (when such an attitude was apparent in the interview interviewees reported that they felt better about the interview). Holmberg (2004, 2009) connects these findings to the concept of therapeutic jurisprudence, which implies promotion of the individual's well-being in order to minimize damage and facilitate rehabilitation. Similarly, Jakobsson Öhrn (2005, 2008) analyzed a series of police interviews with a suspect and found that an empathetic approach by the interviewer stimulated communication while a change towards a more confession-oriented style broke it down.

Furthermore, Kronkvist (2013) has explored the investigative process through the analysis of a homicide case and interviews with police investigators. He found that open information-gathering and humanitarian attitudes were predominant in the interviews, all in line with the attitudes the investigators had expressed. However, Kronkvist (2013) also found evidence for the existence of dominant attitudes and the presence of a "thousand question technique," never mentioned by the investigators but characterized by a large number of questions about details in rapid succession.

In order to create opportunities to separate truth from deception, the interviewing method SUE – Strategic Use of Evidence – has been developed (Hartwig, 2005). The method takes its point of departure from the different strategies used by guilty and innocent persons. If suspects at an early stage are informed about the evidence gained in the investigation, it is likely that guilty and innocent suspects will give similar explanations of their innocence. If the interviewer instead asks questions from the investigative material without revealing the evidence, it is likely that innocent suspects are more prone to give information in line with evidence, while guilty suspects to a greater extent give answers that are contrary to evidence (Hartwig *et al.*, 2007).

In a recently published report ordered by the National Police Board (Granhag *et al.*, 2014) compared suspect interview training in Sweden, the Netherlands, England and Wales, and Norway and concluded that Sweden, unlike the other countries, lacks national coordination and guidelines for training. They suggest the establishment of a general model for interviews with suspects. Swedish research, with its focus on explorations of factors that influence the possibility of gaining reliable information, could contribute to further development of such a model.

Public scandals have not formed a basis for change in Sweden and, interestingly, the Norwegian Police seem to have implemented much more of the knowledge derived from Swedish research. Nevertheless, the need for a discussion of appropriate investigative methods has been pointed out. The Chancellor of Justice concluded in a report that the most important learning from such cases is that it is not only what is done, but *how* it is done, that is crucial.

Conclusion

Even though the cases presented above are not representative of all Scandinavian investigations, it is alarming that they occur at all. In societies with high ideals of justice, it would be expected that some measures would be taken to prevent recurrences. This has seemingly only happened in Norway, even though there are emerging signs of change in both Sweden and Denmark. What can explain these differences between three countries which normally share and cooperate much in the development of the public sector?

All three countries have had public scandals linked to investigative interviewing of suspects. However, the dimensions and implications of the two most famous Norwegian cases was much bigger than the cases in Sweden and Denmark. First of all, the suspect in the Birgitte-Tengs[2] case was convicted at the first court hearing. The fact that he had retracted his initial confession was merely seen as an act to cover up his guilt. His defense lawyers viewed it differently and got the court's approval to assign two of Britain's most influential researchers on interrogation, techniques of manipulation, and false confessions. The result was that the suspect was found not guilty and the Norwegian police were left with humiliation and embarrassment. The second case was, if possible, even more tragic since the suspect, who was deaf, had already served 18 years of his sentence when his innocence was proved. In the following public inquiry his alleged confession and following conviction were defined as a combination of police incompetence in the interviewing of vulnerable suspects and a court case made up of a chain of speculative interpretations of evidence. This was another major blow to the confidence in the Norwegian police and their ability to handle difficult suspect interviews in a professional manner. Both cases were surrounded by massive media attention and indeed were tragic enough in themselves to promote change. However, the public and juridical backdrop created after two previous Norwegian criminal cases, namely the Fasting Torgersen-case[3] and the Liland-case,[4] had already weakened public trust in the Norwegian police and prosecution service. Denmark has not had a public scandal of such dimensions, nor had Sweden until the Thomas Quick scandal emerged.

Another critical issue is how the police organizations have responded to criticism following cases of miscarriage of justice. The top-level management in the Norwegian police acknowledged the lack of updated knowledge by funding Master's degrees in forensic psychology at British universities for one detective from the Oslo police force and one from the National Criminal Investigation

Service (KRIPOS). Not only were the detectives allowed to gather new knowledge abroad, but their ideas for implementing the knowledge in the organization through a compulsory training package inspired by the PEACE model was also backed up from the top-level management both in the police and the prosecution service. This visionary and humble approach taken by the Norwegian Police has not been identified in either Denmark or Sweden. In Denmark the abovementioned scandal has had little, if any, practical impact on the organization. In Sweden the harsh conclusions in the governmental appointed report on the Thomas Quick-scandal (SOU, 2015) will probably bring about some fundamental changes, perhaps even in neighboring Norway. The nature and magnitude of these changes on investigative interviewing remains to be seen. In the abovementioned Tommie Karim case the managers in charge defended their confession-oriented interviews on national TV in the aftermath of the scandal.

Another factor involved might be the fact that the Norwegian Police Academy was organized into a Police University College with its own department for research in the mid-1990s. This development might have reduced a somewhat institutionalized skepticism among the police towards academic knowledge and thus indirectly facilitated a movement towards more scientifically based interview methods in the Norwegian police. Thus, while Norway transformed the basic police training into a Bachelor's level program in 1995, this is still not the case in Sweden, while the Danish Bachelor's degree program was accredited only in 2013. As a final remark it should be kept in mind that it is seemingly not the access to relevant knowledge regarding scientifically based interview methods which explains the differences among the Scandinavian countries, but rather differences in the willingness to grasp it.

Notes

1. The European Credit Transfer and Accumulation System (ECTS) is a standard for comparing the attainment and performance of students of higher education across the European Union and other collaborating European countries and is used to facilitate transfer and progression throughout the Union. For successfully completed studies, ECTS credits are awarded. One academic year corresponds to 60 ECTS credits equivalent to 1,500–1,800 hours of study in all countries irrespective of standard or qualification type.
2. Birgitte Tengs – see: http://en.wikipedia.org/wiki/List_of_miscarriage_of_justice_cases#Norway.
3. Frederik Fasting Torgersen – see: http://en.wikipedia.org/wiki/Fredrik_Fasting_Torgersen.
4. Per Liland – see: http://en.wikipedia.org/wiki/Liland_Affair.

References

Baldwin, J. (1993) "Police interview techniques – establishing truth or proof?" *British Journal of Criminology*, 33: 325–51.

Bonnichsen, H.-J. (2012) *Tvivl på alt og tro på meget. Jagten på sandheden – politiets afhøringsmetoder*. Copenhagen: Rosinate.

Christensen, T. (2011) *Han fikk morderne til at tilstå*. Copenhagen: Lindhardt & Ringhof.

Clarke, C. and Milne, R. (2001) *National Evaluation of the PEACE Investigative Interviewing Course*, Police Research Award Scheme, Report No. PRSA 149. London: Home Office.

CPT (1997) *Report to the Norwegian Government on the visit to Norway carried out by the European Committee for the Prevention of Torture and Inhuman or Degrading Treatment or Punishment (CPT) from 17 to 21 March 1997*. Strasbourg: Council of Europe.

CPT (2000) *Report to the Norwegian Government on the visit to Norway carried out by the European Committee for the Prevention of Torture and Inhuman or Degrading Treatment or Punishment (CPT) from 13 to 23 September 1999*. Strasbourg: Council of Europe.

Fahsing, I. A. and Rachlew, A. A. (2009) "Investigative interviewing in the Nordic region," in T. Williamson, B. Milne, and S. Savage (eds), *International Developments in Investigative Interviewing*. Cullompton: Willan.

Granhag, P.-A., Strömwall, L. A., and Montecinos, S. C. (2014) *Polisens förhör med misstänkta*. Rikspolisstyrelsens utvärderingsfunktion, Rapport 2013: 7.

Gudjonsson, G. H. (2003) *The Psychology of Interrogations and Confessions: A Handbook*. Chichester: John Wiley & Sons.

Hartwig, M. (2005) *Interrogating to Detect Deception and Truth: The Effects of Strategic Use of Evidence*. PhD thesis, University of Gothenburg, Gothenburg.

Hartwig, M., Granhag, P.-A., and Strömwall, L. A. (2007) "Guilty and innocent suspects' strategies during police interrogations," *Psychology, Crime and Law*, 13 (2): 213–27.

Holmberg, U. (2004) *Police Interviews with Victims and Suspects of Violent and Sexual Crimes: Interviewees' Experiences and Interview Outcomes*. Stockholm: Department of Psychology, Stockholm University.

Holmberg, U. (2009) "Investigative interviewing as a therapeutic jurisprudential approach," in T. Williamson, B. Milne, and S. Savage (eds), *International Developments in Investigative Interviewing*. Cullompton: Willan, pp. 149–75.

Holmberg, U. and Christianson, S. Å. (2002) "Murderers' and sexual offenders' experiences of police interviews and their inclination to admit or deny crimes," *Behavioral Sciences and the Law*, 20: 31–41.

Isager-Nielsen, B. (2012) *Efterforskerne – sådan fælder de Danmarks drabsmænd*. Copenhagen: Lindhardt & Ringhof.

Jakobsson Öhrn, H. (2005) *Berätta din sanning: en förhörsledares projekt i förhör med misstänkt person*. PhD thesis, Stockholm, University of Stockholm.

Jakobsson Öhrn, H. (2008) "Results and rapport: a police interviewer's dilemma," *International Investigative Interviewing Research Group Bulletin*, 1: 15–20.

Jakobsson Öhrn, H. and Nyberg, C. (2009) "Searching for truth or confirmation?" *International Investigative Interviewing Research Group Bulletin*, 2 (1): 11–19.

Jönsson, L. (1988) *Polisförhöret som kommunikationssituation*, SIC 23, Studies in Communication. Linköping, Sweden: University of Linköping.

Justisdepartementet (2007) *Fritz Moen og norsk strafferettspleie* (NOU 2007: 7). Oslo: Politi-og justisdepartementet.

Kripos (1998) "Avhør av mistenkte." Unpublished document, National Criminal Investigation Service, Oslo.

Kronkvist, O. (2013) *Om sanningen ska fram. Polisförhör med misstänkta för grova brott*. PhD thesis no. 117/2013. Växjö, Sweden: Linnaeus University Press.

Milne, R. and Bull, R. (1999) *Investigative Interviewing: Psychology and Practice*. Chichester: John Wiley & Sons.

Politiets videnscenter (2007) *Dansk politis afhøringspraksis af vidner og forurettede.* Copenhagen: National Police Commissioners Office.

Politiets Videnscenter (2012) *Dansk politis afhøringspraksis af sigtede.* Copenhagen: National Police Commissioners Office.

Rachlew, A. (1999) "Norwegian Police Officers' Perceptions of Investigative Interviewing: Implications for Training." Unpublished Master's thesis, University of Liverpool.

Rachlew, A. (2003) *Norske politiavhør i et internasjonalt perspektiv*, Tidsskrift for Strafferett, No. 4/2003.

Rachlew, A. (2009): *Justisfeil ved politiets etterforskning – noen eksempler og forskingsbaserte mottiltak.* Doktorafhandling ved det juridiske fakultet Universitet i Oslo. Oslo: Unipub.

Råstam, H. (2012) "Fallet Thomas Quick," *Att skapa en seriemördare.* Stockholm: Ordfront.

Shaw, G. (2001) "Current state of force interview training," in J. Burbeck, *New ACPO Investigative Interviewing Strategy.* Warwickshire Police.

Shepherd, E. and Kite, F. (1988) "Training to interview," *Policing*, 4: 264–80.

SOU (2015) Rapport fråm Bergwallkommissjonen. Stockholm: Statens Offentliga Utredningar 2015: 52.

Statens offentliga utredningar (SOU) (2008) *Framtidens polisutbildning*, Slutbetänkande av Utredningen om den framtida polisutbildningen (SOU 2008: 39). Stockholm: Edita Sverige AB.

Stockdale, J. (1993) Management and supervision of police interviews, London: The Home Office. Police Research Series Paper 5.

Trankell, A. (1972) *Reliability of Evidence.* Vallingby, Sweden: Beckmans.

16 Contemporary developments and practices in investigative interviewing of suspects in Scotland

Stuart Houston, David La Rooy and Annabelle Nicol

Introduction

The interviewing of suspected offenders in Scotland has been subject to considerable change over the years, having been moulded into its current shape and position through courtroom challenges, both within the Scottish legal system as well as across Europe, that have led to significant changes in legislation. Although there have been radical and wide-reaching changes in the structure of the police in Scotland, the requirement to interview suspected offenders has remained unchanged and is still enacted in law. Section 20 of the Police and Fire Reform (Scotland) Act 2012 specifically states it is the duty of a constable, *inter alia*, to prevent and detect crime, bring offenders to justice, to *give evidence* and to attend court. Thus it is within the authority of the police to interview individuals in a manner that will withstand scrutiny of a court and expert opinion.

The criminal law of Scotland differs from that in the rest of the United Kingdom in important respects. Significantly, in Scotland, if a person is arrested they are deemed to be a chargeable suspect and *cannot* be interviewed, whereas in other areas suspects arrested on suspicion of a crime may be interviewed. A suspect, who is required to be interviewed in Scotland, is the subject of a detention under terms of Section 14 of the Criminal Procedure (Scotland) Act 1995, which allows them to be treated as an arrested person. This detention has a maximum time period of 12 hours, which may be extended to 24 hours under the authority of an inspector but this has strict limitations.

This chapter will examine the PRICE model, which has been the model used for suspect interviewing in Scotland since 1995, and look closely at how the Scottish system reached a recognised interviewing model, starting with the case law that went before its use, the structure, training and recent significant changes to the model, and how it compares to the PEACE model used by police forces in other areas of the UK. There are many similarities with England and Wales in terms of the types of crimes that are investigated in Scotland, but as you will see, given that Scotland has a distinct legal system, the particularities of suspect interviewing have been contextualised within the Scottish legal framework.

Background

Historically, the interviewing of suspects in Scotland has been adapted and changed from the outcome of trials, predominantly in the High Court, involving grave offences. The overarching objective has been to develop an interviewing model that elicits evidence that is admissible in court and that can lead to the conviction of the suspect. Of course, it is of the utmost importance that the evidence elicited is reliable and not simply information that leads to conviction.

Research has shown that certain types of questioning are more likely to elicit inaccuracies and produce contradictions. Leading questions by their very nature introduce information, and can be used to 'lead' an interviewee in a particular direction. Loftus and Palmer (1974) demonstrated that manipulating the wording of questions had an effect on the answers given by participants, who had all watched the exact same film of an automobile accident. Suggestive questions imply a particular response is expected from an interviewee and may use some degree of pressure or feedback to get the interviewee to 'go along with' what the interview is saying.

Some individual traits and personality factors make people more likely than others to agree with suggestions made to them. Those who feel a need to obey authority figures and demonstrate behavioural compliance (Richardson and Kelly, 2004; Gudjonsson, 1990), as well as juveniles and individuals with intellectual disabilities, psychological disorders and drink/drug problems are also more vulnerable to the effects of suggestive and interrogative-style questioning (see review by Kassin *et al.*, (2010). A positive correlation between intelligence and memory, and suggestibility (as measured by the GSS – Gudjonsson Suggestibility Scale) has also been found (Gudjonsson, 1983).

Certain techniques used to elicit confessions can also have an effect on a suspect's likelihood to confess to committing a crime. 'Theme development', where the interviewing officer presents the suspect with a reason to confess by providing a moral excuse, justification, rationalisation or minimisation or by laying the blame on someone or something other than the suspect, is a highly effective strategy for eliciting confessions. Use of this method has also been shown to be effective at eliciting both true confessions (Appleby *et al.*, 2011) and false confessions (Russano *et al.*, 2005).

Situational factors while being interviewed may also play a part in eliciting inaccurate information. Davis and Leo (2013) attribute the fact that some suspects become less able to resist and more susceptible to interrogative influence over time to what they term 'interrogation-related regulatory decline' (IRRD). Therefore, even individuals who may start off resisting suggestions become more likely over time to become vulnerable to suggestion, due to the immediate circumstances of the suspect. Acute emotional distress and fatigue or sleep deprivation can cause a failure to self-regulate emotions and cognition. An inability to regulate cognition can impair memory, making suspects more susceptible to suggestive questioning, and this is likely at lower levels of distress than commonly thought. Glucose depletion may also play a role in IRRD. All brain processes depend on the consumption of energy from blood glucose and self-control functions exert a high demand for energy (Galliot and Baumeister, 2007), and individual differences in the availability of blood glucose, such as in the case of diabetes and hypoglycaemia where individuals have less blood glucose available, can render individuals vulnerable to self-regulation failures.

The High Court murder case of *Brown* v. *Her Majesty's Advocate* (*HMA*) is recognised as a significant turning point in the actions of police officers and how they interview suspects. Brown was on trial in 1966 for the murder of a young woman in the Lanarkshire town of Larkhall. During the initial stages of the investigation Brown had been interviewed, along with a number of others, when no suspicion had fallen on anyone. In this first engagement with the police as a witness, Brown provided a brief account of his movements at the time of the murder. After this statement, police discovered a number of discrepancies in his story and invited him to attend a police station, where he was then cautioned under common law. He was not obliged to answer any questions, but went on to provide a statement. After a lengthy period of time, the interviewing officer put a number of inconsistencies in Brown's account to him, and Brown then admitted to the murder, even going so far as to take police officers to an area where he had disposed of some of the victim's possessions.

At trial, Brown was convicted of murder and sentenced to life imprisonment but appealed on the grounds that his confession had been unfairly elicited. During the appeal, the presiding judge Lord Clyde made the following comments:

> Questioning by the police, therefore, which is tainted with any element of bullying or pressure or third degree methods designed to secure admissions of guilt by suspected persons prevents the replies being proved in evidence before the jury at the ultimate trial. For, according to our standards of fair play this would be unjust to the person accused. On the other hand the police have a right, and indeed a duty, to make investigations and to question people in order to find out whether and by whom a crime has been committed, and for the purpose of conducting these investigations to interrogate persons who may be involved. Where exactly the line is to be drawn between legitimate questioning and proceedings which are tainted with undue pressure on or bullying of a person ultimately accused of the crime, may sometimes be a difficult matter. It is not possible to lay down the precise circumstances in which answers given to the police prior to a charge being made are admissible in evidence at the ultimate trial or where they are inadmissible. This is so much a question of the particular circumstances of each case and those circumstances vary infinitely from one another. But the test in all of them is the simple and intelligible test which has worked well in practice – has what has taken place been fair or not?' (Scottish Police Services Authority, 2012: 59)

Although this case occurred nearly fifty years ago, the principles of the findings have gone a long way to setting out the duties and actions in police interviews for a number of years. Although the introduction of the PRICE model has put a lot of emphasis on a described process, the underlying aspect of this case has lived with Scottish officers throughout their careers, as it underlines that it is the police officer's duty not to gain a confession but rather to gain information and that information must be obtained fairly and be usable in criminal proceedings. The objective of the investigative interview with a suspect is not to obtain a confession but is rather an exercise in fact-finding. This particular case paved the way for officers to recognise the boundaries and laid out quite clearly what the purpose of an interview was. It is noteworthy that the year after this judgement the initial Police Scotland Act 1967 was enacted that became the forerunner to the current Police and Fire Reform (Scotland) Act 2012. It is also noteworthy that it was not until 30 years after this case that the Scottish Police College began training the current PRICE model (similar lengthy delays in improving interviewer practice have also been evident with witnesses and victims).

The PRICE model

The PRICE model has been part of the curriculum at the Scottish Police College for all officers attending the facility since 1996. However, the level of training provided to new-start officers and detective officers does vary, with the latter being subject to a week-long course to ensure competency before undertaking any other detective training courses. Although similar in description to the PEACE model, the Scottish system was developed in line with the caution that differs from that used in other parts of the UK. In addition to this, up until 2010 Scottish suspect interviews were conducted without the presence of a legal representative, but this will be subject to further discussion in this chapter.

The main objectives of the PRICE model are to show the value of a structured and organised approach to the interview process and how interviewers can identify and evaluate information learned during the interview process and relate it to other known facts. If followed correctly, the interviewer is able to remain in control of the interview, release information at appropriate times and place information obtained in the correct context in order to be able to determine how the interview should progress to either termination, arrest or charging of the suspect.

The structure is as follows.

Planning and preparation

This is an area where the interviewer can have real control, and the work that is put in at this stage, prior to sitting across a desk from a suspect, should be valued. In many cases planning and preparation are the 'deciding factors' for obtaining successful outcomes. In cases of homicide or other major investigations, it is highly likely that the senior investigating officer will use the services of an interview advisor. This is normally an officer of the rank of detective sergeant, who is a proven investigator and interviewer and has undergone an approved week-long training course provided by the Scottish Police College. This has been in place in

Scotland since the early 2000s and is now recognised as good practice in all major investigations. In the past, this trained officer would compose a plan for others to follow, with appropriate monitoring and support. Through time this role has now evolved and is now more an advisory role, giving support to the officers who conduct the interviews to prepare the plans that are then approved by the senior investigating officer or their deputy.

In more routine cases, the interviewing officer will not require this level of expertise and the officers will produce the plan and conduct the interview. The planning and preparation should always be thorough and although any plan will be submitted as a document in any subsequent case, it is down to the skill of the officers to ensure they cover all the appropriate areas and be flexible to adapt their plan as the interview develops.

The first area to consider in the planning is to have the aim and objective of the interview clear in the mind of the lead interviewer and their corroborating officer. It is essential that both officers know who is taking the lead and when they wish the other officer to enter with any supplementary questions. This allows the interview to be fluid but also, as it is likely to be recorded, it creates a more professional approach. As part of the plan, the officers must ensure that they are aware of all the facts of the case whether these are inculpatory or exculpatory for the suspected person. This demonstrates that element of fairness in ensuring that they are not asking the suspect questions about the offences that is supposition and cannot be verified by facts from witness statements, CCTV or even forensic evidence. In line with this the officers must be aware of the essential elements of the crime in question and what evidence they require to prove it. As part of the plan it is recognised as good practice to write down the essential elements and build the information-gathering section of the interview around the core parts of the crime.

Although these parts of a plan are obvious the most important area that is sometimes overlooked is the welfare of the suspect and the environment for a suspect interview. In addition to the legal requirements of the crime under investigation, the officers must also be aware of any time constraints resulting from when the person was detained for interview, and that they have had their full right to solicitor access explained to them. This should all be under the planning and preparation.

Since 2010, suspects in Scotland have had the right to solicitor access prior to their interview, following the European case of *Salduz* v. *Turkey* (2009). The implications of this recent change will be the subject of discussion later in the chapter.

As is the nature of police work, serious offences will often occur at 'unsocial hours' when officers may have been working long hours during the night, and at times when they may be physically and mentally exhausted. This should always be a consideration in the planning stage, with officers asking themselves 'Am I capable of conducting this interview?' In serious offences, interviews will be subject to review by the Crown Office, the Procurator Fiscal Service (similar to the Crown Prosecution Service in England and Wales), a defence advocate (similar to a barrister in England and Wales) and their legal team, a jury, a sherif (similar to a judge in England and Wales) and the wider public through the media. All these stakeholders, with the benefit of hindsight, could be in a much better state of mental alertness than the police officer who conducted the initial interview. Thus the mental and physical state of the interviewer poses a potential risk to the success of the investigation and should always be considered during the planning phase of the investigation.

Similarly, the planning of an interview should always consider the suspect's needs, for example whether they require any medical treatment, rest to reduce the effect of alcohol or drug abuse, or whether they may need the services of an appropriate adult. Scotland is now a nation with many faiths making up the population and the requirements of suspects in relation to their religious needs for praying or washing should always be given consideration, as should the conduct of the interviewing officers where there are cultural barriers or differences. This is reflective of Lord Clyde's comments in 1966, that in relation to fairness can be added integrity and respect for the suspected person.

The location of an interview should also be considered if it is appropriate for the interview. This can be influenced by the amount of space in the room in the event that other persons are required to be present, for example an interpreter, legal representative or appropriate adult.

Overall, it can be seen from the above that the planning and preparation stage not only has to consider what you are going to ask and seek information about, but also covers all aspects of how the interview is conducted.

Rapport building

Rapport should be established from the first encounter with the suspect and continue throughout the interview. The building of rapport should be displayed in the professionalism of the officers and clearly sets out the roles of the interviewees and interviewers. Rapport-building should never be overlooked as unimportant, research has shown that interviewers' attempts at building rapport were associated with higher levels of suspect responsiveness and cooperation (Bull and Soukara, 2010).

Following the introduction of solicitor access to suspect interviews in Scotland, rapport-building is also seen as part of the disclosure of information to the solicitor. This aspect of professionalism is also relevant in the manner that the interviewing officers explain the interview process to the solicitor, and importantly, set the boundaries of what they expect to be reasonable considerations in the pre-interview disclosure. Any objections the solicitor wishes to raise must be done in a manner that does not deviate from the aim of the interview and allow the police to do their job.

An area of the interview that has caused considerable legal debate is the caution that is provided to the suspect at the commencement, prior to the interviewer asking any questions. In Scotland this varies from other parts of the United Kingdom with the wording being:

> You are going to be asked questions about (crime or offence). You are not obliged to answer, but anything you do say will be noted and may be used in evidence.

In serious crimes this would include the warning that the interview will be both video and audio recorded, although use of this equipment is normally only for interviews conducted by detective officers.

As part of the rapport-building, it is considered good practice to ask the interviewee to repeat that caution back to the interviewer and explain their understanding. In past criminal cases, appeals have been launched due to the suspect being unable to understand what the caution actually means. This should also be seen as a consideration for the interviewer that if the suspect is struggling to understand, there may be some sort of incapacity and the person may require the services of an appropriate adult to facilitate communication in addition to a solicitor also being present. In essence the rapport-building stage should be seen as the opportunity to introduce the interviewers, interviewees and any other persons present and ensure that everyone is aware of the formal interview process that will take place.

Information-gathering

As the central point of the model this is the area where the written plan comes into use and the aim of the interview comes to fruition, to gather information and to enable the suspect to give an account which can include any mitigation or defence. The information-gathering phase is divided into two distinct sections: the suspect agenda where they are given the opportunity to give an account; and the police agenda where interviewers ask the questions that have been pre-planned.

The suspect agenda should start with an *impact question*, clearly stating what it is they are being asked about, which should be in line with the caution they have already been administered. An impact question should be open and an example would be 'Tell me in as much detail as possible about your involvement in (crime or offence).' Frequently, the suspect may not provide a reply to this question, thus a pre-planned back-up question could be, 'Tell me your movements between (times that cover the offence).' This is seen as being fair and transparent because the interviewers are focused on what they are investigating and the relevant times and dates. If at this stage the suspect is willing to answer questions then they should be allowed to provide an account, allowing the interviewers to build up a timeline of movements and an account which may be challenged later in the interview at an appropriate time. Although the interviewers should not challenge any lies at this stage, it is an opportunity to elicit as much information as possible. It is recognised that during the suspect account they may raise key topics that the interviewers had planned to cover in their agenda, but if it is raised by the suspect the officers can seek to gather as much information on the topic as they can.

Once the suspect agenda is exhausted, the interviewers then have the opportunity ask questions about what they ascertain to be important investigative information. This information may be key elements of the crime or offence under investigation or any other essential information, for example the suspect's knowledge of a victim, locus or location, other people, access to vehicles, weapons, money or drugs. The topics that need to be covered are unique to each case but it should be borne in mind that this is the interviewers' opportunity to seek answers, particularly if in the evaluation stage where they may be presenting evidence of identification, particularly forensic evidence linking a suspect with a victim, location or item. It would be unfair if they had not been given an opportunity to provide a legitimate or explainable reason for their presence having been discovered.

Throughout the information-gathering stage, there should be no signs of interviewer bias and all aspects should be probed using the 'wh-' and 'how' questions. At the conclusion of this stage the interviewers should be satisfied that they have asked all the necessary questions.

Confirming the content

Once the information gathering is complete, there is now an opportunity to confirm information that has been provided. This allows the interviewer to restate the critical aspects of the information provided and address any misunderstandings or ambiguities that may have arisen during the course of the interview. The method used in Scotland is referred to as the 'yes/no spiral', where the interviewer provides details and seeks 'agreement' about the information that has been provided. It is important for the interviewer to restate *exactly* what has been said but still remain open-minded and unbiased towards the suspect or their answers.

This stage should allow the interviewer and his/her colleague to perform a 'health check' and ensure that they have covered all areas that they had planned to. In addition, the interviewer may try to anticipate and address possible avenues for defence, surrounding challenges about the questioning, or apparent inconsistencies in the account provided. This phase of the suspect interview can sometimes be quite brief depending on how much information has already been provided by the suspect.

Evaluate and action

The final part of the model allows all of the information to be evaluated and ensure that the interviewers are able to appropriately challenge any inconsistencies that have arisen. This is one of the most important aspects of the interview where the interviewers will be attempting to explain differences between the suspect's account of events with other evidence in the investigation; the suspect's account may then be challenged if there is reason to do so. It is important that the delivery of such evidence is conducted in a controlled manner, and it should never lead to an argument between interviewers, suspects or solicitors. This is the area where the police will hold the answers, and the points of evidence, if not addressed correctly, could render an interview inadmissible in later proceedings.

Specific points of evidence should be put to the suspect one at a time so that the suspect is able to provide an explanation for each. Compared with other phases of the interview model, this is the phase where the police frequently do most of the talking. However, if at this stage someone admits responsibility and confesses to a crime they should be allowed to elaborate and if necessary be further questioned by the interviewer. It should be noted that it is at this stage where the use of forensic identification, CCTV identification or even eyewitness identification can be strategically introduced in order to highlight the evidence or any inconsistencies in the evidence.

The action part of this should be the decision by the officers to move to charge the suspect with the offence, or if necessary release them from detention to allow further investigations to be made.

Training

From the mid-1990s the PRICE model has been the interviewing model taught to all officers who commence service within Scotland and who as part of their initial training are required to attend the Scottish Police College. This has also been repeated in the Detective Training Unit within the college which all detectives in Scotland attend for the Initial Investigators Course. Over the years this course has developed and is now taught after a week-long interview training course on which success must be gained prior to any advancement to further courses within the criminal investigation arena. This includes a number of practical assessments with witnesses and suspects, where the use of actors is essential to provide a realistic but safe training environment (see the Chapter 17 on witnesses and victims in Scotland in Volume 1).

The Scottish Police College has had long-established links with the various organisations, the National Crime faculty, the National Policing Improvement Agency (NPIA) and more recently the National Crime Agency, and in particular with the training of interview advisors. The training provided in this course is replicated from the nationally approved course and the National Interview Advisor was a lecturer on the course. It is now recognised that although the models used in Scotland and the rest of the UK are slightly different there is a great deal of cooperation and crossover with training and this has been shown in recent years with shared training and also the support provided by the National Advisor to senior investigating officers within Scotland.

Cadder v. *Her Majesty's Advocate* (2010)

From the outset for the PRICE model, unlike PEACE, there was no requirement for a solicitor to be present during a suspect interview in Scotland. This became the subject of a legal challenge and a number of sweeping changes during the summer of 2010, which has seen the PRICE model adapting and becoming closer to the UK model. Following the European Court of Human Rights ruling on *Salduz* v. *Turkey* (1999), where it was found that a person who has been detained by the police should have the right to have access to a lawyer prior to being interviewed, unless, in particular circumstances of the case, there are compelling reasons, a number of cases were raised in Scotland that changed the process for interviewing.

The Scottish case that brought about the change was that of Peter Cadder, who having been detained was interviewed in relation to two assaults and a breach of the peace following an incident in Glasgow in 2007. As part of his detention process he declined to speak to a solicitor prior to interview and then went on to make admissions, for which he was charged with the offences. Due to the *Salduz* case, Cadder appealed to the UK Supreme Court that he should have had access to a solicitor. The UK court agreed, quashing his conviction citing that under Article 6 of the European Convention on Human Rights he had been deprived of the right to a fair trial. This has been the most significant change in suspect interviewing since the 1966 case of *Brown*, quoted at the start of this chapter and has seen not just police but courts, lawyers and suspects adapting to a new process. In light of the ruling, emergency legislation was raised within the Scottish Parliament that saw a change in the detention period rising from 6 hours to the 12 hours it is now.

Conclusion

The PRICE model has been used by the police service in Scotland for over twenty years, and although it is very close in its content to the PEACE model utilised in other parts of the UK, unlike the PEACE model it has never been the subject of review (McGurk *et al.*, 1993; Clarke and Milne, 1999). Its use has largely been shaped by case law and changes in legislation that have seen its application develop over time. It still remains the only model for suspect interviewing taught by the Scottish Police College and is recognised by the service as a whole as well as the Crown Office and Procurator Fiscal Service.

As stated throughout, there are differences in the legal system in Scotland which have accounted for the different approach to the interview model. Although the PEACE model could easily be adapted for use in Scotland, it is not something that has been considered and with the ongoing debate over whether Scotland continues as part of the UK, this may remain unanswered for some time.

References

Appleby, S. C., Hasel, L. E. and Kassin, S. M. (2011) 'Police-induced confessions: an empirical analysis of their content and impact', *Psychology, Crime and Law*, 19: 111–28.

Bull, R. and Soukara, S. (2010) 'Four studies of what really happens in police interviews', in G. D. Lassiter and C. A. Meissner (eds), *Police Interrogations and False Confessions:*

Current Research, Practice, and Policy Recommendations. Washington, DC: American Psychological Association, pp. 81–95.

Clarke, C. and Milne, R. (1999) *National Evaluation of the PEACE Investigative Interviewing Course*, Police Research Award Scheme, Report no. PRAS/149.

Davis, D. and Leo, R. A. (2013) 'Acute suggestibility in police interrogations: self-regulation failure as a primary mechanism of vulnerability', in A. M. Ridley, F. Gabbert and D. J. La Rooy (eds), *Suggestibility in Legal Contexts: Psychological Research and Forensic Implications*. Chichester: Wiley-Blackwell, pp. 171–95.

Galliot, M. T. and Baumeister, R. F. (2007) 'The physiology of willpower: linking blood glucose to self-control', *Personality and Social Psychology Review*, 11: 303–27.

Gudjonsson, G. H. (1983) 'Suggestibility, intelligence, memory recall and personality: an experimental study', *British Journal of Psychiatry*, 142: 35–7.

Gudjonsson, G. H. (1990) 'The relationship of intellectual skills to suggestibility, compliance and acquiescence', *Personality and Individual Differences*, 11: 227–231.

Kassin, S. M., Drizin, S. A., Grisso, T., Gudjonsson, G. H. R. A. and Redlich, A. D. (2010) 'Police-induced confessions: risk factors and recommendations', *Law and Human Behavior*, 34: 3–38.

Loftus, E. F. and Palmer, J. C. (1974) 'Reconstruction of automobile destruction: an example of the interaction between language and memory', *Journal of Verbal Learning and Verbal Behavior*, 13: 585–9.

McGurk, B. J., Carr, M. J. and McGurk, B. (1993) *Investigative Interviewing Courses for Police Officers: An Evaluation*, Police Research Series, Paper No. 4. London: Home Office Police Department.

Police and Fire Reform (Scotland) Act 2012. Available at: http://www.legislation.gov.uk/asp/2012/8/section/20/enacted (accessed 12 April 2014).

Richardson, G. and Kelly, T. P. (2004) 'A study in the relationship between interrogative suggestibility, compliance and social desirability in institutionalised adolescents', *Personality and Individual Differences*, 36: 485–94.

Russano, M. B., Meissner, C. A., Narchet, F. M. and Kassin, S. M. (2005) 'Investigating true and false confessions within a novel experimental paradigm', *Psychological Science*, 16: 481–6.

Scottish Police Services Authority (2012) *The Scottish Investigators Guide to Case Law*. Kincardine: Scottish Police College.

17 Police interrogation of suspects in Slovenia

Igor Areh, Sabina Zgaga and Benjamin Flander

Introduction

The Republic of Slovenia, a state surrounded by Austria, Hungary, Croatia and Italy, became an independent state in 1991. Since 2004, it has been a full member of the European Union. After the proclamation of the new constitution in 1991, all legal provisions in force at that time remained, except where they were in conflict with human rights and fundamental freedoms. The Criminal Code and the Criminal Procedure Act are consistent with the European Convention on Human Rights (ECHR).

Police interrogation[1] is a fairly recent procedural institution in Slovenian criminal procedural law. Before 2003, Slovenian police officers were only allowed to gather information from suspects without being able to perform actions for evidentiary purposes, as this was deemed to be completely under the competence of investigating judges. The official explanation for this regulation was that police officers – potentially the most dangerous agents of state power – could not and should not interrogate suspects, since this could only be done by representatives of judicial power.

In practice, however, the results of the aforementioned regulation were quite often the opposite (instead of protecting suspects' rights, the regulation led to violations and was also ineffective). Only after the Act Amending the Criminal Procedure Act was passed in 2003 did Slovenian police officers formally get the right, previously conferred solely on investigating judges, to interrogate suspects accused of criminal offences, but with the obligatory presence of counsel and only when informed of their rights. Even though the new regulation has been criticised by renowned criminal law scholars,[2] it remains in force for now. This chapter expounds how police interrogation is regulated in Slovenian constitutional and criminal procedural law and how it is elucidated by the relevant case law, with special emphasis on the rights and procedural guarantees of suspects/defendants in pre-trial procedure. Also discussed will be the practical aspects of police interrogation, with a special focus on the psychological manipulation of suspects.

Constitutional and legal framework of police interrogation of suspects

Under the Constitution of the Republic of Slovenia, no one may be subjected to torture, inhumane or degrading punishment or treatment. Respect for human personality and dignity is guaranteed in criminal and all other legal proceedings, particularly during the deprivation of liberty. Any person charged with a criminal offence must, in addition to absolute equality, be afforded the right to have adequate time and facilities to prepare his or her defence and to present all evidence assisting the case. Any person charged with a criminal offence is presumed innocent until found guilty by due process of law.[3] Even though this is not explicitly stated in the Constitution, all mentioned guarantees also apply to police (custodial and non-custodial) interrogation of suspects. The so-called Miranda warning is partially contained in Article 19 of the Slovenian Constitution. Under this article, anyone deprived of their liberty must be immediately informed, in his mother tongue or in a language which he understands, of the reasons for being deprived of his liberty. Within the shortest possible time thereafter, s/he must be informed in writing of why s/he has been deprived of their liberty. S/he must be instructed immediately that they are not obliged to make any statement, that they have the right to immediately obtain legal representation of their own free choice and that the competent authority must, on their request, notify their relatives or those close to them of the deprivation of their liberty. Moreover, the Slovenian Constitution prohibits the use of any form of coercion in obtaining confessions and statements and the use of any form of violence on persons whose liberty has been restricted. Any person being interrogated by the police has the right not to incriminate themselves, their relatives or those close to them or to admit guilt. These rather restricted constitutional provisions of the privilege against self-incrimination were expounded by the Constitutional Court of Slovenia in its decision (no. Up-1293/08-24, 2011).[4] Here, the Constitutional Court ruled that the privilege against self-incrimination is primarily realised with the right to counsel and with providing information on the right to silence. Furthermore, it ruled that these two rights constitute an important element of the privilege against self-incrimination even when a person being interrogated by (police) officials has not been deprived of their liberty (see ibid.).

Having undergone several amendments since being passed in 1995, the Criminal Procedure Act defines different methods of obtaining statements from suspects/defendants: police interview or interrogation of a suspect, interrogation of a defendant in a judicial investigation by an investigating judge and a defendant's plea at the main hearing (Criminal Procedure Act 1994). In accordance with the provisions of the original Criminal Procedure Act 1994, police officers were authorised to gather information informally in the form of official notes from a person for whom grounds existed to suspect that s/he had committed a criminal offence, but the final decision of a judge could not be based on this information

(Fišer, 2003). Therefore, police officers were not allowed to formally interrogate (Criminal Procedure Act 1994). The official notes were intended to assist state prosecutors in adopting the decision of whether to pursue criminal prosecution, but were not intended to be seen by the judge deciding the case (Šugman, 2005). Despite the fact that official notes with suspects' statements were officially excluded from the court files, an increasing body of theoretical evidence started to emerge in regard to psychological contamination of the judge with such official notes. This was possible because judges could familiarise themselves with the contents of the said official notes through other applications in the proceedings. In other words, judges could not formally base their decision on official notes, but these undoubtedly influenced their decision-making process (Dežman and Erbežnik, 2003). In its decision (no. U-I-92/96, 2002), the Constitutional Court of the Republic of Slovenia therefore found that the regulations of the Criminal Procedure Act under which a judge could become familiar with the police notes from a pre-trial procedure without being removed from the case violated the right to an impartial trial set out in Article 23 of the Constitution of Slovenia (1991). This constitutional ruling had two consequences. First, a new reason for excluding a judge was introduced into the Criminal Procedure Act, and, second, the legislative authority took advantage of this Constitutional Court decision by introducing a new system of obtaining suspects' statements in pre-trial procedures.

According to the Act Amending the Criminal Procedure Act from 2003, three different situations thus have to be distinguished. Police officers are generally still only authorised to gather information in pre-trial procedure. Firstly, when grounds exist to believe that a *suspect* participated in a criminal offence, police officers are under an obligation to read the Miranda warning to the suspect (Stare, 2004). Information gathered by police officers before such a suspect has had their rights read is entered on the record as official notes, and these have to be excluded from the court files by a state prosecutor (Republic of Slovenia, 2003; Šugman and Gorkič, 2011). Case law confirms this decision (Supreme Court I Ips 31018/2011-420, 2013). In rendering a decision, a judge may not take the official notes into consideration and any evidence based on these notes is excluded (Šugman, 2005; Republic of Slovenia, 2003). There are two further options following the reading of the Miranda warning. If the suspect declares that s/he wants to exercise his or her right to counsel, the interrogation is postponed until the arrival of the counsel or until a time determined by the police, at which point a formal interrogation is conducted (Republic of Slovenia, 2003; Šugman and Gorkič, 2011). After being drawn up and filed into court files, the record of the interrogation is considered evidence and can be taken into account by the judge in rendering a decision. The interrogation is led by a police officer (Šugman, 2006a). However, many legal experts have been critical of this solution and it was suggested that interrogation in the pre-trial procedure should be conducted by a state prosecutor or an investigating judge (Šugman, 2006b).

Even more criticism was directed at the second option, by which a suspect, after being duly informed of their rights, agrees to proceed without counsel present or counsel does not arrive, whereupon police officers question him or her and make an official note (Šugman, 2005). The official note is entered into the court files and the judge may become familiar with it but cannot formally invoke it in passing a decision. The issue of psychological contamination of a judge therefore remains unresolved under the second option (Šugman, 2006a). Also, the official note stays in the court files and may have a certain cognitive effect on the judge, yet the defence is unable to challenge or oppose it, as the judge never invokes it in the grounds for the judgement. This is also known as so-called semi-proof (Šugman, 2006a). Surprisingly, the Supreme Court of Slovenia consistently confirmed the legal regulation stipulating that an official note cannot be considered formal evidence in issuing a judgement, yet it is legal and should not be eliminated from the court files (Supreme Court I Ips 114/2005, 2005). In doing so, a blind eye was turned to the possible actual influence of the official note on the judgement. In selected process instances, official notes could even constitute grounds for implementing formal evidence or for commencing a judicial investigation (Supreme Court I Ips 114/2005, 2005).

Since speeding up criminal procedures was one of the reasons behind introducing police interrogation of suspects, a possible confession of a criminal offence and its effect on the procedure also become relevant. A suspect's criminal offence confession in the pre-trial procedure notwithstanding, competent authorities are required to continue investigating the offence, except in cases resolved through plea-bargaining.[5] Even in such cases, however, a prosecutor is still required to file a direct indictment.

Police interrogations and case law

In passing judgements pertaining to police interrogation, the European Court of Human Rights (ECtHR) primarily considers the following three issues: (1) the right to counsel; (2) the right to remain silent and the privilege against self-incrimination; and (3) prohibited methods of interrogation. These three issues directly relate to Article 6 of the European Convention on Human Rights (1950) guaranteeing the right to a fair trial, and to Article 3 of the same Convention in which torture, inhumane and degrading treatment or punishment are prohibited.[6]

On several past occasions, the ECtHR has ruled against Slovenia due to inhumane treatment by police officers while arresting[7] criminal offence suspects. Conversely, the ECtHR has not yet passed a judgement confirming violations of rights and constitutional procedural guarantees (right to counsel, right to remain silent, the obtaining of statements by use of force or threats, by misleading suspects, etc.) during police interrogations. The same holds true for case law of the Supreme Court of Slovenia and the Constitutional Court of Slovenia. In the case number Up-1293/08-24 (2011), previously mentioned, the Constitutional Court rejected the constitutional complaint of the applicant who was found guilty of illicit trafficking in narcotic drugs by the District Court. The judgement of the District Court was then confirmed by the Higher Court and the Supreme Court of the Republic of Slovenia. In his appeal to the Constitutional Court, the applicant claimed that the testimony of a customs officer was used as evidence against him in the District Court, and that the said testimony contained statements given by the applicant without having duly been told the rights of a suspect in criminal proceedings. In his constitutional complaint, the applicant opposed the Higher Court decision (in which the District Court decision was confirmed) that customs officers were performing their official duty with full authorisation to do so. He stressed that customs officers did not make official notes and that the pre-trial procedure against him had not yet started at that point in time. The Constitutional Court ruled that, for the privilege against self-incrimination, the actual commencement of criminal proceedings is crucial, not its formal introduction. Therefore the privilege against self-incrimination is extended to inspection and monitoring procedures if procedural tasks in these procedures are directed at gathering information for subsequent criminal proceedings or if a criminal investigation is actually being conducted as part of these procedures.

In contrast, the privilege against self-incrimination does not extend to non-criminal (inspection and monitoring) procedures if the activities of officials implementing these procedures do not result in a criminal investigation. Regardless, the evidence legally obtained in non-criminal procedures in these cases (without due instruction on the right to silence), including the defendant's statements, can, according to the Constitutional Court, be used in the criminal proceedings by applying 'greater caution'. When wishing to use such a statement in criminal proceedings, the state (i.e. the prosecutor) must supply evidence that the statement was given as an act of free will.[8] In this particular case, the Constitutional Court ruled finally that criminal suspicion arose only after narcotic drugs were discovered and that all the activities of customs (and police) officers were directed towards a criminal investigation following that point in time, which means that the criminal proceedings had not *de facto* commenced prior to that moment. Because the applicant had made a statement to the customs officer prior to that moment (i.e. at the stage when the customs procedure was not yet part of the criminal proceedings), the customs officer was not under the obligation to instruct the applicant of his right to silence. As the applicant did not claim the use of coercion in his constitutional complaint – he made no claim that he did not answer the customs officer's questions of his own free will[9] – the privilege against self-incrimination was not violated. On these grounds, his complaint was denied by the Constitutional Court.

Police interrogation as a part of investigation procedure: psychological manipulation of suspects

This section discusses the practical aspects of police interrogation. Little evidence exists on how police investigators actually conduct interrogations due to a lack of objective research data and because the suspect's counsel is, in addition to police officers and sometimes a state prosecutor, the only other person present at interrogations. For this reason, analysis of police interrogation in practice will focus on a review of literature designed to assist investigators in their work.

It seems that the literature dealing with the investigation of criminal offences published before the break-up of Yugoslavia in 1991 focuses mainly on obtaining material evidence and refers to, or interprets, legal provisions regulating pre-trial and criminal procedures. When these sources do mention psychological manipulation of suspects, the discourse typically remains on the level of general guidelines with some references to the findings of European and American authors. This brief historical overview of the theory relating to psychological manipulation of suspects is limited to selected comprehensive works by authors who were influential at the time. The influence of an author was estimated from the number of quotations in works by following authors. For the most part, these were legal professionals – psychologists were an exception rather than the rule.

Much has been written on the psychological manipulation of suspects, but the source or authorship of advice offered often remains questionable. Some twenty years ago, the standards for acknowledging sources (citing) on the territory of the former Yugoslavia were poor, so it does not come as a surprise that citations of sources in specialist literature of the time were often missing or incomplete (providing only the author's surname). Moreover, an author's suggestions tended to be based on common-sense suppositions not tested in experiments or on anecdotal evidence, and research results were rarely provided. In the former Yugoslavia, experts in the field tended to closely follow the development of interrogation techniques in other countries. It appears that they were very familiar with and advocated (to a greater or lesser extent) the ideas of Americans Fred Inbau and John Reid (commonly known as the Reid Technique (Inbau *et al.*, 2013). Even when no quotes are given, it is clear that their book *Lie Detection and Criminal Investigation* from 1953 influenced interrogation techniques in the former Yugoslavia. Of course, it was impossible to completely transpose the Reid Technique into practice in the former Yugoslavia as the legal framework at the time – the basis for pre-trial and criminal proceedings – differed significantly from the American legal system. Therefore many ideas typical of coercive interrogation techniques were unacceptable because their use by criminal investigators would have been considered a violation of statutory human rights. It should be mentioned that, in addition to Inbau and Reid's work, the influence of Viennese lawyer Roland Grassberger and his 1950 work *Psychology of the Criminal Proceedings*[10] on criminal psychology was also very influential at the time.

One of the first comprehensive works discussing the psychological manipulation of suspects was published in 1973. Written by psychologist Dušan Putnik, it was a type of manual designed to aid police officers in their work. In connection with interrogation techniques, Putnik stressed the importance of establishing nonverbal cues to deception and of using a polygraph to narrow the number of suspects. Throughout the book, there are numerous references to Inbau and Reid's ideas; it seems, however, that the author is nevertheless being critical of coercive interrogation techniques. Moreover, the work contains several anecdotes, for example about an investigator who was in the habit of having breakfast with suspects and even sharing his meal with them – supposedly to establish a confidential working relationship between the two (Putnik, 1973). For conducting interviews, Putnik suggests the associative method and measuring response time of interviewees, which was most probably taken from the Carl Jung and Franz Riklin treatise *Experimental Studies on Associations of a Healthy Person*[11] (1905).

Another influential work was the book *Criminal Investigation* by lawyer Vlado Vodinelić, published in 1987. Here, the author extensively deals with admissible and inadmissible questions, which may or may not be used in interrogations. Vodinelić recommended various interrogation techniques, for example confronting the suspect with increasingly incriminating evidence, indifferently collecting the suspect's statements and confronting the suspect with contradictory facts and evidence, stressing the advantages of confession, presenting photographs and other physical evidence connected with the criminal offence (also with photos of victims) (Vodinelić, 1987). Interestingly, Vodinelić also suggests obtaining a 'pictorial confession' in which a suspect would draw how they reached the crime scene, the location of objects and events, and their exit route from the crime scene. From the perspective of today's forensic psychology theory, the author's suggested techniques seem more or less like coercive interrogation techniques aimed at inducing suspects' confessions. This does not seem very surprising, considering Vodinelić often quoted Arnold Lichem and his work *The Criminal Investigation: Handbook for the Criminal Police*[12] published in Graz in 1935 – a time when human rights protection standards were significantly lower than today and when little was known of false confessions. The latter holds especially true for lawyers, who would recommend the use of certain interrogation techniques without having at least a basic knowledge of psychology.

An influential authority in the field was also psychologist Zvonimir Roso, who, in 1988, published a book on investigative interviewing containing many suggestions on how to conduct interrogations, but most of them stayed in the domain of unsubstantiated assumptions. Providing arguments for his claims, the author often referred to anecdotal evidence, with valid research sources being rare. Relying heavily on Inbau, Reid, Grassberger, Lichem and Vodinelić, it comes as no surprise that Roso unreservedly recommended the use of projection, minimalisation, rationalisation and empathy simulation, all aimed at obtaining a confession. From the contents of his work, it can be inferred that Roso supported the methods of coercive interrogation more than the other authors previously mentioned, and that he did not point out the many issues connected with coercive interrogation techniques. Interestingly, Roso nevertheless endorsed both audio and video interrogation recordings, a suggestion otherwise not typical of authors advocating coercive interrogation techniques.

Slovenia gained its independence by seceding from Yugoslavia in 1991, and the following year saw the publication of the first book discussing the psychological manipulation of suspects in the newly formed country. In their short treatise, Musek *et al.* (1992) suggested an interview method similar to what is today known as the cognitive interview. They highlight the issue of inadmissible questions and the possibility of identifying deceit with the help of some premises of the criteria-based content analysis (CBCA). The idea behind CBCA is that accounts of real events differ from invented narratives. With CBCA, an account by a witness can be systematically assessed for truthfulness (see Vrij, 2008). Several articles were published after 1991 on the psychological manipulation of suspects, all suggesting an influence from the Yugoslavian authors previously mentioned. In 1997, lawyer Darko Maver wrote the first book in independent Slovenia with an in-depth focus on the psychological manipulation of suspects, taking a critical stance in relation to inadmissible interrogation techniques. Despite frequently drawing from Inbau, Reid and Vodinelić, Maver was more reserved towards their ideas compared to most of his predecessors, and also stressed the issue of false confessions. It came as a surprise to him that, despite having a great evidential value, confession remained relatively rarely discussed in the relevant literature of the time (Maver, 1997).

This has been a brief overview of theory, but what about practice?

Theory into practice

Relatively little is known about how psychological manipulation has been conducted in practice during interrogations, but since the works of the authors mentioned above began to be used in criminal investigator training, theory has at least partially been implemented in practice. The first available Slovenian interrogation manual was published in 2003, but only in the form of internal police guidelines on conducting interrogations which were not made available to the public. Here, ideas from interrogation manuals of foreign authors (e.g. Inbau-Reid, Wicklander-Zulawski, John Walkey) were combined with domestic authors (e.g. Roso and Maver) and contemporary practices on investigative interviewing. Since the ideas of authors favouring coercive interrogation techniques seem to dominate, the manual is controversial on many points. It is suggested that the interview start with open-ended questions, allowing the suspect to freely narrate the details of the event. This is followed by the main part of the interview in which a suspect is confronted with existing evidence. The interview turns to an accusatory style and narrowed questions are used (Štirn and Podvršič, 2003) – a marked influence of the Reid Technique is evident here. In order to obtain a confession, the authors suggest using rationalisation, minimalisation, guilt projection, doubting the suspect's statements and confrontation, among other methods. They also propose the use of other techniques in overcoming the suspect's resistance and denial, such as frequent topic changes, normalisation, sympathising, encouraging confession and stressing the positive aspects of confession. At the same time, the authors warn of using criticism, moralising, abrupt topic changes, threats, blackmail, deceit, of giving promises, lying and constantly interpreting the suspect's statements. The manual also highlights the importance of analysing possible non-verbal and verbal cues to deception in a suspect, but does not suggest using Reid's behavioural analysis interview (BAI). According to the BAI, truthful suspects respond differently to specialised questions than deceptive suspects (Inbau *et al.*, 2013). The authors of the BAI believe that it is a diagnostic tool for detecting deceit. In analysing signs of deception, the authors of the Slovenian manual drew heavily from psychologist Aldert Vrij (Vrij, 2000), but also added a number of verbal and non-verbal signs promoted in interrogation manuals (e.g. Inbau *et al.*, 2013; Zulawski and Wicklander, 1993). It can therefore be assumed that most of the psychological manipulation techniques used on suspects in Slovenia today originate in overly-coercive interrogation techniques. Sadly, there is a lack of research evidence either corroborating or contradicting this fact, so the actual practices of Slovenian criminal investigators can only be deduced from the Slovenian police manual.

Conclusion

In some democratic countries, the last decade and a half has seen significant changes in police law and criminal procedural law, resulting in lower standards for ensuring human rights protection of suspects. These reforms can mainly be traced to the imperative of efficiency and the 'realisation' that having a wide range of rights and procedural guarantees protecting the suspect represents a serious obstacle to fighting crime. Even though it seems that, at least for the moment, legal regulation of rights granted to suspects during police interrogations in Slovenia has successfully bypassed adverse changes, this does not mean that problems do not exist in this segment of criminal proceedings.

The amendment to the Criminal Procedure Act containing the new regulation of police interrogation has been the target of fierce criticism. The critics are particularly concerned about the situation in which a suspect, after being read the Miranda warning, agrees to proceed without counsel present or counsel does not arrive. In this case, police officers are allowed to question the suspect and make an official note containing their statements which stays in the court files, with the defence unable to refute it or challenge its contents. Under special circumstances, the judge deciding the case may also become familiar with the official notes. The critics therefore claim that the issue of psychological contamination of judges – the main reason for amending the Criminal Procedure Act – was not resolved with the amendment. It should also be pointed out that case law in Slovenia rarely indicates examples of prohibited interrogation techniques used by law enforcement officials (e.g. forced statements and confessions resulting from police deception, psychological manipulation, etc.). As there is also a lack of scientific evidence confirming or disputing the use of such police interrogation methods, the actual practices of police investigators can only be inferred from the guidelines provided in the Slovenian police interrogation manual.

Notes

1. This chapter concentrates on police interrogation of persons in pre-trial procedures under the Criminal Procedure Act. In addition, other forms of gathering statements and examining suspects or defendants of a criminal offence also exist in Slovenian legal regulation and practice.

2. Their main concern was that the new legal set-up, giving the interrogation powers previously conferred on the judiciary also to police officers, could affect the level of protecton of the suspect's rights.
3. The Constitutional Court of Slovenia has ruled, much like the European Court of Human Rights before it, that the right to silence and the privilege against self-incrimination are inseparably tied to the presumption of innocence. These two constitutional procedural guarantees supposedly stem from the presumption of innocence (and the right to protection of human personality and dignity).
4. See Constitutional Court of Slovenia decision no. Up-1678/08 (2010).
5. In Slovenia, plea bargaining was introduced into the criminal procedure as late as 2012. Despite being questionable from the perspective of constitutional guarantees, it was adopted relatively fast in case law as it significantly reduces the total length of criminal proceedings. In 2012, plea bargaining was successful in 140 out of 166 cases in total.
6. The results of a comparative analysis (Flander and Zupan, 2012) have revealed that constitutional and statutory regulation of police interrogations in Slovenia exceeds, in some aspects, the case law standards of the ECtHR. The reasons for this are not so much in the potential flawlessness of the Slovenian legal framework but in the fact that the ECtHR case law is guided by the court's endeavours to set minimum standards to those countries which markedly lag behind in this area.
7. See, for example, *Rehbock* v. *Slovenia*, no. 29462/95 (2000) and *Matko* v. *Slovenia*, no. 43393/98 (2006).
8. If the statement was obtained by using force, threats or any similar means, the privilege against self-incrimination is ensured with the prohibition of questioning an official on the suspect's statements and/or with a prohibition to use such statements as evidence.
9. Here, this case significantly differs from the case *Sounders* v. *United Kingdom* on which the ECtHR reached a ruling in the 1990s. In his complaint, the applicant, Mr Sounders, claimed that he had made statements to the Department of Trade and Industry inspection officials under duress, and the defendant (i.e. the state) did not oppose the applicant's claims.
10. *Psychologie des Strafverfahrens.*
11. *Experimentelle Untersuchungen über Assoziationen Gesunder.*
12. *Die Kriminalpolizei: Handbuch für den kriminellen Polizeidienst.*

References

Constitution of the Republic of Slovenia 1991, *Official Gazette*, 33/91-I and later.

Constitutional Court of the Republic of Slovenia (2002) U-I-92/96.

Constitutional Court of the Republic of Slovenia (2011) Up-1293/08-24.

Criminal Procedure Act 1994, *Official Gazette*, 63/94 and later.

Dežman, Z. and Erbežnik, E. (2003) *Criminal Procedural Law of the Republic of Slovenia*. Ljubljana: GV.

Fišer, Z. (2003) 'Selected constitutional issues of the pre-trial procedure', *Zbornik 9. dnevi javnega prava*, 9: 87–101.

Flander, B. and Zupan, M. (2012) 'Paths and shortcuts in the Slovene legal regulation and case law of the European Court of Human Rights', in I. Areh (ed.), *Investigative Interview: Some Law and Psychological Aspects*. Ljubljana: Tipografija, pp. 35–65.

Grassberger, R. (1950) *Psychologie des strafverfahrens* [*The Psychology of Criminal Proceedings*]. Vienna: Springer Verlag.

Inbau, F. E., Reid, J. E., Buckley, J. P. and Jayne, B. C. (2013) *Criminal Interrogations and Confessions*, 5th edn. Chicago: John E. Reid & Associates.

Maver, D. (1997) *Criminalistics*. Ljubljana: Uradni list republike Slovenije.

Musek, J., Polič, M. and Umek, P. (1992) *Introduction to Psychology*. Ljubljana: Ministrstvo za notranje zadeve.

Putnik, D. (1973) *Psychology*. Belgrade: Viša škola unutrašnjih poslova.

Republic of Slovenia, Ministry of the Interior (2003) *Gathering Information from the Suspect – Amendment to the Criminal Procedure Act*. Ljubljana: Ministrstvo za notranje zadeve.

Roso, Z. (1988) *Informative Interview*. Zagreb: Republički sekretariat za unutrašnje poslove SR Hrvatske.

Stare, D. (2004) *Police Interrogation*. Ljubljana: Ministrstvo za notranje zadeve.

Štirn, M. and Podvršič, I. (2003) *Gathering Information from the Suspect*. Ljubljana: Ministrstvo za notranje zadeve.

Šugman, K. (2005) 'On police interrogation and evidential value of the suspect's deposition according to the Criminal Procedure Act', *Pravosodni bilten*, 26: 135–48.

Šugman, K. (2006a) 'The regulation of information gathering from alleged suspects', *Zbornik znanstvenih razprav*, 66: 287–307.

Šugman, K. (2006b) *Basis for a New Criminal Procedure Model*. Ljubljana: Inštitut za kriminologijo pri Pravni fakulteti.

Šugman, K. S. and Gorkič, P. (2011) *Evidence in Criminal Procedure*. Ljubljana: GV.

Supreme Court of the Republic of Slovenia (2005) I Ips 114/2005.

Supreme Court of the Republic of Slovenia (2013) I Ips 31018/2011-420.

Vodinelić, V. (1987) *Criminalistics*. Belgrade: Naučna knjiga.

Vrij, A. (2000) *Detecting Lies and Deceit: The Psychology of Lying and the Implications for Professional Practice*. London: Wiley.

Vrij, A. (2008) *Detecting Lies and Deceit: Pitfalls and Opportunities*. Chichester: John Wiley & Sons.

Zulawski, D. E. and Wicklander, D. E. (1993) *Practical Aspects of Interview and Interrogation*. New York: Elsevier.

18 Investigative interviewing of suspects in Switzerland

Julie Courvoisier, Christophe Sellie and Michel St-Yves

Introduction

The establishment of Switzerland is dated at 1 August 1291 when the cantons of Uri, Schwytz, and Unterwald signed the Federal Charter. Through this commitment, these three first cantons promise *an everlasting covenant against any aggressor*. As the centuries passed, 23 cantons would join them to create what would become the Swiss Confederation.

Until recently, there was no consistency between cantons in their practice and training in investigative interviewing, because each one had its own Criminal Procedure Code.[1] There were important discrepancies between the cantons regarding the application of criminal law that impeded the work of police and justice when the cases were outside the canton (St-Yves *et al.*, 2013). In 1992, a judicial arrangement for mutual legal assistance and cooperation between the cantons was suggested to the cantons and most of them agreed. Then, a code of unified criminal procedure was conceived on 5 October 2007 in Switzerland and was enacted on 1 January 2011. This led to important changes in the practice and training of investigative interviewing.

The aim of this chapter is thus to describe the impact of these changes introduced by the new Swiss Criminal Procedure Code (CPP) and then to give an overview of training and practices on investigative interviewing in Switzerland.

The new Swiss Criminal Procedure Code

Before 2011, there were four models of criminal procedure across the cantons and after several discussions about the choice of the unified model, the legislators decided to adopt the one titled *Prosecution II*. This latter option was already in force in two cantons, as well as in Germany, Italy, the United States, and international criminal tribunals (Kuhn, 2008). This model was chosen not only because it has been adopted internationally, but also due to its efficiency. Indeed, files are now in the hands of a single authority, namely the prosecution.

Since 2011, the prosecutor has held a main position in the new code, being the only master on board throughout the preliminary procedure. Indeed, he/she conducts the investigation and then prepares the indictment required by the court

(Kuhn, 2008; Michaud Champendal, 2010). However, this single insight into a criminal case can cause potential miscarriages of justice (Kuhn, 2008). To counterbalance these broad powers given to the prosecutor, two safeguards were introduced: a court able to order detention measures[2] and immediate access to counsel. This latter institution represents the right for the defendant to be assisted by a lawyer from his/her first police interrogation. Thus, with these two changes, the legislator has strengthened defendant's rights (Cornu, 2010). As the presence of a lawyer in the interrogation is certainly the major innovation of this new code, it is important to describe it here.

Immediate access to counsel

Several debates preceded the implementation of a defendant's right to immediate counsel. Those in favor have emphasized the importance of equality of arms, the control of the interrogation methods used by the police, and the respect for international requirements (Kuhn and Jeanneret, 2011). Those opposed – mainly the criminal prosecution authorities – have highlighted the obstruction to seeking the truth (Kuhn and Jeanneret, 2011).

In the former procedure, the lawyer did not intervene at any time in police interrogation. Now, at the beginning of interrogation, every accused person must be informed that he/she has the right to be assisted by a lawyer of his/her choice. This applies for all offences committed and at the expense of the suspect. However, if the suspect is liable for imprisonment for a period not less than one year,[3] the presence of a lawyer during interrogation is mandatory, whether the suspect wants one or not (Harari and Aliberti, 2011).

Three years after the introduction of the lawyer in the interrogation room, the results have generally been positive. Indeed, police officers and lawyers seem to have adapted to the situation and there has been no real negative impact on confession rates. Solothurn, the only canton which had authorized before 2011 the presence of a counsel during interrogation, also did not seemingly produce any obstruction of justice. Moreover, each professional seem to be satisfied with the system and its introduction in the new federal procedure (Michaud Champendal, 2010). However, the path that led to this current situation was not without pitfalls and some issues remain unresolved. For example, this new code of criminal procedure remains unclear about the real practice of the lawyer in the interrogation room. This produces various interpretations, in particular between police and prosecutors on the one hand and between lawyers on the other. In fact, everyone seeks to read between the lines, in accordance with his/her practice, objectives, and convictions. This has generated, and still generates today, several discussions and exchanges, sometimes tense, to find a common ground. The objective is to get the balance right between the pursuit of the investigation and the search for the truth by the police, while allowing lawyers to act and intervene for the rights of their clients, in order to satisfy everyone. This balance is not easy to achieve, especially when there is a wide room for interpretation in the legal texts. However, even if there are still debates, great strides have already been taken toward conciliation since the enactment of the code.

The immediate access to counsel is laid down in Article 159 of the Code of Criminal Procedure. The first paragraph says that "during a police interrogation, the suspect has the right to have his/her lawyer present who can ask questions."[4] From a police perspective, anyone intervening during interrogation could hinder the work of investigators. Indeed, one of the essential rules of good practice in interrogation is the building of a relationship between the suspect and the interrogator. If the police officer, using various psychological tactics like empathy or active listening, achieves the establishment of a relationship with the suspect, his/her likelihood of obtaining an admission, or even a confession, increases significantly (St-Yves and Landry, 2004; St-Yves, 2014; Vanderhallen *et al.*, 2011; Williamson, 1993). Thus police officers have to remain in control of the interrogation and continue to practice these techniques, while respecting the code and allowing lawyers to *ask questions*. Since it is not in the interest of the lawyer for the interrogation to go wrong or that the suspect finds him/herself in the midst of a war between his/her lawyer and the police, it was first agreed that the lawyer would ask questions only at the end of the interrogation. But even if it helps to avoid breaking the link and the discussion between the police officer and the suspect, these interventions solely at the end are not always beneficial. For example, when rewording or clarifying the words of a suspect are required, it seems inappropriate to do so right at the end, because the end may sometimes be hours later. Thus, how to return precisely and properly to sentences or terms used several hours previously is unclear, as is how not to waste too much precious time discussing what and how it has been said at any time in the interrogation. Thus it is now agreed before any interrogation that the lawyer intervene at the end, but that "he/she also can [...] seek clarification and complement the answers of his/her client to the questions of the police"[5] (Michod, 2010). This also enables the lawyer to fulfill his/her *active* role given by the code, that is he/she is not only present to inform and advise clients of their rights (Mazou, 2012). This leads to the issue of the transcript of the interrogation.

The transcription of investigative interviewing

In Switzerland, currently only the interviewing of young victims is videotaped. By contrast, interrogations of suspects are not recorded, either by audio or video. Thus the interrogator must input everything into the computer while questioning a suspect, or another police officer must be present to do so. Before the presence of the lawyer, the interrogator could easily speak with the suspect with the laptop closed on the table. At the right moment, the police officer could decide to turn on the computer and start to write the protocol. Now it is recommended to say what is noted aloud, so that the lawyer is able to react immediately if he/she thinks that the statements are not being accurately reported (Mazou, 2012; Moreillon and Parein-Reymond, 2013). The code does not require that the statements be reported word for word, but distortions of what is said are prohibited (Dongois, 2014).

However, this question-and-answer sequence said out loud during the transcription creates a very formal aspect to the interrogation. This fear voiced among police officers before 2011 was apparently justified. In an effort to report accurately the words used – a vital aspect for further procedures – the interrogation may lose its relational and human nature. Thus, it will be more difficult for police officers to create a relationship of trust – and confidence – with suspects in such a formal setting. Indeed, when the person interviewed is continually being interrupted, there is the chance of a loss of spontaneity and opportunities for suspects to think of or prepare another version of his/her statement (Cereghetti, 2011). The police officer would also have more difficulty using some of the psychological methods often necessary during interrogation. These methods do not involve trickery or deceit, but are essential to the establishment of a relationship which allows the suspect to feel at ease if he/she wants to talk, especially if the case is serious and/or sensitive. For this reason, a framework that is too formal could limit the building of a context favorable for potential disclosures.

In sum, it is not easy to find the right balance between the accurate drafting of the interrogation protocol in order to please everyone, without losing psychological aspects consistent with the goals of the police. So one can question the benefits of videotaped interrogation, in particular for serious cases.

The place of the lawyer in the interrogation room

Precisely where the lawyer is in the interrogation room was also not specified by the code and has led to many disputes. In order to avoid untimely interruptions by the lawyer, some cantons first required that the lawyer sit behind the suspect to prevent the transmission of stealth messages or action. Others, because of the arrangement and size of the room, had no choice but to seat the lawyer next to his/her client. There are advantages and drawbacks in all cases both for lawyers and police officers, but also for suspects. When the lawyer is next to the suspect, he or she may say something, but also sigh, shake his/her head or roll his/her eyes. The lawyer can do several things that may disrupt the interrogation, break the relationship established between the suspect and the police officer, or inhibit his/her client who may not know what to say or not say. By contrast, this could subdue or reassure the suspect, and could unblock some situations.

When the lawyer is behind his/her client, he/she is similar to a spectator, which may benefit police officers who can work almost like before when lawyers were not present. This would be beneficial if it is necessary to create an intimacy with the suspect, but it is not well perceived by lawyers who wish to emphasize their active role in the new code. Regarding the suspect, the advantages and disadvantages depend on each situation. It may be sometimes useful to have the lawyer next to him/her and other times it has no influence or it can inhibit him/her. As the investigator must remain in control of the interrogation, he/she may decide the place of the lawyer. However, over time and experience, police officers and lawyers have become comfortable with and respect each other's work. As a result, lawyers often sit naturally beside their client.

If the behavior of the lawyer is abusive or too disturbing to the work of the police, investigators must write it down and, if repeated, they may exclude him/her from the room (Guéniat, 2011), although to our knowledge this has never happened. This could be an inconvenience, but also hinder the work of investigation. Indeed, if the lawyer is excluded from the room, the interrogation must stop, even if the suspect agrees to continue. If the interrogation continued, it could be deemed inadmissible in court (Guéniat, 2011; Moreillon and Parein-Reymond, 2013).

Communication between the lawyer and his/her client

The rest of the legal text about the presence of the lawyer is also vague. It says that "the suspect [...] has the right to freely communicate with his/her counsel in case of interrogation conducted by the police"[6] or that "the person who invokes these rights cannot require the adjournment of the interrogation."[7]

With regard to when the suspect can communicate with his/her lawyer, there is consensus that the communication must take place before the interrogation and in private (Kuhn and Jeanneret, 2011; Message CPP, 1175). The lawyer and/or the suspect can also ask for a suspension during the questioning if necessary. Depending on events, for strategic reasons police officers can offer a suspension and a private talk between the lawyer and his/her client. This could be the case particularly if the lawyer is in a position to help the police. For example, if the suspect denies the evidence but it is not a wise move for him/her to do so, it would be better for the lawyer that the suspect stop denying and show willingness to collaborate with the judicial authorities and his/her good faith. It is then often easier to defend him/her in court. In this case, the lawyer becomes a precious ally for police officers and according to the goal of the interrogation, it would be beneficial not only to convince the suspect, but also the lawyer to cooperate. Thus the interrogator must almost duplicate the work: make alliances both with the suspect and the lawyer, sometimes by using different terms depending on who he/she talks to. As a result of this innovation in the new code, the police officer must extend his/her skills and tools to manage not just one but two opponents. For some officers, the motivation for and pleasure derived from conducting interrogations had declined since 2011, but for others it is a new challenge that brings a new dimension to their daily work.

Regarding the duration of any conversation before the interrogation, a consensus has been naturally established since the beginning. There is no set amount of time, but the conversation must have "a certain shortness"[8] (Message CPP, 1175). It generally lasts between 15 and 30 minutes, depending on the seriousness and complexity of the case or if an interpreter is necessary (Michod, 2010), and varies in the light of the circumstances. This conversation must allow the suspect to tell his/her side of story to the lawyer so that the latter may appreciate the situation and give some advice for further procedures (Kuhn and Jeanneret, 2011). At this moment, they do not have access to the criminal file, but in order to keep within the spirit of this innovation, they must be informed of the overall situation (Harari, 2010; Mazou, 2012). Thus police officers provide the identity of the suspect, his/her language and the main elements of the case (Moreillon and Parein-Reymond, 2013). After that, the investigator is free to decide whether to tell them more or not. Again, this decision is strategic and police officers must evaluate the elements available in order to opt for the best solution.

The role of the lawyer

Custody may not last for longer than 24 hours, regardless of the lawyer's availability (Harari and Aliberti, 2011; Kuhn and Jeanneret, 2011; Michod, 2010). Thus, even if their availability is taken into account, the lawyer must arrive within *an appropriate period* (Moreillon and Parein-Reymond, 2013). Therefore, even if it was not required by the code, the cantons have naturally implemented a permanent presence of lawyers (Kuhn and Jeanneret, 2011; Moreillon and Parein-Reymond, 2013).

Apart from these practical and logistical issues that may directly or indirectly impact the practice of police officers and their interrogation techniques, there are other implications of the presence of a lawyer that are sometimes less explicit. For example, it seems easier for police officers to work with lawyers when they have evidence against the suspect. In these circumstances, from experience, lawyers may anticipate further procedures and thus make the suspect aware that lying or denying evidence is not likely to be in his/her best interest. So what about interviewing in order to gain initial information from suspects? What about cases with little or no evidence? In sex crimes, for example, it is often the word of the suspect against the victim – there is rarely physical evidence or witnesses. Police officers interrogating suspects in this kind of case must use tactics based on relationship-building and psychology, not just because of this lack of evidence, but also because of the sensitive aspect of this kind of crime. Indeed, it is not easy to confess, but it is certainly more difficult to confess when the crime committed has a shameful stigma attached (Holmberg and Christianson, 2002; St-Yves and Tanguay, 2009), and to confess quickly. Thus, it is important that police officers take time to build a rapport with the suspect, to speak about things not directly related to the offence, in order to build up trust and make the suspect comfortable to tell his/her story. Creating this intimacy between the interrogator and the suspect is obviously more sensitive when someone else is in the room. And if this person does not understand why the police officer takes time to talk about something other than the case or shows empathy for the suspect, it could have negative consequences for the rest of the interrogation. A big change for Swiss police officers is that they must now, if possible, better prepare the files before questioning the suspect. However, in cases where it is not possible to establish a solid file before the interrogation, police officers must consider other strategies – a more lengthy preparation and planning phase, a deeper analysis of the suspect's personality, motivators and weaknesses, or educating lawyers about interviewing techniques.

The lawyer in the interrogation room may also affect the creation of the relationship between the suspect and the interrogator or hamper the use of psychological methods. This may also play a role in the attitude of the investigator, for example when showing empathy or using tactics like minimization or valorization, familiar techniques in the field (Inbau *et al.*, 2004). Therefore, even though confession rates remained fairly stable in most Swiss cantons after this innovation, the work of the police became burdensome. Questions remain, such as: how to enable police officers to ensure an interrogation while preserving the suspect's rights; how to improve police tactics despite the presence of a third party in the interrogation room; or how to possibly increase confession rates. Some options are now being discussed, envisaged, and even proposed. The quality of evidence should be improved, by doing more work before interrogation in order to be more prepared and equipped in front of the suspect and the lawyer. Indeed, time actually spent by Swiss police officers on preparing and planning an interrogation is very short. This is not something highlighted in their training and practice, and is a step often neglected. Yet, a study by Clarke and Milne (2001) revealed that investigators trained in the use of PEACE, a model which recommends this preparation phase to better plan and deal with legal aspects of interrogations, cited "not having enough time to prepare properly" most often when asked about factors that prevented them from conducting better interviews.

With regard to factors related to internal and external pressures, an awareness program or training of lawyers regarding police tactics should be implemented. The benefit of a confession is not just receiving a reduced sentence. According to most prosecution authorities, the first aim is not necessarily the conviction or the sentence. In fact, it is also important for the person damaged to be recognized as a victim. Thus a confession or an admission may be very important for the victim and/or his/her relatives. In addition to allowing suspects to give their version of the facts, by assuming responsibility for the crime committed and its consequences, they can acknowledge their actions, if have they not already done so. They can better accept their sentence and maybe start rehabilitation work in order not to reoffend.

The role of interpreters

There are four national languages in Switzerland: French, German, Italian and Romansh. In addition, there are different ethnic groups in Switzerland and about 10 percent of the population has a native language other than these four official languages.[9]

The use of an interpreter can lead to some issues, and even more when a lawyer is also present. Indeed, apart from being an intermediary person who may disrupt the momentum between the interrogator and the suspect or not guarantee an accurate translation of what is said, the interpreter can find him or herself in a no-win situation. In Switzerland, according to logistic and practical reasons, it is generally the same person who acts as interpreter throughout the process of interrogation. This person begins to translate what is said during the private conversation between the lawyer and the suspect, which is meant to be confidential. Therefore, while the interpreter should be a *court officer*, he/she is in a private relationship and may then translate the interrogation in the presence of the police (Moreillon and Parein-Reymond, 2013). Ideally, the lawyer should speak the same language as the suspect in order to avoid the intervention of a third party during their private session, or there should be two different interpreters between the private conversation and the interrogation. However, this would often not be practical and would be difficult and expensive (Guéniat, 2011; Kuhn and Jeanneret, 2011; Moreillon and Parein-Reymond, 2013).

However, some lawyers see an advantage to having the same interpreter during the two sessions. It is not always easy for them, especially if they are court-appointed lawyers, to build a confident, trusting relationship with their client during the preliminary conversation. During this short time, they may also need to ensure that the interpreter is appropriate and understood by the suspect. Despite the presence of the interpreter, the suspect may be reassured during this private session in order to confide in the lawyer. Thus, according to most lawyers, it would be inappropriate to break this and almost start over by introducing a new and unknown interpreter. The best solution seems to be to have only one interpreter for everything, but to systematically remind him/her orally of their obligation to professional secrecy (Kuhn and Jeanneret, 2011), or by the signing of a form (Guéniat, 2011).

Current training in investigative interviewing

Changes in this new code of criminal procedure have not only impacted investigative interviewing practices but also training in this field. Moreover, in anticipation of this influence, continuous training was implemented four years before the code was enforced.

Today, in the French part of Switzerland, increasing numbers of police officers are trained to use structured protocols in order to interview witnesses and victims, in particular the protocol of cognitive interviewing using the principles of Geiselman and Fisher (1992, 2014). Regarding interviewing of suspects, all investigators receive an initial training at the Police Academy. More in-depth training is then provided for some, in order to carry out interrogation in accordance with the new code. This latter training, with both theoretical and practical parts, mainly focuses on the understanding of psychological mechanisms involved in interrogation (see St-Yves and Meissner, 2014). The effectiveness of these methods relies on research in this area. The practical section allows police officers to experiment with a protocol including its essential components to effectively conduct an interview with a suspect, that is to say: (1) preparation (and planning) of interrogation; (2) legal aspects (custody, right to have a lawyer); (3) rapport building and communication/gathering information; (4) disclosure of evidence; (5) exploration of the fears and resistance of the suspect; (6) authentication of confession (if needed); and (7) closure of the interview. Training and practice interviewing with suspects are based on good practices within the field of investigative interviewing (for a recent review of research and practice on investigative interviewing, see Bull, 2014; St-Yves, 2014).

Finally, a short section about the psychology of detecting lies and deceit is included to inform police officers about the most objective cues for truth-telling and lies (based on scientific research: see Vrij, 2008, 2014), and to make them realize that care must be taken when assessing someone's credibility.

Aside from receiving training on appropriate ways of questioning witnesses, victims and suspects (using open-ended questions, listening without interruption), police officers are also made aware of the risks associated with investigative interviewing, in particular the contamination of the account by suggestive and leading questions. In addition, they are informed about precautions to be taken with people who are intellectually or psychologically vulnerable, in order to prevent false confessions.

Conclusion

Three years after its beginning, this new code and its direct influence on police interviewing are judged to be positive overall. Indeed, in most cases, an agreement seems to have been reached, thus ensuring a smooth collaboration after working on the initial problems. However, all interviews and suspects are unique, so investigators have to adapt their techniques and practices to each situation in accordance with the type of case, lawyer, or suspect and this task can be more or less sensitive. In addition, despite a cordial cooperation, it should not to be forgotten that police officers and lawyers do not have the same objectives. If the former work for the search for the truth, the mission of the latter is to defend the interests of suspects. These dichotomous goals do not allow a perfect cooperation going in the same direction. Thus there will certainly always be discrepancies between these professions. What might be the possible improvements or recommendations to reduce disparities between them?

The value of what is said during interrogation is not only to obtain a confession for the personal satisfaction of the investigators, but to allow everyone – victims and suspects – to *turn the page* and move on. And even if there is no confession, precious information can come out during the interrogation that can help the result. For this reason, initial and continuous training must be improved, that is for police officers, lawyers, magistrates, interpreters, and all others working in the field of investigative interviewing.

Finally, the issue of videotaped interrogation in Switzerland is the focus of debate among professionals. This practice is now well-established overseas and has recently been adopted in some European countries.[10] Studies on videotaping emphasize a cost-benefit ratio that warrants thinking about the adoption of this practice. Some thought should be given to this issue. Without necessarily imagining a step backward, removing lawyers from the interrogation room but videotaping proceedings may be an additional tool or an acceptable alternative if the lawyer cannot be present with the suspect.

Notes

1. And also a Military Code of Criminal Procedure, a Federal Code of Criminal Procedure and an Administrative Code of Criminal Procedure.
2. Translated from French: Tribunal des mesures de contraintes (TMC).
3. It generally includes the most serious offences of the Swiss Penal Code (homicides, murder, robbery, sequestration, kidnapping, rape, child sexual abuse, arson, etc.). Differences exist between cantons about offences considered in this list not directly established by the Criminal Procedure Code.
4. Translated from French: "Lors d'une audition menée par la police, le prévenu a le droit à ce que son défenseur soit présent et puisse poser des questions."
5. Translated from French: "soit aussi admis [...] à faire préciser et compléter les réponses du prévenu aux questions posées par la police."
6. Translated from French: "le prévenu [...] a le droit de communiquer librement avec son défenseur en cas d'audition menée par la police" (Art. 159 al. 2 CPP).
7. Translated from French: "celui qui fait valoir ces droits ne peut exiger l'ajournement de l'audition" (Art. 159 al. 3 CPP).
8. Translated from French: "une certaine briéveté."
9. For example: Serbo-Croatian, Slovenian, Albanian, Portuguese, Spanish, English, Turkish, Russian, Greek, Macedonian.
10. Interrogations in the UK have been audio-recorded since 1984, but not systematically videotaped.

References

Bull, R. (ed.) (2014) *Investigative Interviewing*. New York: Springer.

Cereghetti, A., interviewée dans "Je ne crois pas à l'impartialité des procureurs," *Plaidoyer*, 6/11 du 3 décembre (2011) Propos recueillis par Suzanne Pasquier.

Clarke, C. and Milne, R. (2001) *National Evaluation of the PEACE Investigative Interviewing Course*, Police Research Award Scheme, Report No. PRAS/149. London: Home Office.

Cornu, P. (2010) "Le nouveau ministère public – son fonctionnement et ses compétences," in R. Pfister-Liechti (ed.), *La procédure pénale fédérale*. Berne: Stämpfli Editions SA, pp. 51–78.

Dongois, N. (2014) *L'erreur judiciaire en matière pénale: Regards croisés sur ses contours en matière pénale*. Zurich: Schulthess.

Fisher, R. P. and Geiselman, R. E. (1992) *Memory-enhancing Techniques for Investigative Interviewing: The Cognitive Interview*. Springfield: Charles C. Thomas.

Geiselman, R. E. and Fisher, R. P. (2014) "Interviewing witnesses and victims," in M. St-Yves (ed.), *Investigative Interviewing: The Essentials*. Toronto: Carswell, pp. 29–62.

Guéniat, O. (2011) "L'avocat de la première heure: ce qui va changer," *Plaidoyer*, 1: 27–30.

Harari, M. (2010) "Quelques réflexions autour du droit du prévenu à la présence de son conseil," in R. Pfister-Liechti (ed.), *La procédure pénale fédérale*. Berne: Stämpfli Editions SA, pp. 79–94.

Harari, M. and Aliberti, T. (2011) Cited in A. Kuhn and Y. Jeanneret (eds), *Commentaire romand du Code de procédure pénale suisse*. Basle: Helbing Lichtenhahn.

Holmberg, U. and Christianson, S. A. (2002) "Murderers' and sexual offenders' experiences of police interviews and their inclination to admit or deny crimes," *Behavioral Sciences and the Law*, 20: 31–45.

Inbau, F. E., Reid, J. E., Buckley, J. P., and Jayne, B. C. (2004) *Criminal Interrogation and Confessions*, 4th edn. Sudbury, MA: Jones & Bartlett.
Kuhn, A. (2008) *Procédure pénale unifiée: reformatio in pejus aut in melius?* Charmey, Switzerland: Les Editions de l'Hèbe.
Kuhn, A. and Jeanneret, Y. (eds) (2011) *Commentaire romand du Code de procédure pénale suisse*. Basle: Helbing Lichtenhahn.
Mazou, M. (2012) "Avocat de la première heure: Quo vadis?" *Jusletter*, 1–15.
Message du Conseil fédéral du 21 décembre 2005 relatif à l'unification du droit de la procédure pénale, FF 2005 1175.
Michaud Champendal, L. (2010) "L''avocat de la première heure' dans la procédure pénale suisse," *Jusletter*, 1–14.
Michod, J. (2010) "Avocat de la première heure et droits de la défense," *Revue de l'avocat*, 8: 323–7.
Moreillon, L. and Parein-Reymond, A. (2013) *Code de procédure pénale. Petit commentaire*. Basle: Helbing Lichtenhahn.
St-Yves, M. (2014) "Rapport in investigative interviews: five fundamental rules to achieve it," in M. St-Yves (ed.), *Investigative Interviewing: The Essentials*. Toronto: Carswell.
St-Yves, M. and Landry, J. (2004) *Psychologie des entrevues d'enquête. De la recherche à la pratique*. Cowansville, Quebec: Les Editions Yvon Blais.
St-Yves, M. and Meissner, C.A. (2014) "Interviewing suspects," in M. St-Yves (ed.), *Investigative Interviewing: The Essentials*. Toronto: Carswell, pp. 145–89.
St-Yves, M. and Tanguay, M. (2009) "The psychology of interrogation: a quest for a confession or a quest for the truth?" in M. St-Yves and M. Tanguay (eds), *The Psychology of Criminal Investigations: The Search for the Truth*. Toronto: Carswell, pp. 9–40.
St-Yves, M., Sellie, C. and Vuidard, E. (2013) "L'interrogatoire de police 2.0: Perspectives nord-américaine et européenne," in *Droits de la personne: la circulation des idées, des personnes et des biens et capitaux. Actes de Journées Strasbourgeoises de l'Institut canadien d'études juridiques supérieures 2012*. Cowansville, Quebec: Editions Yvon Blais, pp. 289–318.
Vanderhallen, M., Vervaeke, G., and Holmberg, U. (2011) "Witness and suspect perceptions of working alliance and interviewing style," *Journal of Investigative Psychology and Offender Profiling*, 8: 110–30.
Vrij, A. (2008) *Detecting Lies and Deceit: Pitfalls and Opportunities*. Chichester: Wiley.
Vrij, A. (2014) "Myths and opportunities in verbal and nonverbal lie detection', in M. St-Yves (ed.), *Investigative Interviewing: The Essentials*. Toronto: Carswell, pp. 225–43.
Williamson, T. (1993) "From interrogation to investigative interviewing. Strategic trends in the police questioning," *Journal of Community and Applied Social Psychology*, 3: 89–99.

North America

19 Interviewing suspects in Canada

Brent Snook, Kirk Luther and Todd Barron

Introduction

As with all police organizations around the world, interviews with suspects and accused persons are integral to the investigation of crime in Canada. To gain an appreciable understanding of suspect interviewing in Canada, it is important for readers to be familiar with the structure and autonomy of Canadian policing. Although there is much autonomy for police officers to use their preferred interviewing practices, there is legislation and case law that provides all interviewers with guidance on what are acceptable and unacceptable practices during custodial and non-custodial interviews. Even though there is a growing body of empirical literature that is starting to inform interviewing practices in Canada, much of what has driven investigative interviewing is based on common-sense notions of what *should* work and, more recently, empirically driven guidance on what *actually* works. There has been a major advancement in Canada over the last five years where the scientifically driven PEACE Model of Investigative Interviewing is challenging previously cherished beliefs and practices. As with any promising development, there has been an anticipated resistance to change; much work is therefore needed to reform investigative interviewing to continue the move from coercive practices (and their seemingly less coercive hybrid derivatives) to an empirically based and ethical model. Consequently, the goal of the current chapter is to provide an overview of the aforementioned current state of affairs.

Canadian policing statistics and autonomy

Public-sector policing in Canada consists of four levels, including municipal, provincial, federal, and First Nations. As of 2013, there were nearly 70,000 police officers in Canada. The Royal Canadian Mounted Police (RCMP) is Canada's largest police organization (and the only federal one) with over 17,000 members – the RCMP is contracted primarily by the provinces (and territories) to service rural areas. The provinces of Ontario, Quebec, and Newfoundland and Labrador have provincial police forces – the Ontario Provincial Police, the Sûreté de Québec, and the Royal Newfoundland Constabulary (RNC), respectively. Outside of the RNC, every major city in Canada is policed by a municipal police organization (e.g. Toronto Police Service, Montreal Police Service, Vancouver Police Service). There are more than 150 police organizations in Canada.

Perhaps most important for understanding police interviewing in Canada, however, is the fact that policing is primarily a provincial responsibility – that is, each province may have its own specific mandates and practices. Granted, policing in Canada is informed somewhat by jurisdictional sharing and numerous organizations such as the Association of Chiefs of Police (responsible for a wide mandate which includes consultation with professional and community partners, advancement of legislative and policy reform), the Canadian Police College (responsible for advanced and specialized police training), and the Canadian Police Knowledge Network (responsible for online training solutions for law enforcement). Within provincial guidelines and the legal rules of interviewing in Canada, each police organization is free to employ any suspect interviewing practice(s) it desires; the extent to which any chosen suspect interviewing approach/tactic prevents a statement from being admitted into evidence ultimately resides with a judge. Such autonomy makes it impossible to make broad, sweeping statements regarding suspect interviewing practices in Canada.

It is also important to note that the choice of interviewing practices of police organizations are influenced by the organization's polygraph examiner(s). The polygraph is used widely in Canada for pre-employment interviews and suspect interviews. Members of organizations who are selected to become polygraph examiners attend a three-month program at the Canadian Police College where they receive extensive training in polygraph examinations and suspect interviewing. Upon return to their organization, they are for all intents and purposes, the expert who sets the organization's interviewing policy and practices.

Custodial and non-custodial interviews

There are two broad types of interviewing in Canada – custodial and non-custodial. A custodial interview occurs when an individual is questioned after being taken into custody by law enforcement officials (i.e. arrested or detained). Custodial interviews are usually conducted in a police station. However, if an individual is questioned by the police without being arrested, but feels that his/her freedom is limited (i.e. psychological detention), this would also be considered a custodial interview. As individuals are deprived of their rights and freedoms during a custodial interview, they must be advised of their constitutional rights under the Charter of Rights and Freedoms (i.e. right to silence, right to legal counsel). By contrast, a non-custodial interview occurs when a suspect is interviewed, s/he is not arrested/detained, and the interview may occur outside the confines of a police station. Individuals undergoing a non-custodial interview do not need to be informed of their constitutional rights.

Non-custodial interviews

When a person is interviewed in a custodial setting, s/he is entitled to the legal safeguards as afforded by the Charter. However, individuals are not afforded these protections when interviewed in a non-custodial setting. Perhaps the most prescient, and most controversial, example of a non-custodial interview is the use of the Mr Big technique.

The Mr Big technique is an undercover police operation and is employed to obtain confessions, or clear suspects, in non-custodial environments. An important aspect of the Mr Big technique is that because it is non-custodial, suspects no longer need to be informed of their legal safeguards (i.e. right to silence, right to legal counsel). Mr Big operations are extremely intricate and elaborate, lasting months or years at a time. Typically, the Mr Big technique involves an undercover officer befriending a suspect and attempting to recruit him/her into a powerful and sophisticated, albeit fictitious, criminal organization (Moore and Keenan, 2013). Once the suspect has agreed to join the criminal organization, undercover officers involve the suspect in a series of escalating fictitious criminal activities, for which the suspect is paid generously (e.g. $100/hour; *R.* v. *Mentuck*, 2000). The purpose of this phase is to demonstrate the extreme wealth, power, and reach of the criminal organization, and also to solidify the suspect's commitment to the criminal organization. In addition to the fictitious criminal activities, suspects are also involved in a number of social scenarios. Social scenarios include attending bars, strip-clubs, and hockey games. Suspects are also treated to all-expenses paid national and international trips (e.g. to Banff, Vancouver, New York), where they stay at lavish hotels and dine at the finest restaurants, with all expenses being covered by the criminal organization.

Once the undercover handler believes that the suspect has committed fully to the organization, the suspect is then interviewed for a higher-level position within the organization. Specifically, the Mr Big technique culminates with a meeting between the suspect and the "Big Boss" of the organization (i.e. Mr Big). The suspect is told that in order to remain part of and move up in the criminal organization, s/he must confess to all of their prior criminal activity. Specifically, the officer attempts to obtain a confession for the serious crime that the suspect is believed to have committed. If the suspect does not confess, s/he will be banished from the organization.

An individual Mr Big operation may utilize as many as 50 police operatives and cost over a million dollars (Kauri, 2013; Smith *et al.*, 2012). While the RCMP has not supplied information on the percentage of Mr Big operations that result in a confession, they have stated that in 75 percent of the operations the suspect is either charged or cleared of the crime. Of the Mr Big cases that are prosecuted in court, the RCMP boasts a conviction rate of 95 percent. In terms of prevalence, the RCMP stated that the Mr Big technique has been used over 350 times as of 2008. While developed in Canada, the Mr Big technique has been used in Australia, New Zealand, and South Africa, and confession evidence obtained from a Mr Big sting has been used in the United States (RCMP, 2011).

On 31 July 2014, the Supreme Court of Canada (SCC) released a decision regarding the admissibility of confessions obtained from the Mr Big technique (*R.* v. *Hart*, 2014). There are two central tenets of the ruling. First, is that the probative value of a confession obtained during a Mr Big operation is a function of the reliability of the confession. That is, the court must assess the circumstances under which the confession was made (e.g. length of operation, presence of threats) to determine whether the confession is reliable. Second, confessions that are obtained by overcoming the will of the accused should be ruled inadmissible – that is confessions that are obtained through coercion should not be used as evidence against the accused. In general, the courts have ruled that Mr Big ploys can be used by police organizations as long as certain procedures are followed.

Custodial interviews

Suspects and accused persons who undergo a custodial interview in Canada are afforded legal safeguards under the Canadian Charter of Rights and Freedoms (henceforth referred to as the Charter), and guidance from case law. That is, suspects must be informed of their right to silence and right to legal counsel, which are derived from sections 7 and 10b of the Charter, respectively. Section 7 of the Charter states that "Everyone has the right to life, liberty and security of the person and the right not to be deprived thereof except in accordance with the principles of fundamental justice." In Canadian case law, the right to silence means that suspects and accused persons must be given a free choice about whether to speak to the police (see *R.* v. *Hebert*, 1990). While those questioned by the police are not lawfully compelled to answer any questions, police officers are also not compelled to cease their questioning (*R.* v. *Singh*, 2007). Thus continued questioning of a suspect after s/he has invoked his/her right to silence is permitted under Canadian case law, and any confession obtained through this manner may still be admissible in court. However, persistent questioning once a suspect has invoked this right may lead to a confession being deemed involuntary (e.g. *R.* v. *S. (D.)*, 2010).

The right to legal counsel is contained in section 10b of the Charter and states that: "Everyone has the right on arrest or detention to retain and instruct counsel without delay and to be informed of that right." As clarified in the subsequent cases *R.* v. *Bartle* (1994) and *R.* v. *Brydges* (1990), prior to being questioned by the police, suspects must be notified of: (1) their right to retain and instruct counsel without delay; (2) information about access to counsel free of charge where an accused meets prescribed financial criteria set up by provincial Legal Aid plans; (3) information about access to immediate, although temporary, legal advice irrespective of financial status ("duty counsel"); and (4) basic information about how to access available services which provide free, preliminary legal advice. In addition, while a suspect does not have the right to have their lawyer present during the interview (*R.* v. *Sinclair*, 2010), they do have the right to contact a lawyer of their choice (*R.* v. *McCrimmon*, 2010) and be given reasonable time to contact said lawyer (*R.* v. *Willier*, 2010).

Case law over the past decade has clarified and provided a precise framework of what police officers are permitted to do during an interview, along with the legal rights afforded to those being interviewed, under the Charter. In saying this, it is also important to mention a key piece of case law, *R.* v. *Oickle* (2000), which outlines the confession rule. The confession rule provides guidance on the factors necessary to determine whether a confession was made voluntarily. If a confession was made involuntarily, it may be excluded from trial. In the *Oickle* ruling, the Supreme Court of Canada stated four factors that should be considered by judges when determining whether a confession was made voluntarily: (1) the extent to which the suspect was of sound operating mind when questioned by the police; (2) the use of threats or promises (e.g. no *quid pro quo* offers); (3) the presence of an oppressive environment (e.g. subjecting the suspect to inhumane conduct); and (4) the presence of police trickery (however, some trickery is permitted as long as it does not shock the community).

We know interviews in Canada have, for the most part, evolved from those that were dominated by physically abusive "third degree" practices to those dominated by psychologically manipulative ones (Leo, 2008; but see *R.* v. *Singh*, 2007, for a recent exception in Canada). In recent years, interviews in Canada have been evolving through the emergence of the PEACE Model of Investigative Interviewing (henceforth referred to as PEACE).

The Reid Technique

The modern-day approach to interrogations in Canada is based largely on the Reid Technique (henceforth referred to as Reid). Reid, a common-sense approach to interrogations, consists primarily of two main phases: the behavioral analysis interview (BAI) (see Masip *et al.*, 2012, and Vrij, 2008, for a review of this process) and the nine-step interrogation (Inbau *et al.*, 2011; Kassin *et al.*, 2007). The accusatory interrogation is comprised of nine steps that aim to elicit a confession from an individual through a psychologically pressure-filled interview (Kassin, 2008; see King and Snook, 2009, for a summary of Reid). Despite the movement away from the use of direct physical force to psychological manipulation, little has changed with regard to protecting innocent detainees from coercive interrogations through the use of Reid (see Horselenberg *et al.*, 2003; Horselenberg *et al.*, 2006; Kassin and Kiechel, 1996; Kassin and McNall, 1991; Perillo and Kassin, 2011; Russano *et al.*, 2005).

The PEACE model: conversation management

As mentioned, interrogation practices are now starting to advance in a meaningful way in Canada through the emergence of the PEACE Model of Investigative Interviewing. PEACE is an acronym which stands for the stages of interviewing, which include (1) Preparation and planning; (2) Engage and explain; (3) Account; (4) Closure; and (5) Evaluation. Beyond the stages, PEACE involves interviewers obtaining complete and accurate information, remaining open-minded, acting fairly, and asking questions to establish the truth of the matter under investigation. Under the PEACE model, the term "interrogation" is intentionally replaced with the term "investigative interview" to reflect a humane and ethical interviewing philosophy. In direct contrast to accusatorial approaches, interviewers are taught to collect information before making decisions (e.g. lay charges), which is more akin to hypothesis testing in science. The role of interviewers who utilize PEACE is that of objective fact-finders as they are taught to avoid confirmatory-seeking interviews, not to attempt to detect deception through behavioral cues, and not to lie or use psychologically coercive tactics to manipulate interviewees. PEACE represents a major departure from the psychologically manipulative interrogation approaches currently in use (i.e. Reid). It does not contain coercive strategies that have been linked to false confessions, and gives detainees a chance to provide a full account before moving to evidence-based challenges (if necessary).

Despite the expansion of PEACE throughout Canada, there is still some resistance. We recognize that – as with any novel or promising development – the implementation of PEACE is not immune from the range of practical challenges and resistance from detractors. Some of the common, yet completely unsubstantiated, arguments and myths surrounding the implementation of PEACE include that PEACE and Reid's BAI are equivalent; PEACE restricts the ability to obtain confessions; Canadian laws are different from UK laws so PEACE will not work in Canada; PEACE is too soft an approach to use on suspects; and that PEACE cannot be used without having evidence against the suspect. Once it becomes clear to police officers that such objections are bogus, the use of PEACE as the model of choice will become clearly evident (see Snook *et al.*, 2014, for a response to these bogus claims).

Empirical data: peering inside the Canadian interview room

We are aware of five studies that provide empirical data on what is happening inside the Canadian interview room. A study by Snook *et al.* (2010a) provided insights into how officers delivered the right to silence and right to legal counsel cautions (i.e. section 7 and section 10b of the Charter, respectively). Their results from an examination of 126 investigative interviews (1995 to 2009) showed that the majority of interviews, but not all, contained the right to silence (87 percent) and right to legal counsel cautions (83 percent). However, police officers tended to deliver the cautions quickly, which could impair the suspect's comprehension of their Charter rights. Suspects invoked their right to silence in 25 percent of the interviews examined, and invoked their right to speak to legal counsel in 31 percent of the interviews examined.

King and Snook (2009) provided the first in-depth analysis into what occurs during police interviews with suspects in Canada. They analyzed 44 video-recorded interviews, which took place between 1996 and 2008. The authors analyzed the interviews to determine how often components of the Reid model and its guidelines (described above) were being used, and how frequently Ofshe and Leo's (1996) influence and coercive strategies were employed. King and Snook found that, on average, the interviews lasted approximately 60 minutes. A general analysis of the video-recorded interviews revealed that a full confession was given in 27 percent of interviews, a partial admission in 23 percent, a denial in 39 percent, and "no comment" in 11 percent; that is, 50 percent of the suspects confessed. Their results also showed that, on average, interviewers used 34 percent of the components composing the nine-step Reid model of interrogation. The most commonly observed influence tactics (Ofshe and Leo, 1996) involved confronting the suspect with existing evidence of guilt (82 percent), offering moral justifications or psychological excuses (64 percent), and using praise and/or flattery (57 percent). The use of coercive strategies was rare, with an average of less than one coercive strategy being used in each of the interviews. Minimization tactics (i.e. minimizing the facts/nature/moral seriousness of the offense) were observed slightly more than maximization tactics, and most interviewers followed the guidelines, suggestions, and themes endorsed by Inbau *et al.* (2011).

A recent study by Snook *et al.* (2012) examined the questioning practices of police officers when interviewing suspects. The authors analyzed 80 transcripts of interviews conducted between 1999 and 2008. They found that the average length of interview was just over 33 minutes. Their results showed that, on average, police officers asked over 96 questions per interview. Nearly 70 percent of all questions asked were closed yes-no and probing questions, while open-ended questions composed less than one percent of all questions asked. In addition, a large majority (i.e. more than 60 percent) of the suspect interviews did not contain open-ended questions. In terms of response length, asking an open-ended question resulted in the highest level of response (i.e. an average of over 90 words). The authors found that the 80–20 talking rule (i.e. suspect should talk 80 percent of the time, interviewer should talk 20 percent of the time) was violated in 100 percent of the interviews, and that in the majority of the interviews, the interviewer spoke more than the suspect. Finally, interviewers obtained a free narrative in 14 percent of the interviews. Overall, however, the authors found that best practices were not being followed – rather than using practices that facilitate the extraction of information, interviewers tended to ask many short-answer questions, asked few open-ended questions, dominated the talking time, and requested free narratives infrequently.

Deslauriers-Varin *et al.* (2011) provided insights into interview practices by talking with offenders. Specifically, they attempted to predict the confession decisions of 221 inmates housed in a Quebec penitentiary. Deslauriers-Varin and colleagues gathered data on the offender's age, ethnicity, education, marital status, parental status, crime seriousness, crime type (i.e. drug, property, violent, sexual), length of prison sentence, number of prior convictions, perceptions of evidence strength, use of legal advice, feelings of guilt, and their confession decision. Nearly 45 percent of the sample confessed their crime. They found that confessors (compared to non-confessors) were more likely to have committed a more serious crime, were more likely to have committed a drug offence, perceived evidence to be stronger, were less likely to use a lawyer, and were more likely to report feeling guilty of their crimes. A hierarchical logistic regression analysis revealed that the likelihood of the offender confessing increased with increasing crime seriousness, number of convictions, strength of evidence, and feelings of guilt. They also found that using the services of a lawyer was associated with a decrease in the likelihood of obtaining a confession. It is worth noting that the offender's self-report data, which was used in their analysis, corresponded to the information contained in official correctional files.

Snook *et al.* (2015) interviewed 100 incarcerated men in a Canadian correctional facility about their most recent police interview, with the goal of identifying the factors that predict confessions and cooperation. The authors collected data on a wide range of variables, including the interviewing style, whether legal advice was sought, the length of the interview, and the suspect's perception of evidence, age, previous conviction, number of convictions, offense seriousness, and attitude toward police. Their results showed that the likelihood of an interview ending in a confession was greatest when the suspect perceived the evidence against them to be strong, when police officers used a humanitarian style of interviewing, and when the interviewee had few previous convictions and had not obtained legal advice. Specifically, using this model predicted that the suspect would confess 79 percent of the time. In terms of self-reported levels of cooperation with the police, the likelihood of cooperation increased with increasing humanitarian behaviors. Conversely, the likelihood of cooperation decreased significantly with increasing experience with the criminal justice system (i.e. number of convictions).

Interview training: personal communications

There has never been a systematic review of interview training across the country. Our personal involvement in interview training, interrogations, and communicating with officers from different provinces provide insights into interview training in Canada. In 2009, for example, the Royal Newfoundland Constabulary (RNC) officially adopted PEACE as their standard of interview training for all members – training includes Tier 1 (three-day course for street patrol); Tier 2 (two weeks for witness and suspect interviewing); Tier 3 Child (one week), Advanced Witness (one week), and Advanced Suspect (two weeks); Tier 4 (three-day quality assurance); and Tier 5 (strategic advisor). This tier-based system ensures that all members of the organization gain fundamental interviewing training, while members in specialized roles receive the necessary training and supervision to function effectively in those roles. This system also assigns ownership of interviewing training to a few highly specialized individuals, whose primary responsibility is oversight of all organization-wide interviewing practices. Five years later, the tiered-based PEACE training system (see Snook *et al.*, 2010b) continues to be taught throughout the organization and is now mandated as the sole interviewing model for that organization.

We also know that PEACE has been adopted by other organizations in Canada including Peel Regional Police (they have trained over 700 members, out of approximately 2,000, at the Tier 2 level) and Niagara Regional Police (they have provided training to nearly 30 members thus far). A number of other organizations also have members that have received PEACE training, including the Canadian Police College (CPC), the Vancouver Police Department, the RCMP, Halton Regional, Durham Regional, Greater Sudbury, the Toronto Police Service, the Canadian Military Police, and the Hamilton Police Service. Despite the spread of PEACE across Canada, personal communications with our policing colleagues suggest that Reid (and its derivatives) is still the dominant paradigm for interviewing suspects. We are also aware that some provinces, for example Alberta, have modified their interview training to incorporate PEACE, but have maintained some persuasion in their approach.

Future directions

There is no doubt that there is continued need to reform the way interviews are conducted in Canada. That reform will only be made possible through the concerted effort of police organizations, academics, and the judiciary. Such reform is beginning to happen in the courts (see *R.* v. *Chapple*, 2012) and many police organizations across Canada (see above). However, because policing is a provincial responsibility, the decision to modernize interview practices will likely have to take place on an organization-by-organization basis. It is understandable that the adoption of a national standard is not a straightforward process.

Greater collaboration between criminal justice researchers and police organizations is also required. Collaborations provide an opportunity for researchers to conduct quality research that is based on a realistic understanding of the conditions under which interviews are conducted. Such partnerships may make police officers more aware of the benefits of empirically derived practices and thus increase their willingness to participate in research and engage academics in the training process.

It is only a matter of time before the psychologically manipulative practices that dominate current suspect interviews become extinct. However, if police organizations choose to use illegitimate versions of PEACE (or similar empirically based models), they will undoubtedly continue to face problems related to false confessions and statement admissibility. The persuasive link between accusatorial or coercive methods and false confessions, and the fact that police officers around the world (e.g. the UK, New Zealand, Norway) are conducting effective criminal investigations with the use of a humane interviewing approach suggests that arguments in favour of mean-spirited tactics are less likely to continue to convince a contemporary and progressive judiciary. The relatively minor costs associated with changing interview policies and practices pales in comparison to the financial, political, and legal costs associated with inadequate investigations and miscarriages of justice.

References

Deslauriers-Varin, N., Lussier, P., and St-Yves, M. (2011) "Confessing their crime: factors influencing the offender's decision to confess to the police," *Justice Quarterly*, 28: 113–45.

Horselenberg, R., Merckelbach, H., and Josephs, S. (2003) "Individual differences and false confessions: a conceptual replication of Kassin and Kiechel (1996)," *Psychology, Crime and Law*, 9: 1–8.

Horselenberg, R., Merckelbach, H., Smeets, T., Franssens, D., Ygram Peters, G. J., and Zeles, G. (2006) "False confessions in the lab: do plausibility and consequences matter?" *Psychology, Crime and Law*, 12: 61–75.

Inbau, F. E., Reid, J. E., Buckley, J. P., and Jayne, B. C. (2011) *Criminal Interrogation and Confessions*. Burlington, MA: Jones & Bartlett Learning.

Kassin, S. M. (2008) "The psychology of confessions," *Annual Review of Law and Social Science*, 4: 193–217.

Kassin, S. M. and Kiechel, K. L. (1996) "The social psychology of false confessions: compliance, internalization, and confabulation," *Psychological Science*, 7: 125–8.

Kassin, S. M. and McNall, K. (1991) "Police interrogations and confessions: communicating promises and threats by pragmatic implication," *Law and Human Behavior*, 15: 233–51.

Kassin, S. M., Leo, R. A., Meissner, C. A., Richman, K. D., Colwell, L. H., Leach, A. M., and La Fon, D. (2007) "Police interviewing and interrogation: a self-report survey of police practices and beliefs," *Law and Human Behavior*, 31: 381–400.

Kauri, V. (2013) "The skinny on Mr. Big investigations," 30 October. Retrieved from http://www.macleans.ca/news/canada/the-skinny-on-mr-big-investigations/.

King, L. and Snook, B. (2009) "Peering inside the Canadian interrogation room: an examination of the Reid model of interrogation, influence tactics, and coercive strategies," *Criminal Justice and Behavior*, 36: 674–94.

Leo, R. A. (2008) *Police Interrogation and American Justice*. Cambridge, MA: Harvard University Press.

Masip, J., Barba, A., and Herrero, C. (2012) "Behaviour analysis interview and common sense: a study with novice and experienced officers," *Psychiatry, Psychology and Law*, 19: 21–34.

Moore, T. E. and Keenan, K. (2013) "What is voluntary? On the reliability of admissions arising from Mr. Big undercover operations," *International Investigative Interviewing Research Group*, 5: 46–56.

Ofshe, R. J. and Leo, R. A. (1996) "The decision to confess falsely: rational choice and irrational action," *Denver University Law Review*, 74: 979–1122.

Perillo, J. T. and Kassin, S. M. (2011) "Inside interrogation: the lie, the bluff, and false confessions," *Law and Human Behavior*, 35: 327–37.

R. v. *Bartle* (1994) SCJ No. 74, 3 SCR 173, 33, CR, 1 SCC.

R. v. *Brydges* (1990) 1 SCR 190, 123 SCC.

R. v. *Chapple* (2012) ABPC. 229.

R. v. *Hart* (2014) SCC 52.

R. v. *Hebert* (1990) 2 SCR 151.

R. v. *McCrimmon* (2010) SCJ No. 36, 2 SCR 402, 77 CR 266 SCC.

R. v. *Mentuck* (2000) MJ No. 69 (QB).

R. v. *Oickle* (2000) SCJ No. 38, 2 SCR 3, 147 CCC 321 SCC.

R. v. *S. (D.)* (2010) OJ No. 5748.

R. v. *Sinclair*. (2010) SCJ No. 35, 2 SCR 310, 77 CR 203 SCC.

R. v. *Singh* (2007) SCJ No.48, 3 SCR 405, 51 CR 199 SCC.

R. v. *Willier* (2010) SCJ No. 37, 2 SCR 429, 77 CR 283, SCC.

RCMP (2011) "Undercover operations – questions and answers," 14 December. Retrieved from: http://bc.cb.rcmp-grc.gc.ca/ViewPage.action?siteNodeld=23andlanguageld=1andcontentld=6943.

Russano, M. B., Meissner, C. A., Narchet, F. M., and Kassin, S. M. (2005) "Investigating true and false confessions within a novel experimental paradigm," *Psychological Science*, 16: 481–6.

Smith, S., Stinson, V., and Patry, M. (2012) "Confession evidence in Canada: psychological issues and legal landscapes," *Psychology, Crime and Law*, 18: 317–33.

Snook, B., Brooks, D., and Bull, R. (2015) "Modelling Self-reported Confessions and Cooperation with Police Interrogators." *Criminal Justice and Behavior*.

Snook, B., Eastwood, J., and Barron, T. (2014) "The next stage in the evolution of interrogations: the PEACE model," *Canadian Criminal Law Review*, 18: 219–39.

Snook, B., Eastwood, J., and MacDonald, S. (2010a) "A descriptive analysis of how Canadian police officers administer the right-to-silence and right-to-legal counsel cautions," *Canadian Journal of Criminology and Criminal Justice*, 52: 545–60.

Snook, B., Eastwood, J., House, J. C., and Barron, T. (2010b) "Dispelling myths and moving forward with PEACE," *Blue Line*, November, pp. 22–4.

Snook, B., Luther, K., Quinlan, H., and Milne, R. (2012) "Let 'em talk! A field study of police questioning practices of suspects and accused persons," *Criminal Justice and Behavior*, 39: 1328–39.

Vrij, A. (2008) *Detecting Lies and Deceit: Pitfalls and Opportunities*. Chichester: John Wiley and Sons.

20 Creating culprits in Mexico City

Gustavo Fondevila

Introduction

There are four hard, simple facts that can straightforwardly explain the lack of a systematic methodology for questioning suspects at the Mexican public prosecutor offices: (1) 98 percent of committed crimes are not reported (Zepeda, 2004); (2) 93 percent of detainees were caught in flagrante (Magaloni, 2007); (3) 46.4 percent of the confessions are obtained through violence or extortion (Prison Population Survey, 2014 – N: 1,256); and (4) 90 percent of those processed were sentenced solely on the accused's confession along with – police – statements as additional evidence (Fondevila, in preparation). There is no need to go any further to see that – except in very few cases – there is no criminal investigation in Mexico City. Public prosecutor offices limit themselves to legally process the cases that they receive and decide to pursue without carrying out any criminal investigation. Without scientific investigation of crimes, the interrogation of suspects in order to obtain new information is not a common tool used in police work. Interrogation is not a method of investigation, but a way of judicializing crimes.

In an environment of impunity, distrust in public security and law enforcement agencies, corruption, violence, and a lack of judicial oversight, police investigators and public prosecutors have no inducement to establish successful criminal investigation systems that comply with the due process of the law. It is not simply a matter of problems regarding training, the absence of internal control, or police culture, but of an entire system that operates with the aim of obtaining judicial outcomes without having to investigate or interrogate as the principal means for obtaining relevant information (Zepeda, 2008). Thus there is no empirical data from direct sources – not even on a national level – that make it possible to approach this issue in a way that goes beyond the local tradition of anecdotes and impressions. As a result, there are no academic studies, publications or even institutional reports on the interrogation techniques or methods of investigation used in Mexico's public prosecutor offices.

Within this context, the aim of the current study is to explain why there is no interrogation system (or methodology) in the Mexico City Prosecutor's Office. The key research question is: How can a prosecutor accuse someone of a crime without an interrogation or criminal investigation? The present chapter is a case study that analyzes the practices of the prosecution in Mexico City.

Methodology

Due to the above-mentioned lack of literature, precedents, and direct sources, this chapter is based on the data obtained through the Prison Population Survey (PPS, 2014) conducted by the CIDE[1] in Mexico City and the State of Mexico in 2002, 2005, 2009, and 2013. The sample size of these four surveys adds up to 5,220 interviewed inmates from 26 different prisons. This survey is a tool for the probabilistic measurement of actual events and opinions. Each poll was designed to follow a random, complex, stratified, multi-stage sampling with a systematic selection of observations and a gender quota. Throughout the different stages, two sampling frames were used: prisons and the inmates at each prison. The inmates who volunteered to participate in this survey were selected based on a list of the inmates at each prison using a systematic skip/sampling process on the initial list during a random startup each day of the survey. This process of systematic skips was performed in three stages: (1) the number of surveys to be applied at each center was determined as a percentage of the total number, that is a proportional allocation was carried out; (2) the total number of inmates was divided by the number of inmates to be surveyed at each prison to obtain the skip interval; and (3) a random number was generated each day to serve as the starting point for the selection process of the inmates to be surveyed. In the event of a refusal to answer the survey, the next inmates on the list were chosen using the systematic skip process. The results of these four surveys are comparable and all of them have a theoretical accuracy of ±5.0 percent with a confidence level of 95 percent. The calculation of the size of the samples takes into account a maximum variability, a non-response rate that was calculated in a pilot test and a design effect (Vilalta, 2013).

The survey covered information about four key aspects to learn the characteristics of the most frequent and common criminal activities, as well as compliance of law enforcement institutions with legal procedures. The four key aspects are: (1) the socio-demographic characteristics of the inmates; (2) the patterns observed over the course of their criminal careers; (3) the performance of the institutions involved in security and law enforcement; and (4) living conditions in prisons.

The survey focuses on gathering information from inmates about their lives both before and since their incarceration. This instrument uses a structured questionnaire for selected inmates to respond voluntarily. Information about their distant past (childhood, family, schooling), their present (criminal networks, work, socialization), the types of crimes they committed at the time of their arrest (types and severity of the offense, amounts robbed or trafficked, use of and access to light weapons, substance and/or alcohol dependence), and the due legal process they faced (police treatment, access to lawyers, type of trial, etc.) is thus gathered from the responses. Finally, the last part collects information about certain aspects of their lives in prison (access to educational programs and/or work, basic services, family visits, etc.).

Although a survey of this nature does not give much direct information about police or judicial interrogation in Mexico, it does generate indirect data out of the direct quantitative empirical information from the perception of the "clients" of the system (the persons questioned): if they were beaten, extorted, asked to change their statements, etc. This information can be weighed against other data, like information from judicial records, preliminary investigations, and so on. Before discussing the findings of the case study, the chapter provides some contextual information concerning the criminal justice (and investigative) process in Mexico.

Historical background

During the Miguel Alemán Valdés administration (1946–52), the Federal Directorate of Security (*Dirección Federal de Seguridad* or DFS) was created as a department of the Interior Ministry (Cuéllar Fernández, 2007). This police corps would rapidly become a kind of state political police in charge of espionage and control of dissident groups. Under the José López Portillo administration (1976–82), this police force would be shaped into the General Office of Crime Prevention Investigation (*Dirección de Investigaciones para la Prevención de la Delincuencia* or DIPD). This singular (political) origin of the judicial police served to establish a sharp division between investigating police and preventive police in Mexico City. The Partido Revolucionario Institucional (PRI) regime never allowed political investigation – or criminal investigation later on – to fall into the hands of a police institution that was not directly linked to the party. This might explain the fact that today the judicial police is one of the institutions that is most resistant to change, as well as one of the most corrupt and ineffective (Naval and Salgado, 2006: 40). It is also one of the least transparent and about which little is known and information is scarce. This structure of preventive police and investigative (judicial) police still exists today.

Who interrogates in Mexico?

The Public Prosecutor's Office (*Ministerio Público*, or MP) is the institution that holds the monopoly of criminal proceedings in Mexico. This means that only by filing a complaint before the MP can citizens expect someone to be prosecuted, judged, and finally punished within the criminal justice system. Hence, the MP is established, at least by law, as the only representative of social interest in criminal matters. Although there is a reform of criminal procedure underway in Mexico City, a mixed criminal justice process still operates: during legal proceedings, the party that accuses (MP) and the party that judges are separate entities (accusatory model). Judges are the ones to ultimately issue a ruling on the guilt or innocence of an alleged criminal offender.

However, prior to the trial, the phase that is led by the MP – the preliminary investigation – exhibits distinct features of the inquisitorial model as both the preliminary investigation and the phase during which a case file is either brought before a judge or filed (whether temporarily or definitively) is the same. Moreover, the current system design prevents judges from looking into all the cases to the same extent since they only have 72 hours in which to issue the corresponding constitutional deadline order,[2] and their workload is not generally reduced to one case at a time. In practice, judges must rely on what the MP sets forth in the preliminary investigation, a fact that is significant because it reflects the MP's lack of judicial control.

Mexican institutional models for public security, law enforcement, and law administration models are quite unique. Security and patrolling the streets are the responsibility of the preventive police, which is part of the Mexico City Ministry of Public Security. Although people can be detained for various reasons, this branch of the police cannot investigate or interrogate people. These tasks are performed by the Mexico City Attorney General's Office, which is specifically in charge of criminal investigation and which formally bring charges against the suspect before the courts. Here, a public prosecutor heads the investigation availing him/herself of the police investigators and expert service areas. The police investigators interrogate suspects and interview witnesses, go to the crime scene, and so on, while expert services analyze the evidence with scientific methods (ballistics, fingerprints, criminalistics, forensics, etc.). If the public prosecutor finds sufficient criminal evidence to file charges, the suspect is sent before the judiciary. All the work carried out before a formal accusation is made encompasses the investigation phase, which closes when the public prosecutor brings the suspect before a judge. As of that moment, the public prosecutor takes on the role of the prosecution in the trial (if the judge decides the case proceeds).

The Attorney General's Office is in charge of the investigation and of filing the accusation. In practice, this means a lawyer handles the investigative strategy and directs it from his/her desk (Magaloni, 2007: 13). This function (MP) replaces the figure of the detective – which does not exist in the city's institutional design (Magaloni, 2006) even though the MP does have investigative police at its disposal to perform these activities. In addition to the absence of such a person devoted to and specialized in investigation, there is a regulatory system in which the preliminary investigations carried out by the MP are practically given full evidentiary value during the trial. In other words, all the evidence gathered during the preliminary stages without any oversight by a judge is deemed as having the full weight of evidence at the trial.

Who is interrogated in Mexico?

To better understand the inner workings of Mexico City's criminal justice system, one should begin by learning who is caught (Bergman *et al.*, 2014). The data from the four surveys conducted found that 31.2 percent of the prison population is between 18 and 24 years old and 23.4 percent is between 25 and 29. Before being detained 91.4 percent had a job (almost half were self-employed in the informal sector on the streets: 56.4 percent in 2013 – N: 1,256). A significant number of these people ran away from home before the age of 15 (32.6 percent in 2013, N: 1,256) because of domestic violence (36.4 percent in 2013) and many also have relatives in prison (32.8 percent) (PPS, 2014).

It is also important to know how they came to be arrested. The survey data revealed that most of the inmates in the metropolitan zone have been accused of committing crimes against property, that is armed robbery (34.9 percent) or simple theft (25.4 percent). In all, theft (in all its different forms) accounts for 60.3 percent of the crimes (Bergman *et al.*, 2014 – N: 1,256). At the same time, 56.4 percent of the inmates were detained in the streets and a vast majority of the inmates (about 7 out of every 10: 69.7 percent) claim that if they had enough money, they could have avoided going to prison because they might have been able to buy their way out of it –regardless of whether or not they committed the crime they were accused of (Bergman *et al.*, 2014 – N: 1,256). This high figure is supported by the fact that almost half of the inmates (46.1 percent) report that at least one police officer asked for money or a possession to free them (Bergman *et al.*, 2014 – N: 1,256).

In short, the vast majority of the people in prison are underprivileged youths working on the streets, who quite probably stole something, were arrested on the street, and could not afford a bribe to avoid being brought before the public prosecutor.

How to create culprits

Once the preventive police bring the detainee to the public prosecutor's office, the interrogations begin in order to decide whether to prosecute. And it is at this moment that the highly dubious institutional practices in Latin America are launched: almost half of the inmates in the surveys (45.6 percent – N: 1,256) claim to have been beaten to render statements or to change their statements from pleading innocent to guilty (Bergman *et al.*, 2014). This high percentage has remained relatively unchanged in Mexico City prisons since these surveys (PPS, 2014) began in 2002 (see Figure 20.1).

The above figures make it possible to assert that the use of violence is one of the key and decisive factors for obtaining confessions of guilt from detainees in Mexico City. Figure 20.2 is even more enlightening because it shows the reasons for the confessions. As can be seen, the number of those who spontaneously pleaded guilty because they actually said they were guilty of committing the crimes was 42.6 percent (N: 1,256) and those who were beaten or extorted (45.6 percent) adds up to an overwhelming 88.2 percent. Almost all the people in Mexican prisons pleaded guilty either because they were guilty or because they were beaten or extorted by the public prosecutor.

If this chapter were solely based on interrogations carried out by the MP, it would only focus on 5.5 percent of the inmates who stated they were persuaded

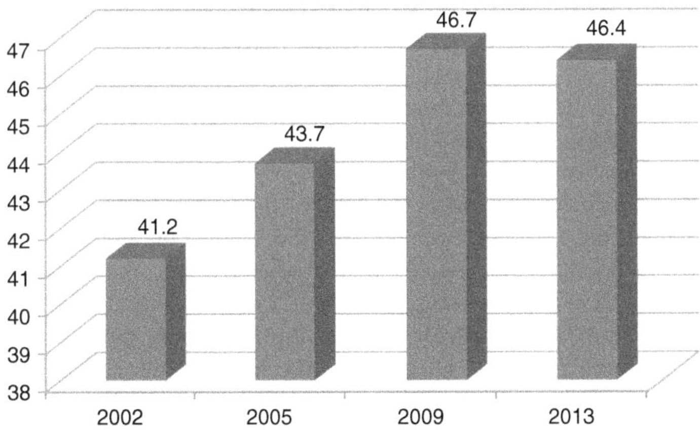

Figure 20.1 Mexico City: Did anyone beat you or use physical force to compel you to render a statement or change your statement (by year: 2002, 2005, 2009, and 2013)?

Source: Calculations based on the 2002, 2005, 2009, and 2013 Prison Population Surveys. Non-responses are not included.

by the MP to confess and 42.6 percent who pled guilty (Figure 20.2). It appears that most of the time, interrogations are not carried out to obtain information but focus on persuading and convincing a detainee to incriminate himself.

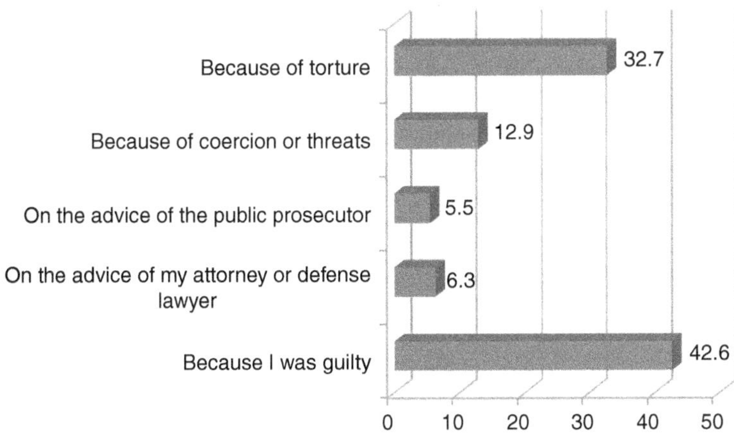

Figure 20.2 Mexico City: Why did you plead guilty?

Source: Calculations based on the 2002, 2005, 2009, and 2013 Prison Population Surveys. Non-responses are not included.

In Mexico City, conviction rates in criminal cases stand at around 92 percent (Court Statistics, 2014),[3] a percentage that is much higher than that of New York City (37 percent in 2012 – CJIR: 2013) or Berlin (79 percent in 2009 – Jehle, 2009: 9). This means that once the trial has begun, the probability of being found guilty is very high. Police corruption chiefly takes place during the early stages of the judicial process (from the moment of detention to the time when the detainee is brought before the judge) as seen in the percentage of police officers who ask for bribes (45.6 percent – N: 1,256; PPS, 2014). They know that once the detainee enters the law enforcement process, the only thing left is to be convicted. Of the total number of case files that were accepted and lawsuits that were initiated (Table 20.1), the courts admitted 72.64 percent of the cases for criminal trial (Court Statistics, 2014). Subtracting the claims that are not pursued by private complainants (who do not give legal follow-up on the claim),[4] out-of-court settlements, etc., which represent 21 percent of all cases, it can therefore be inferred that almost all the cases filed by the public prosecutor's office are admitted into court and almost inevitably end in a conviction (Court Statistics, 2014).

Thus far, law enforcement and criminal justice have been described as working very well for obtaining convictions from case files that include confessions (Seventh Report, 2014). But these case files can have other pieces of evidence. This means that even though there is very little judicial oversight in detentions and the mechanisms for obtaining statements, the judge can order the public prosecutor's office to gather and produce other scientific evidence that supports the confession as a key element of the process. However, as seen in Table 20.2, other than confessions, the only evidence presented in almost every case is statements, which basically consist of two things: (1) a witness *pro forma*, being deputations from the police officers who participated in the detention and the arresting officers; and (2) written testimonies (formal records which are drawn up by the police), i.e. the circumstances of the detention (date and time, etc.). In other words, in 90 percent of the cases, judges admit statements given by the police officers involved in the detention – as the only witnesses of the crimes committed in flagrante – as the only additional evidence other than a confession and these statements only consist of a description of the circumstances surrounding the detention.

Table 20.1 Judicial activity

Mexico City	*2011*	*Total*	*2012*	*Total*
No. of cases filed	20,589	374,659	22,052	345,562
No. of trials initiated	15,641	314,731	16,020	277,238
No. of convictions	16,591	288,728	18,189	246,139

Source: http://estadistica.tsjdf.gob.mx/portal/ (accessed 7 May 2014).

Table 20.2 Type of evidence

Type of evidence	*Average*
Documentary	6%
Expert	4%
Testimony	90%

Source: http://estadistica.tsjdf.gob.mx/portal/ (accessed 7 May 2014).

The mother of all proof

There are many reasons why a system almost completely based on coercive practices can endure and become a common mechanism in law enforcement. As seen above, a confession plays a central and predominant role in both the accusation and the conviction. It is so important that – as seen in Figure 20.2 (Bergman *et al.*, 2014 – N: 1,256) – public defenders themselves have higher rates in obtaining guilty pleas (6.3 percent) than do public prosecutors (5.5 percent). This suggests that public defenders can convince their clients to plead guilty more easily than public prosecutors in the hope of negotiating shorter sentences. In fact, those who plead guilty in the presence of a public prosecutor receive shorter sentences (14 years on average – N: 758; PPS, 2014) compared to those who do so before the MP (19 years on average – N: 415; PPS, 2014).

In Mexico, the weight of a confession has considerably changed over the years. Until a few decades ago, Mexican procedural law considered the maxim of "a confession is the mother of all proof" set in stone. State codes adopted the system for weighing evidence and gave confessions full evidentiary value when substantiated by other evidence and the formal requirements were met. Although these requirements were designed to limit its misuse and give legitimacy to confessions, the high probative value given to confessions and the lack of oversight in obtaining them (in legislation, but especially in practice) directly or indirectly gave way to widescale abuse, much of which was reinforced by controversial court rulings, such as "Confession Before Authorities Without the Competence to It" (Court Opinion 73), "Confession: The Prisoner's Initial Statements" (Court Opinion 78), "Proof of a Confession Obtained under Duress" (Court Opinion 77), and "Retraction of Confession" (Court Opinion 79).

Confession as evidence of guilt is so important that courts do not deem it necessary to present other more scientific evidence to accept the charges against a detainee or a suspect. An example of the role of a confession is seen in the following excerpt of a ruling that set a precedent in 1995:

> When a confession is obtained through physical violence and it is isolated without any other data that corroborates or substantiates it, of course that authority should deny it all value; but if a confession is obtained through blows, and this is corroborated by other data that make it plausible, not

> because of the attitude of police officers should the person responsible who fully confessed his involvement in a given crime be released, naturally without prejudice to the person's right to report the unconstitutional attitude of the law enforcement officers who beat him to the competent authority (Record No. 209400).

This judge's assertion seems to expound everything that is expected from a confession. If the person pleads guilty during the preliminary investigation stage, his/her fate is sealed no matter if he/she can prove that the confession was extracted under torture. Judges' leniency towards public prosecutors and the possibility of presenting preliminary investigations (formal accusations) solely based on a confession of guilt has completely distorted a law enforcement system that was never able to develop a scientific method for interrogating suspects or witnesses. There was never any reason to do so. Resisting any reform, the Attorney General's Office has remained unchanged since around the 1960s.

The use of a confession, however, for the accusing party in criminal trials has gradually become more constricted basically due to the increased attention the media has given to wrongful convictions and constant pressure from the Mexico City Human Rights Commission (through its recommendations to the local Attorney General's Office since the establishment of the commission in 1994).[5] Today, to be considered valid, a confession can only be rendered before the public prosecutor or the judicial authority. Previously, any other authority (naturally including the police) could obtain a confession without any type of judicial oversight (Court Opinion 74). Confessions are no longer given full evidentiary weight because the codes adopted "healthy criticism" or "free" assessment systems that do not obligate the judge to grant full probative value to a confession, but empower the judge to assess it based on his/her experience and critical judgement (although this does not happen in most cases and the judge simply limits him/herself to assuming that the confession obtained from the detainee is valid). This transformation process has taken place within a framework of growing judicialization of the entire criminal procedure. Many of the accused's guarantees were denied him/her during the preliminary investigation. Even then, by means of constitutional reforms and Supreme Court opinions, the guarantees of a defense, non-self-incrimination, and the assumption of innocence, which are vital in the case of a confession, have begun to be extended to every aspect and stage of criminal procedure. The last phase of judicialization will be the implementation of the recent constitutional reforms to criminal matters (oral trials). Through a supervisory judge, the judicial authority will ensure that constitutional guarantees are respected throughout the procedures and that the evidence presented will only be valid if rendered before the judge to hear the case, thus limiting the potential or actual shortfalls in practice within both the Attorney General's Office and police agencies. Meanwhile, in Mexico City, public prosecutors work without any oversight (a supervisory judge, for instance) and the rights of detainees are still not legally protected: the defense scarcely participates in the investigation phase of the proceedings (preliminary investigation).

Conclusions

One piece of information that largely explains how the Attorney General's Office operates in Mexico City is that 93 percent of the detainees are arrested in flagrante (Magaloni, 2007; PPS, 2014). This finding suggests that the agency has all the accused's information at the time of the criminal investigation. In truth, the only crimes that are solved emerge from the detention of a suspect as this means that an investigation was made and brought before a judge who ruled that there was enough evidence to detain a person. The high number of those detained who have been supposedly caught 'red-handed' means that the Public Prosecutor's Office is discouraged from gathering scientific information and analyzing important information in the field or at the crime scene. Any information they do gather is usually gained through the use of coercive practices during interrogations with suspects and other due process violations (Bergman *et al.*, 2014), such as incommunicado detention,[6] the absence of defense attorneys (64.1 percent rendered statements without a lawyer present) and the lack of privacy to speak with a lawyer (59.1 percent), no information on the right to remain silent (63.8 percent), not to speak of the possibility of requesting conditional release during the trial – depending on the type of crime – (86.1 percent), and of course the lack of understanding of the process (three out of every four inmates – 76.4 percent in 2013 – understood little or nothing about the process) (PPS, 2014 – N: 1,256).

Despite this situation, 92 percent of the accusations end in a conviction. This means that the accepted standard of reasonable proof is very low and that judges endorse this situation, does not help to demand or encourage changes in the workings of law enforcement. Moreover, incentives[7] in the judicial system are also aimed at obtaining convictions (Pásara, 2002), which further reinforces the arbitrary nature of the system. In summary, the Mexican case is an example of dubious practices in suspect interrogation.

What's next? Reforms to the criminal justice system

In 2008, the Constitutional Reform to the Criminal Justice System in Mexico was launched.[8] This reform is likely the most ambitious of its kind since the 1917 Constitution[9] and is being introduced gradually (at the moment, some states have already incorporated the new legal system while others, like Mexico City, have yet to do so).[10] The change aims at relinquishing the inquisitorial system and replacing it with an accusatory one that respects the principles of orality, publicity, reply, concentration, continuity, and immediacy.[11] From the perspective of the legislative design of the criminal system, the commitment to democratic change includes the creation of the figure of a supervisory judge (who is responsible for safeguarding the legality of the detention and the respect for the human rights of both the accused and the victim). It also places limitations on the use of pre-trial detention and a new model for the Public Prosecutor's participation in the process, which now has equal standing with that of the accused. The change in legislation is the first step in this in-depth restructuring of the system (Shirk, 2010).

Changing from an inquisitorial criminal system to an accusatory system

The inquisitorial model is predominantly in writing and conducted in secret.[12] The reform seeks to change this system for an adversarial one in which the tasks of investigation and accusation are the responsibility of the public prosecutors. These officials work under the supervision of a new figure called a supervisory judge, who is in charge of safeguarding the rights of those involved in the procedure (both the victim and the accused), and of deciding on the precautionary measures required by the investigation. Cases are judged at an oral and public trial held before an oral court composed of three members, all of whom should not have had any involvement with the case. Moreover, the defense is granted wide-ranging participation in all stages of the proceedings, starting from the investigation phase, in order to make it a truly adversarial process.

Under the new model, public prosecutors cease to have unlimited control over the preliminary investigation as their decisions will be subject to judicial oversight (Arciniegas, 2007). The reformed system is based on the scientific investigation of the crimes (Guillén, 2013). This requires that the quality of the investigations performed by the (current) public prosecutors improve, even to the point of redesigning the investigation itself. Changes to the system include training public prosecutors in criminal investigation (obtaining lawful evidence) and modernizing the prosecutor's expert service system[13] to carry out an effective and lawful investigation of crimes in a way that complies with the judicial supervision to which the agency's performance will be subjected.

So far, the reform has been implemented to various degrees in terms of the progress made in states (for common offenses in each state) and at the federal level (nationwide for federal crimes). For instance, Mexico City has yet to implement the reforms. However, it has been implemented in the State of Mexico, which encircles part of Mexico City and is one of the most populated areas in the country.[14] Although it does not apply to Mexico City, it does give some insight as to the type of changes the reform could bring about in the Federal District. As seen in Figure 20.3, the new judicial process is already showing positive results in the "interrogations" undertaken by the Public Prosecutor's Office (which basically consist of less use of physical force to coerce the "detainees" into rendering a statement or changing their original statement).

Although the data (see Figures 20.3 and 20.4) show that malpractice and unethical tactics are still at unacceptable levels, the new procedure shows a reduction in the excessive use of force at interrogations by the Public Prosecutor's Office.

Improvement has also been seen in interviewees' reasons for pleading guilty. The percentage of confessions obtained under torture dropped from 44.9 percent to 15.4 percent (N: 1,256; PPS, 2014), which gives cause for some optimism regarding the incipient judicial process (Rand, 2014) despite the possible tenuousness of self-reporting data. This reduction in torture is also reflected in a lower sentencing rate, which stood at 75.38 percent in 2013 (Fourth Work Report, 2013: 27).

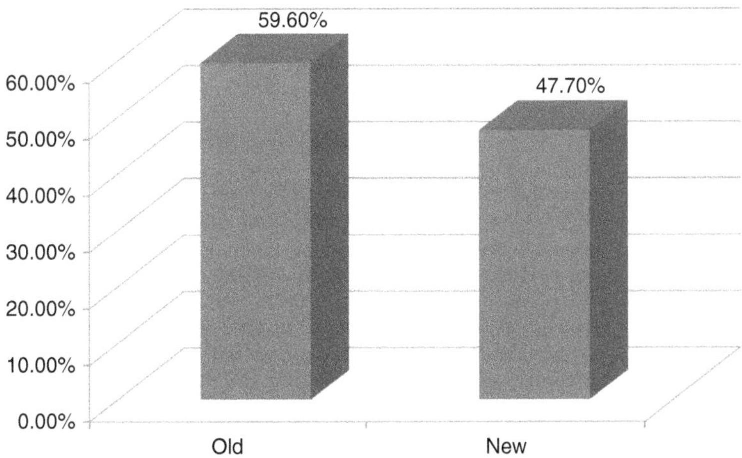

Figure 20.3 State of Mexico: Did anyone beat you or use physical force to compel you to render a statement or change your statement (old and new procedures)?

Source: Calculations based on the 2009 and 2013 Prison Population Surveys. Non-responses are not included.

In summary, in a country where interrogation is not a method of investigation but a means of judicializing crimes, the only way to eliminate torture and extortion is by restricting the incentives that push public prosecutors to obtain higher numbers of confessions, introducing stringent judicial controls, and making trials

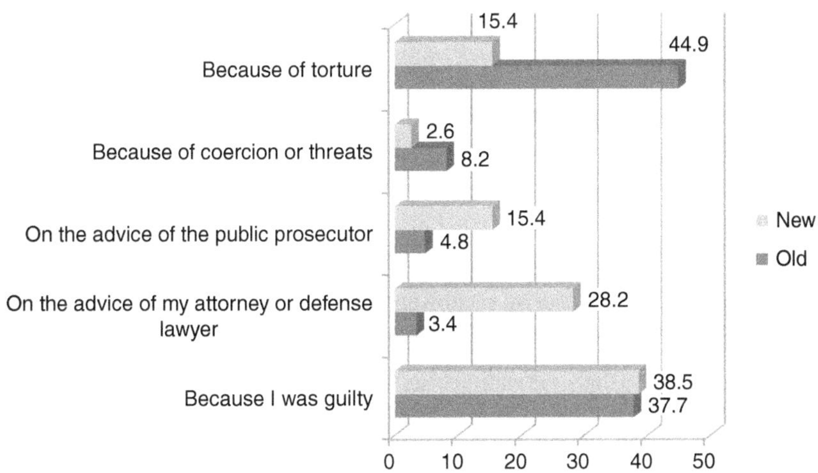

Figure 20.4 State of Mexico: Why did you plead guilty (old and new procedures)?

Source: Calculations based on the 2009 and 2013 Prison Population Surveys. Non-responses are not included.

open to public scrutiny. This is possibly the most important lesson to be learned from criminal reform in Mexico.

Notes

1. Center for Economic Research and Teaching (CIDE), Mexico. See: http://www.cide.edu/ (accessed 3 December 2014).
2. In other words, this is the first stage of the judicial proceedings in which a judge validates or rejects the MP's action prior to a trial and prior to issuing a ruling. There are three types of constitutional deadline orders: a formal order of commitment (during the trial, the defendant is in detention for preventive purposes), an indictment (the accused may be released on bail until appearing for the trial), and an acquittal (the accused is acquitted of the charges the MP ascribed to him/her).
3. The "Court Statistics, 2014" numbers and percentages cited herein were extracted or calculated based on the reports and statistics provided by the Mexico City Superior Court of Justice.
4. These are people who claim to have been victims of crime (most of which are misdemeanors that the Attorney General's Office does not pursue *ex officio*).
5. A good example of this is the case of Gabriel Ulises Valdez Larqué, which in 2009 led the Mexico City Human Rights Commission to issue a recommendation (6/2010).
6. In Mexico, a suspect can be detained for up to 48 hours without any formal accusation brought against him/her. However, he/she does have the right to legal defense from the moment of detention (Mexico City Criminal Code, 2014, and New Code of Criminal Procedures for Mexico City, 2014).
7. For example, the job performance evaluations for promotions are based on outcome efficiency (the number of sentences obtained, etc.), there is no judicial oversight (judge) over the investigation (Attorney General's Office), public defenders are weak, etc.
8. http://www.diputados.gob.mx/cedia/biblio/archivo/SAD-07-08.pdf (accessed 22 March 2014).
9. http://www.juridicas.unam.mx/infjur/leg/conshist/pdf/1917.pdf (accessed 22 March 2014).
10. At this time, the country is experiencing a transition period (from one legal system to another) and it is not yet possible to fully evaluate the results of the new process (although results from the State of Mexico – which incorporated the new system in 2011– are included). The deadline for states to adopt the new system is set for 2016.
11. Continuity means that legal proceedings must be followed without unwarranted interruptions (for example, interrupting a trial for reasons unrelated to the process). Immediacy refers to a speedy trial (without delays or stalling, but meeting the legally established time limits).
12. The entire process is done in writing (not orally) and access to the legal case is not allowed to anyone who is not directly involved with the case, unlike the oral system in which hearings are public and not exclusively done in writing.
13. These experts perform scientific assessments: the reconstruction of the events, ballistics, DNA, etc.
14. The process began in 2009 and ended in late 2011 in the State of Mexico.

References

Arciniegas Martínez, A. (2007) *Policía judicial y sistema acusatorio*. Bogotá: Nueva Jurídica.

Bergman, M., Fondevila, G., Vilalta, C., and Azaola, E. (2014) *Delito y Cárcel en México, deterioro social y desempeño institucional*. Mexico: CIDE.

Cuéllar Fernández, A (2007). Inseguridad: Como illegamos hasta aqui? Seguridad y Riesgo. (Insecurity: How did we get here? Security and Risk) *Revista Entorno 1.11.2007*, 21–25.

Fondevila, G. (in preparation) "Qué hacen realmente los tribunales del DF?".

Guillén López, G. (2013) *La investigación criminal en el sistema penal acusatorio*. Mexico: UNAM.

Jehle, J.-M. (2009) *Criminal Justice in Germany*. Berlin: Federal Ministry of Justice.

Magaloni Kerpel, A. L. (2006) "El detective: eslabón perdido del sistema de investigación criminal en México," in G. Laveaga (ed.), *65 propuestas para modernizar el sistema penal en México*. Mexico: INACIPE.

Magaloni Kerpel, A. L. (2007) *Arbitrariedad e ineficiencia de la procuración de justicia: dos caras de la misma moneda*. Mexico: CIDE.

Naval, C. and Salgado, J. (2006) *Irregularities, Abuses of Power and Ill-Treatment in the Federal District*. Mexico: Fundar. See: http://www.fundar.org.mx/PDF/metagora_eng_long.pdf (accessed 18 December 2014).

Pásara, L. (2002) *Cómo sentencian los jueces en el DF en materia penal*. Mexico: CIDE, DTEJ 6.

Prison Population Survey (PPS) (2002, 2005, 2009, 2013, 2014) Encuesta a Población en Reclusión del Distrito Federal y el Estado de México. Mexico: Centro de Investigación y Docencia Económicas (CIDE). See http://www.biiacs.cide.edu (accessed 11 April 2014).

Rand Corporation (2014) *The Impact of Reform on the Criminal Justice System in Mexico*. See: http://www.rand.org/labor/centers/clasp/research/projects/mexican-criminal-justice-reform.html (accessed 7 May 2014).

Shirk, D. A. (2010) *Justice Reform in Mexico: Change and Challenges in the Judicial Sector*, Working Paper. Mexico Institute, Woodrow Wilson International Center for Scholars and Trans-Border Institute, University of San Diego.

Vilalta, C. (2013) *Inferencia científica y análisis de datos*. México: CIDE.

Zepeda Lecuona, G. (2008) "La investigación de los delitos y la subversión de los principios del debido proceso en México," in A. Alvarado, (ed.), *La reforma de la justicia en México*. Mexico: El Colegio de México.

Zepeda Lecuona, G. (2004) *Crimen sin castigo: Procuración de Justicia Penal y ministerio público en México*. Mexico: Fondo de Cultura Económica y Centro de Investigación para el Desarrollo (CIDAC).

Institutional documents and websites

Código Penal para el Distrito Federal [Mexico City Criminal Code]. See: http://www.aldf.gob.mx/codigos-107-4.html (accessed 4 December 2014).

Compendio Estadístico 2004–2008 [Court Statistics 2004–2008], Tribunal Superior de Justicia del Distrito Federal. See: http://www.poderjudicialdf.gob.mx/work/models/PJDF/PDFs/comunicados/informes_estadisticas/informe_anual_2009/compest2004_2008.pdf (accessed 4 December 2014).

Court Opinion 73, 6th Epoch, p. 165, first section, First Chamber. See: http://sjf.scjn.gob.mx/iusElectoral/paginas/tesis.aspx (accessed 7 May 2014).

Court Opinion 74, Sixth Epoch, p. 167, first section, First Chamber, entitled "Confesión ante la policía judicial" ["Confession before the judicial police"]. See: http://sjf.scjn.gob.mx/iusElectoral/paginas/tesis.aspx (accessed 7 May 2014).

Court Opinion 77, 6th Epoch, p. 169, first section, First Chamber. See: http://sjf.scjn.gob.mx/iusElectoral/paginas/tesis.aspx (accessed 7 May 2014).

Court Opinion 78, 6th Epoch, p. 171, first section, First Chamber. See: http://sjf.scjn.gob.mx/iusElectoral/paginas/tesis.aspx (accessed 7 May 2014).

Court Opinion 79, 6th Epoch, p. 173, first section, First Chamber. See: http://sjf.scjn.gob.mx/iusElectoral/paginas/tesis.aspx (accessed 7 May 2014).

Court Statistics (2014) http://estadistica.tsjdf.gob.mx (accessed 4 December 2014).

Criminal Justice Indicator Report (CJIR) (2013) See: http://www.nyc.gov/html/om/pdf/2013/criminal_justice_indicator_report_summer_2013.pdf (accessed 17 December 2014).

Fourth Work Report (2013) Tribunal Superior de Justicia del Estado de México. See: http://www.pjedomex.gob.mx/web2/img/informes/4oInf_2013/ (accessed 18 December 2014).

Nuevo Código de Procedimientos Penales para el Distrito Federal [New Code of Criminal Procedures for Mexico City] http://www.aldf.gob.mx/codigos-107-4.html (accessed 4 December 2014).

Recommendation 6/2010. Comisión de Derechos Humanos del Distrito Federal. See: http://cdhdfbeta.cdhdf.org.mx/tag/recomendacion-62010/ (accessed 7 December 2014).

Record No. 209400. Location: Eighth Epoch. Instance: Collegiate Circuit Courts. Source: Federal Gaceta del Semanario Judicial de la Federación 85, January 1995. Page: 85. Thesis: VI.2o. J/346. Court Opinion. Matter(s): Criminal. Second Sixth Circuit Collegiate Court. See: https://www.scjn.gob.mx/libreria/Paginas/semanarioauto.aspx (accessed 7 May 2014).

Seventh Work Report of the President of the Mexico City Superior Court of Justice and the Mexico City Judicial Council (2014) See: http://www.poderjudicialdf.gob.mx/es/PJDF/Septimo_informe_2014 (accessed on 4 December 2014).

United States Attorney's Annual Statistical Report. See: http://www.justice.gov/sites/default/files/usao/legacy/2013/10/28/12statrpt.pdf (accessed 17 December 2014).

21 Interrogation and investigative interviewing of suspects in the United States

Christopher E. Kelly and Christian A. Meissner

Introduction

In a country as large and diverse as the United States and one with a decentralized criminal justice system, it would be nearly impossible to have an accurate census of investigative interviewing and interrogation practices of all – or even most – American law enforcement agencies. Interrogators across the nearly 18,000 local and state agencies (Reaves, 2011) who conduct the vast majority of criminal investigations operate through some combination of formal and on-the-job training. The formal training that interrogators receive can range from a few hours of in-house training to popular third-party, multi-day courses such as the Kinesic Interview (Walters, 2003), the Reid Technique (Inbau *et al.*, 2013), or Wicklander-Zulawski and Associates (Zulawski *et al.*, 2001). Even at the federal level, there exists a modicum of standardization across agencies, with the Federal Bureau of Investigation hosting its own training operations at Quantico, Virginia, while other agencies participate in the Department of Homeland Security's Federal Law Enforcement Training Center (FLETC) in Glynco, Georgia.[1] Unlike other countries that have standardized training and practices in investigative interviewing and interrogation, a uniform American system of interrogation is difficult, at best, to identify.

As problematic as it is to be precise (and concise) about American investigative interviewing and interrogation, however, the adversarial nature of the criminal justice system is the common thread running through the various law enforcement agencies in the United States. This adversarial model of criminal justice naturally leads to an accusatory model of interrogation (Leo, 2008), in which extracting confessions is given primacy and a presumption of guilt determines the onset of an interrogation (Meissner *et al.*, 2014). It is by no means universal among American police, but the accusatory model of interrogation is based on psychological manipulation that replaced physical coercion or the so-called "third degree" (Kassin *et al.*, 2010; Leo, 2008). Other hallmarks of the accusatorial model include establishing control over the suspect, using closed-ended questions that confirm what the interrogator already believes to be true, and judging deceit based upon the suspect's level of anxiety (Meissner *et al.*, 2014).

The earliest codification of the psychologically manipulative methods of the accusatorial model was in W. R. Kidd's (1940) *Police Interrogation* manual, though many of the tactics continue to be taught and practiced in contemporary American interrogation. In generic terms, interrogation can be seen as the successive use of three tactics that are geared toward inducing the suspect to confess: *isolation*, *confrontation/maximization*, and *minimization* (Kassin and Gudjonsson, 2004). First, the suspect is left alone prior to questioning in a small room to contemplate the impending interrogation. Next, interrogators present evidence implicating the suspect in the crime, not allowing him to deny the accusations, and foretelling the consequences of non-cooperation. The goal here is to overwhelm the suspect and to maximize his perception of his culpability and the likely consequences therein. In the final step, the interrogator takes a softer approach, offers explanations for the crime that are more favorable to the suspect and that may minimize both the perception of his culpability and the likely consequences that would follow. Together, the methods described here create conditions favorable to the police interrogator achieving the goal of obtaining a confession; however, the methods also leave the suspect vulnerable to being coerced into giving a false confession (Kassin *et al.*, 2010; Meissner *et al.*, 2014).

A related – but no less critical – factor in the shift from physically abusive to psychologically manipulative methods in American interrogation was the landmark *Miranda* v. *Arizona* (1966) decision (Leo, 1992). In *Miranda*, the Supreme Court reaffirmed the rights of custodial suspects against self-incrimination and imposed upon the police the well-known requirement of reminding suspects of said rights prior to questioning. In the years following the decision, the law enforcement community (and adherents to more conservative crime control measures generally) argued that the new rules would hamstring police investigations. These fears have proven unfounded, as research has consistently demonstrated that suspects overwhelmingly waive their *Miranda* rights and offer admissions and confessions (Cassell and Hayman, 1996; Feld, 2013; Kassin *et al.*, 2007; Leo, 1996). A compelling reason for this is that the police quickly became adept at delivering the warning and convincing suspects that it is in their best interests to waive their rights (White, 2001).

The American model of accusatorial interrogation is sharply contrasted with the information-gathering approach most associated with police in the United Kingdom. Whereas American police interrogations are guilt presumptive, confrontational, and rely heavily on psychological manipulation (including the disallowing of denials), systems in the United Kingdom and elsewhere rely on information-gathering techniques that do not presume guilt, that establish rapport, and use principles of investigative interviewing that allow the suspect to freely offer his or her account and that present evidence in a strategic manner (Meissner *et al.*, 2014). The information-gathering interviewing strategy, also known as the PEACE model (Planning and preparation; Engage and explain; Account; Closure; Evaluation) (Clarke and Milne, 2001), was developed in an attempt to curtail miscarriages of justice brought on by coercive and accusatorial methods (see Clarke and Milne, this volume, for much more information on PEACE).

The current chapter on American interrogation begins with a focus on the descriptive and observational research of contemporary interrogation in the United States. We then analyze these practices in light of what are known to be the most effect methods of investigative interviewing and interrogation. In the final portion of the chapter we examine training practices in the United States, with a focus on accusatorial methods, and then look to the future of American interrogation. We conclude with an observation that American interrogation is at a crossroads with regard to the practice of interrogation and the nascent, but perhaps increasing, influence of evidence-based practices.

American interrogation in practice: descriptive research

In this section we focus on several major studies that have systematically catalogued interrogation practices in the United States through one of two methodologies: self-reported surveys and observational/content analyses. These studies paint a picture of American interrogation which, when compared with most other countries' practices, highlight the differences between accusatorial and information-gathering models. As discussed below, observational studies of American interrogation are relatively rare; however, several recent projects (e.g. Cleary, 2014; Kelly *et al.*, 2013a; Russano *et al.*, 2014) are contributing to a contemporary perspective on interviewing and interrogation in the United States.

The pre-eminent survey of police interrogators was conducted by Kassin *et al.* (2007) in which 631 police interrogators[2] were asked to report their usage of 16 techniques, most of which were drawn directly or adapted from common interrogation manuals. The most common techniques reported by investigators included isolating the suspect from family and friends, conducting the interrogation in a small room, identifying contradictions in the suspect's story, and building rapport. Those techniques considered to be the most coercive or manipulative were reported to be employed very infrequently: using physical intimidation or threats of consequences for non-compliance, lying to the suspect about having failed a polygraph, or expressing frustration or anger. Interestingly, despite the interrogators' rare use of lying about a polygraph, Kassin *et al.* reported that their sample was more willing to use deception about having other types of evidence of the suspect's guilt (mean of 3.11 on a five-point scale). The 16 techniques were further reduced to four factors (*isolation, rapport, and minimization*; *confrontation*; *threatening the suspect*; and *presentation of evidence*). Analyses suggested that "investigator characteristics associated with a tendency to presume guilt are predictive of more frequent use of psychologically manipulative and confrontational techniques …" (Kassin *et al.*, 2007: 395).

More recently, Redlich *et al.* (2014) developed a survey consisting of a large number of specific techniques used by interrogators in the United States and other countries. Their sample included a wider variety of interrogators than Kassin *et al.* (2007), such as federal agents (e.g. FBI, Department of Homeland Security) and military interrogators, in addition to state/local police interrogators. Redlich *et al.* based their survey on an interrogation taxonomy (Kelly *et al.*, 2013b) that identified approximately 70 unique and specific techniques that were sorted into six "meso-level" domains: *rapport and relationship building*, *context manipulation*, *emotion provocation*, *confrontation/competition*, *collaboration*, and *presentation of evidence*. Whereas Kassin *et al.* asked participants to rate how often they would build rapport with suspects, Redlich *et al.* included nine different indicators of rapport building, four of which were the most frequently employed techniques (meet the suspect's basic needs, show kindness, build a bond with the suspect, be patient). Redlich *et al.* found that *rapport and relationship building* and *emotion provocation* were the two most frequently used domains, while *confrontation/competition* and *context manipulation* were the least frequently employed domains. Furthermore, Redlich *et al.* demonstrated that while the interrogation methods favored by participants varied across interrogation contexts, the *rapport and relationship building* domain served as a primary tactic regardless of context.

In a survey of police interrogators from ten jurisdictions around the United States, Reppucci and colleagues focused on several of the more coercive interrogation methods of the accusatorial model, including ineffective methods for detecting deceit, and examined how the use of them varied depending upon the age of the suspect (Meyer and Reppucci, 2007; Reppucci *et al.*, 2010). Techniques such as observing body language or speech patterns to detect deception, asking questions repeatedly, and minimizing the seriousness of the crime were reportedly used by a majority of interrogators and at a remarkably stable rate across age groupings of suspects. Although using deceit and presenting false evidence were comparatively less favored in these studies, approximately 30 percent of respondents stated that they used these techniques.

Survey research can be quite useful for understanding interrogators' perceptions of the techniques they utilize; however, this methodology comes with the caveat that the results may be biased due to social desirability or other such influences. This is particularly true of behaviors that can be considered coercive or especially manipulative as some interrogation techniques can be. Accordingly, observational research (e.g. content analysis of live interrogations, recordings, transcripts, or case files) is necessary and has been conducted to a limited degree in order to triangulate the actual practices of American interrogators.

Unlike the United Kingdom, for instance, where the recording of police interviews is mandated, American police have historically operated under no such uniform requirement. Like nearly all other law enforcement and criminal justice policies in the United States, the recording of police interrogations varies across states and practices within many states vary by jurisdiction. Fewer than ten states require custodial interrogations to be recorded, though others strongly encourage the practice (Kassin *et al.*, 2010; Sullivan, 2010). Although there has been an increase in the number of jurisdictions requiring video recording of interrogations, including such federal agencies as the Federal Bureau of Investigation and the US Department of Defense, the vast majority of police interrogations conducted in the United States involve no audio or video record of the event. This lack of recordings has resulted in a relative dearth of observational studies from which to draw strong conclusions about American interrogation practices. As a point of comparison, it is perhaps because of the United Kingdom's law requiring police to record their interviews that there is a comparatively larger body of similar British observational research.

One of the earliest observational studies of interrogation, however, was Leo's (1996) seminal work from two US police departments. This landmark study demonstrated the value of systematically observing, cataloging, and analyzing actual interrogations for scientific purposes. In general, Leo found that fewer than six of the 25 interrogation tactics he identified were employed in an average interrogation session. The most commonly occurring approaches included *appealing to the suspect's self-interest* and *confronting the suspecting with evidence*, two very prominent tactics found in accusatorial interrogations. Moreover, Leo reported that four tactics were significantly associated with providing incriminating information: *appealing to the suspect's conscience*, *identifying contradictory information*, the *use of praise or flattery*, and the *use of moral justifications*.

Focusing on suspects aged 16 and 17, Feld (2013) similarly coded 307 interrogations conducted in Minnesota. He grouped interrogation techniques into the dichotomous categories of *minimization* and *maximization* and reported that the most commonly employed techniques (or strategies or questions) were *confronting the suspect with evidence*, *accusing the suspect of lying*, *urging the suspect to tell the truth*, and using *Reid Behavioral Analysis Interview (BAI) questions*. Feld categorized these as maximization techniques (i.e. those designed to increase the suspect's fears or anxiety), and noted that tactics from the minimization category were relatively less frequent in his sample (e.g., *neutralization*, *appealing to the suspect's self-interest*, and *showing empathy*). Although differences between the Feld (2013) and Leo (1996) studies may be attributed to police perceptions of effective techniques for juvenile versus adult suspects, other research has demonstrated that, by and large, a suspect's age is irrelevant with respect to interrogation methods (Meyer and Reppucci 2007; Reppucci *et al.*, 2010; Redlich *et al.*, 2004).

In sum, whether it is through survey or observational research, American interrogation methods are largely – but not exclusively – associated with an accusatorial and psychologically manipulative approach. In the next section, we examine the effectiveness of these methods in light of existing laboratory research in order to draw conclusions of interrogation practices in the United States.

Assessing the effectiveness of American interrogation practices

More than fifty years ago, the publication of a landmark manual on *Criminal Interrogation and Confessions* (Inbau and Reid, 1963) marked a significant point in the history of American interrogation practices. For better or worse, the accusatorial model embodied within this manual became the benchmark for law enforcement practices widely used within the United States. In the following paragraphs, we review the state of the literature with respect to the accusatorial model of interrogation, and compare its effectiveness with that of alternative methods emerging from the practices of other countries. One antecedent to change in other countries has been the role of accusatorial methods in eliciting high-profile false confessions from innocent suspects (Bull and Milne, 2004).

In the United States, social scientists and legal scholars have documented hundreds of cases involving wrongful conviction over the past several decades (Scheck *et al.*, 2000). In 25–30 percent of these cases, innocent suspects were induced to provide a false confession or admission that ultimately led to conviction (Drizin and Leo, 2004; Garrett, 2011). Given a growing awareness of the false confession phenomenon, social scientists began systematically assessing what factors may lead an innocent person to provide a false statement, including the unique characteristics of the individual that may render them more vulnerable to police questioning and the powerful influence of certain interrogation techniques that could produce false confessions. Detailed reviews of this literature are available to the interested reader (see Kassin *et al.*, 2010; Kassin and Gudjonsson, 2004; Lassiter and Meissner, 2010); however, a brief discussion of the role of accusatorial interrogation methods is provided below, given its relevance to assessing the efficacy of police interrogation techniques.

A significant body of research stemming from both experimental paradigms in a laboratory setting (Kassin and Kiechel, 1996; Russano *et al.*, 2005) and archival analyses of known false confessions (Drizin and Leo, 2004; Garrett, 2011; Ofshe and Leo, 1997a, 1997b) suggest that accusatorial methods of interrogation can significantly increase the likelihood of a false confession (Kassin *et al.*, 2010). For example, techniques designed to *maximize* a suspect's perception of the evidence against him (such as presenting false evidence or bluffing about the potential for incriminating evidence; see Horselenberg *et al.*, 2003; Nash and Wade, 2009; Perillo and Kassin, 2011; Redlich and Goodman, 2003) and those that attempt to *minimize* a suspect's perceptions of his culpability or the likely consequences if he were to confess (by implying leniency or offering face-saving excuses; see Horgan *et al.*, 2012; Klaver *et al.*, 2008; Russano *et al.*, 2005) have both been shown to increase false confessions by innocent suspects. A strong belief in the suspect's guilt on the part of the investigator has also been shown to exacerbate the use of accusatorial methods (Kassin *et al.*, 2003), promote beliefs in deceptive behaviors (Meissner and Kassin, 2002, 2004), and ultimately increase the likelihood of inducing a false confession (Narchet *et al.*, 2011). Indeed, the psychological factors leading an innocent person to provide a false confession have been shown to involve both perceived social pressure to confess aroused by the interrogator and the potential consequences associated with confessing (vs. not) (see Houston *et al.*, 2014; Yang *et al.*, in press).

While documenting techniques that may produce a false confession represents an important contribution to both theory and practice, recent research has also begun to identify those psychological processes associated with true confessions (Houston *et al.*, 2014) and to identify those methods of interrogation that might produce diagnostic confession statements from guilty suspects (Meissner *et al.*,

2014). For example, Horgan and colleagues (2012) distinguished between minimization and maximization techniques that influenced suspects' perception of the likely consequences associated with confession, observing that approaches devoid of "manipulating consequences" produced more diagnostic outcomes (i.e. an increased likelihood of true confession and a reduced likelihood of false confession). True confessions were largely a product of participants' feelings of guilt or remorse and their beliefs of the evidence against them – a finding that is quite consistent with a host of laboratory studies (Houston *et al.*, 2014), as well as surveys of false confessors (Gudjonsson and Sigurdsson, 1999; Redlich *et al.*, 2011).

More recently, a growing number of empirical studies have begun to assess the diagnostic utility of information-gathering approaches to interrogation such as the PEACE model used in the UK and other countries (Meissner *et al.*, 2014; see Clarke and Milne, this volume). Both experimental research (Evans *et al.*, 2013; Narchet *et al.*, 2011) and field studies in the UK (Soukara *et al.*, 2009; Walsh and Bull, 2010) have demonstrated that information-gathering methods of interrogation – which involve the development of rapport, good elicitation strategies, positive confrontation, and strategic evidence presentation methods – produce more diagnostic outcomes by increasing the likelihood of eliciting true confessions while reducing the likelihood of eliciting false confessions. Additional studies have demonstrated the importance of developing rapport, or a "working alliance," between the interrogator and the subject, particularly given its importance in facilitating suspect disclosures (Alison *et al.*, 2013; Evans *et al.*, 2014; Goodman-Delahunty and Howes, in press; Goodman-Delahunty, 2014; Redlich *et al.*, 2014; Vanderhallen and Vervaeke, 2014; Walsh and Bull, 2012a, 2012b). Finally, strategic evidence presentation strategies have also been developed to facilitate disclosure by guilty subjects, demonstrating that late (or gradual strategic) disclosure of evidence is more likely to produce admissions that distinguish innocent from guilty suspects (Hartwig *et al.*, 2014; Smith and Bull, in press).

Taken together, the above research is consistent with a meta-analysis of the available literature by Meissner and colleagues (2014) that compared the diagnostic utility of accusatorial and information-gathering methods of interrogation. While both methods were rather effective in producing "confessions" in observational studies of real interrogations (when compared with a set of control techniques that were common to both), experimental studies that manipulated guilt and innocence showed that information-gathering approaches yielded a higher rate of true confessions while reducing the risk of false confessions.

American interrogation at a crossroads: future directions for research and training

Interrogation in the United States is currently at a crossroads – the methods used by law enforcement, military, and intelligence communities over the past 50 years were developed through prior experience and perceptions of effectiveness that are largely devoid of scientific validation or assessment. Recent studies, however, have called the relative efficacy of these approaches into question, with data suggesting that the use of accusatorial methods of interrogation can compel false confessions from innocent persons. This research has also begun to assess the role of alternative approaches to interrogation that appear to improve the diagnostic value of information elicited from suspects – methods that improve the development of rapport, encourage cooperation and communication, use positive confrontation and strategic presentation of evidence, and rely upon more reliable cues to deception.

The United States government via its High-value Detainee Interrogation Group (HIG), a multi-agency group with components from the Federal Bureau of Investigation, the Defense Intelligence Agency, and the Central Intelligence Agency, has recently invested in a five-year research program aimed at developing a scientific understanding of interrogation that might leverage theory, methods, and metrics drawn from the cognitive, behavioral, and social sciences. To date, more than 60 research studies have been supported through this effort, with many of the findings reflected in the current chapter. While investigators began this research in their laboratories, the HIG facilitated further assessments of the methods with federal law enforcement and military training facilities in the US, leading many of these facilities to begin integrating the more effective, science-based methods into their curriculum. The HIG has also developed "research-to-practice" training packages that are being made available to other federal, state, and local entities as they work to disseminate the research findings and improve practice in this area.

Our own interactions with military, law enforcement, and intelligence personnel in the US suggest that practitioners are eager to identify ethical, evidence-based methods of interrogation that will improve their ability to collect information from non-cooperative individuals. While further research and development will be vital to creating a robust understanding of the influence of key facets of an interrogation (see Evans *et al.*, 2010) – including the role of language and culture (Kelly *et al.*, in press), the influence of contextual or environmental factors, and an understanding of factors that might lessen resistance and improve rapport development – a monumental paradigm shift is perhaps in the offing. Rooted in cutting-edge research and increasing cooperation between researchers and practitioners, the treatment of non-cooperative suspects in the United States appears to be incrementally moving toward a new model of interrogation and away from the psychologically manipulative methods of the past half-century.

Notes

1. This is to say nothing of the country's human intelligence (HUMINT) apparatus, though an Executive Order commanding all federal-level interrogators to conform to the standards of the Army Field Manual 2-22.3 was issued by President Obama in January 2009.
2. Although this chapter is concerned with American practices, it should be noted that the Kassin *et al.* (2007) sample included a small proportion (< 10 percent of the total) of Canadian police investigators.

References

Alison, L. J., Alison, E., Noone, G., Elntib, S., and Christiansen, P. (2013) "Why tough tactics fail and rapport gets results: Observing Rapport-Based Interpersonal Techniques (ORBIT) to generate useful information from terrorists," *Psychology, Public Policy, and Law*, 19: 411–31.

Bull, R. and Milne, B. (2004) "Attempts to improve the police interviewing of suspects," in G. D. Lassiter (ed.), *Interrogations, Confessions, Entrapment*. New York: Springer, pp. 181–96.

Cassell, P. G. and Hayman, B. S. (1996) "Police interrogation in the 1990s: an empirical study of the effects of Miranda," *UCLA Law Review*, 43: 839.

Clarke, C. and Milne, B. (2001) *National Evaluation of the PEACE Investigative Interviewing Course*, Police Research Award Scheme. London: Home Office.

Cleary, H. M. D. (2014) "Police interviewing and interrogation of juvenile suspects: a descriptive examination of actual cases," *Law and Human Behavior*, 38: 271–82.

Drizin, S. A. and Leo, R. A. (2004) "The problem of false confessions in the post-DNA world," *North Carolina Law Review*, 82: 894–1007.

Evans, J. R., Meissner, C. A., Brandon, S. E., Russano, M. B., and Kleinman, S. M. (2010) "Criminal versus HUMINT interrogations: the importance of psychological science to improving interrogative practice," *Journal of Psychiatry and Law*, 38: 215–49.

Evans, J. R., Meissner, C. A., Ross, A. B., Houston, K. A., Russano, M. B., and Horgan, A. J. (2013) "Obtaining guilty knowledge in human intelligence interrogations: comparing accusatorial and information gathering approaches with a novel experimental paradigm," *Journal of Applied Research in Memory and Cognition*, 2: 83–8.

Evans, J. R., Houston, K. A., Meissner, C. A., Ross, A. B., LaBianca, J. R., Woestehoff, S. A., and Kleinman, S. M. (2014) "An empirical evaluation of intelligence-gathering interrogation techniques from the United States Army Field Manual," *Applied Cognitive Psychology*, 28: 867–75.

Feld, B. (2013) *Kids, Cops, and Interrogation: Inside the Interrogation Room*. New York: New York University Press.

Garrett, B. L. (2011) *Convicting the Innocent: Where Criminal Prosecutions Go Wrong*. Cambridge, MA: Harvard University Press.

Goodman-Delahunty, J. and Howes, L. M. (in press) "Social persuasion to develop rapport in high stakes interviews: qualitative analyses of Asian-Pacific practices," *Policing and Society*.

Goodman-Delahunty, J., Martschuk, N., and Dhami, M. (2014) "Interviewing high-value detainees: security cooperation and reliable disclosures," *Applied Cognitive Psychology*, 28: 883–97.

Gudjonsson, G. H. and Sigurdsson, J. F. (1999) "The Gudjonsson confession questionnaire – Revised (GCQ-R): factor structure and its relationship with personality," *Personality and Individual Differences*, 27: 953–68.

Hartwig, M., Granhag, P. A., and Luke, T. J. (2014) "Strategic use of evidence during investigative interviews: the state of the science," in D. C. Raskin, C. R. Honts, and J. C. Kircher (eds), *Credibility Assessment: Scientific Research and Applications*. Waltham, MA: Academic Press, pp. 1–36.

Horgan, A. J., Russano, M. B., Meissner, C. A., and Evans, J. R. (2012) "Minimization and maximization techniques: assessing the perceived consequences of confessing and confession diagnosticity," *Psychology, Crime and Law*, 18: 65–78.

Horselenberg, R., Merckelbach, H., and Josephs, S. (2003) "Individual differences and false confessions: a conceptual replication of Kassin and Kiechel (1996)," *Psychology, Crime and Law*, 9: 1–18.

Houston, K. A., Meissner, C. A., and Evans, J. R. (2014) "Psychological processes that distinguish true and false confessions," in R. Bull's (ed.), *Investigative Interviewing*. New York: Springer, pp. 19–34.

Inbau, F. E. and Reid, J. E. (1963) *Criminal Interrogation and Confession*. Baltimore, MD: Williams & Wilkins.

Inbau, F. E., Reid, J. E., Buckley, J. P., and Jayne, B. C. (2013) *Criminal Interrogation and Confessions*, 5th edn. Burlington, MA: Jones & Bartlett Learning.

Jayne, B. C. and Buckley, J. P. (1999) *Investigator Anthology: A Compilation of Articles and Essays About the Reid Technique of Interviewing and Interrogation*. Chicago: John E. Reid & Associates.

Kassin, S. M. and Gudjonsson, G. H. (2004) "The psychology of confession evidence: a review of the literature and issues," *Psychological Science in the Public Interest*, 5: 35–69.

Kassin, S. M. and Kiechel, K. L. (1996) "The social psychology of false confessions: compliance, internalization, and confabulation," *Psychological Science*, 7: 125–8.

Kassin, S. M., Goldstein, C. J., and Savitsky, K. (2003) "Behavioral confirmation in the interrogation room: on the dangers of presuming guilt," *Law and Human Behavior*, 27: 187–203.

Kassin, S. M., Drizin, S. A., Grisso, T., Gudjonsson, G. H., Leo, R. A., and Redlich, A. D. (2010) "Police-induced confessions: risk factors and recommendations," *Law and Human Behavior*, 34: 3–38.

Kassin, S. M., Leo, R. A., Meissner, C. A., Richman, K. D., Colwell, L. H., Leach, A. M., and La Fon, D. (2007) "Police interviewing and interrogation: a self-report survey of police practices and beliefs," *Law and Human Behavior*, 31: 381–400.

Kelly, C. E., Abdel-Salam, S., Miller, J. C., and Redlich, A. D. (in press) "Social identity and the perception of effective interrogation methods," *Investigative Interviewing: Research and Practice*.

Kelly, C. E., Redlich, A. D., and Miller, J. C. (2013a) *The Dynamic Process of Interrogation*, Final Report to the High Value Detainee Interrogation Group, Washington, DC.

Kelly, C. E., Miller, J. C., Redlich, A. D., and Kleinman, S. M. (2013b) "A taxonomy of interrogation methods," *Psychology, Public Policy, and Law*, 19: 165–78.

Kidd, W. R. (1940) *Police Interrogation*. New York: Basuino.

Klaver, J., Lee, Z., and Rose, V. G. (2008) "Effects of personality, interrogation techniques and plausibility in an experimental false confession paradigm," *Legal and Criminological Psychology*, 13: 71–88.

Lassiter, G. D. and Meissner, C. A. (2010) *Police Interrogations and False Confessions: Current Research, Practice, and Policy Recommendations*. Washington, DC: American Psychological Association.

Leo, R. A. (1992) "From coercion to deception: the changing nature of police interrogation in America," *Crime, Law, and Social Change: An International Journal*, 18: 35–59.

Leo, R. A. (1996) "Inside the interrogation room," *Journal of Criminal Law and Criminology*, 86: 266–303.

Leo, R. A. (2008) *Police Interrogation and American Justice*. Cambridge, MA: Harvard University Press.

Meissner, C. A. and Kassin, S. M. (2002) "'He's guilty!' Investigator bias in judgments of truth and deception," *Law and Human Behavior*, 26: 469–80.

Meissner, C. A. and Kassin, S. M. (2004) "'You're guilty, so just confess!' Cognitive and behavioral confirmation biases in the interrogation room," in G. D. Lassiter (ed.), *Interrogations, Confessions, and Entrapment*. New York: Kluwer Academic, pp. 85–106.

Meissner, C. A., Redlich, A. D., Michael, S. W., Evans, J. R., Camilletti, C. R., Bhatt, S., and Brandon, S. (2014) "Accusatorial and information-gathering interrogation methods and their effects on true and false confessions: a meta-analytic review," *Journal of Experimental Criminology*, 10: 459–86.

Meyer, J. R. and Reppucci, N. D. (2007) "Police practices and perceptions regarding juvenile interrogation and interrogative suggestibility," *Behavioral Sciences and the Law*, 25: 757–80.

Miranda v. *Arizona*, 384 US 436 (1966).

Narchet, F. M., Meissner, C. A., and Russano, M. B. (2011) "Modeling the influence of investigator bias on the elicitation of true and false confessions," *Law and Human Behavior*, 35 452–65.

Nash, R. A. and Wade, K. A. (2009) "Innocent but proven guilty: using false video evidence to elicit false confessions and create false beliefs," *Applied Cognitive Psychology*, 23: 624–37.

Ofshe, R. J. and Leo, R. A. (1997a) "The social psychology of police interrogation: the theory and classification of true and false confessions," *Studies in Law, Politics, and Society*, 16: 189–251.

Ofshe, R. J. and Leo, R. A. (1997b) "The decision to confess falsely: rational choice and irrational action," *Denver University Law Review*, 74: 979–1122.

Perillo, J. T. and Kassin, S. M. (2011) "Inside interrogation: the lie, the bluff, and false confessions," *Law and Human Behavior*, 35: 327–37.

Reaves, B. A. (2011) *Census of State and Local Law Enforcement Agencies, 2008*. US Department of Justice, Office of Justice Programs.

Redlich, A. D. and Goodman, G. S. (2003) "Taking responsibility for an act not committed: the influence of age and suggestibility," *Law and Human Behavior*, 27: 141–56.

Redlich, A. D., Kelly, C. E., and Miller, J. C. (2014) "The who, what, and why of human intelligence gathering: self-reported measures of interrogation methods," *Applied Cognitive Psychology*, 28: 817–28.

Redlich, A. D., Kulish, R., and Steadman, H. J. (2011) "Comparing true and false confessions among persons with serious mental illness," *Psychology, Public Policy, and Law*, 17: 394–418.

Redlich, A. D., Silverman, M., Chen, J., and Steiner, H. (2004) "The police interrogation of children and adolescents," in G. D. Lassiter (ed.), *Interrogations, Confessions, and Entrapment*. New York: Kluwer Academic, pp. 107–26.

Reppucci, N. D., Meyer, J., and Kostelnik, J. (2010) "Police interrogation of juveniles: results from a national survey of police," in G. D. Lassiter and C. Meissner (eds), *Interrogations and Confessions: Current Research, Practices, and Policy*. Washington, DC: American Psychological Association.

Russano, M. B., Meissner, C. A., Narchet, F. M., and Kassin, S. M. (2005) "Investigating true and false confessions within a novel experimental paradigm," *Psychological Science*, 16 (6): 481–6.

Russano, M. B., Narchet, F. M., Kleinman, S. M., and Meissner, C. A. (2014) "Structured interviews of experienced HUMINT interrogators," *Applied Cognitive Psychology*, 28: 847–59.

Scheck, B., Neufeld, P., and Dwyer, J. (2000) *Actual Innocence*. Garden City, NY: Doubleday.

Smith, L. L. and Bull, R. (in press) "Exploring the disclosure of forensic evidence in police interviews with suspects," *Journal of Police and Criminal Psychology*.

Soukara, S., Bull, R., Vrij, A., Turner, M., and Cherryman, C. (2009) "What really happens in police interviews of suspects? Tactics and confessions," *Psychology, Crime and Law*, 15: 493–506.

Sullivan, T. P. (2010) "The wisdom of custodial recording," in G. D. Lassiter and C. Meissner (eds), *Police Interrogations and False Confessions: Current Research, Practice, and Policy Recommendations*. Washington, DC: American Psychological Association, pp. 127–42.

Vanderhallen, M. and Vervaeke, G. (2014) "Between investigator and suspect: the role of the working alliance in investigative interviewing," in R. Bull (ed.), *Investigative Interviewing*. New York: Springer, pp. 63–90.

Walsh, D. and Bull, R. (2010) "What really is effective in interviews with suspects? A study comparing interviewing skills against interviewing outcomes," *Legal and Criminological Psychology*, 15 (2): 305–21.

Walsh, D. and Bull, R. (2012a) "Examining rapport in investigative interviews with suspects: does its building and maintenance work?" *Journal of Police and Criminal Psychology*, 27: 73–84.

Walsh, D. and Bull, R. (2012b) "How do interviewers attempt to overcome suspects' denials?" *Psychiatry, Psychology and Law*, 19: 151–68.

Walters, S. B. (2003) *Principles of Kinesic Interview and Interrogation*. Boca Raton, FL: CRC Press.

White, W. S. (2001) *Miranda's Waning Protections: Police Interrogation Practices after Dickerson*. Ann Arbor, MI: University of Michigan Press.

Yang, Y., Madon, S., and Guyll, M. (in press) "Short-sighted confession decisions: the role of uncertain and delayed consequences," *Law and Human Behavior*.

Zulawski, D. E., Wicklander, D. E., Sturman, S. G., and Hoover, L. W. (2001) *Practical Aspects of Interview and Interrogation*, 2nd edn. Boca Raton, FL: CRC Press.

Conclusion

Interviews and interrogations of suspects – obtaining the truth, not just confessions

David Walsh, Allison D. Redlich, Gavin E. Oxburgh and Trond Myklebust

Increasingly, over the last twenty years or so, we have learned more about the interviewing and interrogation practices of police and law enforcement officers when they question those suspected of crimes. However, almost exclusively, our awareness has focused on the UK, the USA, Canada and Australia. Much less is known about interview and interrogation practices elsewhere around the world, especially in non-western countries like the Middle and Far East. There also appears to be a strong link between the countries where researchers are from and the amount of scientific knowledge we previously held about a particular country's practice. Furthermore, a clear correlation exists between the lack of knowledge and those countries which are alleged (with strong anecdotal evidence) to use torture and other degrading forms of treatment towards those being questioned as suspects of crimes. As such, the training of interviewers is absolutely vital in every aspect and this is an area that many chapters have highlighted.

The editors' endeavours have resulted in obtaining contributions concerning suspect interviewing and interrogation from parts of the world hitherto unknown to the public (such as Slovenia, Iran and Mexico). Even in highly developed countries such as Germany, Belgium, Switzerland and France, it is the case that we have been unaware of interview and interrogation practices. As such, the chapters in this volume consistently enlighten and inform us. Indeed, it is the global reach in this volume that is its groundbreaking feature. Nevertheless, we recognise only too readily that in many parts of the world, knowledge about practice still remains either hidden or unethical (or both). The Human Rights Watch organisation (http://www.hrw.org) report concerns regarding the treatment of prisoners by police and security forces in more than twenty countries in 2014 alone that largely relate to the regular practice of confessions being extracted by either physical or psychological torture that tend to result in convictions (with either none or little else by way of evidence offered to support the confession). However, only two of these countries (France and the USA) are covered in this volume. This is not to suggest that the volume falls short in its coverage, as our expectations were that we would cover just a fraction of the 195 countries in the world. Rather, such absence reminds us all of the size of the task remaining in influencing established practices that are known to: (1) be unethical;

(2) cause false confessions; and (3) undermine notions of social and criminal justice.

What limited knowledge we have from academic studies also suggests that unethical practices, more focused upon obtaining confessions than gathering reliable accounts, pervades common practice, with its attendant risks of gaining false confessions and, subsequently, miscarriages of justice. For example, Broadhurst *et al.* (2013) refer to how police interrogations in Cambodia usually result in confession with little by way of corroborative evidence, while Vadackumchery (1998) suggests that training and practice in India is far from satisfactory. (See also Thilalgaraj (2002) who reports frequent custodial violence by Indian police officers, while Ramakrishnan (2013) suggests that such violence in Indian police interrogations, while deplorable, is often accepted as necessary both by the public and the police.)

Cases involving known miscarriages of justice that have been so pivotal in transforming practice in, say, England and Wales, have had little effect in some countries, where it seems interrogational practices that prompted such errors still seem resilient to change (see, for example, O'Mahoney (2002) with regard to the Republic of Ireland). Indeed, even where such powerful bodies (such as the European Court of Human Rights) have directed that change must occur across the European Economic Area (EEA) (e.g. in the *Salduz* ruling, which directed that suspects must be given the right to legal advice before questioning) responses have been varied, inconsistent and slow, despite this ruling taking place in 2008. Certain chapters that refer to countries in the EEA in Volume 2 bear witness to this reluctance, while others suggest that some form of response has been made to this ruling (though often well short of the universal availability to legal advice that occurs in England and Wales and the USA).

The above suggests a stark and depressing picture of contemporary practice around the world when the police interview suspects of crime. However, as this volume has shown, there are parts of the world that have developed a more ethical approach in the past few years. Moreover, even in countries such as the USA, the recording of interviews has gradually increased, while research developments suggest a gradually changing picture (particularly when those studies are undertaken in collaboration with law enforcement practitioners). These are features that have been found to be crucial in advances elsewhere in the world (as has the introduction of legislation that effectively outlaws the practice of torture). These legislative changes have been noted, for example, in Malaysia, Taiwan and the United Arab Emirates, where positive efforts have also been made to professionalise policing (Farrar, 2013; Hou, 2013). Elsewhere (e.g. Romania and Ghana), authors have written about the practice of investigators when they interview/interrogate, even if some of these efforts seem somewhat simplistic and naive when compared to the literature available from researchers and practitioners based in Western countries. However, they still represent early steps toward a more professional, scientific and ethical direction (see, for example, Anim-Danquah, 2013; Olteneau, 2011, 2013). Furthermore, in the USA, where concern has often been raised over the practice of investigators, the recent Senate

Committee report exposed and severely criticised some of those less savoury practices, recognising their shortfalls in obtaining reliable accounts (Senate Select Committee, 2014).

The practice of increasing the research-base relating to interviewing through scientific study cannot be overemphasised, particularly when undertaken collaboratively with practitioners. We argue that the knowledge established through scientific perspectives represents a basic foundation for practitioners. Our contention is that such collaborative research efforts need to be relentless in their pursuit of ethical practices which are more efficacious in gaining reliable accounts from interviewees and in gradually changing practices worldwide. We have seen from this volume that countries with well-established traditions of investigation and criminal justice (such as Australia, Canada, the UK and the Scandinavian countries) are gradually recognising, or have even changed, their approaches (usually in the face of judicial ire over flawed interrogation techniques that either would likely have (or did) lead to miscarriages of justice). In England and Wales, the introduction of appropriate legislation, audio/video-recording and the PEACE model of interviewing have, together, led to more skilled practice and quite probably the removal of unethical practices often found in studies before their introduction (see Bull, 2014).

It is also no coincidence that since their implementation in England and Wales, no false convictions that relate to inappropriate questioning techniques have resulted, in contrast to the previous situation before their introduction. Indeed, the use of the PEACE model, when used skilfully, has been associated with those interviews that tend to yield more comprehensively detailed accounts from suspects (Walsh and Bull, 2010). Further studies conducted elsewhere in the world have reinforced this perspective (see, for example, Meissner *et al.*, 2012), while reminding us of the need for continuing research. Nevertheless, it should come as no surprise that information-gathering, as an interview objective, is one increasingly being accepted around the world, with the PEACE model (or its derivatives) becoming incrementally viewed as the preferred model to train investigators (for example, New Zealand, Norway and the Netherlands – see this volume). Yet there remains much to do. In England and Wales, the performance of investigators, while avoiding oppressive and confession-centred techniques that can cause false confessions, still remains problematic with regard to certain skills, such as: (1) rapport-building; (2) summarising; (3) confronting suspects; and (4) developing an effective interview strategy/structure, despite their training (see Clarke and Milne, this volume).

Explanations as to why this picture appears to persist remain elusive (as does the resolution of the problem). It therefore behoves us as researchers to persist in working with practitioners in order to continue to develop the PEACE interview model (or similar) that succeeds in practice in avoiding false confessions and overcoming false denials while gathering accurate, reliable, relevant and comprehensive information. As the two volumes show, this remains a global challenge. Without the skilled interviewing of victims and witnesses, opportunities to fully establish what happened, by whom and to whom are not fully exploited. In turn, history has taught us that tactics that are argued to prompt false confessions from suspected offenders unequivocally succeed in creating further victims while allowing the guilty to go unpunished. Dostoyevsky (1862) famously wrote that the way society treats its prisoners is a measure of civilisation in that society. We would agree. However, we would further argue (before the point of incarceration in the criminal justice process) that another judgement should be made. How civilised a society is should be measured by how it treats its victims, witnesses and suspects.

References

Anim-Danquah, E. (2013) *Principles of Interrogation*. Bloomington: Authorhouse.

Broadhurst, R., Bouhours, T. and Keo, C. (2013) 'Crime and justice in Cambodia', in J. Liu, B. Hebenton and S. Jou (eds), *Handbook of Asian Criminology*. New York Springer, pp. 167–82.

Bull, R. (ed.) (2014) *Investigative Interviewing*. New York: Springer.

Dostoyevsky, F. (1862). *The House of the Dead*. Ware: Wordsworth.

Farrar, S. A. (2013) 'Crime and criminal justice in Malaysia', in J. Liu, B. Hebenton and S. Jou (eds), *Handbook of Asian Criminology*. New York: Springer, pp. 231–46.

Hou, C. (2013) 'An overview of the criminal justice system in Taiwan', in J. Liu, B. Hebenton and S. Jou (eds), *Handbook of Asian Criminology*. New York: Springer, pp. 297–308.

Meissner, C., Redlich, A., Bhatt, S. and Brandon, S. (2012) *Interview and Interrogation Methods and Their Effects on True and False Confessions*. Oslo: Campbell Systematics Reviews.

O'Mahoney, P. (2002) *Criminal Justice in Ireland*. Dublin: Institute of Public Administration.

Olteneau, G. (2011) 'The importance of evaluating and using the specific behavioural manifestations of the individuals investigated within judiciary investigations', *International Journal of Criminal Investigation*, 1: 75–86.

Olteneau, G. (2013) 'Suggestibility in interview and interrogation: considerations about the use of smile', *International Journal of Criminal Investigation*, 3: 7–22.

Ramakrishnan, N. (2013) *In Custody: Law, Impunity, and Prisoner Abuse in South Asia*. New Delhi: Sage.

Senate Select Committee (2014) *Report of the Senate Select Committee on Intelligence: Committee Study of the Central Intelligence Agency's Detention and Interrogation Program*. Washington, DC: United States Government.

Thilalgaraj, R. (2013) 'Criminal justice system in India', in J. Liu, B. Hebenton and S. Jou (eds), *Handbook of Asian Criminology*. New York: Springer, pp. 199–211.

Vadackumchery, J. (1998) *Police Interrogation: Dos Which the Police Don't*. New Delhi: APH Publishing.

Walsh, D. and Bull, R. (2010) 'The interviewing of suspects by non-police agencies. What's effective? What is effective!', *Legal and Criminological Psychology*, 15: 305–21.

Index

Page numbers in italic refer to figures and tables.

For Product Safety Concerns and Information please contact our EU representative GPSR@taylorandfrancis.com
Taylor & Francis Verlag GmbH, Kaufingerstraße 24, 80331 München, Germany

www.ingramcontent.com/pod-product-compliance
Lightning Source LLC
LaVergne TN
LVHW011114300926
849160LV00008B/383

* 9 7 8 1 1 3 8 0 6 6 0 8 3 *